Radical Shelley

Radical Shelley

*The Philosophical Anarchism
and Utopian Thought of
Percy Bysshe Shelley*

MICHAEL HENRY
SCRIVENER

PRINCETON UNIVERSITY PRESS

Princeton, New Jersey

Copyright © 1982 by Princeton University Press
Published by Princeton University Press, 41 William Street, Princeton, New Jersey
In the United Kingdom: Princeton University Press, Guildford, Surrey

All Rights Reserved

Library of Congress Cataloging in Publication Data will be
found on the last printed page of this book

This book has been composed in Linotron Sabon
Clothbound editions of Princeton University Press books are printed
on acid-free paper, and binding materials are chosen
for strength and durability

Printed in the United States of America by Princeton
University Press, Princeton, New Jersey

To Mary Ann

Contents

Acknowledgments

I AM GREATLY indebted to many teachers, critics and scholars, but I wish to pay special attention to the following: my dissertation committee, Irving Massey, John Dings, and Arthur Efron (my doctoral dissertation, *The Paradox of Hope in Shelley's Poetry*, was the earliest version of what eventually became the present study); Kenneth Neill Cameron, for his pioneering work on Shelley's politics; John P. Clark, for his study of Godwin's anarchism; Daniel J. Hughes, for articles on Shelley's imagery; and Donald H. Reiman, whose textual and critical studies, and advice have been so helpful. E. P. Thompson's historical writing, and Raymond Williams's literary criticism have decisively altered my sense of the complex relationship between "literature" and "society." I also wish to thank my fellow participants in the Literature and Society Program (1972-1976) at the State University of New York at Buffalo, for making graduate school such an interesting experience, one of whose results is this book. I am grateful for my colleagues at the Wayne State University English Department who have been both encouraging and intellectually challenging.

The following libraries I thank for their professional courtesies: Lockwood Library, State University of New York at Buffalo; the University of Wisconsin at Milwaukee Library; the Duke University Library; the Detroit Public Library; and especially the Purdy Library, Wayne State University.

The Wayne State English Department and a Wayne State University summer grant have assisted in the completion of the book, which was typed by Margaret Maday, who did an exceptionally fine job.

I have used, whenever possible, the Norton Critical Edition of Shelley's prose and poetry edited by Donald H. Reiman and Sharon B. Powers (New York, 1977). I have relied on Frederick L. Jones's edition of Shelley's letters (Oxford: Clarendon Press, 1964) and have cited from letters and other material in *Shelley and His Circle, 1773-1822*, edited by Kenneth N. Cameron and Donald H. Reiman (Harvard University Press and the Carl and Lily Pforzheimer Foundation, 1961-1973). For Shelley's prose, I have used the Julian edition (Roger Ingpen and Walter Peck, eds., *The Complete Works of Percy Bysshe Shelley* [1926-1930; rpt. New York: Gordian Press, 1965]). For William Godwin's *Enquiry Concerning Political Justice*, I have used the three volumes edited by F.E.L. Priestley (University of Toronto Press, 1946).

A portion of Chapter One appeared in a slightly different form in "Godwin's Philosophy: A Revaluation," *Journal of the History of Ideas*, 39 (1978), 615-26. The editor has given me permission to use this material.

I do not include a bibliography because numerous bibliographies are readily available and my footnotes are sufficiently extensive.

Finally, I thank Charles Baxter, Ross Pudaloff, Daniel J. Hughes, Tom Morris, Donald H. Reiman, and John P. Clark for having read the manuscript in one form or another and offering useful suggestions; to them I am especially grateful, although I am of course responsible for whatever errors the book contains. I also want to thank Mrs. Arthur Sherwood, literature editor at Princeton Univesity Press, and Judith May, the copy editor.

Introduction

AT ONE TIME Shelley was mistakenly viewed as no more than a disciple of William Godwin, whose political ideas he supposedly translated into poetry. The last five decades of Shelley scholarship have laid to rest this oversimplification by illustrating other philosophical influences, and showing how the poetry and prose are related to the times in which they were written.[1] Godwin's anarchist philosophy, however, was such a decisive influence on Shelley that it is necessary to reexamine the relationship, but this time with the benefit of knowing the full complexity of Shelley's literary situation.[2] Shelley was Godwin's most critical student, thoroughly understanding his philosophical anarchism so that he made it his own, eventually revising it to meet the requirements of new political problems and to accommodate his own political insights. Viewed in terms of the entire radical tradition, and not just Godwin's anarchism, Shelley's political philosophy becomes more comprehensible, acquiring a coherence that maintains itself from the beginning to the end of his literary career.

Shelley tried to separate interests and politics so that his political philosophy would articulate universal values, not material or selfish interests. At the time, however, the political conflict was clearly one of material interests, with a disenfranchised majority, mostly poor, struggling to wrest power away from an entrenched ruling elite of aristocratic families. Since material concerns were so dominant, it seems "utopian" for Shelley to disengage interests from politics because neither the rich nor the poor were in a position to recognize universal values. Shelley, however, believed that conditions were favorable for going beyond power politics. He consistently supported the English reform movement in its struggle for parliamentary reform, but also tried to sway the movement toward libertarian ideas he believed free from the taint of class interests. Perhaps the most interesting feature of Shelley's political writings is the attempt to maintain a reasonable balance between achieving realizable goals and moving toward an anarchist ideal.

Although Shelley believed he was speaking for universal concepts, he never could transcend his social conditioning as a member of the titled gentry whose economic interests were rooted in the land and whose cultural assumptions were of the leisure class. "Radical" Shelley was, in many ways, quite un-radical, so that with considerable justification Donald Reiman calls him an agrarian reactionary.[3] Yet, when located in the historical context of both English politics and nineteenth-century radical thought, then Shelley's politics, in all their contradictory complexity, are an important contribution.[4] Shelley is in a line of visionary radicals whose perception of what is socially possible is "utopian" in the sense that it is thoroughly beyond the confines of the established order. Since so many nineteenth-century socialists were indeed visionary, then Shelley becomes a by no means irrelevant example. It is important to disclose the aristocratic, agrarian, and biased aspects of Shelley's radicalism, but one should not be surprised to find such features. Is anyone free from the conditioning of society? When, however, one situates Shelley in his historical context, one can appreciate his efforts, however imperfect.

"Philosophical anarchism" is a precursor of the nineteenth-century anarchism of Proudhon, Bakunin, and Kropotkin, a tradition which culminated in the Spanish revolution of the 1930s; but it is also within the tradition of democratic socialism. Especially as revised by Shelley, philosophical anarchism establishes a political ideal, a utopia, toward which society is moving in stages; it rejects a millenarian logic whereby utopia could be achieved immediately; it accepts politics as a process of gradual reforms and compromise, as well as ethical idealism. Shelley's attempt to strike a workable balance between the possible and the ideal is more characteristic of democratic socialism than of anarchism. Nevertheless, his preference for direct democracy, his repudiation of "Jacobin" centralism, and his libertarian critique of militarism and other forms of authoritarian coercion are quite remote from the more "Fabian" styles of democratic socialism and more consistent with the "participatory democracy" hailed by the anarchistic New Left.

Shelley believed that the economic infrastructure had been sufficiently developed to permit an egalitarian community without poverty or excessive toil. Therefore, he concentrated on the conditions of freedom, rather than the preconditions; his "visionary" radicalism, then, is grounded on the assumption that equality is possible.[5] Although Shelley was wrong about the preconditions, he explored in interesting ways the conditions of freedom. Utopian speculation is an important, if especially ambiguous, enterprise; while it sustains desire for social change, and encourages activism, it also has a legacy of authoritarianism. As a radical before Marx, however, Shelley shows a remarkable sense of utopia's problems and the necessity to move toward utopia in stages rather than all at once.

To consider human agency important, as I do, is not to dismiss determinant factors (determination, as Raymond Williams and E. P. Thompson remind us, means "establishing limits," not causing effects).[6] In the present study of Shelley, I pay close attention not only to historical determinants, but to psychological ones as well, especially the Oedipal configurations of Shelley's—and the reform movement's—political idealism. Shelley's literary career is incomprehensible without taking into account his search, sometimes desperate, for a sympathetic audience. Moreover, consideration of his personal life, as one can imperfectly understand it, is unavoidable if one wishes to perceive Shelley's work contextually. Despite all the factors that humanize Shelley and bring him down to earth, I consider his radicalism to be important enough to study closely and to learn from. An angel, ineffectual or otherwise, Shelley was not; a complex and visionary political writer and poet, he certainly was.

Radical Shelley

ONE

Visionary Radicalism
and Radical
Culture

THE PATTERN of development typically established for the English romantic poets is the transition from naive political radicalism to literary romanticism, informed by a faith in imagination and sober conservative skepticism. Although there is a limited truth to this oversimplification, it distorts the actual process the poets experienced. Distortion becomes myth when the Enlightenment (rationalist, mechanistic, revolutionary) is contrasted with Romanticism (imagination and feeling, organicism, conservatism).[1] This is especially misleading in dealing with a poet like Shelley, whose work reflects a growing pessimism even though he never ceased being a political radical. The central conflict from the 1790s to 1832 is not between styles of thinking, more or less "romantic," but between "Old Corruption"—that is, the institutions of the English ruling class—and an ever growing number of people who opposed it. Unless one examines the English radical culture Shelley was a part of, that native tradition of radicalism he modified, then it will be impossible to make sense of Shelley's complex development.

When Shelley was expelled from Oxford in 1811, there already existed a rich radical tradition which he was making his own. In 1809, Sir Francis Burdett revived the 1790s' radicalism by introducing his proposal for parliamentary reform in the House of Commons. The decade of the 1790s, however, was a different era, whose radicalism was crushed and driven underground by repression. But what Burdett started grew into a movement of nearly revolutionary proportions after 1815, and even though it, too, was defeated, its configuration was not the same, nor was the defeat as thorough.

One can begin a study of 1790s' radicalism by tracing the origins of a small group of reform Whigs, such as Fox, Grey, Sheridan, Erskine, and the Duke of Norfolk (the latter was the patron of Percy Shelley's father, Timothy, M.P. and later baronet). Although there was agitation for political change before the American war of independence (the Wilkes affair in the 1760s, Wyvill's association of freeholders, and Major Cartwright's call for universal manhood suffrage in 1776), the most serious attempt to launch a reform movement came with formation of the Society for Constitutional Information in 1780. The SCI had three basic demands: (1) political rights for Dissenters by repealing the Test and Corporation Acts; (2) annual parliaments; (3) better representation for the middle class. The SCI acted as a pressure group on parliament, urging their Whig allies to press for reform. Although reform proposals were easily defeated in parliament, the reformers did not take the revolutionary step of appealing to the lower classes for assistance—a step the French reformers took in 1789. The early successes of the French Revolution inspired the English reformers to take a more militant stand on reform, but the ruling class was more intransigent than ever. Edmund Burke's defection from the progressive Whigs signaled the impossibility of reform as long as France was revolutionary. Burke's *Reflections on the Revolution in France* exerted a powerful influence against not only the French Revolution but English reform as well. To grant a parliamentary reform, however moderate, during the Revolution, was to concede legitimacy to the logic of democracy at a time when the ruling order had to be defended.[2]

Although the revolution in France moved the ruling class rightwards, it had a strong "left" influence on the reform movement, which acquired in 1792 a plebian organization, the London Corresponding Society. The tradesmen, artisans, and laborers of the LCS introduced a new democratic element into English reform politics, which had previously been dominated by the prosperous strata of the middle class. However united by an opposition to Old Corruption, the radical culture possessed a wide range of different perspectives. Although there is continuity in the radical culture from the Foxite Whigs to the artisans of the LCS, distinctions have to be made. The most significant dividing line is between those who would be completely satisfied with moderate reform and those who would not. At one pole there was the republican artisan, a follower of Thomas Paine, while at the other pole was the aristocratic Whig, like the Duke of Norfolk, who wanted a constitutional monarchy (with a House of Lords), slightly modified to allow some middle-class participation. In the 1790s, these opposing views sometimes clashed. For example, the Duke of Norfolk was a landlord hated by the Sheffield area democrats because of the Duke's policies of enclosure and rent-gouging. The Duke who was publicly admonished by the King for his "radical" declamation concerning the "sovereignty of the people" is the same one who, without a qualm, drove poor laborers from their land in order to increase his profits.[3] But these diverse elements did not always meet head-on. A 1790s' radical pamphlet, which seems typical, blurs class distinctions.[4] Equal weight is given to lower-class issues (impressment, indirect taxation, Poor Law administration, game laws, union rights, enclosures, education for the poor, provision for the aged) and middle-class issues (religious tolerance, poor rates, land taxes, abolition of monopolies, debtors prison, legal reform, better provision for curates). The differences, which were real and would become more apparent after 1815, were somewhat softened in the 1790s when conservative opinion was so much stronger than radical culture.

To the left of the Foxite Whigs, but to the right of the revolutionaries in the LCS, William Godwin and Mary Wollstonecraft articulated a visionary radicalism which Percy Shelley, a decade later, was to adopt and revise. Two features of this radicalism are distinctive and clarify its uniqueness within the broader radical culture: its gradualism (and rejection of revolution and direct action); and its emphasis on literary and cultural radicalism (as opposed to political or economic radicalism).

Thomas Paine, in *The Rights of Man*, and John Thelwall, at LCS meetings, proposed to go beyond gradualism by staging mass demonstrations and even an extra-parliamentary "Convention." Imitating the French example, they appealed directly to the lower classes for support in challenging the power of Old Corruption. Coleridge, however, like Godwin, was fearful that this approach would lead to the revolutionary "excesses" of a *sans-culotte* democracy. In *Conciones ad Populum* (1795), Coleridge recommends that educated reformers plead *for* the oppressed, but not to them. It is dangerous to appeal to the self-interest of the lower classes before the "purifying alchemy of Education" has had a chance to "transmute the fierceness" of ignorance into "virtuous energy."[5]

The question of gradualism or militant action was the occasion for a split in the LCS in 1795, with the majority faction going with

Thelwall, and the rest adhering to Godwinian ideas. The LCS, under Thelwall's leadership, could mobilize a crowd of 100,000 in London to protest against the government. When the government contemplated more repressive legislation, Godwin wrote an interesting pamphlet which criticized Thelwall and the LCS for what he called demagoguery. Godwin goes so far as to recognize the right of government to restrain the activities of the LCS. "The collecting of immense multitudes of men into one assembly, particularly when there have been no persons of eminence, distinction, and importance in the country, that have mixed with them, and been ready to temper their efforts, is always sufficiently alarming."[6] Although Godwin recognizes the repressive nature of the legislation contained in Pitt's and Grenville's Bills concerning treason, sedition, and unlawful assembly, as we would expect him to, his primary motive is to plead for moderation in the reform movement. John P. Clark summarizes the issues thus: "Godwin sought in the pamphlet to convince radicals to become more moderate in their methods of seeking reform, to convince the public that repressive legislation is undesirable, and to convince the government that repression is unnecessary."[7] By 1795, however, the left was in no position to influence state policy, no matter what it did. Considering the weakness of the left, Godwin's moderate position was both prudent and realistic, despite the elitist nature of his argument.

Thelwall and others in the LCS, however, believed that only by appealing directly *to* the poor, as Paine had done, as the French had done, could they develop a movement capable of changing society. The implications of the Paine-Thelwall strategy are revolutionary, while the Coleridge-Godwin method is reformist. The key factor is the status of the laborer who, for Godwin, lacked the leisure necessary for cultivation of reason; therefore, the reformer had to address the educated classes first. When the reformer directed attention to the laborers, he would speak to them as individuals, not as a class. Paine and Thelwall were not much more egalitarian, however, because they believed they truly represented the interests of the lower classes, from whom they sought active support. It had become a radical tactic since the Wilkes agitation for a politician to use the so-called "mob" to frighten parliament into activity.[8] The two different positions, then, are much closer than is apparent at first glance because both assume that the poor themselves are incapable of rational activity unless it is directed by educated radicals.

Rejecting the "coercion" of politics, Godwin promulgated a cultural politics instead, elevating culture and education far above economic and political action. One reason for Godwin's optimism concerning culture was the expanding literacy at the time. The reading public was growing to such an extent that Wordsworth, in the *Lyrical Ballads* Preface, and Coleridge, in 1816, could complain of the debauched taste of popular culture, the evil effects of "the circulating libraries and the periodical press."[9] Sidney Pollard writes that "between about 1815 and 1835, . . . at least two-thirds even of the factory proletariat could read."[10] The swelling wave of literacy seemed to be ushering in a new era. Middle-class men and women had witnessed the emergence and growth of their own culture in the eighteenth century, and now the lower classes were "improving" their intellect with literary culture. Godwin and Wollstonecraft envisioned a middle-class cultural revolution, spreading in both directions, converting and transforming both rich and poor to the supposedly universal truths of nature, reason, and feeling. Defenders of the old order, however, were alarmed by the increasing literacy. Confirming conservative fears was the popularity of Thomas Paine's answer to Burke, *The Rights of Man*. At a time when the sale of 40,000 to 80,000 copies meant a spectacular circulation for a pamphlet, the 200,000 or so copies sold of Paine's essay represented a quantum leap. By 1809, an estimated 1.5 million copies of Part Two alone were in the United Kingdom.[11] In fact, Part Two disturbed authorities the most because in Paine's simple prose style he criticized English political institutions and proposed to advance reform by convening an extra-parliamentary convention.

If Godwin and Wollstonecraft had little faith in, and much fear of, the laboring poor to whom Paine appealed, they had an almost religious reverence for the power of intellectual culture to humanize whomever it contacted. To comprehend their view of culture, one must turn to the eighteenth-century novel, where so much middle-class culture came to be articulated.[12] Because it was a form less cluttered with rules and standards, the novel attracted numerous middle-class "amateurs," especially women, in the last three or four decades of the eighteenth century. The new novelists wanted to make some money as well as express in literary terms their own unique concerns. One can speak of a thriving middle-class culture from Richardson's *Clarissa* to Ann Radcliffe's gothic romances. The sentimentality, sensationalism, and "vulgarity" of the novel and romance were assertions of middle-class cultural identity. "The

7

repression of feeling," J.M.S. Tompkins writes, "though it was a mask of breeding in high life, was not yet a universally accepted standard of behaviour,"[13] certainly not by the readers of *The Man of Feeling* and other tear-jerkers. In the 1790s, however, with the emergence of the so-called "Jacobin" novelists like Bage, Inchbald, Holcroft, Godwin, and Wollstonecraft, the political implications and direction of middle-class culture became controversial.[14] As the battle raged between Jacobins and anti-Jacobins, the problematic word was *reason*; to anti-Jacobins, it signified a demonic force that threatened the family, patriotism, religion, property, and virtue itself. The controversy was not between styles of thinking more or less "rational," but was instead a political and cultural conflict, with Holcroft and others arguing for certain radical values that were subversive of what the Jacobins called custom, superstition, and prejudice. There is no deficiency of feeling in the Jacobin novels, but there are also a number of attacks on male superiority, the power of the land-owning class, and even class hierarchy itself. *This is what upset the conservatives*, not the presence or absence of "feeling."

A VISIONARY RADICALISM

However much one modifies the statement, it remains true: Godwin, more than any other radical, influenced Shelley's political philosophy. Cameron has written of the important influence of Paine and the reform movement. McNiece has shown the way Shelley's ideas and poetry were affected by the literature of the French Revolution.[15] Godwin, however, remains the central figure; only by an in-depth exploration of his thought can one see how important an influence he had on Shelley. He was more than just an influence, because as a visionary radical Godwin encountered many of the same contradictions and dilemmas Shelley too would encounter. Of Godwin's—and Mary Wollstonecraft's—works, Shelley read more, and more often, than any other radical author;[16] moreover, he incorporated more of their ideas than those of any other author. Shelley, then, was attracted to their visionary radicalism at the expense of Whig liberalism, moderate reform, and Painite or utilitarian republicanism. In three important areas their visionary radicalism was to the left of even Paine's republicanism. First, *Feminism*.[17] Neither middle-class nor working-class radicalism was much concerned with the rights of women, especially the equality Wollstonecraft argued for. Although Bentham favored female suffrage, his utilitarianism was inconsistent with a more radical feminism, which tied the liberation of women to an attack on economic inequality and the destructive effects of the "commercial spirit."[18] Second, *Property*. Paine was content with slightly modified laissez-faire capitalism, as was Wordsworth in 1793.[19] Indeed, at the time, this was a progressive, antiaristocratic position. The LCS and SCI concentrated on political questions, not economic or social issues. Despite what their opponents said about Jacobin levelers, the 1790s' radicals were not opposed to capitalism or inequality; at the most, they favored certain kinds of welfare legislation and different taxation policies, while Godwin argued for a kind of socialism. Third, *Perfectibility*. As one traverses the political spectrum, one sees radicals stopping at various points where they declare "liberty" has been realized. The moderates want to retain a King and House of Lords, while the republicans want to preserve aristocratic as well as bourgeois property; indeed, one of the "rights" of man declared by the French Revolution was the right of bourgeois property. Influenced by Condorcet and Fawcett, Wollstonecraft and Godwin believed in perfectibility, the infinite possiblities of progressive change.[20] Their vision of what society might become generated their critique of the established order. Rejecting revolution, they put their hope in evolutionary change directed by educational and cultural activity. By changing consciousness they hoped to alter institutions, which would pave the way for further improvement.

However much their radicalism appealed to Shelley, it possessed three problems that would trouble him: the abstract individual, culture, and evolutionary social change. There is a disturbing congruence between the demand to sever one's organic connections for the sake of radical change and the tendency of the Industrial Revolution to destroy organic culture in order to create abstract labor. It is not necessary to romanticize organicism, as Burke did, to see that it set limits upon exploitation. Sidney Pollard concludes that "the modern industrial proletariat was introduced to its role not so much by attraction or monetary reward, but by compulsion, force and fear."[21] Both agrarian capitalism and the new industrialism depended upon abstract labor, that is, a work force without specific or organic identity. In a feudal economy, the personal ties between lord and tenant, priest and parishioners, are crucial to maintain and reproduce the social order, but landless laborers on a capitalist farm are wage-workers, no more than that; in fact, in

9

the 1790s, most of them were additionally degraded by receiving supplements to their inadequate wages under Poor Law provisions established by the Speenhamland system. The early factories were run with child labor which factory owners purchased from poor houses and orphanages. Those children without parents and those without rich parents were the least able to protect themselves, the most abstract available work force vulnerable to maximum exploitation. Godwin's novel *Fleetwood* (1805) eloquently protests against the use of child labor in the section dealing with Ruffigny and the silk mill. Pauper children were the perfect examples of abstract labor because they had no organic family connections, no sense of traditional values with which to oppose the morality of laissez-faire. But visionary radicalism also wants to eliminate "custom" and "prejudice." The individual with visionary radical beliefs is motivated by rational benevolence, but is not connected with any particular social group or class. The attempt to ground a utopian dialectic on an individualistic basis places a great burden on liberatory culture, some of whose ambiguities have been pointed out by Raymond Williams.[22] Furthermore, Godwin's rejection of revolution or political struggle leads to a theory of social change that tries to dispense with ordinary politics. Although Godwin was not unaware of these problems, it was Shelley who investigated them in a more thorough way.

To appreciate fully the quality of the visionary radicalism Shelley inherited, one must examine Godwin's philosphy and then some of the novels written by Godwin and Wollstonecraft. These two aspects of visionary radicalism, philosophical and fictional, complement each other, as one discovers that Godwin the radical and Godwin the romantic are not opposites.

GODWIN'S PHILOSOPHY: THE DIALECTIC OF STASIS AND FLUX[23]

If one is to discover the elements of Godwin's philosophy that attracted Shelley and made him one of the foremost radical thinkers of the 1790s, one has to forget, as Shelley scholars are not apt to do, the miserable personal relations between father- and son-in-law. If Godwin treated both Mary and Percy poorly, one must temporarily declare the irrelevance of those facts, and examine Godwin's own writings, where one finds a remarkably astute defense of subjectivity and a fine awareness of the historical forces that were threatening subjectivity.[24]

Godwin's unfortunate diction has caused some misunderstanding of his philosophy, particularly in his use of two key problematic words, "necessity" and "perfectibility." It has been a common error to assume that Godwin meant that man, guided by "necessity," was moving inevitably toward perfection. In fact, however, Godwin finally dropped the word "perfectibility" in favor of "the progressive nature of man"—which was all he meant in the first place[25]—and held subtle and complex views about necessity. F.E.L. Priestley says that Godwin actually believes in free will, despite the overt statements to the contrary. The important controversy concerning free will, according to Priestley, hinges on the nature of motive. For Godwin, motive derives from the power of reason, but for Holbach, Helvétius, and Bentham, motive derives from the properties of matter; the nature of motivation is the significant issue.[26]

After one dispels the phantom "Godwin" who, according to one of his detractors, gave birth to "reason dehumanized" and "cool insanities,"[27] one starts to understand how such a philosopher attracted the romantic poets, especially Shelley. John Middleton Murry went so far as to equate Godwin's "reason" with the "imagination" of the romantic poets.[28]

A key to Godwin's philosophy is his dialectic of stasis and flux. Etymologically, similar words and concepts emerge from the root words *stasis* and *stare* (Latin, "to stand"): state, estate, static, station, stationary, stagnate, status quo, stability, statute, staid, stale, and standardized. Each word has its own kind of immobility which Godwin opposes with his principle of flux. The tendency of stasis is to arrest the enquiry of mind; fix it at some stationary point; appropriate the authority and power formerly aspects of subjectivity; reify the self into an object and political subject; and commence a new dialectic, not of enquiry but of prejudice. At one pole, the self is in danger of being abolished, while at the other—the pole of flux—it is stasis, government, and hierarchy that are in danger of extinction.

Godwin's dialectic proceeds from the antithetical natures of mind and government. He bids the reader to

contrast the nature of mind, and the nature of government. One of the most unquestionable characteristics of the human mind, has appeared to be, its progressive nature. Now, on the

11

other hand, it is the express tendency of positive institution, to retain that with which it is conversant, for ever in the same state.

The war against stasis will be waged by "incessant industry, by a curiosity never to be disheartened or fatigued, by a spirit of enquiry to which a philanthropic mind will allow no pause." The most important thing is "that we should never stand still, that everything most interesting to the general welfare, wholly delivered from restraint, should be in a state of change, moderate and as it were imperceptible, but continual." Nothing is worse than "an institution tending to give permanence to certain systems and opinions." Governmental stasis breeds revolutionary upheaval "by violently confining the stream of reflection, and holding it for a time in an unnatural state."[29]

But Godwin does not see stasis as something wholly external to man. The struggle between stasis and flux is rooted in the human condition. In an 1831 essay entitled "Of Belief," Godwin locates a primary source of evil in the problematic qualities of thinking. "We frame propositions, and, detaching ourselves from the immediate impressions of sense, proceed to generalities." The process of detachment is at once the hope for enlightenment and the source for so much folly and evil. In being able to formulate abstract thoughts and distinguish ourselves from animals, "we pay a very high price."[30] Godwin here reminds one of Rousseau's criticism of thinking. For Godwin, it is only by detaching ourselves from immediacy that we are free to subject propositions to the criteria of reason, benevolence, and justice; but this same liberation from the senses also has produced the horrors of civilization, such as war and inequality. Furthermore, mind has, according to Godwin, a *"vis inertiae"* that resists stimulation and makes mental detachment even that much more difficult.[31] An additional obstacle for fluxional enquiry is the authority of stability: if something is true, presumably it does not need to and will not change.[32] The ideals of revision and the open mind are essential to enquiry, but they can also seem to be rationalizations for inept and confused thinking.

Political Justice pivots around human fallibility. *Because* the human condition is problematic and because truth is so difficult to ascertain, Godwin finds it necessary to adopt a utopian anarchism. Since truth is not apparent, it becomes the goal of a project of enquiry, a process of trial and error, and comes from "that happy collision of understandings" which should have no end.[33] Godwin has taken the assumptions of Milton's *Areopagitica* and carried them to a logical extreme; what Milton and Protestant individualism started, Godwin finished, but concluded with his anarchism. He exchanged static, linear, top-down hierarchy for a democratic pursuit of truth. Just as the reforming Protestant sought to abolish mediating structures between God and man, so Godwin seeks to remove such barriers between people.[34] The aim of political science, in fact, is to simplify or eliminate political structures, decentralize as much as possible, until government ceases to be the overwhelmingly powerful source of prejudice that it has become. The authority that government exerts is due only to its power, not its philosophical acumen. What the Catholic Church was to the Protestants, government is to Godwin: it inhibits communication and impedes the search for truth.

According to Godwin, each mind's subjectivity is unique because each person's experience is unique, and the only truths each mind knows are particular truths; each case is *sui generis*. In *Political Justice*, Godwin says that "ideas are to the mind what atoms are to the body. The whole mass is in a perpetual flux; nothing is stable and permanent; after the lapse of a given period not a single particle probably remains the same."[35] "Everything," according to Godwin, "in man may be said to be in a state of flux; he is a Proteus whom we know not how to detain."[36] If mind is Protean and fluxional, then it follows that perception is essentially subjective. "Two men view a picture. They never see it from the same point of view, and therefore strictly speaking never see the same picture."[37]

Since mental flux is continual, even in sleep, the self is never entirely the same from one moment to the next. Nothing is perceived or experienced, however, discretely in unrelated segments, but rather we view a coherent context that is constantly modified. As Godwin says, adumbrating Dewey's "funding effect," "every idea that now offers itself to the mind, is modified by all the ideas that ever existed in it."[38] It is with some relief that the reader of *Political Justice* comes across some modification of the fluxional principle; Godwin admits that certain "resting-places for the mind" are permissible as long as we realize that these points of stasis, these theoretical conclusions, are only tentative, liable to be overthrown by later enquiry and further revision.[39]

Godwin's literary theory also places a high value upon process. In a controversy with his wife, Mary Wollstonecraft, he believed "incident" and she thought "feeling" was the most important element in a novel. Both opposed the giving of "sermons" in the novel.[40] The critical controversy over the changed ending of *Caleb Williams* has revolved around Godwin's motives; did he alter the ending due to political fear or was he more interested in aesthetic unity? Mitzi Meyers, with whom I agree, believes that Godwin changed the ending, just as he revised *Political Justice*, as a result of his enquiry and concern for unity.[41] The most significant treatment of literary process by Godwin is the essay, "Of Choice in Reading," in *The Enquirer*.[42] Godwin discusses the tension, even contradiction, existing between the author's intention and the actual effect the text has on the reader. What he calls the work's "genuine tendency" is not always the same as what the author intended or thought was the purpose. Aesop, Homer, Milton, and Rowe all created works that reveal this tension between intended "moral" and "genuine tendency."[43] Furthermore, Godwin has not been duly credited for developing the "Satanic" reading of *Paradise Lost*.[44] Godwin says that Milton's God is "so merciless and tyrannical a despot" that one must hate Him.[45] He thus opens up literary criticism to subjective response, a sensitivity to the creative process, and antiauthoritarian critique. Godwin was fascinated with the creative process from which can emerge unexpected and even unacceptable material as the byproduct. As is well known, he started writing *Political Justice* with the intention of showing how government can benefit humanity, and discovered instead, in the process of composition, that only the absence of government could be truly beneficial.

The creative process exposes the mind to stimulation by new evidence: old ideas are challenged, and new ideas are allowed to grow. In an 1801 essay, he says, "I had learned indeed that enquiry was the pilot who might be expected to steer me into the haven of truth."[46] His commitment to enquiry and the creative process caused him to dissent from the liberal tradition. His dissent can be seen clearly in his critique of law. A *sine qua non* of the liberal philosophy is the sanctity of law, along with due process, trial by jury, the right to a lawyer, and so on. But to Godwin none of this stands up to the criterion of justice. Liberal theory has a faith in indirection; there is nothing *intrinsically* worthwhile in the legal procedures, but they are necessary for the benefits they produce and the evils they avoid. Godwin's criticism of Burke, Rousseau, French materialists, Montesquieu, and of the philosophers of "self-love" (*amour propre*) dealt precisely with the idea that liberal theory tried to legitimize, namely, that political justice can be achieved indirectly by means other than reason and enquiry.[47]

In Godwin's critique of law, we can see his subjective dialectic at work. Law is perceived as an agency of stasis in conflict with mind's creativity, and an actively evil force as well. The coercion of law first "annihilates the understanding of the subject upon whom it is exercised, and then of him who employs it."[48] By imposing stasis, law generates a dialectic of unreason in both directions; the state becomes more irrational and the self tends to perceive what was once intersubjective as dominated by coercion, brute force, and power. For Godwin the coercion of property is almost synonymous with the coercion of law; of property he says, "the immediate tendency of the established administration, is to persuade men that reason is impotent."[49] If reason is impotent, then subjectivity, too, is powerless. The self is precariously wedged between accepting the omnipotence of objectivity, or asserting itself in violent action.

Law demystified is, in Godwin, no more than a set of opinions on what is proper social behavior; philosophically, a law has the same status as an opinion. But law hypostasizes opinion; it transforms an opinion whose origin was specific into a universal truth, with all the power of the state behind it. There is no reasoning with the law. The dialectic of reason gives way to the stasis of unreason. What is the point of thinking in a world where subjective preference is irrelevant?

Law freezes and immobilizes the dialectic of reason. What must remain a process to maintain its vitality becomes, now, a physical thing in the social universe that subjectivity must evade as one evades a wild animal on the prowl; in fact, Godwin actually uses the phrase "wild beast" to describe government.[50] Opinion reified operates as brute force through the court system, the judge, the jury, the prison, the executioner. But worse even than that, law is opinion mystified; it possesses the aura of authority; it enters subjectivity not as just any other hypothesis but as an extension of objectivity; there is the danger of the subjective realm becoming a projection of the objective realm.

It may be superfluous, at this point, to mention how much Godwin's conception of law differs from that of Bentham. A comparison is valuable, nevertheless, because it will reveal just how wide the chasm is between Godwin's libertarian dialectic and the dominant culture. Although Bentham was in his time a radical, he appears in retrospect a prophet, and one of the architects of bureaucratic mentality and behaviorism.

Godwin knew little of Bentham's work in the 1790s, but sometimes *Political Justice* reads like an attack upon Bentham. Repudiating the very essence of Bentham's philosophy of law, Godwin maintains that "delinquency and punishment are, in all cases, incommensurable," contrary to Bentham's essential premise that crime and punishment, like pain and pleasure, are quantifiable. The Newtonian moralist sought to formulate the calculus of pain and pleasure; and the ideal legislation embodied the perfect calculus. Godwin also asserts that no "two crimes are ever alike" and that to try to classify them and arrange them systematically is absurd, thus denying that there can ever be a calculus of crime and punishment.[51] He goes on to declare that there should be "no code but the code of reason" and, in a footnote, adds a *reductio ad absurdum*: "It would therefore become necessary to formulate not only a particular legal code for each citizen, but a new law for every crime."[52]

Bentham's perspective is succinctly expressed in his notion of the ideal prison, the Panopticon. The warden-guard can see all, at all times, from above, without being seen. From the vantage point of the legislator, others are visual objects to be controlled. The implicit assumption is that the legislator knows what is best for the legislated. Bentham says, "To be incessantly under the eyes of the inspector is to lose in effect the power to do evil and almost the thought of wanting to do it."[53] Benthamite law, too, is to operate like a pair of eyes, constantly reminding people what is right and wrong. The Benthamite legislator is not a part of the system his panoptical gaze defines. Instead, subjectivity is relegated to the role of designing the structure by which subjectivity itself is obliterated.[54]

The anarchistic simplification of social structures which Godwin recommends to replace the artifice of law and government has its parallel in literary theory. He says that literary style should be "free from unnecessary parts" and that it should be "the transparent envelope of our thoughts."[55] Godwin once again secularizes a notion from his Nonconformist heritage: he gives to the Puritan plain style an anarchistic twist, altering the emphasis for the sake of a pure and democratic humanism. The priority he gives to communication in literary theory also implies an educational theory. Education and enlightenment are of the utmost importance for Godwin, as Burton Pollin has demonstrated.[56] Pollin delineates the problems Godwin's position entailed, especially the wide gaps between his anarchistic theory and the practical political alternatives available at the time. As Pollin says, Godwin's utopian theories have implications that lead to a pessimism he only *fully* expressed in his fiction.[57] It is this aspect of Godwin, where utopia leads to pessimism, that I find especially interesting in relation to Shelley.

One must distinguish between a primary and a secondary pessimism. The pessimism of Swift and Malthus is primary: they both believe social improvement is impossible because the nature of things is arranged against any progress.[58] Malthus's pessimism leads to a kind of secondary optimism—at least for wealthy people. Because improvement is impossible, the rich do not have to make any sacrifices. Godwin as well as Shelley was an adamant opponent of primary pessimism. A proposition which neither Godwin nor Shelley ever retracted asserted: "there is no evil under which the human species can labour, that man is not competent to cure."[59] It is more accurate to call Godwin a utopian and not a revolutionary, because Godwin is able to create images of what could or should be; he is not able to show precisely how these images can be translated into action. A major source of Godwin's and Shelley's secondary pessimism is an anarchistic rejection of revolution. Revolutionary theory assumes that social ideals can be instituted immediately and by force, if necessary. From the first edition of *Political Justice* (1793) to his last book, *Thoughts on Man* (1831), Godwin never ceased reminding his readers that revolution was unacceptable.

Instead of revolution, he pinned his hopes on progress, cultivation of truth, and sincerity. His notion of progress is best epitomized in his analysis of the origins of language.[60] Godwin agrees with Rousseau's *Discours sur les origines du l' inégalité* that the extremely complex operations performed by language could not have been created except by centuries of collective effort—slow, laborious, imperceptible. Godwin prefers this kind of social development because it does not require any extraordinary effort; there is no need for politics or special actions; one merely does what one would do normally, regardless of progress or of any other historical trend alien to experienced values. He characteristically wants to narrow the distinction between politics and ethics at the expense of politics.

His idea of progress must be sharply contrasted with the optimistic idea of "progress" characteristic of the Victorian era. Certain changes exhibit progress, but there is no necessary and inevitable march of improvement from primitive to modern times. In fact, progress can be reversed, subject to historical "vicissitudes of flux-reflux."[61] Greece and Rome, for example, achieved states of development that, in some areas at least, have yet to be matched. He does see, however, an unbroken tide of progress since the Renaissance, and he has high hopes for its continuing. His reasons were by no means naive: he saw the printing press as a revolutionary invention.

An important aspect of progress was its precariousness. The existence and vitality of progress were caught between the threatening forces of political institutions and revolutionary upheaval. However much he sympathized with revolutionaries and even conceded that, as the last resort of all last resorts, he would sanction revolution,[62] he saw things which, paradoxically, make revolution reactionary. First, a revolution is not libertarian. Civil liberties and the freedom of enquiry diminish during revolution; hence, revolution retards intellectual progress. Second, revolution sets in motion what he calls "the passions"—revenge, hatred, fear, selfishness—which go unchecked by reason. Third, revolution is illusory: it pretends to usher in the golden age when, in fact, it cannot. Godwin is not an absolute pacifist. That revolution kills people is not, in his view, a *prima facie* case against it.

> The abuses which at present exist in political society are so enormous, the oppressions which are exercised so intolerable, the ignorance and vice they entail so dreadful, that possibly a dispassionate enquirer might decide that, if their annihilation could be purchased, by an instant sweeping of every human being now arrived at years of maturity, from the face of the earth, the purchase would not be too dear.[63]

His idea of revolution as illusion came from his analysis of oppression, which he saw as *essentially* "mental." That oppression was essentially psychological did not mean that poverty, prisons, and war were figments of the imagination. Indeed, the only absolute evil in his philosophy is pain, which, no matter what the context, is always evil. Rather, Godwin believed that if a majority of people were truly convinced that the government was illegitimate, then it would be a rather simple matter to enact the transfer of power. He believed that the achievement of revolutionary consciousness virtually constituted the revolution; if the oppressed ceased honoring the oppressor, then the chains would fall. *Either* the people are not really enlightened, do not really wish to enjoy freedom, and therefore the revolution is, in fact, a *coup d'état* of ambitious politicians

who speak a "revolutionary" rhetoric, *or* the people fully enlight-
ened really desire freedom and the oppressor's hold on them is
precarious, so precarious that revolution is not even necessary.[64]
Revolution also engenders the illusion that just one "grand revo-
lution" will solve all the problems. This vain notion is especially
"pernicious" because the individual's efforts for social improvement
should be constant and perpetual. Social reform is a continual proj-
ect, a process that should never cease. Still, one cannot evade the
pessimism that is contained in Godwin's critique of revolution.
Human evil is too great to be eliminated readily or easily. He sees
oppression as an eternal possibility, a potentiality always there:
"there will be oppressors, as long as there are individuals inclined,
either from perverseness, or rooted and obstinate prejudice, to take
party with the oppressor."[65] This is essentially the theme of *Pro-
metheus Unbound*.

Godwin's pacifist and libertarian scruples did not prevent him
from assenting to a violent revolution *if* such a thing could really
create a much better world. But he did not see how revolution could
perform what seemed like magic. In lieu of revolution and in ad-
dition to the silent works of progress, Godwin proposed cultivation
of truth and sincerity. He uses the stale metaphor of mind-as-garden
and spatial images of depth and elevation to describe the cultured
mind. But this trite vocabulary works in a new way, and he makes
a convincing case for what Roger Poole has called "deep subjec-
tivity." This subjective space, or "sphere of discretion" as Godwin
called it,[66] is the precondition for constructive thought. Without
the creative potentiality of subjective space, the self is at the mercy
of the prevailing mechanical objectivity. Godwin urges that we
"should remove ourselves to the furthest distance from the state of
mere inanimate machines, acted upon by causes of which they have
no understanding."[67]

Godwin's commitment to culture and cultivated subjectivity con-
tained no illusions whatsoever about the prerequisites of enlight-
enment. Poverty and protracted manual labor did not allow for the
leisure and energy absolutely necessary for cultivation of mind. The
solution was to reduce the hours of labor, spread the work equitably
through the different social strata, and reduce labor through a dim-
inution of luxury and the utilization of machinery.[68] Such a solution
seemed apparent and reasonable to Godwin; so why all the fuss?
He might have been surprised by the tenacity with which the wealthy
clung to their prejudices (as Godwin might put it), but he never

underestimated the evil of economic inequality: it brought out the best of his stern wit. For example, when asserting that the state is a class state, owned by and run for the rich, he says, "robbery and other offences, which the wealthier part of the community have no temptation to commit, are treated as capital crimes."[69]

Cultivating the truth was the means by which stagnation was to be dissolved. Enlightenment acquired heroic dimensions in Godwin's hands. No time is to be lost pursuing the truth, no matter into what inconvenient nooks and crannies the truth happens to lead. It is an aggressive adventure, but only superficially similar to Benthamite and utilitarian heroism. The images of utilitarian adventurism that come to mind are at odds with anything that Godwin would find acceptable: the legislator peering down from the eye of the Panopticon; the imperialist forging his way into Africa; James Mill and friends composing the legal code for conquered India; Kay-Shuttleworth creating one more statistical chart. Godwin, on the other hand, was far more conservative in his adventurism than Bentham. His utopian vision reveals his essentially conservative nature: he envisions a decentralist federation of "parishes," small communities in which each person does a small amount of labor. He would prefer to do without a technological innovation if it meant more manual labor and less leisure. The only legal machinery in each parish (and even this was to be phased out as soon as possible) was the jury, an *ad hoc* committee to act in an emergency whenever the need arose. He was willing to put up with disorder and inconvenience if it meant doing without punishment and prisons. The real business in life was enlightenment and humane association, and society should be cleared of the obstacles put in their way.[70]

It is here that one finds the greatest contrast with both the Marxist dialectic and capitalist development. Marx was no enemy of technological improvement as such, but he envisaged a socialist revolution using this technology to abolish scarcity. Contrary to Marx's faith in large-scale industrial production, anarchists have traditionally distrusted economic enterprises so centralized or massive that they cannot be controlled directly by the community. Furthermore, rather than accept the teleology of capitalist technology (that is, assume that the evolution of the machine must proceed without interference, as though it were an operation of nature), Godwin insists upon the priority of certain values: leisure, equality, sharing toil, direct democracy.

Godwin's joint doctrine of sincerity and cultivation of truth further removed his program from the conventionally academic. The doctrine of sincerity provides an outlet for immediate gratification; revolution, in a sense, is now, and commences as soon as one is willing. His doctrine of sincerity sounds like a call for the abolition of the superego. The goals are transparence between self and others and what he called "self-approbation" or, in psychological terms, becoming one's own father and authority. Shame, secrets, and repressed feelings are to be let go.

> Reserve, deceitfulness, and an artful exhibition of ourselves, take from the human form its soul, and leave us the unanimated semblance of what man might have been . . . were not every impulse of the mind thus stunted and destroyed. If our emotions were not checked, we should be truly friends with each other.[71]

One effect of insincerity is the corruption of language, the very medium of enlightenment; insincerity has the tendency "to cut off all commerce between the heart and tongue."[72] He did not subscribe to the ascetic and puritanical view that "regardless of the consequences, one must be sincere." Nevertheless, he could not see a way to reach a compromise between absolute sincerity and a prudent insincerity.

However original and brilliant Godwin's critique of society, it leaves dilemmas unresolved which Shelley would inherit. For example: if leisure is necessary for truth-seeking, and the lower classes have no leisure, then there must be an economic reorganization; but this very reorganization depends on an enlightened people. Godwin was unable to get out of a circle of imperatives, oughts, and conditionals. The philosophies of Holbach, Helvétius, and Bentham were, in contrast, optimistic because they saw human nature as a knowable quantity that could be manipulated to produce certain effects. Since it was man's nature to seek pleasure and avoid pain, man would inevitably achieve a high degree of happiness. Although Godwin often used the language of utilitarianism, he could not be farther away from their optimism.[73]

The gap between "truth" and "reality" reappeared in *Thoughts on Man*, where he discussed Necessity and Immaterialism. Although he agrees with Jonathan Edwards and Berkeley, he admits that these truths are impractical; indeed, in the actual world, we have to act as though we have free will and a conviction of matter's reality.[74] There is substance to what Judith Shklar says of Godwin. Godwin's

21

ethics, she claims, destroy ethics as philosophy because Godwin does not accept general rules at all, only unique particulars.[75] In a sense, Shklar is correct. If the only truths are particular, then what Godwin leaves us with is a procedure guiding us away from general, static falsehoods. Furthermore, if human nature is problematic and unique as Godwin thought it was, and if truth is so difficult to discover that any and all mediating structures between people have vicious tendencies, then Godwin seems to have led us close to atomistic subjectivism. How can there be community or commonality if so little can be taken for granted? The French materialists left us, at least, with a common human nature.

But in answer to these criticisms, one can say that Godwin was not interested in a "community" achieved at the price of subjectivity and reason. And, yes, human nature *is* problematic, so much so that "disorder" can be preferable to "order" in some instances. The real power of Godwin's thought is negative, its ability to destroy the pseudo-rationality behind social concepts supportive of the established political order. Nevertheless, the anxiety we feel after understanding Godwin is real and complex. For one thing, the implication seems to be that interpretation and critique are all that one can do and still remain within the boundaries of reason and the subjective dialectic. That is to say, language seems to be the only objective instrument through which reason can operate in the world. Shelley will reject this excessive valuation of language and extreme intellectualism. Secondly, another implication seems to be that "reason" can be practiced only under conditions of leisure. While it is admirably humane that Godwin criticized the circumstances under which working people had to labor, it is also a limitation of his own perspective that he sees *only* irrational possibilities coming from workers themselves. Shelley will try to correct this bias also.

GODWIN'S NOVELS

Godwin's novels provide an interesting perspective on his philosophy, because when the subjective dialectic first enters the fiction, it is through the introspective romanticism of Rousseau. Godwin not only read and reread Rousseau's *Confessions*, he also attempted to compose a similarly confessional work on his own life. Although he never completed the project or published what he wrote, his introspection went far enough to reveal what seems to be the emotional center of his literary life. Concerning his state of mind as a youth before becoming Samuel Newton's student, Godwin writes:

> It was scarcely possible for any preceptor to have a pupil more penetrated with curiosity and a thirst after knowledge than I was. . . . Add to this principle of curiosity a trembling sensibility and an insatiable ambition, a sentiment that panted with indescribable anxiety for the stimulus of approbation. The love of approbation and esteem . . . pervaded my mind.[76]

The words "curiosity," "thirst after knowledge," "insatiable ambition," and "love of approbation and esteem" direct one's attention immediately to the narrator-protagonists of Godwin's novels who possess these qualities. Furthermore, one can hear an echo in this passage from *Political Justice*'s praise for the restless intellect. In *Political Justice*, however, "curiosity" is a virtue, while in the autobiographical passage and in the novels, it is fraught with anxiety.

Godwin's overcoming of organic connections involved superseding first his father, a small-town, Dissenting minister, and then a succession of father-figures, including Samuel Newton. As discussed earlier, the doctrine of sincerity implied the goal of becoming one's own father by refusing to be swayed by the restraining voice of shame. The fearless enquirer, however, cannot extirpate the anxiety of having become fatherless. In the autobiographical passage, the young Godwin wants the approval of his teacher Newton, but the ambivalence of the desire is obvious. Although he can try to alleviate the anxiety to please Newton by conforming to Newton's idea of a good pupil, he can also conform, obtain approval, and then reject Newton (which is what Godwin actually did), to pay Newton back for all the anxiety and dependence he had been forced to endure. Love and power are mixed here in such a way as to defy separation. On the one side is love, dependence, inferiority, and on the other is hate, independence, and superiority.

If Godwin's "curiosity" can be traced back to a reaction against his father's neglect, then it becomes a desire to be loved by a more worthy father. But this desire too is ambivalent because as soon as one is loved by the ideal father, one has to acknowledge the real father's rejection and the impossibility of reconciliation; one has to face the extent to which one was hurt by the father. Furthermore, after one paternal rejection, the son is wary of other rejections, so that although young Godwin "trembles" for Newton's approval, he also dislikes his dependence upon Newton and his power of approval.

It is not my purpose to psychoanalyze Godwin but to suggest a psychological dialectic at work in the philosophy, and especially the novels. Godwin's own crisis, which seems to be reproduced in some form in *Caleb Williams*,[77] corresponds to social phenomena with similar configurations. Laissez-faire meant the end of paternalism, so that numerous people were forced into "becoming their own fathers" whether they wanted to or not. Although declining, the institution of apprenticeship was still current in Godwin's lifetime. With so many runaway apprentices, it was obvious that the absolute control over apprentices was both resented and difficult to enforce.[78] The absolute control of husband over wife was another customary relationship under attack. In the late eighteenth century, individualism affected many facets of social life.

The novels that arise from these psychological origins present an essentially social experience. The isolated, abstract self, whether powerless like the child laborer Ruffigny or omnipotent like the alchemist St. Leon, is a problem with important social implications. Radicals were asking people to abolish their organic connections with custom and superstition, and to overthrow their emotional ties to the oppressor class and its institutions. At the same time factory owners were demanding that artisans and peasants sever all connection with their organic culture and become a disciplined industrial proletariat. In response to the new exploitation and economic distress ushered in by capitalist agriculture and laissez-faire, workers appealed to the state as a traditional, organic class; they called upon the state to fulfill its ancient obligations to regulate the economy according to ideals of justice. The state, however, declared that labor was "free," that it would be an injustice to tamper with the organic workings of the market.[79] According to laissez-faire and the Ricardians, organic nature exists only in the market, in the law of supply and demand, in free trade, and so on. It no longer exists between classes or in social and political life.[80]

The most abstract self is the powerless laborer, whom Godwin depicted as Ruffigny in the novel *Fleetwood*. The pauper child is vulnerable in its poverty and its youth. Once Ruffigny loses the protection of a loving parent, he becomes an instrument of labor in the silk factory. Subjectively, Ruffigny views himself as other than an instrument because he has had other kinds of experience which he remembers and in which he roots his identity (working-class radicalism was also nostalgic for a prior mode of existence it considered superior to capitalistic dominance). He opposes to the instrumental logic of the factory his memories of play, the images of a past rural life in Switzerland, the pleasures felt in his body and expressed by his imagination. The main difference between him and his fellow workers is that he entered the factory at the age of eight, while they became "hands" at the age of four—standard practice at the time in the English silk mills.[81] He runs away from the factory to preserve his identity as other than instrumental, as someone who dreams, remembers, reflects, and enjoys, as someone with subjective depth. The only way he is able to escape further exploitation is to acquire a protecting patron. Ruffigny pathetically hopes for the patronage of the French King, of whose kindness he is so certain. Even to the young Ruffigny, it is clear that "free labor" only means free to be exploited. He is saved from a life of degradation only by the lucky happenstance of befriending Fleetwood senior, a man of benevolence, sensibility, and even more crucial, great wealth. Only by acquiring a worthy father with *social power* does Ruffigny keep himself from perpetual exploitation.

A similar example of abstract labor comes from Mary Wollstonecraft's novel, *Maria, or The Wrongs of Woman.* Wollstonecraft's Jemima is one notch below Ruffigny: she is female. As a poor orphan, she lacks any kind of familial protection, so that she is an abstract person *par excellence*. Physically beaten, exploited as an apprentice, raped, treated always as an instrument, Jemima somehow survives in London as best she can, stealing or selling her body. She escapes the hardships of proletarian life only be becoming the manager of a private madhouse; that is, she ends her own oppression by imprisoning other people. The novel suggests no third or middle course. The only way Jemima quits her job as jailkeeper is as the servant of middle-class Maria. Jemima insists upon service as the necessary condition of Maria's protection. But as a woman who has violated the rules regulating middle-class wives, as someone who has defied the wishes of her husband, Maria needs protection as much as Jemima does. Even though Wollstonecraft died before completing the novel, it is hard to imagine a plausible happy ending because Maria, too, is powerless, "abstract" by virtue of her leaving her husband. Henry Darnford is the protector for the duration of the completed narrative, but his presence is disturbing because of its necessity. The novelist also felt this uneasiness because in one projected ending, Wollstonecraft has Darnford betray Maria, who then has to plead her case by herself.[82] The isolated, abstract self needs to find a home, however artificial, lest society impose its utilitarian, instrumental logic on this specimen of free labor. Jemima is an abstract self by virtue of her class, sex, and family situation, while Maria exchanges the organic identity of wife for the abstract identity of feminist. The utopian promise implied in the narrative is the overcoming of universal domination by the community of the oppressed—Jemima, Henry, Maria. By telling their stories to each other, by sharing their histories, they make possible an association based on solidarity rather than hierarchy. That this is no more than a promise, overwhelmed by the omnipresence of domination, is made clear when each one gravitates away from egalitarian community and toward the established social roles of servant, husband, wife.

In Godwin's novels, there is not even a hint of possible utopian community. Indeed, community is always false, inauthentic, something whose contradictions render it inevitably destructive. The only relationship with utopian promise is between the text and the reader. The voice of the narrator appeals to the reader on terms of equality, as a fellow victim of society with contradictory movements. Like the utopia concealed in Kant's notion of reason, Godwin's community is of the disenchanted, those who face the truth, no matter how unpleasant.[83]

The four novels I will be discussing (*Caleb Williams*, 1794; *St. Leon*, 1799; *Fleetwood*, 1805; *Mandeville*, 1817-1818), all of which Shelley read, are narrated in the first person. Whether Godwin's method of narration derives more from Rousseau, Sterne, or Richardson, or even from one of his fellow "Jacobin" novelists, the important thing is the isolated "I" who speaks to the reader. The "I," however, is in every instance a deceived narrator, whose narration self-destructs in ways apparent only to the reader. Caleb, St. Leon, and Mandeville end their stories in a hopeless situation, so that their narrations mark their final public existence before they pass into the ineffable privacy of death or silence. Even the happy ending of *Fleetwood* might have been otherwise if the protagonist's wife had not been supernaturally patient and forgiving. These isolated narrators, duped and victimized by the social order whose institutional irrationality they reproduce in consciousness, speak to the reader as realists who want to smash illusion and face the truth. They, however, cannot see the whole truth which we, as readers and not participants, can see.

So-called reality has to be disenchanted because it is a network of lies and distortions. To use structuralist parlance, it is a text designed to trap the naive reader who cannot interpret. Not even one's own impulses that are experienced as facts of nature can be accepted at face value because they are products of a contradictory society. Caleb's curiosity, St. Leon's ambition, Fleetwood's jealousy, and Mandeville's misanthropy are not innate qualities which each brought into the world at birth, but represent a complex process of mediation between society and desire. The disenchanting power of the novel rests with its ability to show these qualities in their full, self-destructive career.

The paradox of Godwin's novels is that the naive character, although trapped, coerced, and deceived, is unaware of alternatives, so he or she experiences reality from the perspective of epistemological certainty. In *Caleb Williams*, both Laura and Collins refuse to believe Caleb's innocence because it will subvert their worldview. They prefer to dismiss evidence that complicates their criteria of judgment than to question their *system* of judgment.[84] Although Marguerite suffers in *St. Leon*, she does so in a context of normality. If her husband had fulfilled his role of good husband, then she would never have complained; she never doubted the social foundation upon which happiness rested. The contrast in *Fleetwood* is between the husband who suffers because of a jealousy he creates and the wife who suffers because of his jealousy. The self-destructive character is forced to doubt his own impulses, while the innocent victim has a secure identity. Likewise, Mandeville destroys himself and those he loves, but only he is fully aware of how guilty and perverse he is. His victims are only aware of their own innocence. In Godwin's novels, to be an innocent victim is a fortunate occurrence.

Political Justice depicts society as ideological: Burke's organic society is a system of power relationships, none of which can be justified according to ideals of justice and rational benevolence. The naive citizen who rejects radical reason cannot avoid the fate of oppression, either as victim or victimizer. Behind the so-called sacred rights of obedience, deference, and property, Godwin discloses self-interest, coercion, and deception. If society must be interpreted in order to perceive it accurately, then the question of authenticity becomes central. Lionel Trilling pointed to the machine and inordinate wealth as principal causes of anxiety over authenticity, but there are other distressing social developments.[85]

27

The dominant economic tendency in Godwin's lifetime (1756-1836) was the shift from a land-based to a capital-based economy. The enormous national debt contracted to finance the wars of the eighteenth century and against Napoleon facilitated the movement of wealth from land to banks. Manipulation of laws, ultimately words on pieces of paper, became a primary means by which wealth was transferred and reproduced. Virtually every radical in Shelley's day criticized the baneful consequences of "paper money." The question of "paper" became significant for peasants because squatters and tenants without the proper legal documents were told by enclosure agents they had no rights to the land; the concept of traditional rights meant nothing in court. Forgery was a capital offense, and one of the most famous criminal cases of the 1820s involved forged Bank of England notes.[86] If economic rights were no longer rooted in concepts of organic community, hereditary tenure, and mutual obligation, then they became dependent instead on manipulation of words.[87] Although there were abuses in the old system, the new system allowed for greater uncertainty and more opportunities of deception. It is no accident, surely, that *St. Leon*, *Fleetwood*, and *Mandeville* all involve at least one episode in which hereditary property is threatened by gamblers, duplicitous relatives, and scheming lawyers. It is also appropriate that the social ideal in *Political Justice* is not a complex, industrial society, but a small village. The greatest source of inauthenticity was not inordinate wealth *per se*, but *abstract* wealth that produced rapid social change impossible to control.

Another reason for epistemological doubt is historicism. If individuals are shaped by institutions which, in turn, are modified during historical development, then neither "self" nor "society" is ever the same.[88] If change is constant, then upon what foundations can ethics rest? In *Caleb Williams*, the ethical ideals of Falkland are historically specific and represent the values of a landed aristocracy. The ideals of honor and reputation self-destruct because they rest upon inequality which Falkland can exploit to his advantage when it suits him. St. Leon's excessive desire for fame and reputation is carefully accounted for in the narrative (early death of his father, a passionate attachment to his mother who encouraged "chivalry," and so on), but it is also historically specific. Loyalty to King, aristocratic property, patriarchal family, and the master-servant relationship are all ethical norms in the world the novel portrays, but all of these are institutions *Political Justice* criticizes mercilessly. If, as Godwin believes, one's moral life determines one's real value as a human being, then ethical relativity seems to undermine the centrality of ethics.

The conflict between historicism and ethics is most apparent in *Mandeville, A Tale of the Seventeenth Century*, where the morally attractive characters invariably take the "wrong" religious and political positions. Although Godwin in fact favored the Independents and Cromwell, his morally superior Clifford is a Catholic convert and a royalist. Mandeville's morally perfect sister, Henrietta, is both apolitical and nonsectarian, almost as though her purity depended on her withdrawal from the public sphere. Mandeville, however, cannot understand how his perfect sister could fall in love with and marry someone so ethically odious as a Catholic. The suggestion of the novel is that ethics and politics are independent of each other. Clifford is virtuous not because of his religion or politics, but solely because of his private life, his actual relationships with others. And even if Mandeville had been a republican and an Independent, he would have been as morally bankrupt as he actually was as a royalist and Presbyterian. Furthermore, the virtue of Clifford and Henrietta cannot be translated into the public realm, where virtue is powerless even to modify the destructive misanthropy of Mandeville.

At the center of *Mandeville* is not ethics but self-destruction. An explanation for the fact that each of Godwin's novels is narrated by a self-destroying protagonist is authenticity. In other words, the alienation of the extreme situation is an attempt to discover and experience authentic reality, which normal society tries to bury in falsehoods. Trilling, Miyoshi, Bataille, Massey, Sontag, and numerous others, especially in the existentialist tradition, have written on the extreme situation as an avenue to knowledge inaccessible otherwise.[89] The wager is something like this: in exchange for a false happiness, the nihilist gets authentic suffering; instead of a false identity which mystifies contradictory social relations, a true identity based on misery and isolation; instead of the lie, the truth. I am distorting the voluntary element here because it is not the characters who choose to be nihilistic, it is Godwin who chooses to write about them. But the implication seems clear enough: in a contradictory society only a contradictory self can perceive the authentic configurations of reality. The problem with characters like Clifford and Henrietta is that the happiness they promise announces a premature closure, a permanent separation of ethics and politics, self and society, private and public. As Hegel sees Rameau's nephew, so Godwin sees his nihilistic narrators: their negative transcendence disrupts spirit so that it can reconstitute itself later and on a higher level.[90]

Godwin, as a necessitarian, traces Mandeville's misanthropy to his traumatic past: the massacre of his parents by the Irish Catholics, his upbringing in the gloomy atmosphere of his uncle's estate, his education at the hands of a fanatical (but good-natured) Calvinist. The determining past, then, is dominated by the existence of loss, the loss of parents, of a happy home, of a pleasure-oriented childhood. At one point when Mandeville is flattered into a brief optimism, he says of himself: "I am not lost in loss itself."[91] But, of course, he is. Destroying all possibilities of normal happiness, he preserves his special identity as victim, as someone who has lost everything and so is nothing. Through misanthropy he enshrines his love for his dead parents and the grief over his lost childhood. By refusing to forget, he roots his identity in loss.

Of his irrational hatred of Clifford, he says, "He is a part of myself, a disease that has penetrated to my bones, and that I can never get rid of, as long as any portion of consciousness shall adhere to the individual Mandeville."[92] Clifford, then, is Mandeville's other self, his opposite, the self he can never become as long as he maintains his identity as victim. Benevolent, warm, forgiving, friendly, Clifford betrays no consciousness whatsoever of evil, contradiction, or trauma. Clifford is the person Mandeville would have become if he had not been Mandeville. Godwin's ethics must acknowledge Clifford as virtuous, but Godwin's sympathy is with Mandeville. The trauma of loss is truer to the actual historical situation than the Shaftesburean sensibility of Clifford. After all, it is easier to be perpetually charming if one has had no traumatic experiences. Mandeville's negativity insists upon the reality of suffering as the essence of experience, not to be forgotten. By refusing to forget, he locates the trauma of loss at the center of consciousness, so that the ethics of benevolence and sensibility seem remote from the reality of lived experience.

The greatest contrast with the fate of the nihilist is the happy marriage. Mandeville's insanity derives from the marriage of his sister and Clifford; he also undermines his own marriage. Like Coleridge's Mariner or Goethe's Werther or Rousseau's St. Preux, Godwin's narrators are excluded from "domestic bliss." When Fleetwood finally does marry, he cannot enjoy the happiness of the relationship, but tries his hardest to destroy it with his jealousy.

Although St. Leon is married to a woman of perfection, Marguerite, he threatens to destroy the relationship first by gambling away his estate and then by following his Faustian impulses. I think there is no question that Godwin loved Mary Wollstonecraft, whose death was the greatest loss of his life. The persistence of isolation in the novels cannot be reduced, however, either to Godwin's own grief or to hypothetical ambivalence. I think, rather, that Godwin could not reconcile the happiness of marriage, representing a typical novelistic-literary closure, symbolic of resolution, with the social misery that seemed so much truer, more authentic, more necessary to be remembered.

The most interesting treatment of self-destruction is in *Caleb Williams*. As a member of the lower classes, Caleb Williams can be either a loyal, naive servant, who accepts the social norms at face value, or an inquisitive, rebellious figure, animated by curiosity. Those critics who blame him for his curiosity and even portray him as the principal villain of the novel are exercising a misplaced moralism. It is the society, not any one character, who is the real villain in *Caleb Williams*. Neither aristocratic honor (Falkland), the master-servant relationship, nor sincerity (Caleb Williams) can save the characters from tragedy, which derives from severe contradictions, not from individual moral inadequacy.

The ambiguity of benevolence is that it is discretionary, since it rests upon hierarchical foundations. Although Fleetwood senior befriended the powerless Ruffigny, he certainly did not have to. Late eighteenth-century literature was obsessed with benevolence, defining its limits and propriety, but it was clear that by benevolence the age of sensibility did not mean equality. In fact, inequality is tied to benevolence in an inextricable way. Feelings of gratitude and pity have little meaning except in conditions of inequality. Fleetwood rescuing the poor orphan, middle-class Maria befriending proletarian Jemima, Falkland trying to protect Miss Melville and the Hawkins family: this is benevolence. Young Godwin's ambivalence towards his teacher Newton is similarly grounded in a hierarchical relationship. The real negation of benevolence is not malevolence or self-love, but solidarity, the community of the oppressed on terms of equality. Of gratitude, Godwin says in *Political Justice*, it "is no part either of justice or virtue."[93]

Gratitude and obedience are appropriate kinds of behavior for a servant with a good master, which Falkland undoubtedly is. The actual historical tendency, as I have already noted, was in the op-

31

posite direction, away from the organic relationships such as master-servant and toward class antagonism (the atavistic quality of the Sam Weller-Pickwick relationship in Dickens cannot be exaggerated). The Falkland-Williams relationship is an interesting example of social tension because it shows that even a good master and a fairly good servant could not avoid tumultuous conflict. If a villain like Tyrrel were used to demonstrate the irrationality of aristocracy, it would be ineffective because his failings are so obvious. It is the very *structure* of the master-servant relationship that breeds the tragedy of the novel, not the specific qualities of each character. If Falkland and Caleb were equals, Falkland would never have assisted Caleb in the disclosure of his secret. He allows Caleb's curiosity to bear fruit because he knows how much more powerful he is in comparison to his servant. Likewise, Falkland's secrets would not have the delicious attraction they possess for Caleb if he were not an underling, a social inferior. Clearly, knowledge for Caleb is a method of acquiring power that society has structured out of his reach.

There is only one way to explain why Falkland neglected to kill Caleb and remove the one person who could implicate him in Tyrrel's murder, and that is Falkland's own desire for disclosure. The Gothic remorse Falkland wrapped around himself after Tyrrel's death, and the subsequent trials are symptomatic of his divided self.[94] Although aristocratic honor necessitated concealment of his crime, a higher system of ethics called for utter sincerity. He uses Caleb Williams to live out his own ambivalence, confessing his crime only after he has tortured Caleb long enough to make his guilt insupportable. Jacqueline Miller is correct in saying that Caleb never extricates himself from the rhetorical strategies of his "author," Falkland, but Gerald Barker is also right when he refuses to accept the justice of Caleb Williams's self-condemnation at the novel's end.[95] The narrative has not liberated the narrator from oppression—if anything, it has intensified his misery—but the ambiguity of innocence and guilt, as they are deconstructed in the novel, has laid a foundation upon which an undistorted ethics can arise. Falkland's self-destructive oppression of Caleb Williams is the only way he can exorcise the introjected ideals of aristocracy. By persecuting Caleb, Falkland represses that part of himself which condemns as criminal his cover-up of Tyrrel's murder. As Freud said, repression is never wholly successful and is, in fact, a way of remembering, so that eventually Falkland ends the tension by confessing. It is pointless to condemn Falkland's evil, because the novel develops it as a psychological necessity.

Similarly irrelevant are ethical judgments of Caleb's curiosity (as though he could have chosen not to be curious!). Caleb exchanges the organic ties of master-servant for the abstract identity of free individual; or, one should say, he tries to make the exchange. When he poses as his own person, he inevitably fails because in this particular society the aristocracy dominates. Neither Laura nor Collins, as I mentioned earlier, believes in Caleb's innocence, because to doubt the aristocracy's prerogative rights brings into question the whole society. For them, naiveté is better than disintegrative skepticism. In hiding, as he puts on the various disguises of the outsider, it is obvious that Caleb's only authentic identity is negative, as someone who cannot play his accepted social role. By ceasing to be the loyal servant, Caleb destroys his only available social role in organic society. Whether or not he tells the truth about his master is inconsequential compared to his disloyalty to his master. He yearns to be his own person, independent of Falkland, but it is clear that the only human being with whom he can have a close relationship is his master and persecutor, Falkland. The only identity he can have is in relation to Falkland, as rebellious servant. In an aristocratic society, a rebellious servant defined by an outraged master *is* a rebellious servant. The "facts" are irrelevant because no fact is prior to aristocratic power. That Caleb is something other than his social role only he and the reader know.

The lesson of the novels is the necessity of epistemological doubt. The organic, the normal, the institutional, the very surface of reality cannot be trusted. Only by means of the critical interpretation of experience provided by the narrative of someone who is, in a fundamental sense, an outsider, can the authentic features of society be perceived. The images with which Godwin and Wollstonecraft leave us make closure impossible. Their novels expire, they do not conclude. They reveal the contradictory nature of a society that presents itself publicly as just and rational, but whose hidden essence is suffering and exploitation. If the novels point anywhere, it is to that society, where any authentic closure will or will not take place.

CONCLUSION

By the end of the revolutionary decade English "Jacobinism" was only a memory. So successful was the Pitt repression that in 1801

Godwin could speak of the democratic movement as completely dead.[96] In the cultural struggle for the hearts and minds of the middle classes, the anti-Jacobins were victorious. So hostile was the public to anything Jacobin that Godwin had to publish his books under pseudonyms, and Godwin's friend Holcroft had to leave England. One result of the 1790s was to unite "respectable" opinion behind an antidemocratic consensus because the alternative was considered more fearful. However moderate the English "Jacobins" like Godwin actually were, they also introduced something frightful into public discourse. If reason, justice, and benevolence, rather than custom, prejudice, and self-interest, were to provide the logic structuring institutions, then there was nothing to guarantee the prevention of English *jacqueries* and *sans-culotte* democracy. A Yorkshire freeholder, a Dissenting factory owner, a republican intellectual, a Foxite Whig, or a prosperous merchant might indeed have many grievances against Old Corruption, but—with the assistance of much propaganda and effective repression—they came to view the evils of Old Corruption as more bearable than the possibility of social revolt. The kind of aggressive reformism practiced by the English Jacobins came to be associated with the possibility of social insurrection. When "reform" reappeared in 1809, reformers were at pains to separate what they wanted from the "illegitimate" demands of revolutionaries. The fear of revolution and the hardening of "respectable" opinion against "innovation" were a legacy of the 1790s that Shelley had to contend with.

TWO

The Making
of a Philosophical
Anarchist

(1809-1813)

INTRODUCTION

UNLIKE his Platonism or skepticism, which have long been taken for granted, Shelley's anarchism has received spotty acknowledgment by critics, even though his politics have been closely scrutinized.[1] When critics have discussed Godwin's influence, they have rarely perceived Godwin's anarchism as existing in relation to an anarchist tradition.[2] Before a self-consciously anarchist movement emerged in the latter part of the nineteenth century, anarchism existed in two forms, one philosophical and the other millennial. One can trace an anarchism from Diogenes and the Cynics, and even from the Taoists, to various heretical theologians, to some Enlightenment philosophers including Godwin.[3] This philosophical tradition was a movement of rebellious individuals who defied secular and religious authority. Millennial anarchism was a tradition of mass movements of religious heretics who wanted a paradise on earth with direct democracy and the abolition of secular and spiritual hierarchies.[4] Shelley discovered millennialism in the literature about the French Revolution, but he also found it within himself, as an unextinguishable desire for a world far better than the one in which he lived. Murray Bookchin identifies the millennial aspects of an intuitive anarchism this way: "Viewed from a broad historical perspective, anarchism is a libidinal upsurge of the people, a stirring of the social unconscious that reaches back, under many different names, to the earliest struggles of humanity against domination and

35

authority."⁵ While Godwin's principal contribution to anarchism was refining the philosophical tradition to a degree of consistency and inclusiveness that it had not possessed before, Shelley effected one of the first syntheses between the philosophical and millennial traditions.

Shelley's willingness to use specifically political means—reforms and political (rather than social) revolution—to advance liberty and equality does, however, estrange him from the main currents of nineteenth-century anarchism. In this respect, he anticipates the Marxian approach, whose ideal is a classless anarchy, but whose means of getting there are political and indirect, mediated rather than immediate.⁶ In Godwin's model of social change, he assumes that social consciousness can be educated progressively by philosophical radicals; this consciousness can be translated into political institutions, thus influencing consciousness in new ways, permitting further advances. If Shelley adumbrates Marx, so does Godwin. The critical difference between Shelley and Godwin is this: the former is much more activist than the latter, more eager to intervene socially with philosophical insights, and more willing to risk the dangers of revolution. Within Shelley's own anarchism, however, there are two different emphases, mediation and rebellion. When he concentrates on mediating the ideals of utopia, his approach is closer to Marx than Bakunin, even though he is following the anarchist logic of William Godwin. But when he emphasizes the Ideal, trying to translate as directly and immediately as possible the millennial vision into language or action, his political style is rebellious, in the tradition of antinomians who exist outside the bounds of *Realpolitik*. Shelley never fully resolved the tension, which is embodied in his concept of the poet-prophet or philosophical reformer, who exists between actuality and potentiality.⁷ He is at once a philosophical rebel, like Godwin, and a millenarian, impatient to drag heaven down to earth or pull earth up to heaven. He is both an enlightened rationalist, sensitive to the particulars of historical evolution, and a Dionysian anarchist, whose world-view is Manichean.

ZASTROZZI AND THE PROBLEM OF IDENTITY

Shelley did not just happen to read *Political Justice* and automatically become a radical. He had to be already psychologically inclined in a rebellious direction, or the ideas of *Political Justice* would have provoked boredom or anger. Shelley himself draws a distinct line between the wild fantasies of gothic romance and the serious literature he produces after having rejected the gothic, but one must not ignore the continuities between the one and the other. *Zastrozzi*, his first gothic romance, is superior to the later *St. Irvyne* because *Zastrozzi* is at one with its gothic impulse, whereas *St. Irvyne* bears considerable evidence of Shelley's loss of interest in the gothic mode. When he abandons the gothic, he does so only in the sense that he supersedes it, absorbing and incorporating whatever is vital for him in that tradition. Gothic elements are evident in Shelley's later work, most notably *The Cenci*. But what makes *Zastrozzi* interesting in relation to social radicalism is the way it explores the issue of psychological identity.

The question of identity resolves itself in social terms. One is a landlord, husband, father, peasant, king, or merchant. Identity derives from familial and social role. If, however, one's socially sanctioned identity no longer corresponds with one's own subjective concept of self, then there is identity crisis, and one must discover identity by exploration. Godwin presents us with two kinds of identity, the person of rational and disinterested benevolence who has transcended all familial and social determinations, and the obsessive rebel, whose pursuit of knowledge entails extreme experiences that take place beyond the boundaries of what is socially acceptable. It is this latter concept of self that Shelley's gothic is capable of exploring.

Zastrozzi, the product of a sixteen-year-old, is derivative and immature, but presents an adumbration of the older Shelley's preoccupation with desire, identity, and rebellion.[8] Since the novel is not well known, I will give a summary. Verezzi is a prisoner of Zastrozzi, whose henchmen, Ugo and Bernardo, transport the sleeping prisoner to a desolate cavern, where he is chained, and given only bread and water. He has no idea why he is a captive; indeed, his ignorance is part of the terror. A violent storm precipitates a rock slide, which causes the cavern to collapse (a similar catastrophe liberates Cythna in *The Revolt of Islam*, VII, st. xxxviii). His guards, assuming Verezzi dead, leave the cavern. Thus abandoned, he begins to starve, and eventually loses consciousness, but Zastrozzi has him retrieved from the cavern, just in time to save his life. He is nursed back to health at a country cottage, from which Verezzi makes an escape when Zastrozzi is away. Dodging Ugo and Bernardo, he makes his way to Passau, where he collapses from fatigue, but luckily, a peasant woman comes by who is in need of a laborer, and Verezzi acquires both a job and a lodging. Zastrozzi and his men are unsuccessful in finding their prisoner, but they meet their employer, La Contessa di Laurentini, hereafter known as Matilda. It turns out that Matilda wants Verezzi kidnapped because she is passionately in love with him, and to get him, she will do *anything* (this is the "unbounded and disgusting passion" alluded to by an irate reviewer of the novel).[9] The plan is for Zastrozzi to capture Verezzi and murder Julia, Verezzi's true love and fiancée.

Matilda's castle is not far from Passau, and just when she is close to throwing herself into the river in a fit of love-sickness, Verezzi shows up and restrains her. She confesses her love for him, but he politely turns her down and reminds her of his undying devotion and responsibility to Julia. Most of the novel (Chapters V through XIII—there are only seventeen chapters) is devoted to the slow but successful seduction of Verezzi by Matilda. While he is at her castle, she tells him that Julia has died. He immediately loses consciousness and slips into an illness from which he only intermittently recovers. He is forever on the verge of losing consciousness. Contemplating suicide, hoping for death, he somehow survives, nursed and encouraged by patient Matilda, whose jealousy and frustration give her "excruciating agony." After many weeks of unsuccessful attempts to seduce her sickly lodger, she carries out a scheme planned by the diabolical Zastrozzi—who has been, apparently, busy all this while trying to kill Julia. First, it is arranged that an apparent assailant will try to stab Verezzi, but Matilda intervenes in the nick of time, and it is she who gets stabbed instead. While the assailant scurries back into the forest, Verezzi is stunned by her gesture of love, and overwhelmed by the degree of Sensibility she displays. Second, he "happens" to overhear an apparently spontaneous soliloquy she delivers, lamenting her anguished passion, and he, being sensitive, is of course deeply moved by both deeds, and finally falls in love with her. After marrying, they enjoy "sensual and Lethean ecstasies" for about a month, but she still feels anxious about Julia who, Zastrozzi finally reports, is now a poisoned corpse.

But then an emissary from the Inquisition requires Matilda's appearance in court. Terrified, she flees with Verezzi—both disguised—to Venice. It turns out that Zastrozzi had deceived Matilda, because in Venice, she and Verezzi discover Julia, alive. Understandably upset, they have a lovers' quarrel which she apparently wins until Julia walks into the room. Unable to tolerate the situation, Verezzi plunges a dagger into his chest and dies. With the same dagger, Matilda kills Julia. The Inquisition learns of these events and arrests Matilda, who, with noble and aristocratic disdain, refuses to confess, in much the same manner as Beatrice faces the Inquisition in *The Cenci*. But then, in her cell, she begins to soften after dreaming that an angel recommends repentance, which would help her avoid eternal damnation. Called before the Inquisition again, she tries to persuade Zastrozzi, who has also been captured, to renounce his diabolical atheism, which he proudly and defiantly asserts to the end.

In his final speech, Zastrozzi lays bare his secrets. It turns out that all along, he has been avenging his mother's honor, which was sullied when Signor Verezzi, although impregnating her with Zastrozzi, did not marry her. Already having killed Verezzi senior, he manipulated events to culminate as they did, since he gained more pleasure by provoking his half-brother's suicide than he could have obtained by simply murdering him. Expressing no regrets, defiantly atheistic, he is put on the rack, laughs, and dies.

Only with great reluctance and caution can one take this delightful novel seriously. But one has to, I think, because the parallels with similar patterns in the mature poetry are too striking to ignore. Zastrozzi and Verezzi represent two different ways of acquiring identity. Zastrozzi is a committed actor, dedicated to the concealment of subjectivity and manipulation of other people. Verezzi is the opposite, a devotee of Sensibility, one who allows his feelings to lead him where they will. The former fights against nature and God, creating his own existential ethics, while the latter tries to become a part of nature without violating social conventions. Speaking to Matilda, Zastrozzi defends his ethics in an extraordinary speech. Defending artifice and role-playing, he says,

"My maxim, therefore, . . . through life has been, wherever I am, whatever passions shake my inmost soul, at least to *appear* collected. I generally am; for, by suffering no common events, no fortuitous casualty to disturb me, my soul becomes steeled to more interesting trials. I have a spirit, ardent, impetuous as thine; but acquaintance with the world has induced me to veil it, though it still continues to burn within my bosom. Believe me, I am far from wishing to persuade you from your purpose. No—any purpose undertaken with ardour, and prosecuted with perseverance, must eventually be crowned with success. Love is worthy of any risque—I felt it once, but revenge has now swallowed up every other feeling of my soul—I am alive to nothing but revenge. But even did I desire to persuade you from the purpose on which your heart is fixed, I should not say it was wrong to attempt it; for whatever procures pleasure is right, and consonant to the dignity of man, who was created for no other purpose but to obtain happiness; else, why were passions given us? why were those emotions which agitate my breast and madden my brain implanted in us by nature? As for the confused hope of a future state, why should we debar ourselves of the delights of this, even though purchased by what the misguided multitude calls immorality?"[10]

The image of the ardent soul burning through the veil, the Miltonic satanism, the ideas on pleasure, Nature, the dignity of man, the future state, and morality are hardly adolescent. The defense of role-playing proceeds from the assumption that the social world is hostile and ignorant. Presenting a public self is his way of protecting his "inmost soul." With the public world as pure falsehood, and private self as pure subjectivity, desire can obtain what it wants only through manipulation. Although he claims to be a hedonist, pleasure is hard work; it is something "obtained" and "procured"; emotions "agitate" and "madden"; and desire is something requiring "perseverance" and "ardour," even "risque." Delight is something wrested away from a hostile environment. The barrenness of society has political, even revolutionary implications, but there is also an enormous burden put upon the individual to create a meaningful world because nothing can be expected from society.

To Verezzi, Julia represents social normalcy, marriage, traditional love, whereas Matilda seems to be sexual pleasure incarnate, one who lives only for her desire. Verezzi is attracted to both, but he does not want to choose; rather he lets events test his emotions until a "choice" unfolds. He is also, obviously, attracted to intense frustration and conflict that threaten the ego. Indeed, the novel creates innumerable opportunities for Verezzi and Matilda to be *on the verge*. Whether they are on the verge of madness, death, orgasm, suicide, or losing consciousness, their familiar situation is of unbearable tension. A plausible inference is that there is something irresistibly attractive about this kind of extreme experience, which places the self in a situation that the self does not control. They both seem to will themselves into situations where forces more powerful than the will create additional stress. The hidden purpose of the conflict is to discover the nature of what Zastrozzi called "those emotions which agitate my breast and madden my brain." Matilda chooses to let herself be ruled by her sexual passion, with the hope that the obsession will lead to real fulfillment. Similarly, Verezzi allows himself to live through an ambivalence in order to discover his true identity, which turns out to be truly divided.

With all three characters, identity comes from "within" or as a consequence of passionate opposition to social norms. Unlike this painful quest for meaning, society has nothing to offer, so the individual has to create his own system of values. The problem with the novel is that the search lacks depth and seriousness, but the outlines of an authentic quest are present. One tension in the story is between the will that controls the ego, and the passions that try to destroy the ego, which is also imperiled by the false banalities of society. Verezzi kills himself, Matilda recants, and Zastrozzi is executed—the fates of the characters prefigure the difficulty the Shelleyan idealist will encounter, who had the nearly impossible task of creating a meaningful world in opposition to a society empty of value.

The message of Shelley's gothic is that society as it is possesses little value. Telling Godwin of his transition from gothic to philosophy, Shelley says that as a result of *Political Justice*, "I found that in this universe of ours was enough to excite the interest of the heart, enough to employ the discussions of Reason."[11] Before *Political Justice* he preferred fantasy, but afterwards hopes to *transform* society. Both Verezzi's passivity and Zastrozzi's willfulness can provide a psychological impetus for such a transformation. Receptivity, unbearable tension, and ego loss are depicted in Shelley's later poetry, where the process of inspiration involves an inevitable collapsing after an achieved coherence.[12] Asia in *Prometheus Unbound* is heroically receptive to dreams and voices which do not originate from her will. Will, however, is another instrument of creative spirit: Zastrozzi's proud will prefigures other rebellious figures, such as Ahasuerus in *Queen Mab* and Prometheus. One could say that Zastrozzi is the rational man whose rebellion is controlled by the will, and Verezzi is the obsessive rebel, whose search for repose is a process of discovery.

ATHEISM AND ARISTOCRATIC ANARCHISM

As in fiction, so Shelley in "real" life tested the limits of aristocratic identity with a combination of passivity and defiant will. The ultimate result was his being expelled from Oxford and banished from his home, Field Place. There is no evidence that he wanted to leave Oxford, where he could do as he pleased. So painful was the notion of being permanently alienated from his family that Shelley, as late as May 1813, was still trying unsuccessfully to find a means of reconciliation with his father.[13] Nevertheless, the whole point of *The Necessity of Atheism* was provocation. The essay's actual ideas, hardly revolutionary, derive entirely from Locke and Hume, whereas the title is far more militant. If ideas come from the senses, as Locke claims, then the idea of "God" cannot derive from sense-impressions. Since belief is not voluntary, there can be no "criminality" attached to unbelief. The essay concludes on a note of high philosophical purpose, with a commitment to "Truth."[14] At this time Shelley was a deist, and not yet—like Hogg—an atheist, but by sending the essay to the school officials and displaying it at the Oxford bookstore, they obviously intended to test the extreme limits of the school's tolerance.

Before the expulsion from Oxford in March 1811, Shelley was already developing rapidly into a rebel. On November 19, 1810, he orders Godwin's *Political Justice*, a book he probably first read at Eton the previous year under the guidance of Dr. Lind. The inconclusive state in which he left *St. Irvyne*, which he published anyway in November 1810, was due to Shelley's lack of interest in the gothic mode. Unhappiness with the gothic might have been precipitated by Godwin's *St. Leon*, on which *St. Irvyne* is partially modeled. Although *St. Leon* has gothic elements, it is primarily a Jacobin novel, whose "unity of design" and intellectual seriousness distinguish it from the more popular romances of Lewis and Radcliffe. On December 18, 1810, Shelley is contemplating what seems to be a Jacobin novel, "a Novel . . . principally constructed to convey metaphysical & political opinions by way of conversation." Moreover, "it shall receive more correction than I trouble myself to give the wild Romance & Poetry."[15] Perhaps influenced by *Political Justice*, *St. Leon*, or both, Shelley is expanding his literary interests beyond gothic romances. That Godwin was on Shelley's mind at this time is also indicated by a letter of December 20, 1810, where he alludes to Godwin's publisher as an acceptable substitute for the unreliable Stockdale. From this same letter it is apparent that Hogg and Shelley had even been trying to find Godwin's address in order to correspond with him.[16]

One dimension of the Hogg-Shelley relationship and their quest for answers to theological questions, especially God's existence or nonexistence, is clearly psychosexual. The brothers leagued together in an Oedipal struggle challenge the authority of their own fathers, the Oxford dons, and God himself. The rapidity of Shelley's intellectual development at Oxford might be explained by the relationship with Hogg. They stimulated each other, confirmed each other's self-confidence, egged each other on, and went much further in a rebellious direction than either would have gone individually. The homoerotic element is important, providing perhaps an extra source of energy to assist them in so recklessly opposing the Oxford authorities.[17] Hogg's radicalism melted away shortly after the Oxford expulsion under pressure from his father; it seems that Hogg needed Shelley's companionship in order to sustain his radicalism. (A simpler explanation would be economic: Hogg had to be a lawyer in order to make money, so he had to forsake radicalism, whereas Shelley could live on his inheritance.) Hogg's attempted seduction of Harriet in 1811 and the resulting histrionics on both sides certainly indicate sexual ambivalence being worked out. Shelley, however, after the Oxford expulsion, continued to resist the authority of his father and developed a deep and enduring form of radicalism. Even when Hogg had completely abandoned radicalism, he was still attracted to women connected with Shelley—first Mary Godwin, with whom he apparently did have sexual relations, and finally Jane Williams, with whom he lived after the deaths of Shelley and Captain Williams.

Shelley's interest in Godwin, metaphysics, and rebellion was not simply an Oedipal phase, although it certainly was that too. On March 2, 1811, shortly before the atheism pamphlet resulted in his expulsion, Shelley wrote to Leigh Hunt, who had recently been acquitted for the third time of antigovernment libel. Shelley now imagines himself taking a seat in Parliament once he is old enough, so that it is safe to say he does not foresee the Oxford expulsion or the alienation from his family. He does perceive the need for a "methodical society" comprised of "rational liberty" advocates who could then "resist the coalition of the enemies of liberty." To further this goal, he proposes a meeting to begin organizing. The references in the letter to Illuminism and the French Revolution indicate some thought on the issue of political intervention.[18] To extrapolate from this letter, it seems that Shelley was imagining himself working with the moderate reform movement—Burdett, the Hunts, and the remnants of the Foxite Whigs.

If Shelley or his father had been more willing to compromise, they could have been reconciled and decisively altered Shelley's future. As it was, however, he refused to accede to his father's demands, which included apologizing to Oxford and promising not to call Christianity into question publicly. Cut off from his family and Oxford, he had to fend for himself intellectually and emotionally. Godwin's anarchism would be psychologically attractive to Shelley during this crisis because *Political Justice* refers all disputes to the umpire of reason. Shelley could mediate his Oedipal conflict through the language of rational utility, relieving some guilt and allowing himself to develop a more secure identity. In the letters between Shelley and his father, Percy is usually (but not always) cool-headed and reasonable, trying to push the center of debate away from considerations of custom and obedience and toward philosophy. By disobeying his father on philosophical, rather than just personal, grounds, Shelley strikes a balance between will and passivity. He is at once a willful rebel and a victim of prejudice. Many a rebel in Shelley's writings will possess this kind of balance between Verezzian helplessness and Zastrozzian strength.

Godwin's Oedipally useful anarchism provided a philosophical justification for disobeying the orders of paternal authority. Whatever is not founded in reason has no legitimacy in Godwin's system. But if Shelley's letters are any indication, he did not subscribe to the main tenets of Godwinian anarchism until at least the June 25, 1811 letter to Elizabeth Hitchener. Before that, Shelley seems to be more of an antinomian, aristocratic anarchist, whose logic is quite distinct from Godwin's utilitarian and egalitarian assumptions. In an April 25, 1811 letter to Hogg, he uses "perfectibility" to refer to personal development, whereas Godwin's perfectibility is always in relation to social progress.[19] In two other April letters to Hogg, he says that Christianity is necessary for repressing the vices of the "Canaille," but unnecessary for the illustrious few like himself and Hogg.[20] In a May 9, 1811 letter to Hogg, he develops this position by first misreading Godwin, and then disagreeing with him. He mistakenly identifies the principal criterion of Godwin's ethics as "expediency," which is a falsification of Godwinian rational utility. Shelley says that only "motive" matters, not the consequences, even though Godwin had been at pains to insist upon both benevolent motive and utilitarian consequence as necessary criteria for justice. The letter's purpose is to justify free love for the virtuous elite, whose motives are pure, and who do not need restrictive laws.

Whereas Godwin fuses ethics and politics, Shelley in this letter demands that they be kept separate. There is total freedom for the virtuous few, but not for the corrupt and selfish many.[21]

The most likely source for this un-Godwinian anarchism is Robert Clifford's translation of Abbé Barruel's *Memoirs, Illustrating the History of Jacobinism.*[22] Adam Weishaupt's sect of Illuminists is especially anarchistic in Barruel's treatment.[23] The *Memoirs* were a good source for many heresies the pious Frenchman loathed, but which greatly interested Shelley. Conviction of one's own blessedness leading to the practice of free love is standard antinomianism. The aristocratic twist Shelley gives to it is partially a way of finding common ground with his past experience. He is not socially dangerous, he is telling himself, because he wants freethinking and fearless liberty for himself only. Furthermore, Shelley was infected with the biases of the aristocracy, some of which were starting to be eroded. But in May 1811 he was still an aristocratic snob.

Godwinian anarchism, although with an intellectualist bias in some ways prejudicial to the poor, is nevertheless egalitarian. Antinomian anarchism offers personal salvation from externally constituted authority and tends to be socially disruptive. It has also been egalitarian, but it is not necessarily so. Between Godwin's concept of utility and the antinomian concept of salvation there is a great difference, which is a creative tension in Shelley's later work.

REVISING GODWINIAN ANARCHISM

In a series of letters to Elizabeth Hitchener, Shelley articulates the main features of a philosophical, Godwinian anarchism. A special revisionary process begins on January 3, 1812, when Shelley starts corresponding directly with Godwin. Shelley matured politically and developed his own kind of anarchism as a result of his relationship with Godwin and experiences and events including the Irish expedition, the arrest and imprisonment of their servant Dan Hill, the Tanyrallt attack, government surveillance of Shelley's political activities, the Luddite insurrections, and the repression of journalists such as Eaton and the Hunts.

The letter to Elizabeth Hitchener of June 25, 1811 is the first certain evidence of Shelley's egalitarian anarchism. He writes: "I am no aristocrat, or any *crat* at all but vehemently long for the time when man may *dare* to live in accordance with *Nature* & *Reason*, in consequence with *Virtue*."[24] He has come to the con-

clusion that religion is the principal obstacle to the emergence of a
new society organized by reason and inquiry, which are two God-
winian passwords. But the emphasis on nature points to the Illu-
minism he read about in Abbé Barruel.

Shelley's growing maturity is apparent in a July 13, 1811 letter
where he has gone far beyond the snobbery of his "Canaille" state-
ment of April. He gave a beggar some food, and then tried fruitlessly
to engage him in conversation. He realizes the inhumanity of aris-
tocratic "benevolence" and understands the beggar's reluctance to
treat Shelley in a friendly way. Only egalitarian social change can
create the conditions permitting friendly intercourse among all peo-
ple because inequality poisons every human interaction.[25] Words-
worth, around this same time, was defending the humanizing effects
of alms-giving, as opposed to the logic of laissez-faire and the Mal-
thusian arguments against public assistance. Shelley is not opposed
to poor relief, but looks beyond the mere palliative of an assistance
which perpetuates inequality. Echoing *Political Justice* and *The En-
quirer*, he suggests in a letter of July 25, 1811 that the ideal of
perfect equality may not be attainable, but it must be striven to-
wards because inequality is the root cause of social misery. He tells
Elizabeth Hitchener that 500,000 "aristocrats" force nine and one-
half million other citizens—the poor—to labor for them.[26] Like
Godwin, Shelley foresees equality resulting from the diminution of
aristocratic opulence. Following Adam Smith's labor theory of value,
Shelley believes that wealth is the product of living labor, so that
the wealthier the individual, the more labor he in fact controls. To
diminish excessive wealth is to diminish labor and increase the
leisure of the laboring poor.

The issue of money reappears on October 26, 1811, when he
makes the Godwinian argument that possessing wealth as a re-
sponsible steward is acceptable under the criterion of utilitarian
justice.[27] Money, Shelley says, "commands labor, it gives leisure,
& to give leisure to those who will employ it in the forwarding of
truth is the noblest present an individual can make to the whole."[28]
Writing to Godwin, Shelley says that if he and his wife worked for
a living "at the loom or the plough," they would be "less useful to
our species."[29] He adds: "Probably, in a regenerated state of society
agriculture & manufacture would be compatible with the most
powerful intellect & most polished manners," but not now in this
society.[30] Godwin was not the one to challenge this view, to be
sure. Unlike George Ripley, Tolstoy, Morris, or Kropotkin—radi-

cals of a later generation—Shelley never subjected the dichotomy and hierarchy of manual and intellectual labor to a critique. Shelley inherits Godwin's intellectualist bias and only slightly revises it, but never in relation to the possibility of his working for a living. Nevertheless, for Shelley to believe that his wealth was held in a utilitarian stewardship was, for the time, a progressive view in comparison to the typically aristocratic attitude of doing whatever one wished with one's own.

In the letters to Elizabeth Hitchener before he corresponded with Godwin, Shelley's anarchism is for the most part Godwinian, except for its millennialism. Shelley imagines the "golden age," similar to "the millenium of the Xtians," although his own millennium—the "omnipotence of mind over matter"—is "the task of human reason." The full triumph of mind will culminate " 'when the lion shall lay down with the lamb.' "[31] One reason, I think, that Shelley preferred the first edition of *Political Justice* to the other two[32] is that it possessed the most enthusiasm for the triumph of reason. The most inflated claims for the omnipotence of mind are in this edition, where Godwin gets as close as he ever does to millennialism. Shelley is inspired by the millennial hope of the French Revolution, to which he is turning for political orientation just about the time he begins corresponding with Godwin. A day before he writes Godwin for the first time, he tells Elizabeth Hitchener that he is working on a tale exploring the failure of the French Revolution.[33] For Shelley, Godwin exists as a thinker who articulated some of the revolutionary decade's most enduring ideas, which need critical revaluation because the revolution failed.

Before Shelley begins corresponding with Godwin, he knows Godwin's work so thoroughly that he can suggest to Elizabeth Hitchener an order in which to read the principal works (*The Enquirer, St. Leon, Political Justice,* and *Caleb Williams*).[34] He demonstrates a better understanding of Godwin's thinking than he did when he thought "expediency" was Godwinian in a new letter where he contrasts Paley's utilitarian criteria in ethics with Godwin's emphasis on motive. He declares the Godwinian faith succinctly: *"Every prejudice conquered every error rooted out, every virtue given is so much gained in the cause of reform."*[35]

On January 3, 1812, Shelley begins a correspondence with Godwin that alters his life decisively. Ironically, the elopement with Mary, Godwin's daughter, is the event which generates a hostility between the two men that never entirely disappears. From January

1812, to July 27, 1814, when Mary and Shelley elope, Godwin's influence on Shelley was equivocal. Perhaps the only good thing Godwin did in person was to expand and deepen Shelley's literary interests by insisting that he study the great authors of Greece, Rome, and Elizabethan England. On the other hand, Godwin discouraged Shelley's political enthusiasm and reinforced the most dubious aspects of Shelley's radicalism. If he had listened to Godwin, Shelley would not have published anything; would have reconciled with Sir Timothy; would have joined the Whigs; would not have written the distinctively Shelleyan kind of poetry that he did write; would not have tried to intervene at all in the political and social struggles of the day. And this, from the radical philosopher of the revolutionary decade! Although Shelley did not like to admit it, Godwin had changed. Through his wife Harriet we learn how Shelley feels about Godwin. Harriet writes to Catherine Nugent (an Irish working woman) that Godwin "thinks himself such a very great *man*" that he will not allow any of the Godwin daughters to visit the Shelleys because Godwin has not yet personally met the Shelleys.[36] According to Harriet, Godwin

> too, is changed, and [filled] with prejudices, and besides, too, he expects such universal homage from all persons younger than himself, that it is very disagreeable to be in company with him on that account, and he wanted Mr. Shelley to join the Wig party and do just as they pleased, which made me very angry, as we know what men the Wigs are now. He is grown old and unimpassioned, therefore is not in the least calculated for such enthusiasts as we are. He has suffered a great deal for his principles, but that ought to make him more staunch in them, at least it would me.[37]

Extreme political repression was simultaneous with Godwin's discouragement of radical politics, especially the plans for an "association" of philanthropists that Shelley had in mind. Prudence and safety were certainly on the side of Godwin, who provided Shelley with an opponent against whom he could test and clarify his ideas, so many of which, ironically enough, could be traced back to Godwin's writings. On no major issue did Godwin actually change Shelley's mind, but Godwin did force Shelley to defend himself with more rigor than he might have had to otherwise.

A key disagreement between them is their respective interpretations of what went wrong with the French Revolution. According to Godwin, the only acceptable means of advancing social progress is individual discussion, because protest movements invite revolutionary violence and "tumult." Hostility to associations is a "pillar" of *Political Justice*; to make the poor aware of their oppression is to risk their taking "redress of grievances into their own hands." The libertarian philosopher should not exhort the poor to act, but should search "into the hidden seeds of things" and view phenomena for root causes from a disinterested standpoint.[38] One must learn "to put off self, and to contribute by a quiet, but incessant activity, like a rill of water, to irrigate and fertilize the intellectual soil."[39] There is either a quiet, peaceful agitation, or revolutionary chaos. The problem with the French Revolution and the English 1790s was politics, not a certain kind, but any kind. In the third edition of *Political Justice*, Godwin admits that revolutions cannot be prevented entirely, but the longer they are postponed the better. In the first edition, he did not advocate revolution, but he defended it as being preferable to prolonged stagnation. The philosopher must not retreat from the fray, but must make his presence felt. Shelley could be expanding upon Godwin's very own ideas of the first edition when he formulates an association of philanthropists. Shelley's analysis of the failure of the French Revolution is that there were not enough philosophical reformers—revolutionary intellectuals with high and pure ideals. Nor were they well organized, so that they did not have a great impact on the Revolution, whose bloodshed, chaos, hatred, and authoritarianism they could not prevent.

Shelley's novel *Hubert Cauvin*, which was to analyze the failures of the French Revolution, might have portrayed someone like Shelley, a rebel with ideals, trying to influence the course of the revolution. It probably shared similarities with *Laon and Cythna*, another reworking of the French Revolution theme. Perhaps he never published the novel because he was not sure enough of his own ideas to defend them from Godwin's criticism. By January 7, 1812, the novel seems well under way, and nine days later, he says that the novel will be printed in Dublin "cheaply."[40] Although he abandoned *Hubert Cauvin*, he did not abandon his concern with the French Revolution.

Godwin and Shelley had a major argument over Shelley's Irish expedition, especially his appeal to the Irish poor (*An Address to the Irish People*) and his call for an association (*Proposals for an Association of Philanthropists*). Godwin rejected out of hand any

attempts to address the poor, and rested his hopes instead on in-
dividual discussions with other members of the educated classes.
Shelley, however, is trying to mediate the truths of philosophy from
a privileged realm (where philosophy exists as one of the prerog-
atives of the leisure class) to the lived experience and consciousness
of the laboring poor. He tells Godwin the Irish pamphlet is con-
sistent with *Political Justice* because the essay contains "the benev-
olent and tolerant deductions of Philosophy reduced into the sim-
plest language."[41] He is not afraid that the Irish will turn into an
irrational mob once their interests and prospects are philosophically
analyzed. In truth, Shelley is not nearly as fearful of revolution as
Godwin. Writing to Elizabeth Hitchener from Dublin, he says that
these are the undeniable truths: "the equality of man, the necessity
of a reform and the probability of a revolution."[42] As Godwin
continues to throw water on Shelley's revolutionary fire, Shelley
turns to Paine for inspiration. On February 14, 1812, Paine's works
are being culled for useful quotations, with the ultimate result prob-
ably being *Declaration of Rights*, a leaflet designed specifically for
the eyes of the poor. Around this same time he is planning for a
popular audience the *Biblical Extracts*, which would "reject all the
bad, and take all the good of the Jewish books," as well as "the
moral sayings of Jesus Christ" liberated from "the mystery and
immorality which surrounds them."[43] Shelley thinks about his au-
dience, because he wants to be an effective social reformer. Of the
Irish pamphlet he says that "it is intended to familiarize to the
uneducated apprehensions ideas of liberty, benevolence *peace* and
toleration. It is *secretly* intended also as a preliminary to other
pamphlets to shake Catholicism at its basis, and to induce Quak-
erish and Socinian principle[s] of politics without objecting to the
Christian Religion, which would do no good to the vulgar just now
..."[44] Shelley has considered the problems of rhetoric, audience,
communication of ideas, the consciousness of the poor, and stages
of development, as any serious-minded reformer would do.

His ideas for an association of philanthropists are also well con-
sidered. The full connotations of the word "philanthropist" are
hard to recover, but they include notions of disinterested benevo-
lence, international solidarity, love of humanity, and philosophical
perspective.[45] He answers Godwin's most serious criticism of as-
sociation by saying that there will be no *"unnatural unanimity"*
because of the principle of minority secessions; that is, if a dispute
cannot be resolved to the satisfaction of a minority, it can split off

and operate on its own. This kind of network of small groups loosely federated anticipates by many years the affinity group concept developed by the Spanish anarchists. In *Proposals for an Association* he says: "Godwin wrote during the Revolution of France, and certainly his writings were totally devoid of influence, with regard to its purposes. Oh! that they had not!" Had there been more philosophical radicals, "France would not now be a beacon to warn us of the hazard and horror of Revolutions. . . . I consider it to be one of the effects of a Philanthropic Association, to assist in the production of such men as these, in an extensive developement of those germs of excellence, whose favourite soil is the cultured garden of the human mind."[46] The poor are to be progressively educated by an elite of philosophical radicals working in association.

The difference between Shelley's association and the political associations of the day, like the Catholic Committee or the Hampden Clubs, is that Shelley's association provides an organization for visionary and philosophical radicals, whose social criticism and ideals far exceed the particularistic demands of the interest groups. Shelley wants universal liberation, not just a slightly modified status quo. Throughout his life, he looked to liberation movements in other nations with unbounded enthusiasm, because for him social renovation was an international process. When Shelley's associations do not become reality, the idea of world revolution does not pass away, but enters the realm of poetry, aesthetics, and the imagination. When Godwin articulated his philosophical anarchism he hedged it with an antipolitics and intellectual bias so extreme that by the time Shelley met Godwin the latter was hardly distinguishable from the liberal Whigs. Shelley rediscovered this anarchism, and breathed new life into it by attaching it to the social movements of the day. Association is one solution to the problem of political mediation—a problem Godwin dismisses when he accepts only individual discussion.

Shelley's specific proposal for an Irish association could not give rise to immediate results because the Catholic Committee absorbed most the leisure-class advocates of reform. For Shelley to attract radicals—like Lawless and Catherine Nugent—who might have composed an association, he would have to live in Ireland and make a real commitment to the Irish situation, something he was not willing to do. He never contemplated staying in Ireland, but as a temporary visitor he accomplished as much as he could reasonably have expected. Once he returned to England from Ireland he could have formed an association, but did not. He continued to agitate in his own way, but the problem of mediation continued under the weight of enormous contradictions. In Devonshire Shelley launched radical pamphlets in balloons and bottles, a method of propaganda which painfully bears witness to his isolation.

Although Shelley thought Ireland was a beacon of "liberty," he did not see any philosophical value in the Luddite uprisings, which were dismissed as hunger riots. Taking a close look at his comments on the Luddites and other "manufacturers," one discovers that Shelley associates town laborers with filth, dirt, disease, hunger, starvation, and ugliness. Writing to Medwin on November 26, 1811, Shelley says he does not want to live "near any *populous manufacturing dissipated* town," nor near any barracks.[47] Precisely such places were erupting in Luddite rebellions at that time. Writing to Elizabeth Hitchener, December 26, 1811: "The manufacture[r]s are reduced to starvation. My friend, the military are gone to Nottingham—Curse light on them for their motives if they destroy one of its famine-wasted inhabitants." This is clear enough. He then continues: "Southey thinks that a revolution is *inevitable*; this is one of his reasons for supporting things as they are.—But let *us* not belie our principles." The aristocrats "may feed & may riot & may sin to the last moment.—The groans of the wretched may pass unheeded till the latest moment of this infamous revelry, till the storm burst upon them and the oppressed take furious vengeance on the oppressors."[48] The aristocrats are breeding their own destruction, but the revenge of the oppressed is a product of the oppression itself and seems beyond judgment. Although these are sound ideas, Shelley is missing the significance of the Luddite uprisings. They were attempts by the laborers to resist the laissez-faire practices of maximum exploitation sanctioned by the state. The laborers wanted to regulate the textile industry in a more humane way, seeking to maintain the high quality of the products but not allow profiteering. Having exhausted the parliamentary protest method, the laborers used direct action to combat the economic policies that were ruining their lives. Shelley was hardly unique in being blind to the nature of Luddism, because class prejudice alone made it extremely difficult for anyone in the leisure class to be fair to the Luddites. Nevertheless, Shelley could not mediate between a philosophical anarchism and Luddism. The Irish situation was easier to think about because it had been a standard Whig cause for years (even though his father had voted against Emancipation five times)[49] and also because Shelley was distanced from the actual Irish problems. Luddism struck too close to home.

Shortly before going to Ireland, Shelley writes to Elizabeth Hitchener from the Lake country. His class prejudice and the ambiguity of his radicalism are apparent in the following sentences:

> at this Keswick tho the face of the country is lovely the *people* are detestable. The manufacturers with their contamination have crept into the peaceful vale and deformed the loveliness of Nature with human taint. The debauched servants of the great families who resort contribute to the total extinction of morality. Keswick seems more like a suburb of London than a village of Cumberland. Children are frequently found in the River which the unfortunate women employed at the manufactory destroy.[50]

Shelley's father could have written this, word for word, because it lacks imaginative sympathy, not to mention radical understanding. Shelley's response is aesthetic, written from the narrow perspective of the aristocrat who assumes that a beautiful prospect is his birthright. The beauties of nature are, in this instance, objects of aristocratic consumption, and the laborers' existence interferes with aristocratic pleasure. This is simply an opposition to industrialism on narrowly aesthetic grounds. Only when Shelley expands his social aesthetic and transcends his class bias can his anarchism rest on a more solid foundation. The process of overcoming his aristocratic heritage is gradual, uneven, and partial. However, Shelley, unlike so many others in his class, was starting to overcome some of these prejudices.

Another factor is important for Shelley's politics: repression. Almost as soon as he began his career as a political writer he expressed fears of imprisonment, and even martyrdom. His fear was by no means melodramatic, but a sober evaluation of the sociopolitical conflict that was going on in England at the time. From the 1790s, when Shelley was born, to the year of his death, 1822, the government was incessantly mobilized against democratic change of any kind. After the agitation of the 1790s was repressed, the next moment of social crisis was in 1811, when Luddism flared up with unprecedented fury. To put down the initial Luddite uprisings of 1811-1812, the government used a force of 12,000 soldiers, which was six times larger than any force used before to suppress domestic rebellion, and even larger than many of the armies the British were meeting on the Continent.[51] The advocates of law and order were hardly unprepared, however, because they had constructed 155 new military barracks between 1792 and 1815, usually in the so-called "Jacobin" areas. If the government ruled by consent in 1792, then, according to E. P. Thompson, by 1816 "the English people were held down by force."[52] Behind the Luddite struggle was a conflict between two kinds of political economy. In the first ten years of the nineteenth century, while labor unions were banned, workers in the cotton and wool trades pleaded with parliamentary committees for relief and more effective legislation to regulate the industry. Competition and unscrupulous employers had depressed wages to an alarming degree. Even the more prosperous workers were deprived of half their wages by indirect taxation, some of which helped pay for the new barracks. Parliament responded to the workers by abolishing all the paternalist legislation that had previously existed and which had been a modest kind of protection, and then used the committee hearings for investigating seditious and illegal trade-union activity.

Successive crop failures in 1809, 1810, 1811, and 1812, in conjunction with the economic crisis precipitated by war with America, created a desperate situation that even a benevolent government would have had a hard time dealing with. In 1812, wages dropped as low as 7 to 9 shillings a week, while a quatern loaf of bread cost 1s. 8d.[53] There was, however, no government relief or regulation of the textile trade. Instead, there was repression. In April 1812, eight people in Manchester were hanged after a food riot: four for mill-burning, three for house-breaking, and a woman for stealing potatoes.[54] In January of the next year, seventeen Yorkshire Luddites were hanged, while six others were sentenced to transportation. Journalists too felt the power of repression; Leigh and John Hunt, William Cobbett, Peter Finnerty, and Daniel Isaac Eaton were all jailed during this period.

After the end of the French wars, there was more economic depression and a resurgence of the reform movement. Between 1816 and 1820, there was an ongoing struggle between the government and the reformers, as England came close to revolution—just how close is still a matter of controversy. Between 1811, when Shelley was expelled from Oxford and the Luddites began to "regulate" the textile industry, and 1822, when Shelley died and most the reform leaders were silenced or in jail, 1,107 people were executed in Wales and England, only 210 of them for murder.[55] One also has to add those killed by the armed forces, such as the eleven killed in Manchester at the Peterloo Massacre, or the people sentenced to transportation who died on their way to Botany Bay, or those who died from "jail fever," a common danger of imprisonment. There are also no reliable figures on how many starved to death, died from malnutrition, or were killed in work accidents.

There were other, less violent forms of social control. In 1815, the newspaper tax was raised to 3-1/5d, one of the "taxes on knowledge." In 1817, Habeas Corpus was suspended again, and the "Gagging Acts" were passed. At the end of 1817, three workers were hanged for participating in the Pentridge Rebellion, inspiring Shelley to write one of his protest pamphlets. The greatest activity, however, was in 1819, when the reform movement culminated its agitation with the huge Manchester demonstration which became the Peterloo Massacre. Afterwards, the government, still unwilling to grant any concessions, only increased repression even more. The passage of the notorious "Six Acts" at the end of 1819 temporarily stalled the reform movement, at least one phase of it. The leaders were jailed, the journals and newspapers were regulated and taxed almost out of existence, and the movement itself was divided between radicals and moderates. The Queen Caroline Affair of 1820 was the occasion for both a trivialization of the movement and a new opportunity for further agitation. To give some idea of the level of repression that existed then, I offer the incredible statistic concerning Richard Carlile, his shopmen and shopwomen; in their struggle for a free press—free to publish works like *Queen Mab*, Byron's *Cain*, and *The Rights of Man*—they spent a total of 200 years in prison.[56]

The issue of imprisonment is a good place to make a transition back to Shelley, because prison was a significant threshold in his political thinking. Radicals of the period had to face the possibility of imprisonment as a matter of course. What, if anything, was worth going to jail for? It is interesting that only a few who were imprisoned once made a return trip. After the "Six Acts" of 1819 were passed, a second conviction for libel brought with it banishment from the British Empire. If one had enough money, one could enjoy a number of privileges in jail that are unheard of now, such as totally free correspondence and almost unlimited visiting rights. But, in addition to the health problems already alluded to, prison sentences often meant financial ruin. John and Leigh Hunt, for example, were fined 500 pounds and had to make a security deposit of 750 pounds to insure good behavior for five years. They would have spent even longer than two years in jail if they had not paid all the fines. These were enormous sums of money, even for prosperous journalists.[57] Just how effective these repressive measures were may be ascertained by the example of William Cobbett. After Habeas Corpus was suspended in 1817, he fled to America, apparently unwilling to risk another prison sentence and financial ruin.

Shelley was aware of the dangers of repression even before the publication of *The Necessity of Atheism*, when he wrote to Leigh Hunt about the wisdom of forming "a methodical society . . . to resist the coalition of the enemies of liberty."[58] The idea of a "society" reappeared a year later in Ireland, where he proposed an association of philosophical reformers who, unlike Daniel O'Connell's Catholic Committee, would go beyond a limited concern for Catholic Emancipation and Repeal of the Union Act. By going beyond O'Connell's Committee (which, as moderate as it was, was having its own legal problems), Shelley's group of philanthropists would undoubtedly have been greeted by government prosecution, even if it had remained within the nonviolent framework that Shelley insisted upon. In the pamphlet itself there are references to the possibility of enduring persecution, sacrificing personal interests, confronting danger, being imprisoned, and even executed. But it is significant that when Shelley finally rejected the idea of an Irish association, in a letter to Godwin, he never once mentioned the issue of repression.[59] Whereas the Luddite destruction of stocking-frames was specifically designed to raise wages and bring the employers into line, and the Irish had a vested interest, obviously, in the reforms they were agitating for, Shelley's own interests in social change were less clearly defined. Going to jail, then, became an ethical problem for Shelley, while for Lancashire weavers or Irish Catholics, prison was one of the dangers of struggling for survival.[60]

If one is to include all the instances of repression suffered by Shelley, one has to start with his expulsion from Oxford and his banishment from Field Place for having published and not recanted his argument against Christian faith. He could have been prosecuted for blasphemous libel if his youthfulness and social position had not been mitigating factors.[61] When he delivered his speech at the Fishamble Theatre in Dublin on February 28, 1812, a government spy dutifully took notes which were then sent to the Home Office.[62] From Dublin Shelley mailed a trunk to Elizabeth Hitchener, then still residing in Sussex; because of insufficient postage, the trunk remained at Holyhead, Wales, where a customs surveyor opened it and found pamphlets seditious and blasphemous enough for him to initiate extraordinary action. The Home Office was sent copies of the pamphlets and a copy of Harriet Shelley's letter to Elizabeth Hitchener who, after the Sussex Postmaster-General was alerted, was spied upon.[63] The spying was not without effect because "rumors" began to circulate immediately afterwards, and Elizabeth's position as a schoolteacher was becoming problematic. Although Shelley had wanted her to join them in Lynmouth (where he himself was being spied on), it seems that the rumors and the spying forced the issue.[64]

While at Lynmouth, Shelley wrote a pamphlet protesting the imprisonment of Daniel Eaton, who had published one of Paine's works. This open letter to Lord Ellenborough, the judge of the case, was an example of Shelley's new caution. According to Newman I. White: "Had the *Letter to Lord Ellenborough* been published, it might very well have brought a government prosecution upon the author; Shelley was quite aware of this and took considerable precautions. 'The Letter' was printed under his personal supervision, without the name of either author or printer."[65] Apparently Shelley was not cautious enough, because "only fifty copies (out of a printing of one thousand) escaped being burned by the alarmed printer."[66]

The greatest alarm for the Shelley circle was the arrest in Barnstaple on August 19, 1812, of Dan Hill, their fifteen-year-old servant whom they had first employed in Dublin. He was tried and convicted for distributing radical pamphlets written by Shelley, although Dan did not reveal the authorship to the authorities. He received six months in prison, the penalty for not paying the 200-pound fine. Shelley was in no position to pay for Dan's release; he had a hard enough time paying "fifteen shillings a week to keep Dan in necessary comforts" for the six months.[67] If Shelley's authorship of the pamphlets had been known, he would have faced far more serious charges than Dan had. A typical sentence, if he had been brought to trial, was two years in jail and a large fine and security deposit insuring good behavior.

The Barnstaple authorities of course communicated with the Home Office, so that by 1813, there was already a substantial file on Shelley. Interestingly, there are no letters or other testimony that might reveal how he felt about Dan's arrest, but in a situation like this, actions speak as loudly as words; along with his female entourage, Shelley immediately fled Lynmouth. They settled in Tremadoc, Wales, where Shelley was to have the worst scare—or the most well-performed hoax—of his life. Which one it was is not clear. It is possible that Shelley staged the Tanyrallt attack to provide an excuse to leave Wales and his debts. It is also possible Shelley was attacked, so I want to pursue that possibility for now. On February 26, 1813, Dan Hill returned from prison. That night, Shelley heard a noise downstairs and intercepted an intruder, who fired a pistol and pierced Shelley's nightgown, while Shelley's own pistols misfired. The event, known to biographers as the Tanyrallt Affair, has been variously interpreted. I will give Richard Holmes's account, which I will paraphrase.[68] The local quarry owner and largest employer, Robert Leeson, was an archconservative, whom Shelley had insulted by refusing to meet with him socially. Leeson learned of Shelley's radicalism and acquired one of his pamphlets, which he sent on to the Home Office. As a son of a rich Irish landowner, Leeson was not amused by Shelley's ideas on Ireland. There was some labor unrest in Tremadoc, and not far away, a mere two hours' ride, rioting in the Leyn Peninsula led to the execution of two workers in 1813. It was, of course, the period of the Luddite uprisings. Less than a month before the Tanyrallt attack, seventeen Yorkshire Luddites had been hanged. A week before the attack, Leigh and John Hunt were sent to prison for libeling the Prince Regent. Holmes suggests that the intruder was sent there by Leeson, who wanted him to gather pamphlets and other incriminating material, probably in preparation for a case of libel to be brought against Shelley. Also, Leeson wanted Shelley and his radical influence out of the area. The government depended on civilian cooperation in repressing political opponents. In 1802, for example, the Society for the Suppression of Vice was organized by Wilberforce to search for antireligious blasphemers and seditious radicals in order to bring them to court. It is altogether plausible that the government encouraged Leeson to obtain evidence, even though there is no proof of it.

After the attack, Shelley very nearly had a nervous breakdown (or feigned having one) and fled to Ireland as soon as he could. Once again, we have no detailed reflection by Shelley on this episode, so we must guess. If Holmes and other critics who believe it was a real attack are correct, then this must have been terrifying. Particularly since the attack occurred in the context of the Luddite uprisings and mass hangings by the government, the Tanyrallt Affair made Shelley realize that radical politics entailed more serious consequences than getting expelled from college. There were about forty hangings in the early Luddite period.

This was certainly not the last time he had to deal with repression, which makes itself felt in everything Shelley ever wrote, including the poetry. Although he never formed an association of philanthropists, he certainly took numerous risks, even after the Tanyrallt episode. One could even consider *The Liberal*, the joint project of Leigh Hunt, Lord Byron, and Shelley, a kind of association, and this is one of the last things Shelley worked on before his death.

Although it cannot be attributed solely to the repression, an aristocratic, antinomian anarchism persisted in Shelley's thinking. Even though he thoroughly understands Godwin's ideas, and has formulated his own concepts, Shelley still dreams of a utopian retreat from political conflict and wishes he could dwell with the happy and virtuous few, far away from the corrupt world of oppressor and oppressed.[69] Shelley's yearning for a realm of purity untainted by "the restless turbulence of interested feelings" is recurrent, and provides some of the impulse for poems like *The Witch of Atlas* and *Epipsychidion*.

PHILOSOPHICAL ANARCHISM AND THE POLITICAL WRITINGS OF 1812

The Irish pamphlets, the *Declaration of Rights*, and *Letter to Lord Ellenborough* are political essays articulating a philosophical anarchism, which relates to Godwin's philosophy and Shelley's revision of those ideas. The first essay, *An Address to the Irish People*, uses the issues of Catholic Emancipation and Repeal of the Union Act as a pretext to discuss the more universal, philosophical issues of human emancipation. The year 1812 was an opportune time to stress "universal" liberation because, as a recent critic has shown, there was then a concerted effort at Catholic-Protestant unity.[70] The essay goes from the concrete particular to the universal, discovering the Ideal within the world of experience. Shelley protests the oppression of the Irish Catholics, but locates this in a historical context, so that the social ills are not peculiar to the Irish, but symptomatic of more general tendencies. However worthy of success, neither Catholic Emancipation nor Repeal of the Union Act will comprise the full liberation of the Irish, especially the laboring poor Shelley's essay specifically addresses. The tightrope Shelley is walking is the line between violent revolution and reforms that are merely "temporizing" and time-serving.[71] He tries to defuse fanaticism and narrow reformism by shifting the focus from the particular to the universal: from Catholic oppression to religious intolerance, from Irish oppression to inequality, from institutional laws and practices to universal human truths.

The most radical deviation from Godwin is not in the essay's content, but in its style, mode of presentation, and intended audience. As is clear from his protesting letters to Shelley, Godwin thought that nothing but mischief could come from addressing the poor about their oppressed condition. Although Shelley said on March 18, 1812 that he would no longer address "the illiterate,"[72] he said this more to mollify Godwin than to establish a principle he fully believed in. He continued to address the poor later in 1812 and also in 1819, when he again tried to reach a popular audience. To illustrate their differences, one can compare two typical tropes they like to use. A favorite Godwinian trope, but also employed by Shelley and others, is cultivation of mind: by means of study, conversation, and solitary reflection, the individual cultivates the mind with knowledge just as the farmer cultivates the land. The process is slow, organic, certain, with a harvest in autumn, barring a climatic disaster. A favorite, but by no means unique, trope of Shelley's is fire and light imagery signifying the creative mind. Daniel J. Hughes has lucidly discussed the "fading coal" image as it relates to Shelley's conception of the creative act, but this trope can be found even in the first Irish pamphlet. "Oh! Ireland . . . thou art the isle on whose green shores I have desired to see the standard of liberty erected, a flag of fire, a beacon at which the world shall light the torch of Freedom!"[73] The enlightened mind gives off light and heat, which can ignite other minds in a fiery apocalypse of libertarian revolution.

Although the content of the Irish pamphlet is pure Godwin, Paine's influence is also felt, but more as an inspirational model than anything else, because Paine's ideas are not systematically incorporated as Godwin's are. Paine, however, would represent a more activist mode of propaganda than Godwin. The essay's critique of religion exceeds the moderate argument for toleration, whose liberalizing virtues are not emphasized. Mistaking a nationalist feeling for something more philosophical, like the freethinking of some of the United Irishmen who had been defeated earlier, Shelley misread the minds of the Irish Catholics, whom he considered ready to part from their Catholicism.[74] Shelley divides religion into its true aspects—ethics and "good works"—and its false, institutional aspects. Paraphras-

ing Paine, Shelley says that the best religion produces the best be-
havior.[75] He then takes a historical look at the issue of religious
persecution, of which the oppression of the Irish Catholics is only
one example. He discusses the Catholic persecution of heretics, and
the Reformation which tried to correct the church's abuses but
which also created new sources of intolerance and injustice. The
point is not the relative superiority of Catholic or Protestant, but
the corrupting influence of power, regardless of who possesses it:
"although rational people are very good in their natural state, there
are now, and ever have been, very few whose good dispositions
despotic power does not destroy."[76] The root problem is alienating
one's own rational capacity to an externally constituted authority
which mediates between divine law and individual experience. Shel-
ley's bold criticism of the priesthood is that it usurps the religious
liberty of the individual and creates a stultifying institution in the
place of personal judgment. "Can there be worse slavery than the
depending for the safety of your soul on the will of another man?"[77]
As priests usurp human power by their authoritarian mediation, so
do they promote intolerance to justify their privileged access to
divine wisdom. Shelley uses Godwinian arguments to refute intol-
erance. First, the coercion of intolerance is ineffective because it
employs force and does not persuade by means of reason. Second,
since belief is involuntary, under the sway of necessity, it is pointless
to penalize those whom a majority deems mistaken in their religious
convictions.[78] If religion's true role is to identify right and wrong,
then the institutional form of the religion is secondary. The mere
existence of laws and institutions has no bearing whatsoever on
genuine ethics because laws "cannot change virtue and truth . . .
because they are unchangeable."[79]

The existence of a truth independent of and superior to the legal
institutions of society is a key anarchist assumption. Godwin greatly
expanded Paine's suggestion that government and society were dif-
ferent and separable. Echoing both Paine and Godwin, Shelley says
that only the "vices" of humanity make government a necessary
evil.

When all men are good and wise, Government will of itself
decay, so long as men continue foolish and vicious, so long
will Government, even such a Government as that of England,
continue necessary in order to prevent the crimes of bad men.
Society is produced by the wants, Government by the wicked-

ness, and a state of just and happy equality by the improvement
and reason of man.[80]

By means of moral and institutional reformation, society can ex-
pand its dominion at the expense of Government, until rational
anarchy has completely supplanted the nation-state. As members
of society, people are universal subjects, part of all humanity, but
as Irish Catholics, people can be sectarian and nationalistic.

Catholic Emancipation applied only to the Irish upper classes,
since the poor majority were excluded from political power as were
the English poor. The Repeal of the Union Act would directly assist
the poor because of, presumably, reduced taxes. Shelley concen-
trates the latter half of the essay on the issue of inequality, something
the Catholic Committee never mentioned. The root cause of crime,
unhappiness, and all the ills which government can try to repress
is inequality, which cannot, however, be abolished immediately.[81]
The present task for the poor is to acquire virtue and wisdom by
means of study, discussion groups, and education in order to lay
the foundation for future equality. Institutions will change as the
popular consciousness changes. Meanwhile, the poor should be
patient, nonviolent, practicing a heroic forbearance despite inevi-
table repression and provocation. He wants the poor to resist tyr-
anny, but stop short of revolution. He acknowledges the severe
obstacles to gradual, progressive change, especially the denial of a
free press. Shelley's tightrope is that line between reformism and
revolution. Godwin was certain that one would inevitably topple
over into revolution, whereas Shelley was willing to take that risk
because continued oppression was even more unacceptable.

As a whole, the pamphlet is a remarkable adaptation of God-
winian anarchism to suit the particular occasion of Irish oppression.
The least satisfactory aspect of the essay is its assumption that the
Irish poor, while capable of being enlightened, are devoid of a
worthy culture. It is also troubling that Shelley keeps urging the
Irish poor to keep on working regularly and without interruption,
as if they might be tempted to engage in strikes. Shelley was not
just ignorant of Irish culture: his assumptions insured that he would
never have to examine it. He also urges the poor to forsake drink
and idle play during their leisure hours in favor of self-improvement
and intellectual culture.[82] In Godwin's *Political Justice* is also the
conviction that no real change in the consciousness of the laboring
classes can take place until they enjoy far more leisure than they

do at present. One can appreciate Shelley's eagerness for the poor to acquire intellectual knowledge, but his inability to conceive of a material basis for this acquisition makes his proposal abstract.

Proposals for an Association of Philanthropists provoked Godwin's ire more than the first pamphlet, even though its intended audience was not the poor. The association would be more radical and philosophical than the Catholic Committee, although the immediate goals would be Catholic Emancipation and Repeal of the Union Act. It would also agitate for universal emancipation, debating ideas, educating the poor, and generating other associations.[83] Shelley rejects Godwin's tactic of complete reliance on individual discussion: "individuals acting singly, with whatever energy can never effect so much as a society."[84] Shelley wants an intelligentsia, organized in associations, to guide social change in Ireland and England.

Shelley revises Godwin's ideas rather than invents wholly new ones, because Godwin himself admits that individual virtue *alone* will not change society effectively.[85] Although even the first edition of *Political Justice* speaks against the evils of political association, Shelley is certainly correct in finding libertarian arguments in favor of association. Association is a tactic to embody the Godwinian ideas of social change. The elitist concept of revolutionary intellectuals is pure Godwinism in that it assumes that rationality derives only from the mind of the intellectual, separated from labor. Kropotkin would find most libertarian not the intellectuals like Paine and Condorcet, but the *sans-culottes* of the Paris sections and the *jacqueries*; they practiced a direct democracy far in advance of the more bureaucratic ideas of even the most enlightened intellectuals.[86] Shelley, however, perceives direct democracy as a future goal, not a historical possiblity for the present. He is nevertheless hopeful. Whereas Godwin's rational utility emphasized disinterested benevolence, Shelley's "philanthropy" is an active, positive "love," a universal sympathy.[87] Although Shelley expects government repression, he disavows violence and recommends nonviolent resistance. Although government may call Philanthropy a crime, it is not: "Conscience is a Government before which, all others sink into nothingness."[88] Shelley also repudiates the idea of secrecy, and wants to have all the group's proceedings public and open to scrutiny. Its goal is not seizure of power, but the dissolution of government and inequality by means of social reforms and enlightened social consciousness.

Another interesting dimension of the essay is the language, specifically where it anticipates Shelley's poetry. Irish reforms, of little value by themselves, are necessary steps in a universal movement of social renovation. A millennial note is unmistakable: "I behold the lion lay down with the lamb, and the infant play with the basilisk."[89] Another millennial trope is the transformation of social ills into allegorical symbols, like "the eyeless monster bigotry."[90] As anticipations of the millennium and allegorical symbols, social events lose their autonomous status. The millennium is an event that Shelley too will enjoy, as a fellow participant in a universal apocalypse.

A Declaration of Rights, composed and printed in Dublin, differs from the Irish pamphlets in that Ireland is never mentioned in the entire broadside, which belongs as much on a Barnstaple as on a Dublin wall. In diction, intended audience, and format, the *Declaration* is close to *An Address to the Irish People*. In fact, Shelley identified "farmers" as the readership he hoped to gain for the *Declaration* in Devonshire. It is the most Painite piece of literature he ever wrote because of its stress on rights. An argument in *Political Justice*, Book II, Chapter 5, is directed against the notion of rights and in favor of rational utility—duties, not rights. Paine, however, is in the political tradition that emphasizes popular rights, as the title of his most famous book indicates: *The Rights of Man*. A person, according to Godwin, has no positive rights as such because they would imply a category of actions exempt from the criterion of "reason."[91] Moreover, "the voice of the people is not . . . 'the voice of truth and of God' " because "universal consent cannot convert wrong into right."[92] The Lockian notion of rights—doing "what we will with our own"[93]—is unacceptable because the concept of justice has the authority to overrule merely selfish preference. Godwin, however, defends negative rights, that is, the right of private judgment.[94] Out of Paine's notion of "rights" comes the right of resistance and the call to revolution when tyrants have violated the rights of the "third estate." Godwin wants to discourage revolutionary upheaval, and thus he emphasizes reason and justice. Paine appeals to the self-interest of the oppressed, whereas Godwin appeals to the supra-individual concept of utility, which exists beyond the merely egoistic self-interest.

The *Declaration* possesses both Godwinian and Painite concepts of rights.[95] Theses X through XV discuss passive rights and civil liberties, the moral freedom of the individual to pursue the truth wherever it may lead; this is mostly Godwinian. The first nine theses reject the rights of government, and analyze the concept of legitimate authority. These are mostly Painite pronouncements on the rights of the governed, although there are some Godwinian emphases: there is the "right" to perfect the government (V); the coercion with which the "rights of man" must be secured should be "as slight as possible" (VII); when government resorts to force rather than reason to enforce its will, it is a sure sign of irrationality (VIII); no one "has a right to disturb the public peace by personally resisting the execution of a law, however bad" (IX). The sixteenth thesis is a marvelous example of the broadside's Godwin-Paine mixture. The first sentence, "The present generation cannot bind their posterity," is a prominent idea from *The Rights of Man*, whereas the second sentence, "The few cannot promise for the many," alludes to the Godwinian argument against promises. The ethical foundation of politics (XVII-XIX) is Godwinian, but other theses are Painite, and some could have been written by either philosopher. Even the final thesis, a stirring anarchist declaration, has Painite echoes: "The only use of government is to repress the vices of man. If man were to-day sinless, to-morrow he would have a right to demand that government and all its evils should cease."

The *Declaration* is Shelley's most extreme attempt to popularize radical ideas and to translate anarchist ideals into a form potentially understandable to an extensive audience. Philosophical anarchism has become a series of aphorisms. The divergence from Godwin, especially as he is in 1812, is dramatic. Shelley is willing to use republican concepts from Paine as a way of leading up to more libertarian ideas. The broadside is not philosophically rigorous, to say the least, but it is consciously political at every point. Shelley wants to dislodge the reader from whatever point on the political spectrum he or she happens to have arrived at. He cares more that he move the reader somewhere leftward, toward anarchism, than whether every statement is thoroughly libertarian. Shelley is an activist, desiring movement, and he is willing to experiment.

The *Declaration* went as far in a popular direction as Shelley ever ventured, at least until 1819. That the *Declaration* was one of the items for which Dan Hill was arrested is the ultimate irony.

A Letter to Lord Ellenborough was written in June 1812, well after the prosecution of Daniel I. Eaton for having published some of Paine's deistic works. Addressed to the intellectuals, the members of the leisure classes, the *Letter*'s diction, rhetorical techniques, and argumentative logic are all designed to apply anarchist principles to a particular instance of injustice in such a way that the readership will be moved in a libertarian direction.

Shelley claims that Ellenborough had no right to condemn Eaton solely for publishing opinions contrary to the established religious doctrines. He then situates this specific act of judicial intolerance in the context of the perennial struggle between inquiring, unrestrained philosophy, and superstitious custom,[96] thereby suggesting the familiar Godwinian antinomy between free mind and static institution. Another Godwinian argument against the punishment of deism is that since belief is involuntary, coercion is powerless to persuade the individual of an opinion's validity.[97] Using the criterion of rational utility, Shelley wonders rhetorically whether the fearless inquirer ought not to be the beneficiary of patronage rather than the victim of persecution because, after all, the philosopher is trying to bestow selfless knowledge upon humanity.[98] The *Letter* goes beyond arguing for mere toleration of dissident opinions, especially in its latter pages, where it argues against the rationality of institutional Christianity. Showing the influence of Paine and Holbach, Shelley condemns Christianity as an institution which has survived not by means of its philosophical rigor, but by force and fraud, violence and persecution. Lord Ellenborough, as a defender of Christianity, is playing the part of the Inquisition, suppressing the opposition by dictatorial means. The social forces Shelley depicts are Custom on the one side, and Philosophy on the other; a new social world depends on the overcoming of Custom and the victory of Philosophy.

Despite its form as a letter, it embodies no intention whatsoever of trying to persuade Lord Ellenborough to change his ways. The strategy is quite simple: The *Letter* aims to carry someone already sympathetic to the plight of Eaton (who was, at the time, a popular opponent of Old Corruption) beyond a merely emotional enthusiasm for Eaton, and toward a philosophical comprehension of the issues at stake. The problem is not one bigoted judge, but the systematic judicial opposition to philosophy, and the cultural bias against fearless inquiry. The real victim is not Eaton, but the entire society, since it is deprived of courageous truth-seekers.

Although Godwin himself was a freethinker, he did not emphasize that aspect of his philosophy until his last work, *Christianity Unveiled*, which Mary Shelley was afraid to publish even after Godwin's death.[99] In the next chapter I will discuss Shelley's complex response to Christianity as he formulated his own kind of free-thinking, but it is worth noting that religion is of far greater concern to Shelley. Godwin's predominant audience in the 1790s was the Nonconformist middle classes, the Dissenting intellectuals from Norwich, Birmingham, Bristol, and London. Although some of these intellectuals had reached freethinking conclusions, many had not, and perhaps Godwin did not want to emphasize something guaranteed to alienate his reader. By Shelley's time, secularist ideas had spread because of Paine's influence, and a laboring-class tradition of freethought was beginning to emerge.[100] Also, undoubtedly influenced by the example of the French Revolution in which the church and priesthood were principal targets of revolutionary attack, Shelley identified Christianity as one of the most important enemies of liberty, equality, and philosophy. Christianity was the cultural vehicle through which the ruling aristocracy legitimated its domination of the laboring classes; Christianity preached to the lower classes the virtues of obedience, deference, and hope in the afterlife, thus serving the interests of the rich.

QUEEN MAB

Shelley produced a work of lasting importance to the nineteenth-century socialist movement: *Queen Mab*. Ironically, in view of its later popularity among radical workers, Shelley printed the poem privately, hoping that, at best, it might be read by young aristocrats, but he knew the work was far too bold for open publication. The poem was to have a very different fate. In 1815, Shelley, as I argue elsewhere, wrote a long review of *Queen Mab* for *The Theological Inquirer*, in which he quoted almost a third of the poem.[101] Certain revisions of *Queen Mab* were published with *Alastor* in 1816. And in 1821, a London bookseller brought out a pirated edition of *Queen Mab*, which marked its official existence in the political world because the publisher, Clark, was prosecuted. Richard Carlile, a working-class radical, also brought out an edition of *Queen Mab*. Thereafter, illegal editions of the poem were far more numerous than any legal editions of Shelley's poetry, at least in the nineteenth century. The poem became a weapon in the battle of ideas during the heroic age of English socialism, when Owenites, secularists, Chartists, and radicals of different persuasions read it in cheap editions, as *Queen Mab* became a part of socialist culture. Shelley relies on conventional literary devices to communicate his unorthodox message. Alternating between lyrical forms borrowed from Robert Southey's escapist romances and the more traditional blank verse of Milton, Shelley constructs a dream allegory in which Ianthe, who is sleeping, is visited by the Fairy, Queen Mab. The Queen discloses the evils of the present and the past, and reveals a portrait of the utopian future, when full Godwinian equality has replaced the evils of war, competition, greed, and superstition. The poem's philosophical assumptions are not contradictory, but coherent in a sophisticated way. The attentive student of Godwin's philosophy will notice that the poem has an un-Godwinian emphasis on "nature," which comes from Holbach. Once "nature" passes from Holbach's text to Shelley's poem, the concept undergoes certain changes so that it actually complements Godwinian ideas. In *Political Justice* the fundamental ground upon which the entire argument rests is the nature of human mind, its "natural" tendencies when allowed to develop without the repression of coercive institutions. The mind's capacity to reason is the basis for egalitarian community which can dispense with the stultifying procedures of static law. Nevertheless, the assumption behind the premise that fluxional mind can generate human community is that "nature" not only presents no insuperable obstacles to reason, but is itself rational. If the world is knowable, and the self capable of knowing it, then Godwin discloses a typically eighteenth-century belief in the goodness of nature. So, although Godwin rarely alludes to nature, and stresses instead the creative powers of mind, his philosophy rests on the foundation of nature's rationality. Shelley discovered Holbach on his own, even though it was by critically engaging the *philosophes* like Holbach that Godwin developed his own ideas.

The rationality of nature was an ideological weapon with which the *philosophes* and French revolutionaries delegitimated monarchy, aristocracy, and the Catholic Church. Materialistic naturalism was the metaphysical alternative to Christianity, whose ideas lent support to the *ancien régime*'s complex system of deference and hierarchy. Once God is dislodged as the center of the universe, so too, at the secular level, are King, the bishops, and the nobles. For these and other political reasons, Shelley turns to "nature" in *Queen Mab*. The anthropomorphic God of Christianity is the "prototype of human misrule" (VI, 105),[102] the spiritual image of monarchical despotism. By substituting nature for God, Shelley offers an alternative to "human misrule."

The rationality of nature serves many purposes in the poem. The cyclical transformations of matter (" 'There's not one atom of yon earth / But once was living man' " [II, 211-12]) serve to emphasize a common humanity, and demystify the artificial distinctions of social hierarchy. Nature also provides images of order worthy of imitation: "The universe, / In nature's silent eloquence, declares / That all fulfil the works of love and joy,— / All but the outcast man" (III, 196-99). If joyous self-fulfillment is the lesson of nature, then Shelley is urging the outcast man to act accordingly. Another of nature's voices bids humanity to change society. As the seasons change every year, undergoing death and rebirth, so should social institutions perish and enjoy a rebirth with injustice purged. As in "Ode to the West Wind," the natural power that transforms autumn into winter, and winter into spring is a revolutionary force: "the imperishable change / That renovates the world" (V, 3-4). Still another lesson from nature derives from the contrast between natural innocence and corrupt institutions. The innocence of children is undermined by militaristic toys, war games, and religious superstitions (IV, 103-20). There is a Rousseauistic dichotomy between natural goodness and institutional corruption: if institutions are so structured as to reflect natural innocence, then social suffering can be definitely abolished.

There is one final use that Shelley assigns nature in *Queen Mab*. Drawing upon pastoral and millennial mythology, he portrays his utopian society as a renovated, erotic nature. In Canto VIII, Shelley inaugurates the vision of utopia with a description of nature. One millennial myth suggests that complete social harmony must wait for the readjustment of the earth's polar axis, so that extremities of heat and cold, dryness and wetness, will be abolished along with social injustice.[103] As in *Prometheus Unbound*, Shelley here precedes the description of his utopian society with a description of renewed nature: " 'The habitable earth is full of bliss' "(VIII, 58). Frozen wastes become " 'heaven-breathing groves' " (VIII, 59-69). Utopian deserts become teeming " 'with countless rills and shady woods / Corn-fields and pastures and white cottages' " (VIII, 75-76). Moreover, every creature is now vegetarian, with predatory violence banished from the world; even poisonous vegetation has disappeared (VIII, 77-87; 124-33). This new nature, from which all objectionable traits have been eliminated, is the same one that appears in *Prometheus Unbound*. The entire earth becomes a loving, nurturing mother, at whose breast her "children" not only receive love, but act out the essence of this maternal utopia, which is lovemaking and play. " 'All things are recreated, and the flame / Of consentaneous love inspires all life: / The fertile bosom of the earth gives suck / To myriads . . .' " (VIII, 107-10). The identical thing happens in *Prometheus Unbound*, whose fourth act is an extended celebration of the earth-mother's children now fully liberated from the domination of the repressive father, Jupiter. Nature becomes a vehicle through which Shelley's utopian impulse expresses itself in its psychosexual intensity.

As an image to signify equality—not equality under law, but Godwinian equality—eroticized nature is appropriate, because with a post-scarcity equality there is no basis for competition. With a pacifist nature, the principle of play becomes the quintessential utopian activity. Play is, to use Kant's phrase, nonpurposive pur-posiveness, activity that is in itself pleasurable and which does not seek beyond itself for justification. Play counteracts Godwin's ex-treme rationalism and too exclusive emphasis on intellectually util-itarian activity, and more importantly establishes a nonutilitarian rationale for poetry itself as linguistic play. (For images of play in the poem, see IX, 12-22, which describes the end of "toil"; IX, 50-56, which depicts the course of passion; IX, 114-29, which portrays children playing in the ruins of an abandoned prison).

Shelley's poetry from *Queen Mab* to *The Triumph of Life* has a philosophical dualism that is a familiar Shelleyan constant. The dualistic pronouncements in *Queen Mab* (I, 130-56; IV, 139-53; IX, 232-33) are consistent with his concept of nature throughout the poem. The position is somewhat paradoxical, but it is not mud-dle-headed. Necessity, or the spirit of nature, operates through the material world and in the human mind. Matter undergoes trans-formations according to the laws of necessity (VI, 146-238); mind, too, as Godwin illustrates, is moved by the strongest motive and has no freedom to disobey that motive. There is, however, another dialectic at work in society, the conflict between "spirit" and "sen-sualism." Human spirit follows the laws of nature and obeys the authority of reason, whereas "sensualism" is the logic of exploi-tation and domination. The exercise of tyrannical power is the pursuit of an illusory pleasure, a vain attempt to procure lasting happiness and immortality (III, 22-106). The oppressor, violating nature's laws, cannot be happy, and will never achieve the immor-tality granted to the virtuous. What gives meaning to human life is not mere human existence, but the spirit in which people live their lives. The virtuous individual has the will to resist domination.

"Nature, impartial in munificence, / Has gifted man with all-sub-duing will" (V, 132-33). Virtue and will war against wealth and power. The virtuous person is the anarchist who "commands not, nor obeys" because "Power, like a desolating pestilence, / Pollutes whate'er it touches; and obedience, / Bane of all genius . . . Makes slaves of men, and, of the human frame, / A mechanized automaton" (III, 175-80). The pursuit of wealth, like that of power, corrupts the individual in a fatal way, whereas the person of virtue has "consciousness of good, which neither gold, / Nor sordid fame, nor hope of heavenly bliss / Can purchase." Moreover, the ideal rebel lives a "life of resolute good, / Unalterable will, quenchless desire / Of universal happiness . . ." (V, 223-27).

Shelley's is an ethical dualism, even though it is expressed in the language of metaphysics. Ianthe's spirit participates in the dream allegory because her virtuous life earned her the good fortune of being chosen by the Queen (I, 123-29). Although the poem denigrates the "mere" body, it celebrates the body that loves and plays, so that any idea of an ascetic, pleasure-denying elevation of spirit at the expense of sexuality could not be further from the meaning of *Queen Mab*.

Queen Mab provides an ethical argument against monarchical society and in favor of rational anarchy. Shelley's stress on the evils of monarchy might seem ill-chosen, because most historians today agree that monarchical power was diminishing considerably; the real power lay in the hands of the great Whig and Tory families. Nevertheless, monarchy was still powerful because of royal patronage and the enormous wealth distributed at the discretion of the royal bureaucracy. The great aristocratic families worked through the royal system to maintain and expand their influence. The critique of monarchy in Canto III is not just a protest against absolutism, but an attack on Old Corruption and its foundations. The poem criticizes the belief that absolute political power gives the ruler happiness and immortality, neither of which he can achieve because such power is contrary to nature's laws. Monarchy breeds a class of courtiers—placemen, pensioners, royal bureaucrats—who consume the wealth created by agricultural and industrial laborers. Using Godwin's critique of luxury and drawing upon the popular resentment against royal corruption, Shelley argues that the "gilded flies" and "drones" live off the toil of workers, whose excessive and dehumanizing labor is necessary to keep the courtiers in luxury. Abolish "luxury" and the laborers will not have to work as hard.

The royal bureaucracy was financed mostly by taxes on consumer goods, so that the laborers actually did subsidize the courtiers. The king and courtiers, according to Shelley, are misguided by precedent and custom, and violate natural and ethical laws. The libertarian rebel, however, sacrifices the ephemeral and illusory pleasures of "sensualism" for the more enduring and satisfying happiness of "virtue." Although kings cannot achieve immortal fame, the "virtuous man" can; he "leads / Invincibly a life of resolute good, / And stands amid the silent dungeon-depths / More free and fearless than a trembling judge . . ." (III, 153-55). Fearless, strong, benevolent, and eloquent, the rebel is nevertheless defeated by monarchical power, but in his martyrdom he gains a victory over oblivion. The virtuous rebel is guided by the ideals which will be realized in the future, on the ruins of disintegrated, "unnatural" monarchy.

The critique of "luxury" did not stop at the royal bureaucracy, but extended to the entire social practice of "Commerce." The fifth Canto, the poem's best, turns into poetry Godwin's "Book VIII, On Property," of *Political Justice*. Under selfish Commerce, the human soul is sacrificed to the production of commodities: "All things are sold," even love. Alluding to Adam Smith, Shelley laments that the creative potential of the laborer is sacrificed to the "wealth of nations" and to the making of nails and pins. Gold is a "living god" which dominates the entire society, corrupting everything. "Natural kindness" and "boundless love" are repressed in every individual during the scramble for wealth. The rich, as well as the poor, are sacrificed to the idol of selfish gain. With the totality of society infected with the commercial spirit, Shelley proposes a new god, "virtue," to replace the old one. The libertarian rebel escapes the cash nexus by transcending self-interest and acting on the ideals of humanity. Virtue requires no "mediative signs" and generates a new kind of commerce—love, or what one could call symbolic reciprocity. "Good words and works" are freely exchanged under conditions of social equality. Whereas Commerce mechanizes and reifies human spirit, the reign of virtue permits the unrepressed growth of spirit.

Two "notes" to *Queen Mab* bolster Shelley's attack on Commerce. The first, entitled "And statesmen boast / Of wealth!", recapitulates the ideas of Canto V, and adds a critique of landed wealth as well. "English reformers exclaim against sinecures,—but the true pension list is the rent-roll of the landed proprietors."[104] Moreover, "The nobleman, who employs the peasants of his neighbourhood in building his palaces . . . flatters himself that he has gained the title of a patriot by yielding to the impulses of vanity."[105] But aristocratic luxury does not stimulate "the wealth of nations" in which everyone takes a happy part; rather, it generates an excessive amount of labor to which the poor are subjected, so that they are deprived of healthy leisure by this unnecessary toil. The poor do not work to create socially useful products, but labor solely for the benefit of the wealthy.

Nevertheless, Shelley's greatest ire is against commercial wealth, as is apparent in the vegetarian note. Shelley opposes meat-eating not only for psychological and physiological reasons, but for political and economic reasons. To produce a consumable piece of livestock, it is necessary to use ten times more vegetable matter than required to feed people directly with vegetables.[106] In other words, if one acre of pasturage could produce meat sufficient to nourish one person, then that same acre, if utilized for vegetarian purposes, could provide for ten people. (Although Shelley's factor of ten is exaggerated, his idea has been seriously articulated by modern ecologists.) If less meat and wool, too, are produced, then more land will be available to feed people, and the poor will not have to labor for superfluous luxuries. Like Godwin, Shelley wants to simplify the economy in order to increase the leisure of the poor and to shorten the working day. Such a society has to be agrarian, but cannot permit capitalist farming for profit. Agriculture must be freed from Commerce, the real culprit. "The odious and disgusting aristocracy of wealth is built upon the ruins of all that is good in chivalry or republicanism."[107]

Shelley traces the root of monarchical society to Commerce, where he applies the axe of philosophical anarchism. His concept of the libertarian rebel stresses individual effort. There are three different types in the poem's theory of history: the oppressors, the oppressed, and the libertarian rebels. The poem's utopian speaker is herself outside of history, above and beyond it, immune to the exigencies of social life. A feature of Godwin's anarchism that had a lasting influence on Shelley was disinterestedness; the philosophical anarchist has to transcend mere self-interest and determine the genuine interests of humanity, according to the criterion of justice. Shelley actually was an aristocratic rebel who repudiated—but not completely—his own class, and who championed the rights of the oppressed from whom, however, he always remained at a distance. The social gulf between someone like Shelley (from the titled gentry,

Eton and Oxford), and someone like Dan Hill, his Irish servant, was so wide that even the purest, best intentioned idealist could never fully close it. The Queen Mab figure accurately reflects Shelley's position as the aristocratic, disinterested rebel, distinct from both the oppressors and oppressed. From Queen Mab to Laon to Prometheus to Ahasuerus to the "sacred few" of his last poem, Shelley's image of the ideal rebel is consistently one of the ethically pure individual liberated from the contaminating influences of self-interest. Whereas the egoist is at the mercy of selfish desires, pursuing power and wealth, the Shelleyan rebel denies self-interest and identifies instead with humanity as a whole, thus rejecting the merely phenomenal world of apparent reality for the ideal world of immutable justice and virtue. In *Queen Mab*, this ethically ideal realm is closely identified with nature's laws, but in later poems, it takes on a more humanistic coloring. This ideal realm, however, is never a mystical haven which can substitute for the transformation of the social world. The ideal world is the ethical standard by which society is judged and accordingly restructured. Although it is unlikely that the social world will ever coincide exactly with the ideal world, Shelley still believes that one must try to approach perfection.

A good example of the Shelleyan rebel is Ahasuerus of Canto VII. Unlike Queen Mab, Ahasuerus is a victim, and therefore passionately involved in the struggle against injustice. His being cursed with eternal life puts him on the margins of society that are remote from Queen Mab's placid throne. The alienated man *par excellence*, Ahasuerus crushes Judaeo-Christianity with intellectual satire reminiscent of Blake's antinomian attacks. God, as portrayed by the Wandering Jew, is a sadistic bully whom only the feeble-minded could wish to worship. God's power, however, Ahasuerus does not deny, even though he resists it. An existential rebel, he defies an authority he cannot overcome and refuses to grant any ethical legitimacy to the divine power of which he is a victim. In his final lines, Ahasuerus anticipates the rebellion of Shelley's Prometheus, who also resists "omnipotent" power.

> Thus have I stood,—through a wild waste of years
> Struggling with whirlwinds of mad agony,
> Yet peaceful, and serene, and self-enshrined,
> Mocking my powerless tyrant's horrible curse
> With stubborn and unalterable will,
> Even as a giant oak, which heaven's fierce flame

Had scathed in the wilderness, to stand
A monument of fadeless ruin there;
Yet peacefully and movelessly it braves
The midnight conflict of wintry storm,
  As in the sun-light's calm it spreads
  Its worn and withered arms on high
To meet the quiet of a summer's noon.
                                                     (VII, 254-66)

First, the blank verse here is perhaps the best in the entire poem. The poetry derives its energy from the language, not from the ideas alone. The self-objectification of Ahasuerus in the oak metaphor is an excellent way to demonstrate his peaceful serenity and complex immobility. He counters God's curse of perpetual life with perpetual defiance, turning the curse of never dying, an impotent immobility, into the majesty of never submitting. He achieves his own self-created stasis by consecrating his rebellion and condemning his judge and oppressor. He anticipates the stationary defiance of Prometheus by, literally, *enshrining* his *self*. Another echo of *Prometheus Unbound* can be heard in the scathing of the giant oak; the "lightning-blasted almond tree" in Act II is a prophetic sign of Prometheus's deliverance (II, i, 135).

Ahasuerus refuses to accept God's judgment; he, in turn, judges God; and thus his power is appropriately imaged as a sturdy oak. Another interesting source of excitement is the fire imagery. There is "Heaven's fierce flame" that is destructive and sadistic, like Jupiter's thunderbolt. Ahasuerus must endure the fire of tyranny, the misuse of fire. Another torture is the absence of fire, the withdrawal of light and warmth, the "Midnight conflict of wintry storm." (Prometheus, too, will endure the torture of fire's absence in Act I of *Prometheus Unbound*.) The last three lines, however, promise a rebirth and deliverance. The sunlight and summer's noon present the hope of fire's return, not as a thunderbolt, but as a healing and nurturing presence. Neither Milton's Satan nor the Ahasuerus of legend ever had hope of liberation, as Shelley's Wandering Jew has.

Neither Queen Mab nor Ahasuerus is an accurate portrait of the mediating bard because the one is too detached, and the other not detached enough. The poem only anticipates the experience of inspiration that will become so important later. The utopian purpose of poetry, however, is spelled out in Canto V, where the living god, Gold, has killed sympathy between people, so poetry will try to revive it. Against the tyranny of gold and the selfish ego, the poem enlists the will and the imagination of the poet. Since Shelley believes that neither the tyrants nor their victims can initiate the movement toward utopia, it will have to be the outsider, the poet with strength and benevolence, who will point the way. At this stage, Shelley has the same sense of the poor's passivity as Godwin. Indeed, the importance of literary culture and the inspired bard are, in part, responses to the assumed ignorance and passivity of the lower classes. Not even Luddism changed Shelley's mind.

CONCLUSION

From *Zastrozzi* to *Queen Mab*, Shelley has developed into a writer and social theorist of remarkable maturity. At the age of twenty, he is more politically sophisticated than most poets ever become. He has revised Godwinian anarchism in a Shelleyan direction, so that by 1813, he is no longer a "disciple" of Godwin, but a thinker and activist fully on his own. The ethical basis of his philosophy, which is well defined, is to remain a Shelleyan constant. The configurations of his "divided self" are clearly delineated and will never completely fade. The passionate instability of Verezzi vies with the detached control of Zastrozzi; the disinterested benevolence of Queen Mab is the polar complement of the Verezzian Ahasuerus (although he, too, has some Zastrozzian qualities). A distinctly aristocratic anarchism, which posits a privileged elite above the *canaille*, is something usually subordinate to a social anarchism, but the aristocratic qualities of Shelley's thought are never entirely superseded. The principal task he assigns himself in the early period is mediation of the ethical ideals that, fully realized, would create a utopia; this is a project to which he continues to dedicate himself until his death. The various inner contradictions Shelley experienced throughout his literary and political life—even the yearning for an escape beyond the phenomenal world—never overturned his primary goal: to help create a new society.

THREE

Romanticism
and Religion
(1814-1817)

INTRODUCTION

BY THE END of 1813, Shelley's situation was as follows: his major literary-philosophical statement, *Queen Mab*, was too seditious and blasphemous to be published; he was unable to form a political "association"; and when he tried to propaganize on his own, he was ineffective. Although Shelley's earliest phase was immensely productive, it was also a dead end. To continue in politics and literature he would have to find better ways to express his philosophy.

In early 1814 Shelley published a small edition of *A Refutation of Deism*, a freethinking dialogue in the tradition of Hume and Holbach. The essay seems to have made no impression on the public, who had another chance to read the anti-Christian critique in 1815, when *The Theological Inquirer* published it, along with a review of *Queen Mab*. An event of major consequence intervened between *A Refutation of Deism*'s first and second appearances: the elopement of Shelley and Mary Godwin. The collapse of Shelley's first marriage and his falling in love with Mary had an effect on the relationship between William Godwin and Shelley. From the moment they eloped to Europe in the summer of 1814, to the day in late December 1816, when they finally married, Mary and Shelley were bitterly estranged from Godwin. Shelley's disillusionment with Godwin began before mid-1814, but the disintegration of the relationship shocked the poet, with whom Godwin refused to speak (although in letters he asked Shelley for money). From philosophical mentor to archenemy, Godwin's transfiguration did nothing to weaken

Shelley's philosophical anarchism which, even before the elopement, was a completely Shelleyan creed. Shelley had by now learned most of what Godwin had to teach and he was beginning to explore other philosophical and literary perspectives. The ancient Greek philosophers, Rousseau, Berkeley, Hume, and Plato were by no means anti-Godwinian thinkers (Godwin urged Shelley to study all of them), but they provided an independent strain of images and ideas from which the poet could make a uniquely Shelleyan synthesis. From late 1813, when he was writing *A Refutation of Deism*, to early 1817, when he was probably finishing the so-called *Essay on Christianity*, he refined and deepened the philosophical foundations of his anarchism; moreover, a unique pattern was clearly emerging from his diverse writings in prose and poetry. A central experience becomes the process of inspiration, the direct communion with a divine presence that exists in nature and humanity. Inspiration leads to an ethical idealism whose ultimate goal is an anarchist utopia. The problem of mediation, however, is difficult to resolve because the inspired poet, like the anarchist prophet, falls between the ideals of perfectibility and the actual historical situation. The poet-prophet has to translate the apocalyptic ideals into an earthly language capable of being understood by mortals. If he allows the ideal vision to dominate every other consideration, then he will write in a language few people can understand. If he concerns himself more with audience expectations than visionary purity, then he is in danger of eclipsing the vision.

A turning-point comes with the writing of *Alastor*, which signifies a transition from a radical rationalism to a new, "romantic" synthesis. With *Alastor*, Rousseauistic and Wordsworthian pantheism enters the mainstream of Shelley's public writing, so that the crucial experience becomes not just enlightenment but inspiration. Many poems in the Esdaile Notebook also bear evidence of pantheism, so that clearly it was something Shelley wrote about before *Alastor*. Just how much before is hard to tell, because of the uncertain dating of most of the Esdaile poems.[1] The assumptions of rationalism defined the problem as one of communication. Provide the necessary and correct information, and then the unenlightened would be converted to enlightenment. The word itself, "enlightenment," suggests a self-sufficient source of truth filling an empty space. The inspiration paradigm assumes a divinity in man and nature which is capable of being excited into actuality by any number of experiences, poetry and expository prose being only two of them. Inspiration, as Shelley perceives it, is an inconstant wind and a fiery apocalypse, an indeterminate process of discovery. The *philosophe* takes knowledge from one place—his own mind—and transfers it to another place—another mind. Post-*Alastor* Shelley, however, supplements a mechanistic epistemology with a conviction that the living subjectivity of the reader must experience and perceive the truth before it can be "learned."

The *Alastor* breakthrough in late 1815 leads to the Genevan summer of 1816, the height of Shelley's worship of Rousseau, Wordsworth, and Coleridge. Romantic naturalism opens an exit to political reaction and merely private consolation for the tragedies of history and existence. In *Alastor*, "Mont Blanc," "Hymn to Intellectual Beauty," and the so-called *Essay on Christianity*, Shelley makes a unique synthesis of the rationalist and romantic strains of radicalism. Pantheistic spirit and ecstatic communion with nature do not lead to quietism, but to an insurrectionary demand for destroying the old world and building a new one. In this period, after *Queen Mab* and before *Laon and Cythna*, Shelley continues to develop in the same direction as he did earlier, searching for points of mediation from libertarian ideals and divine beauty to history and existence.

A REFUTATION OF DEISM

Coming after the unpublishable *Queen Mab*, *A Refutation of Deism* is especially interesting for its rhetorical strategy, which is clever and deceiving. Expensively printed, it even disavows in the preface any interest in reaching "the multitude" who are likely to "misconstruct" this novel "mode of reasoning."[2] The title (against deism) and the preface ("It is attempted to shew that there is no alternative between Atheism and Christianity") are designed to attract a naive Christian, who expects to read an antifreethinking essay in which Christian truth overwhelms infidelity. Instead, Shelley has written an ingenious dialogue between a deist who destroys the logic of Christianity, and a Christian who destroys the logic of deism. If indeed there is no alternative between atheism and Christianity, the logical reader must accept atheism (or a skeptical agnosticism).[3] Shelley has achieved a remarkable degree of duplicity so that he not only circumvents government repression (by appearing to uphold the established order), but undermines orthodox thinking.

Like the *Biblical Extracts*, *A Refutation of Deism* turns biblical quotations against Christian institutions. Whereas the *Biblical Extracts* culled libertarian passages to undermine Christianity, the *Refutation* cites passages which are especially barbarous to ridicule Christian assumptions. Wanting to be an effective social reformer, Shelley recognizes the necessity of rhetoric, using language to provoke the reader through the experience of reading into perceiving the truths; ineffective propaganda simply announces that something is true, without providing the necessary experience by which its truths could be perceived. Nevertheless, whether stated directly or indirectly, the truths Shelley writes are the same, and rhetorical ploys do not alter the philosophical anarchism which is the basis of these truths. Although *Queen Mab* is more straightforward than the *Refutation*, both works speak for the same ethical idealism.

The wretched moral qualities Theosophus attributes to the atheist are, ironically, those qualities Shelley always identifies with his ethical hero, in *Queen Mab* and all his other works. For the atheist, "private judgment" is the "criterion of right and wrong"; the odious infidel, unafraid of punishment, "dreads no judge but his own conscience."[4] The atheist has all the qualities Shelley identifies as necessary for the ethical hero, who uses his own reason and conscience to discover the laws of nature in order to construct a rational society based on love.

Eusebes, by attacking deism, actually upholds a philosophical skepticism, not the Christian orthodoxy he tries to defend. In his exposition of Christianity's many virtues, he recurrently attacks reason and philosophy by praising the sufficiency of faith. When Eusebes says that Christianity has discovered as "delusive vices" the "genius, learning and courage" of the philosophical tradition, the irony is obvious.[5] Indeed, as Christianity is portrayed in the dialogue, it is an antisocial source of all that is hostile to the true interests of humanity. Antisexual, otherworldly, militaristic, intolerant, punitive, anti-intellectual, Christianity has been an unmitigated disaster ever since its political success in the third century, A.D. Although some of Christ's moral views, shorn of their mystical trappings, are admirable, they are also nothing more or less than part of the philosophical tradition of ethics[6] (Shelley develops this line of thinking in greater detail later in the *Essay on Christianity*). That, however, is the full extent to which one can praise Christianity. Scientific naturalism is a far more humane system of explaining the universe. Natural phenomena are explicable by laws, not all of which we know at present; nevertheless, the lack of complete knowledge is no excuse for a retreat into superstition.[7] Human phenomena are also subject to necessity: belief is involuntary; the basis of perception is sensation; the mind has to be persuaded by the strongest motive.[8] Historical hermeneutics can find internal evidence within the Bible indicating that Gospels were written well after Christ's death, not by eyewitnesses.[9] An anthropological account of polytheism adequately explains why people would project power onto the gods in response to their inability to control the world.[10] In Eusebes' antideism argument, he denies that good and evil exist independently of the human mind, because the mind creates good and evil in the act of perception.[11] By this, however, Shelley is not suggesting a subjectivistic world-view, an infinite plurality of "truths," or the unknowability of the world. Rather, he is being a consistent humanist. Only when perception creates good does good exist; only then will evil ever be conquered. If good and evil existed absolutely, outside and independent of human perception, then indeed Christianity would accurately describe the moral universe, with a creator God and an evil Satan.

If people are to gain control of history and direct its development toward the fulfillment of human needs, then they have to forsake the fatalistic notions of theism. If God has created the world, then humanity can never be certain that its own deeds will not someday be superseded by the greatest power. Anthropomorphism makes the irrationalities of religion seem plausible. At this time, Shelley has not developed any of his pantheistic notions, although there are hints of pantheism in Eusebes' comments on matter not being inert.[12] Pantheism, however, never threatens his humanism. Indeed, a painful thing about Shelleyan inspiration is that the divinity merely inspires; the poet is the one who has to translate this apocalyptic experience into words. There is not much difference between the "nature" of the *Refutation* and the "divinity" which emerges in Shelley's later work. The movement toward divinity and away from natural law is toward a more consistent humanism. Regardless of nature's laws, it is finally people who must create the social utopia if a utopia is to exist. The inspiration model Shelley adopted from 1816 onwards embodies the utopian dilemma: an ideal society, created by desire and imagination, inspires an effort to transform the actual historical world into an ideal society. Needless to say, Shelley's going from nature's laws to inspiration is hardly an accommodation with Christianity or any other organized religion, nor does it signify a retreat from a philosophical anarchism. Rather, it marks the mature development of Shelley's radical ideas, his refusal to be dogmatic, and his ability to grow.

Another aspect of Christianity that interested Shelley at this time is developed in a fragment of an unfinished novel. *The Assassins*, written in the summer of 1814 while Shelley was in Europe with Mary and Claire, was apparently to have been a "romance" about a interaction between the Wandering Jew and a utopian community of Christian anarchists called "Assassins." A major focus, if one can surmise from the fragment, would have been the contrast between the exemplary moral life of the utopians and the corrupt social world from which the Wandering Jew has come. Resembling Gnostics, the Assassins acknowledge "no laws but those of God" and "modelled their conduct towards their fellow-men by the conclusions of their individual judgment on the practical application of these laws."[13] They fused together a "submission to the law of Christ" and "an intrepid spirit of inquiry." Practicing complete equality, they lived according to the doctrines of "benevolence and justice," not the institutional laws and customs formulated by a secular power.[14] After leaving Jerusalem, they settled in a remote valley where they prospered and were protected from the outside world. Within this favorable environment, the utopians could develop the full extent of their moral nature.

"To love, to be beloved, suddenly became an insatiable famine of his [the Assassin's] nature, which the wide circle of the universe, comprehending beings of such inexhaustible variety and stupendous magnitude of excellence, appeared too narrow and confined to satiate."[15] This expanding circle of love was a perpetual triumph over the "commercial spirit" of selfish egoism. The Assassins "knew not to conceive any happiness that can be satiated without participation, or that thirsts not to reproduce and perpetually generate itself."[16] If, however, they were to mingle with other social beings, framed by very different social customs, they would find themselves at war with that society, either as victims of persecution or uncompromising revolutionists.[17]

The purpose of the romance seems to be propagandistic, introducing radical ideas to a popular audience attracted by gothic trappings. One form of Christianity, which has worked its malevolence through the Wandering Jew, is confronted by a utopian and anarchistic heresy; between the two there can be no compromise. Presumably Shelley would delineate the fine moral sensibility of the

Assassins to illustrate that virtue depends on motives entirely different from those animating orthodox Christians. The Assassins possibly would alter their own concepts if confronted with the perversions of Christian doctrine. All one can know for sure is that Christianity, in its dominant mode, would be attacked as inconsistent with the highest ethical ideals which, supposedly, Christ tried to promulgate.

The *Refutation of Deism* enjoyed a second existence as the opening article of an ephemeral journal, *The Theological Inquirer*, which was published between March and September 1815. There was also a long review of *Queen Mab*, a third of which was quoted, written by an "F." who also wrote an "Ode to the Author of *Queen Mab*." The journal's editor, "Erasmus Perkins," was really George Cannon, with whom Shelley collaborated to some extent.[18] With the *Refutation of Deism* between the covers of a freethinking journal, its ironic mode is transparent and its true readership made plain. It is too subtle to affect a Christian's blind faith, but its arguments are effective against deism, the dominant mode of freethinking at the time. Since there had to be cooperation between Shelley and the editor of the journal, one can infer that in 1815 Shelley was trying to reach a wider, more responsive audience for two of his most important works.

ALASTOR

The Godwinian dimension of *Alastor* has gone almost unnoticed, even though it provides a bridge linking the pantheistic naturalism with the elegiac lament for the "beautiful soul," the Visionary whose quest ends in death.[19] In the novels of Godwin and Holcroft, the solitaries lead tragic lives because, despite their many admirable qualities, they cannot break out of the egoism within which they are imprisoned and thus sundered from a sympathetic community. Godwin's Falkland derives his egoism from his aristocratic honor; St. Leon, from his Faustian greed and ambition; Fleetwood, from his jealousy. Holcroft's Anna St. Ives and Frank Henley actually do succeed, after many thousands of words, in converting the selfish egoist, Coke Clifton, to rational altruism. And the moral status of Hugh Trevor's picaresque adventures hinges on his ability to forgive, forbear, and refrain from revenge, lest his "egoistic" impulses drag him down to the same barbarous level as the selfish avatars of Old Corruption like the Earl of Idford or the Bishop of Wakefield.

The tragic conflicts produced by the liberatian novelists of the 1790s point to the necessity of changing society. Precisely the same kind of didactic point is being made in *Alastor; or, The Spirit of Solitude*, in which one Shelleyan solitary, the Visionary, is destroyed in an attempt to personalize the Absolute.

Godwin and Shelley take social alienation for granted because in an unjust society only the rebel upholds true rationality, but they do not accept private solutions to the problem of estrangement. The *Alastor* Visionary, properly educated by the pantheistic spirit of nature, tries to possess absolutely the spirit of beauty and truth. The Visionary's fate is not even remotely exemplary, contrary to what some critics have suggested. Indeed, just the opposite is true. The narrator who survives and tells the tale is the true hero because only he initiates the communitarian act of sharing, and only he knits the fabric of an organic connectedness between people. The exemplary hero is the mediator, the individual who, though alienated from an inauthentic society, is vitally connected with nature and an emergent society of which he is an active, creative agent. Although unworthy of imitation, the *Alastor* Visionary's death is tragic, to be understood in necessitarian terms, not with moralistic labels. The Visionary's tragic flaw—an inability to love—generated the vision which, after it fled, plunged him into a state of death-in-life, whose culmination was actual death. The narrator's sympathy for the Visionary is justified because a beautiful soul is being destroyed in its misguided quest for the Absolute.

There is a dramatic contrast between the mediating narrator, whose nature-worship leads to imaginative humanism, and the apocalyptic Visionary, whose "natural piety" is short-circuited by repressed sexuality. In the preface Shelley makes clear his preference for the Visionary's mistaken quest over the merely egoistic pursuit of selfish gain that typifies the gentlemen of the leisure class. The narrator and Visionary both reject the established social order whose basis is "blood and gold," and both find in nature a pantheistic spirit that links them in a mystical bond to all living things. The narrator, however, is ethically superior to his egoistic comrade.

Wordsworth and Coleridge, like Godwin, are important influences in *Alastor*.[20] In *The Excursion*, the Intimations of Immortality Ode, "Tintern Abbey"—verbal echoes of which are found all through *Alastor*—the pantheistic spirit of nature is a consolation for failures of existence and politics. By the act of memory, Wordsworth can recover a sense of lost vitality. In *The Excursion*, Wordsworth's despondent Solitary, however, cannot accept the failures of social life. The fatalistic acceptance of suffering and injustice advocated in the poem is, despite its incisive social criticism of laissez-faire industrialism, what led Mary to write in her journal, after they both read the *Excursion*: " . . . much disappointed. He is a slave."[21] Shelley wants to synthesize a pantheistic naturalism and an ethical idealism. The Visionary is also similar to Coleridge's Ancient Mariner, from their initial tragic deed (killing the albatross, ignoring the Arab maiden), to their experience of death-in-life and their supernatural boat journeys. Even the ethical point, that all life is sacred, is the same in both poems, but the differences are equally striking. The Mariner expiates his guilt by telling his tale, whereas the Visionary feels no guilt whatsoever. Coleridge is fascinated with the effects and process of guilt, whereas Shelley delineates the consequence of error from the perspective of a tragedian. The Mariner passes successfully from death-in-life to life and social connections; Shelley's Visionary, however, is fated to die one of the most beautiful deaths in literature. He returns to nature and the source of all life in a way reminiscent of Asia's descent into the origins of existence in *Prometheus Unbound*. Once the Visionary enters the shallop, he is driven by powerful forces into the deepest recesses of nature. When he finally reaches "home," he has achieved a victory over the dualistic split between subject and object, man and nature, desire and fulfillment. Becoming "one" with nature is to die, because the essence of living is struggle and conflict. "Hope and despair, / The torturers, slept" (639-40) signifies one possible resolution of spiritual estrangement. The other possibility, the one embodied in the narrator, is to transform the social world so radically that spirit will find a home in society, not in death.

An interesting romantic borrowing is the concept of inspiration, a primary event in "Kubla Khan" and alluded to frequently by Wordsworth. For both Coleridge and Wordsworth, inspiration is a process during which the poet is inspired by the power of nature so that he creates a strong poetry; there is a transfer of energy. Shelley, however, distinguishes in *Alastor* between two kinds of inspiration, one of which is an aberration. The "good" inspiration occurs when inauthentic modes of experience are suddenly replaced by true modes. The narrator, at the poem's begining, announces his "brotherhood" with natural objects and declares his filial devotion to the maternal spirit of nature. The process by which he loses his false social identity and acquires his "natural" identity is, then, a "good" inspiration. In a passage reminiscent of "Hymn to Intellectual Beauty," the narrator says that he has tried unsuccessfully to find the secrets of nature by means of magic and alchemy, although now he is content to invoke the "breath" of the "Great Parent" to inspire his poetry and attune it harmonically with the pantheistic nature-spirit (20-49). Whereas the narrator ceases to quest after the Absolute and contents himself with natural piety, the Visionary does not. He begins with the "good" inspiration of nature-communion which purifies his perceptions, but he also has an "unnatural" inspiration. Oblivious to the Arab maiden's love, the Visionary continues his quest until nature—his own—has its revenge. Fusing his frustrated sexual desires and his greed for knowledge, he dreams of a beautiful, veiled woman like the Abyssinian maid of "Kubla Khan." The subliminal eroticism of "Kubla Khan" becomes explicit in *Alastor* when the Visionary tries to unite sexually with his dream-woman. After he awakens from his dream, he does not learn the lesson of nature, about which the narrator is quite clear:

> The spirit of sweet human love has sent
> A vision to the sleep of him who spurned
> Her choicest gifts. He eagerly pursues
> Beyond the realms of dream that fleeting shade;
> He overleaps the bounds.
> (203-207)

The erotic dream is an inspiration that so estranges the Visionary from natural existence that he is transported into death-in-life, the ultimate consequence of which is actual death. The "bounds" existed for both narrator and Visionary, so that both could choose whether to "overleap" or remain within them. The situation Shelley is investigating is the plight of the solitary rebel, the aristocratic dissenter, who can choose whether to be aristocratic or egalitarian, apolitical or political, uninvolved or activist, pamphleteer or poet. It is not surprising Shelley was attracted to the Visionary's resolution, but he rejected it as unethical. Moreover, the pathos of the elegiac conclusion derives from the necessity of struggle and tension which the narrator and reader must endure as social beings within temporality. The union of subject and object, and the reconciliation of nature and man, which the dying Visionary symbolizes, are both utopian images that promise a happy resolution sometime far in the future. The elegiac tone with which the poem concludes signifies the narrator's refusal to accept loss or find compensation. Com-

paring the conclusions of "The Ancient Mariner," or the Intima-
tions of Immortality Ode (or virtually any of Wordsworth's tragic
poems), one immediately sees the dramatic differences. Whereas
Coleridge and Wordsworth integrate tragedy into everyday life,
reconciling ethics and history (usually by means of fatalism), Shelley
cannot allow tragic loss to be temporized. The narrator laments
the departure of a beautiful soul whose loss is irreplaceable. The
poem, like *Caleb Williams*, ends in tension, and tries to enlist the
reader in a spiritual alliance. Shelley wants to awaken in the reader
those sympathetic, imaginative qualities whose full development
will have, hopefully, immense social consequences. The reader is
asked to discriminate among three levels of existence: the egoistic
pursuit of selfish gain, the misguided quest for the Absolute, and
natural piety. Shelley expands the scope of this piety to include
being sexually responsive, as interested in other people as in the
secrets of nature and wisdom. However tempted Shelley was by the
idea of escape from temporality and existential conflicts, he rec-
ognized that there was no escape, except in death.

The imagination, by taking one out of one's own limited sphere
and into the drama of human existence, as the poem *Alastor* does,
can initiate a civilizing process which educates the social affections.
It is the narrator of *Alastor* who is heroic, because without his
mediating activity the Visionary's self-involved tragedy would be
lost to oblivion. Moreover, the narrator's stance is exemplary in
relation to the quest of the Visionary, whose "generous error" is
tragic. Like the libertarian novelists of the 1790s, Shelley portrays
someone with many admirable qualities whose tragic flaw leads to
a "self-centered seclusion" which is the very antithesis of the poem's
controlling ethic. Unlike the "Jacobin" novelists, however, Shelley
has a dynamic sense of nature as a source of apocalyptic energy;
they would have concluded the poem shortly after the Visionary
awakens from his dream. The boat journey affirms the beauty,
power, and erotic vitality of nature, which still remains, even at the
poem's end, a source of potentiality which the Visionary misused.
The power and beauty of nature can, if properly mediated, act as
a revolutionary social force. The tragedy of *Alastor* is that this
process does not happen.

ESSAY ON CHRISTIANITY

The themes developed in *Alastor* are explored in "Hymn to In-
tellectual Beauty," and "Mont Blanc," both written at Geneva in

the summer of 1816. There is a fresh influx of impressions from the Swiss landscape, his constant companion Byron (whom he tries to convert to the "religion" of Wordsworth and Coleridge), and the writings of Rousseau, especially *La Nouvelle Héloïse*. The passionate intensity with which Shelley promoted his romanticism can be gauged by Canto III of *Childe Harold*, Byron's brief but deeply felt experience with pantheism.[22] Neither before nor after Shelley's propagandizing did Byron ever go so far in a Shelleyan-Wordsworthian direction. Shelley believes that the libertarian social philosophy he derived from Godwin has new supporting evidence from Wordsworthian-Rousseauistic naturalism.

By the end of Shelley's Genevan summer his libertarian philosophy is closely linked with the creative imagination and the experience of inspiration. Returning to England in September, he finds the country on the brink of revolution. This new factor inspires him to reformulate his politics and take into account the radical movement of the laboring classes unofficially led by "Orator" Hunt, the Spenceans, and Cobbett, and a rejuvenated moderate reform movement of the "respectable" classes, headed by the independent Whigs in Parliament, the Hampden Clubs, and the Hunts' *Examiner*. The text which represents Shelley's effort to restate his position in the light of pantheism, the creative imagination, inspiration, and the resurgence of democratic forces is, I believe, *Essay on Christianity*. After this, which he never publishes or even finishes, he is ready to act and write on the principles articulated in the *Essay*: the two Hermit of Marlow pamphlets and *Laon and Cythna*.

Although the *Essay on Christianity* has received considerable commentary, it has rarely been intensively analyzed. A line of argument, from Robert Browning to Ellsworth Bernard and Bennett Weaver, stated a case for Shelley's Christianity.[23] This futile effort depended somewhat on the *Essay on Christianity*, which was frequently cited—not by Browning, who wrote before the *Essay*'s publication—but never fully interpreted. The question of Shelley's Christianity is now, fortunately, a dead issue. There has been, however, some useful commentary on the *Essay*. A. H. Koszul, in what is still the best edition of the work, has some excellent notes.[24] James Notopoulos has researched the Platonic elements;[25] David Clark has footnoted many of the sources;[26] and Kenneth Cameron has written one of the few extended analyses of the *Essay*.[27] I want to argue that the *Essay* is not an essay at all, but an unfinished *fragment* that should be treated as such. Next, I wish to establish the context—biographical, philosophical, political, and theological—within which the fragment acquires meaning. Then I shall analyze the different sections of the fragment, and finally offer some conclusions. The fragment, as I interpret it, reveals the workings of Shelley's mind at an interesting juncture in his development, between the Genevan summer of 1816 and the completion of *Laon and Cythna* in 1817. It is an important transitional work which records the process of Shelley exploring new possibilities and re-valuating old ones.

Shelley never wrote an *Essay on Christianity*, a title invented by Lady Shelley in 1859. The wife of Percy Florence Shelley, Lady Shelley published the *Essay on Christianity*, in *Shelley Memorials*.[28] It is not even a good title for the fragment left in the notebook. "God, Christ, and Equality" would be closer to the mark. Shelley himself entitled two of the three parts; one he called "God" and the other, "The Equality of Mankind." Even with a more accurate title, the fragment does not comprise an essay. Although everyone, even Lady Shelley, acknowledges that the "essay" is in fact fragmentary, readers still persist in treating it as an essay rather than a fragment. Shelley could have finished it if he had wanted to; *he did not want to*. That Shelley did *not* write an "essay" on Christianity is a fact that we should try to account for, or at least accept. He *began* to write such an essay, made several false starts, apparently found a workable concept, then dropped the project. That is the actual process Shelley underwent in 1816-1817, the probable dates of his work on the theological fragment. Why did he abandon the project? I think he reached an impasse where the fragment was neither a freethinking discourse nor anything sufficiently free from that genre's limitations to warrant publication. The conclusions arrived at in the fragment pointed to well-conceived public statements on politics and to a visionary poetry embodying an ethical idealism translated into potentially popular forms.

The dating of the fragment is not absolutely certain, but 1816-1817 is at least highly probable. Notopoulous offers late 1816 or early 1817, while Koszul, Reiman, and Cameron suggest 1817. If one sets aside the idiosyncratic guess of Clark—1810-1813—then it seems that the fragment was probably written between late 1816 and 1817: some time after returning from Switzerland in 1816 and before the completion of *Laon and Cythna* in 1817.[29] To bolster the case for an 1816-1817 dating—and I believe the fragment was written before March of 1817—I offer the observation that the high

89

praise found there for Rousseau is consistent with Shelley's view of Rousseau during the summer of 1816, when the poet visited the various spots in Switzerland where Julie and Saint-Preux had played out their tragedy.

The problem for Shelley in 1816-1817 was not first principles, but trying to refine his position and discover appropriate public forms for expressing his ideas. In a letter written near the end of 1817, Shelley apologizes for the imperfections of *Queen Mab*, but says also:

> It is the Author's boast & it constitutes no small portion of his happiness that, after six years [a typical exaggeration] of added experience & reflection, the doctrines of equality & liberty & disinterestness, & entire unbelief in religion of any sort, to which this Poem is devoted, have gained rather than lost that beauty & grandeur which first determined him to devote his life to the investigation & inculcation of them.[30]

His first principles, a revised Godwinian anarchism, had been established for a number of years, well before the 1816-1817 period. The way he has phrased the statement is reminiscent of "Hymn to Intellectual Beauty": "I vowed that I would dedicate my powers / To thee and thine" (61-62). Shelley's dedication of his ideas entails two separate but connected processes, "investigation" and "inculcation." For inculcating the ideas of equality, liberty, disinterestedness, and freethinking, what were the appropriate public vehicles? Poetry or prose? What audience should Shelley address? What rhetorical strategies were suitable, both effective and consistent with high philosophical purpose? The problems of inculcation, not just investigation, were vexing Shelley while he was writing the fragment.

The fragment of 1816-1817 is part of Shelley's ongoing project of finding appropriate ways to express his libertarian ideas. Although the fragment displays the important influence of Godwin, it never once cites his name or alludes to any of his works. This curiosity can again be explained by the unfriendly relations between Godwin and Shelley. Shelley's situation, then, in 1816-1817, was this: he was still very much a follower of Godwin's major ideas, which by now had become fully his own, but he was hostile to the man himself. The haggling with Godwin over money might have sharpened Shelley's interest in the dichotomy of God and Mammon. Indeed, the ascetic simplicity advocated by Diogenes, Rousseau, and Christ no doubt struck a responsive chord in the Shelley of this period.

The political context of this time is also important. The year 1816 saw increased activity by the movements for parliamentary reform. A notable feature of 1816-1817 was the emergence of a popular, democratic reform movement that frightened many Whig and moderate reformers.[31] Shelley, writing to Byron on November 20, 1816, expresses a fear that social revolution might break out. Although Shelley does not want a revolution, he does want radical reform. On March 4, 1817, the government enacted its Habeas Corpus Suspension Act, and on March 31 banned seditious meetings. This repression was in response to riots and numerous, large meetings for reform held all over the country. The political upheaval makes it inevitable that Shelley's mind will be on politics. Specifically, Shelley wants to explore strategies for social change short of social revolution, but conducive to radical change nevertheless.

Another biographical context is meaningful for the fragment: the suicide of his wife Harriet, and the subsequent Chancery suit over Shelley's children by Harriet. Although Shelley does not include any of Diogenes' misogynistic remarks in the fragment, Diogenes of Sinope was a notorious woman-hater. That Diogenes gets such a long speech in the fragment might be due to Shelley's barely unconscious hostility to women and the guilt they had aroused in him. In the notebook, on folio 6, prior to the theological fragment, is a jotted comment: "The similitude of doctrine between Jesus Christ and the Cynics on the subject of marriage and love."[32] Also, after the theological fragment, Shelley wrote in this same notebook a "fragment on Marriage." That Shelley was unhappy with the institution of marriage is hardly surprising. (Diogenes the Cynic advocated the abolition of the family, a community of wives, and free love—possibilities that might have appealed to Shelley in this tragic period.)[33] I think, too, the ascetic ideal of disengagement from worldly affairs was appealing, since Shelley himself was embroiled in such affairs far beyond what he found comfortable. Surely one motive for moving away from England in 1818 was to simplify his life. Lastly, the Chancery suit raised the specter not just of losing custody of his children, including William, but also of going to jail for having written *Queen Mab*. On January 11, 1817, writing to Mary, he says he is afraid the Westbrooks will bring a bill against *Queen Mab*, resulting in his imprisonment as "an atheist & a republican."[34] On January 30, 1817, to Claire Clairmont, Shelley sounds as if he is certain he will go to jail.[35] Even as late in April 23, 1817, he is still worried about a criminal information against *Queen Mab*.[36] Despite his fears, Shelley was not very cautious; he published his Hermit of Marlow pamphlet in early March 1817, an extremely dangerous time to test the government's will, and also composed *Laon and Cythna*, a defiantly seditious and blasphemous poem. Nevertheless, he was afraid he would go to prison and lose his children, so that he might have found it easy to identify with the martyrdom of Christ.

The theological fragment of 1816-1817 is comprehensible within the terms and interests of a philosophical anarchism. That it was, at one time, considered evidence for Shelley's orthodox Christianity is certainly amusing, since such a view could not be further from the truth. Instead, Shelley was probing various philosophical and rhetorical tactics to undermine Christianity and replace it with an uncompromising humanism. Specifically, the fragment can be put under the following headings: (a) a philosophical critique of religion, Christianity, and Jesus Christ; (b) the redeemable aspects of Christian ethics; (c) an alternative to Christian metaphysics.

The fragment has three principal foci. The first, the philosphical critique of religion, is something Shelley worked on early in his career and continued until the end of his life. In the fragment, he advances his understanding beyond the perspective of *A Refutation of Deism*, and anticipates the religious insights of *Prometheus Unbound* and *A Defence of Poetry*. The second concern is also an old one. Shelley once contemplated publishing the *Biblical Extracts*, which was to include quotations from the Bible illustrating various radical doctrines.[37] His concept was to use certain strains of Judaeo-Christian thought to undermine the institutional constructs that were historically dominant. In the fragment he goes beyond the *Biblical Extracts* idea by situating the redeemable aspects of religious thought within the tradition of Western philosphy. Socrates, Plato, Diogenes the Cynic, and Rousseau were all exponents, in varying degrees, of the radical ideas discernible in some of Christ's statements. Lastly, metaphysics: Shelley had long been interested in an alternative to the metaphysics of orthodox Christianity. The essay for which he was expelled from Oxford was primarily a metaphysical inquiry. More recently, in the summer of 1816, he had investigated the problem of divinity in "Mont Blanc." The fragment begins where "Mont Blanc" left off, and points toward the metaphysical solutions of *A Defence of Poetry*.

The fragment, I suggest, starts out as an attempt at another *A Refutation of Deism*, that is, a philosophical critique of Christianity in the deist-freethinking tradition. Shelley, however, in 1816-1817, brings to this mode ideas and perceptions that did not exist in 1814, when *A Refutation of Deism* was first published. Each part of the fragment breaks off at particular points that are suggestive. I will try to reconstruct the process of thought that each part represents. Although Shelley did not write a freethinking essay in 1816-1817, he generated ideas and concepts that one can see embodied in other works published in 1817 and later. There is even a significant anticipation of the ethical stance he develops in his last two poems, *Hellas* and *The Triumph of Life*.

SECTION 1 (f. 7–f. 7ᵛ)[38]

The first section is clearly in the freethinking tradition. Shelley, after Spinoza and Paine, distinguishes between Christ's ethical doctrines, which deserve sympathetic attention, and institutional Christianity, which needs to be demystified. Neither Volney nor Holbach tried to salvage radical ideas from Christianity. In *Histoire Critique de Jésus Christ*, Holbach portrays Christ as a confidence man whose magical tricks were inspired by madness, greed for power, or both. In *Le Bon Sens de Curé Jean Meslier*, he argues for the complete adequacy of reason and nature, both of which are sufficient for practicing virtue; religion is not just unnecessary, it is the archenemy of true philosphy. And in *Système de la Nature*, Holbach makes an extended argument for naturalistic materialism.[39] Shelley, in *Queen Mab* and *A Refutation of Deism*, borrowed numerous ideas from Holbach, but by 1816-1817 his influence is negligible. For Holbach, Christianity is a superstition imposed upon a passive society by violence and fraud; there is, then, no truth at all to be found in Christianity. Although Shelley agreed with much of Holbach's analysis, he did not believe that *all* of Christianity was simply and exclusively a fraudulent superstition.

Shelley had for a long time distinguished between Christ's ethical ideas and the supernatural mystification which was institutional Christianity. The *Biblical Abstracts*, planned in early 1812, was a work whose principal assumption was the separability of Christ's ethical ideas and Christian institutions. From 1812 to 1817 the Bible Society debated the wisdom of having published and widely distributed to the poor copies of the Bible without liturgy or commentary. Shelley's *Biblical Extracts* would have aided readers in their interpretation. The year 1812, then, was an appropriate time to interpret the Gospels from a radical point of view.[40] *Queen Mab*, written about the same time as the no longer extant *Biblical Extracts*, at first takes the Paine-Spinoza position, and then, in a retracting footnote, aligns itself with the Holbach-Palmer tradition.[41] In *A Refutation of Deism*, the Holbachian position reigns dominant. The closest Shelley comes to the Paine-Spinoza position is when Theosophus says,

> I am willing to admit that some few axioms of morality, which Christianity borrowed from the philosophers of Greece and India, dictate . . . rules of conduct worthy of regard; but the purest and most elevated lessons of morality must remain nugatory . . . so long as the slightest weight is attached to that dogma which is the vital essence of revealed religion.[42]

It is revealing to see what Paine and Spinoza do with the ambiguity of Christianity. In the first part of *The Age of Reason*, Paine's Christ is an exponent of equality, "a virtuous reformer and revolutionist," whose radical ideas were subverted by the "Christian Mythologists" of the Church.[43] Paine, however, does not greatly develop the contrast between Christ and his Church, almost ignoring it in the second part. Paine's ultimate commitment is to scientific materialism within a deistic metaphysics, so he is not overly concerned with redeeming Christ's ethics. Spinoza is much closer to Shelley's position of 1816-1817. In the *Theologico-Political Treatise* (a translation of which Shelley worked on for years), Spinoza rejects the supernatural aspects of Christianity—miracles, mysteries, oaths, etc.—and locates true religion in good works, the practice of justice, benevolence, and maintaining ethically correct conduct. True religion is true ethics, so that the ethical ideas in the Bible are indeed worthy of study. Spinoza, however, did not put much trust in Scripture, which he showed to be unreliable, fragmentary, and mutilated; rather, he believed the word of God was more legible in the minds and hearts of living people, whose mutual tolerance and search for truth were better religious safeguards than any form of sectarian religion.[44]

The centrality of ethics, rather than scientific materialism, makes Spinoza, not Paine, the most important parallel in 1816-1817. I say parallel rather than source or influence, because it is after the theological fragment had been written that Shelley took up the project of translating the *Tractatus Theologico-Politicus*. Mary's journal records Shelley working on a translation in November, 1817; January, March, April, and June of 1820; and November of 1821. For Shelley, Christ is first and foremost an ethical paragon, whose ideas can be saved only by demystifying Christianity and locating Christ in the philosophical tradition.

The first section of Shelley's theological fragment breaks off where he begins to discuss the supernatural events following Christ's death. Nearly every freethinker in the tradition deals with the issue of "miracles," which have to be accounted for in a rational way. There is a surviving fragment on miracles which seems to have been written around the time of *A Refutation of Deism*. The speaker in the fragment, which seems to be a dialogue, says: "I am inclined to think the miracles related in the Bible sprang from three great sources, of imposture, fabrication and a heated imagination."[45] It is the last possibility that seems prominent in the final sentence of the fragment under consideration: "The philosopher may attribute the application of these events *to* the death of a reformer or the events themselves to a visitation of that Universal Pan who." As Koszul remarks, the sense here is not clear. It seems to mean something like this: either natural prodigies were blamed on the murderers of a popular reformer, or the prodigies themselves were the confused perceptions of a social "panic" due to the disturbing nature of Christ's ideas. (I read "Universal Pan" as a Greek pun rather than an allusion to Thomas Taylor's pagan revival—Koszul's suggestion; "Universal Pan" also appears, but not as a pun, in *The Witch of Atlas*, stanza IX, line 113.)

There is a fragment which Ingpen and Peck, as well as Clark, append to the text of the so-called *Essay on Christianity* immediately after the "Universal Pan" sentence.[46] I think they are mistaken, and not just on grounds of textual integrity. The actual theological fragment which breaks off at "Universal Pan who" does *not* explore any further the issue of miracles. The fragment which editors have inserted after the first section does not investigate miracles but the historical moment of Christ's birth and the emergence of Christianity. The kind of analysis Shelley undertakes here reminds one of *A Defence of Poetry* and *A Philosophical View of Reform*. This extraneous fragment seems part of a historical treatment of "progress." Showing the dialectical interaction between the decline in politics, art, and private life, this fragment shares the dialectical assumptions of *A Philosophical View of Reform* and *A Defence of*

Poetry. Contrasting the republican virtues of disinterestedness with selfish sensualism, the fragment echoes the dichotomy between imagination and Mammon which is developed in *A Defence of Poetry*. The sophisticated sense of historical change which Shelley shows here points to 1819-1821, not 1816-1817. Specifically, the fragment asserts that "other effects indirectly favorable to the progress of mankind sprung from the same causes." He goes on to say: "Good and evil subsist in so intimate an union that few situations of human affairs can be affirmed to contain either of the principles in an unconnected state."[47] This dialectical sense of history is something Shelley acquires only after considerable thought and revision; it is not something prominent in his work of 1816-1817. Indeed, historical change at this period is more of a cause-effect process initiated by moral reform. There are anticipations of historical dialectics, but nothing consistently and coherently delineated in 1816-1817.

The reason Shelley broke off the investigation of miracles was that he realized it was something that had been done many times by other freethinkers, including himself in *A Refutation of Deism*. In the next part of the fragment he claims he cannot investigate miracles because of the repressive political atmosphere, but I do not think we have to take this seriously. Shelley, rather, had to believe that such a commonplace critique of miracles did not need to be done again. If I am correct in placing the "miracles" fragment near the composition of *A Refutation of Deism*, then Shelley would already have written two critiques of miracles. Why do it again? The important concept in the first part of the theological fragment of 1816-1817 is not miracles, but the ethical ideas of Christ "the reformer."

SECTION 2: "GOD" (f. 8ᵛ–f. 24)

Shelley here discusses many issues, but fundamentally he makes the following points. (1) The God of Christ is not a Jehovah, a punitive, law-ridden, anthropormorphic demon (Blake's Nobadaddy); it is instead both an ideal of ethical perfection and an ineffable, but benignant "presence" in the universe with which "the pure" can have communion. (2) The essence of true religion, as preached by Christ, is the practice of justice and virtue, guided by the "divine" ideals of ethical perfection. (3) The reformer who, like Christ, wants to overturn the false gods of nationalism, war, revenge, cruelty, and so on, cannot practice utter sincerity, but must accommodate his or her public declarations to the prejudices of the audience. Such, briefly, is the second section.

I want to begin with the last point because it helps to explain the other two. The meditation on rhetoric begins near the bottom of folio 20, immediately after Shelley has written "To Belong To Some Other Part / Introduction." He feels a need, at this point, to "introduce" his projected essay because he realizes how unorthodox his Christ actually is in comparison to the Christ of the churches or even to the Christ in the New Testament. In a canceled passage which was to have begun the "Introduction," Shelley wrote: "In the picture which [is] here attempted to be delineated of his system and his character the most liberal construction is carefully put on those circumstances which have been considered most equivocal."[48] To explain the discrepancy between the "real" Christ and the "actual" Christ, Shelley asserts that reformers can never practice utter sincerity. Considering how the fragment evolves, one can see the irony of Shelley drawing attention to his own sleight of hand: he is turning Christ into a Shelleyan radical precisely because he is so eager to reach an audience at a level where it can respond sympathetically. As becomes clear in the third and final section, "Equality of Mankind," Shelley had no intention of trying to create a new Christian sect. As he admits in the third section, Christ is neither an original nor the most profound thinker in the ethical tradition. The reason Shelley concentrates on Christ, rather than, say, Pythagoras, Socrates, Diogenes, or Rousseau, is fairly obvious: England is a Christian country. While Shelley himself is practicing a kind of rhetorical duplicity, he calls attention to it by showing how Christ also "misrepresented" his ideas.

The meditation on rhetoric, then, begins with the sentence, "It cannot be precisely ascertained [in] what degree Jesus Christ accomodated his doctrines to the opinions of his auditors, or in what degree he really said all that he is related to have said."[49] Shelley then develops the latter part of the sentence for a number of paragraphs before returning to the question of rhetoric. In these paragraphs he follows the hermeneutic path of Spinoza in trying to analyze the contradictions of Scripture. Finally, however, in folio 23, he returns to the issue:

Jesus Christ did what every other reformer who has produced any considerable effect upon the world has done. He accommodated his doctrines to the prepossessions of those whom he addressed. . . . He said—However new or strange my doctrines

97

may appear to you, they are, in fact only the restoration and re-establishment of those original institutions and ancient customs of your own law and religion.[50]

The problem for the reformer, then, is to communicate novel ideas in such a way that they are not rejected out of hand as totally absurd. One tactic is to pose as a restorer of pure traditions fallen into corruption. There was, in fact, an especially powerful strain of late eighteenth and early nineteenth-century radicalism that sought to restore the old Saxon liberties lost at the Norman invasion and never fully recovered thereafter. It has been rare for a popular radical movement to do without some form of revolutionary "remembrance" whereby the status quo is unacceptable because it has deviated so far from an ideal located in the past.[51] Shelley is doing the same thing; he is contrasting the true Christ with the corrupt Christian establishment in order to promote social changes that can appear as restorations rather than innovations.

As this meditation continues, its unacknowledged source seems to be Godwin, specifically his ideas on sincerity, Book IV, Chapter VII, *Political Justice*. Shelley says:

All reformers have been compelled to practise this misrepresentation of their own true feelings and opinions. It is deeply to be lamented that a word should ever issue from human lips which contains the minutest alloy of dissimulation . . . or any thing but the precise and rigid image which is present to the mind. . . . But this practise of entire sincerity towards other men would avail to no good end, if they were incapable of practising it towards their own minds.[52]

And then Shelley explains the inadequacy of utter sincerity. "In fact, truth cannot be communicated until it is perceived. The interests therefore of truth required that an orator should so far as possible produce in his hearers that state of mind in which alone his exhortations could fairly be contemplated and examined."[53] Some of Shelley's own experiences must have increased his distrust of utter sincerity. Most importantly, by 1816-1817, he had already felt the effects of government and social repression. There is a curious paragraph which seems to reflect Shelley's acute consciousness of the repression and his own possible danger. First, he declines to investigate the issue of miracles because their truth or falsehood would have no effect on the verity of Christ's ethical doctrines. But then he says he would discuss miracles, except that he is afraid of doing so. The "connection of the instance of Jesus Christ with the established religion of the country in which I write renders it dangerous to subject oneself to the imputation of introducing new gods or abolishing old ones. . . ." Shelley then says that even the "metaphysician and the moralist," however moderate, may still end up like Socrates—"the bowl of hemlock for the reward of his labours."[54] Here is an interesting confluence: Christ, Socrates, Shelley. And immediately after Shelley states his explicit fear of becoming a martyr like Christ comes his paragraph criticizing utter sincerity, which I have been analyzing.

The doctrine of utter sincerity, then, is inadequate for two reasons; it fails to address the problem of repression and it fails to take into account the subjective experience of responding to new ideas. Although Godwin speaks mostly in favor of sincerity, he does admit that "truth" cannot be "communicated absolutely pure,"[55] so that perhaps Shelley expanded Godwin's own concession to rhetoric. As he sought alternatives to sincerity, Shelley began, perhaps inadvertently, to develop his theory of imagination. Truth has to be perceived before it can be communicated. The audience is an audience of subjects, with their own perceptions, not empty vessels to be filled with radical philosophy. The "orator" should produce a state of mind perceptive to new ideas; *that* is the rhetorical task. Indeed, during this whole period, from *A Refutation of Deism* to the theological fragment, Shelley has pondered the rhetorical difficulties facing the libertarian writer. He keeps returning to this problem because he has yet to find a definitive solution.

The ultimate purpose of Shelleyan rhetoric, however, is iconoclastic and subversive. Once Shelley's Christ has insinuated himself into the prepossessions of his audience, he then "tramples upon all received opinions, on all the cherished luxuries and superstitions of mankind. He bids them cast aside the chains of custom and blind faith by which they have been encompassed from the very cradle of their being, and become the imitators and ministers of the Universal God."[56] Thus the section titled "God" ends, after which begins the final section, "Equality of Mankind." The direction in which Shelley is going is clear by now. The possibility of repression and the sensibility of the audience are factors the reformer contemplates in order to be effective. The *kind* of social change Shelley wants is an anarchism in which each individual is both imitator and minister of the highest ethical ideals of philosophy. Although he envisions the abolition of all churches and institutional coercion, Shelley is not abolishing authority, which he calls the "Universal God." Like Godwin, he believes in objective ideals which society can learn to acknowledge. Neither Shelley nor Godwin is the kind of anarchist who rejects all authority except subjective desire. There is only one God, and not a pantheon of subjectivist gods.

The metaphysical speculations on divinity that precede the meditation on rhetoric and sincerity become more comprehensible now. I want to examine the ontological and epistemological arguments in light of the ethical doctrines announced at the end of the fragment.

Although sometimes Shelley distinguishes between Christ's concept of God and his own, usually the two are the same. Shelley offers the following concepts of divinity. (1) "God is some universal being, differing both from man and from the mind of man."[57] (2) God is "the interfused and overruling Spirit of all the energy and wisdom included within the circle of existing things."[58] (3) God is "something mysteriously and illimitably pervading the frame of things."[59] (4) God is virtue, or the highest ethical ideals and practices, or "the overruling Spirit of the collective energy of the moral and material world."[60] (5) The God of Christ is "the Power from which or thro which the streams of all that is excellent and delightful flow: the Power which models as they pass all the elements of this mixed universe to the purest and most perfect shape which it belongs to their nature to assume."[61] (Shelley rejects the idea that God possesses a will, however.) (6) Heaven is "when pain and evil cease, and when the benignant principle unt[rammel]led and uncontrolled, visits in the fulness of its power the universal frame of things."[62] (7) God "is a model thro which the excellence of man is to be estimated, whilst the *abstract* perfection of the human character is the type of the *actual* perfection of the divine."[63] (8) God is "the principle of all good, the source of all happiness, the wise and benevolent creator and preserver of all living things."[64]

Shelley has a fairly consistent concept of God as something apocalyptically human, but also as something more than human—a benignant presence—that pervades, visits, shapes, and preserves. (I think one must assume Shelley did not really mean that God was a "creator" of living things in (8). We must assume that the poet's language ran away from him temporarily, because if God is creative, it has will, thus entailing the problem of anthropomorphism—something Shelley consistently argues against.) If God is both human

100

and cosmic, an ideal and a presence, transcendent and immanent, then there are no metaphysical obstacles to human perfectability. Indeed, not only are there no obstacles, but the ontological nature of the universe is such that perfectability is a historical possibility.

Shelley's metaphysical assumptions are not original, but his synthesis and ultimate use of these assumptions are distinctly Shelleyan. Spinoza, Wordsworth, Coleridge, Southey, Plato, and Rousseau are some of the probable sources of Shelley's concepts, but none of these authors followed his ideas to the exact conclusions that Shelley did. There are important hints of Shelleyan conclusions in these sources, however. In chapter five of *Tractatus Theologico-Politicus*, Spinoza distinguishes between the universal moral law which is Christ's ethical doctrines, and the laws of society. If people followed their reason, and obeyed the authority of moral law, then there would be no need for government. Government, however, is necessary to repress and restrain the egoistic sensualism of human nature. The millennial *possibility* of moral law replacing secular law is something Spinoza is aware of. Only Spinoza's low estimate of human nature turns him against the anarchist possibility.

Another interesting source is Rousseau, so highly praised in the fragment. From *Émile* Shelley could have gotten the Savoyard Vicar's emphasis on an intuitive experience of divinity; and from *La Nouvelle Héloïse*, which he read religiously at Geneva in the summer of 1816, he would have absorbed many ecstatic passages linking love of nature with human love, both of which were "divine" in some sense. An even more intriguing source is *Le Contrat Social*. Although there are scattered throughout Rousseau's political works numerous hints of anarchism, the suggestive passage in *Le Contrat Social* seems directly related to Shelley's own meditations in the theological fragment. In Livre IV, Chapitre VIII, Rousseau ponders the fate of a society of ethically pure Christians. They would not need a government, according to Rousseau, because their allegiance would be to God, not the State. Rousseau does not believe a society of pure Christians could exist, because of the Christian commitment to the world of spirit. But even if such otherworldly Christians could form a utopia, it would be fatally vulnerable to attack from a Catiline or a Cromwell, some authoritarian figure who would dominate the Christians. Pure Christians could not both resist a tyrant and remain loyal to their spiritual ideals.

I think Shelley might very well have contemplated this passage with serious attention. In *A Refutation of Deism*, Theosophus seems to have this passage in mind when he says, "a whole nation of Christians (could such an anomaly maintain itself a day) would become, like cattle, the property of the first occupier."[65] Shelley's reply to Rousseau would be something like this. Christ's ideas, truly purified, reveal a commitment to *this* life, not to the other world beyond this one. Therefore, Rousseau's major objection is removed. The very curious passage on Caesar and Brutus (f. 13ᵛ–f. 14)[66] is perhaps ultimately related to Shelley's trying to overcome Rousseau's arguments. Shelley defends Brutus's killing of Caesar on the grounds of justice, an essentially utilitarian sense of justice. Caesar's assassins would have sacrificed themselves if to do so would have promoted justice. In other words, they did not kill Caesar out of revenge, but out of concern for the good society. This is Shelley's unorthodox illustration of the ideas in Matthew 5:43-45.[67] When related to Rousseau's strictures against a Christian utopia, however, the Brutus passage makes even more sense. True followers of Christ's ethical ideas, Shelley is arguing, would remove a tyrant without violating their ideals; indeed, they would be acting on those ideals, not contradicting them.

Numerous critics have studied Shelley's working through the assumptions of Wordsworth, Coleridge, and Southey, and his revising of their ideas in a Shelleyan direction. One point I want to make is that however far Shelley "swerves—to use the Bloomian terminology—from his sources, his theology is not as idiosyncratic as it might appear at first glance. Elaine Pagels, writing recently on the Gnostics, argues that the Gnostic churches were suppressed because of the sociopolitical implications of their religious ideas.[68] If spiritual authority could be learned directly through contact with spirit, then there was no need for a church hierarchy. If the Gnostics relied primarily on their own experiences with divinity, then no church establishment could ever erect an institutional authority which the Gnostics would recognize as legitimate. The direct democracy, feminism, and freer sexuality of the Gnostics threatened the Catholic Church in a fundamental way. This strain of Christianity did not wholly die with the Gnostics, but was recurrently revived in various millennial forms before, during, and after the Reformation. Each revival, of course, caused great social and political disruption of authoritarian institutions.[69]

Shelley's analysis of the problem of evil is somewhat reminiscent of Gnostic doctrine. The egoist, the "narrow and malevolent spirit,"[70] shuts himself off from the benignant influences of divinity. Like

Blake's Urizen, he separates himself from the divine interconnectedness and unity. According to Christ and the facts at hand, Shelley argues, "some evil Spirit has dominion in this imperfect world. But," he assures us, "there will come a time when the human mind shall be visited exclusively by the influences of the benignant power."[71] Similarly, the Gnostics believed the world of created nature to be inferior to the world of the divine spirit; they too believed the mind could slough off the influences of the material world and experience instead a spiritual resurrection. I do not want to push the parallel between the Gnostics and Shelley as far as some have done,[72] because Shelley's ultimate point is that the evil Spirit is institutional Christianity and other authoritarian social institutions, all of which he wants abolished. Shelley is a social critic, not a mystic, so he wants the institutions abolished thoroughly, in society as well as in individual minds.

To summarize the important aspects of the second part: Shelley replaces the concept of an anthropomorphic deity, who punishes and rewards, with theological assumptions that offer no obstacles to human perfectibility. He also rejects complete sincerity as a means of working toward perfectibility, thus justifying his own rhetorical practices. Finally, he reaches the conclusion that Christ's ultimate intention was revolutionary, to overturn the old Law and institute a new society whose authority is derived from moral law. What kind of moral law? To answer this question, Shelley wrote the next section, "Equality of Mankind."

SECTION 3: "EQUALITY OF MANKIND" (f. 25–f. 33ᵛ)

This section is fairly easily summarized. Inequality is the root cause of injustice and social misery, but it cannot be abolished immediately by political coercion. Contrary to the community of goods advocated by Plato and practiced by the early Christians, Shelley recommends an exemplary social life undertaken by philosophical individuals who will promote the "universal benevolence" necessary to supplant inequality. He envisions a gradual, progressive, evolutionary increase in the practice of justice and virtue coinciding with the decrease in inequality and governmental coercion. When the social affections develop to an extraordinary degree, then ethical idealism will have replaced political legislation, leaving society as a utopia of egalitarian anarchy. Christ, then, turns out to be a philosophical anarchist. Theology has become political

103

and economic philosophy. Lady Shelley's title now appears as deceptive as it was intended to be because it is clear that Shelley's primary interest in this fragment is not Christianity, but social reformation.

Godwin was hardly the first to advocate "equality," and indeed his own egalitarian commitment was a mild one in comparison to that of others. Enlightenment thinkers discussed communist equality with a high degree of sophistication and earnestness,[73] while some radicals in France and Great Britain in the 1790s put forward communism as an immediate political option, not simply as a utopian ideal. Godwin and Shelley consistently opposed insurrectionary communism, and their philosophical anarchism can be understood as a way of preserving the communist ideal without submitting to what they perceived as the violent chaos of revolution.

The section begins with a quotation from Luke 4:18, which Shelley interprets with his own theological assumptions. The "spirit of the Lord" which is "upon" the prophet is that same benignant spirit of the previous section and is identical with the Intellectual Beauty of the 1816 "Hymn." Indeed, that poem seems the most appropriate gloss on this Biblical extract. In stanza 5 of the poem the spirit "falls" on Shelley, who then vows in stanza 6 to "dedicate" his powers to "thee and thine." The process of inspiration is one in which the prophet is "visited" by the spirit, which convinces him or her to "preach." In the previous section, Shelley had inquired into the method by which one should preach, and rejected utter sincerity. In this section, he asks about the actual content of the message, equality.

Christ, Plato, and Diogenes agree that the root cause of social misery is inequality: "They saw that the great majority of the human species were reduced to the situation of squalid ignorance, and moral imbecility, for the purpose of purveying for the luxury of a few, and contributing to the satisfaction of their thirst for power."[74] Shelley, however, distinguishes between two different egalitarian remedies. Plato's "law" would distribute power and property equally, but "Diogenes devised a nobler and more worthy system of opposition to the system of slave and tyrant."[75] Then Shelley launches a lengthy speech by Diogenes, who elucidates an alternative to Plato's communist republic. The speech (f. 25ᵛ–f. 27) is mostly Shelley's own ideas, with only a few of Diogenes' own words inserted. The poet's Diogenes is much more egalitarian and libertarian than the Cynic portrayed by Diogenes Laertius, his primary source for the thought of Diogenes of Sinope. The speech can be condensed into the words of Shelley's "Hymn to Intellectual Beauty": "Man were immortal, and omnipotent" if "Love, Hope, and Self-esteem" were not inconstant. If the self enjoys self-esteem, it will not need to worship a tyrant. If the self does not worship "Mammon"—the egoistic pursuit of wealth and power—it can instead pursue "God"— love, virtue, justice, knowledge. Rather than abolish inequality by institutional means, Diogenes proposes an exemplary life practiced by philosophical individuals. The goal is the moral reformation of the person, whose ethical practices must change before inequality is diminished. Instead of struggling with each other over objects of wealth and power, people in an egalitarian society will enjoy the infinite pleasures of wisdom and loving community.

Notable in this Godwinian rejection of Platonic communism is the fundamentally agrarian assumption that equality does not require industrial development. Marx believed that only complete industrial development through the domination of nature could create a productive capacity sufficient to meet everyone's needs without anyone having to be exploited. In Shelley's day there were certainly democratic proponents of industrial development—Bentham, for example. Both Godwin and Shelley reject an equality tied to industrial expansion, and attach it instead to moral improvement. To achieve equality, they recommend a level of consumption that would entail a low level of industrial productivity. To promote enlightenment they advocate less labor, more leisure. One can trace this kind of anti-industrial approach to equality to figures like Thoreau, Tolstoy, and Morris. Marxist philosophers of the Frankfurt School (Adorno, Horkheimer, Marcuse) have argued that the ultimate, if inadvertent, logic of dominating nature is hostile to the best interests of humanity. The present ecological crisis indicates the need to revise industrialism so that it no longer endangers the continuation of life on the planet. In short, the agrarian perspective of Godwin and Shelley, even if it coincides with the immediate economic self-interest of Shelley, the landowner's son, is a serious and important component of radical thought, one that is becoming more, not less, relevant.

One must also note, however, that such a perspective does indeed relieve Shelley of some discomfort over his personal wealth. In folio 32, Shelley alludes to Matthew, 19:16-30, where a young man of wealth comes to Christ asking how to be saved. Christ tells him: "If thou wilt be perfect, go *and* sell what thou hast, and give to the poor, and thou shalt have treasure in heaven." However generous Shelley was with his money—and he was indeed generous, and lived quite simply for a man of his high social position—he did not sell his property and give it to the poor. Furthermore, he criticizes the early Christian attempt at communism as futile because the community of goods did not coincide with a moral reformation. Instead, Shelley puts forward the Godwinian idea of stewardship: not a community of goods, but the ethically correct distribution of goods according to the philosophical perceptions of each "steward." This idea is also consistent with the ancient concept of social responsibility associated with the paternalistic landowners. Another echo of aristocratic paternalism can be heard in Shelley's use of the ideas of benevolence and moral sense. Although he goes beyond the hierarchical assumptions of the benevolist school of ethics, he still uses their vocabulary, which makes one recall landowners assisting the unfortunate and needy. One should note, however, that even if this is self-serving on Shelley's part, it is nonetheless socially significant, because benevolent paternalism was something that was declining precipitously, and had been in decline all during the eighteenth century. It is not often that we link Shelley's political thinking to the "Tory humanism" of Wordsworth or Coleridge, but the parallel is there to be drawn.

Another agrarian thinker is brought into the fragment as part of the egalitarian tradition: Rousseau. Shelley's hero of 1816 is not less, but greater than Christ; Rousseau's ideas are "more connected and systematic."[76] His strictures against civilization, however, cannot be interpreted as a type of primitivism. A moderate simplicity of living, a rejection of Mammon, and a pursuit of philosophy are all that Rousseau really meant. Shelley states the assumptions of the rational Enlightenment quite unequivocally. Uncivilized man is "pernicious and miserable"; thus Shelley rejects the myth of the egalitarian Golden Age.[77] Moreover, the "nature of man" has progressed from the earliest times because of the increase in knowledge. With greater knowledge there is more equality, more justice, and more virtue. Like Godwin, from whom he derived most of these ideas, Shelley links moral growth with the increase in knowledge, not simply with a re-education of the corrupted instincts. Although one cannot forget the numerous calls for purity and for a Wordsworthian "wise passiveness" toward nature, one cannot forget either that Shelley is still firmly within the assumptions of the rational Enlightenment.

106

CONCLUSION

The theological fragment is not only agrarian in perspective, but it also provides a rationale for Shelley's alignment with the moderate reform movement. If Diogenes' approach to social change is more reliable than the Platonic-institutional approach, then gradual, not revolutionary, change is preferable. Moreover, the proponents of moderate reform among the "respectable" classes were closer to Shelley's concept of the self-governing, independent citizen than the more desperate, often hungry, poorly educated laborers. The farmers, shopkeepers, tradesmen, professionals, and prosperous artisans were property owners, not proletarians. They had a stake in preserving society while reforming it. Shelley was afraid that a revolution would install a demagogic regime upheld by the class hatred of the poor; needless to say, he and other gentlemen of leisure would lose their privileges in such an upheaval. The better course was a steady, gradual, but persistent drive toward perfectibility.

Diogenes' approach assumes molecular, organic creation of the new society "within the shell of the old" by means of the individual's principled disengagement from unjust institutions and other exemplary conduct. The "practice" of equality will precede its institutionalization. This essentially Godwinian approach is qualified, of course, by the necessity of mediation and rhetoric. Whereas Shelley stresses emphatic mediation in the two Hermit of Marlow pamphlets, he presents an uncompromising vision of the Ideal in *Laon and Cythna*.

107

FOUR

The Hermit
of Marlow

(1817)

INTRODUCTION

SHELLEY never moved closer than the periphery of the reform movement of his day, but in 1817 he attempted to play an active role as pamphleteer and poet. If any of these writings had been popular, perhaps he would not have left England in 1818, never to return. The first "Hermit of Marlow" pamphlet displays an acute sense of everyday politics, even a nearly Machiavellian shrewdness one rarely associates with Shelley. Read in terms of English politics, *Laon and Cythna* is a much less ideal but more politically relevant poem than has been usually suggested. In the second Hermit of Marlow pamphlet, Shelley has a new appreciation of the laboring classes. Luddism came and went without workers making a significant impression on Shelley's consciousness, but the proletarian insurrections of 1817 inspired him.

The events of 1816-1817 could easily have had an opposite effect, of frightening Shelley away from radical politics. The year 1816 saw steadily increasing economic misery. Massive unemployment (especially for discharged sailors and handloom weavers), and high prices for bread and meat, partially caused by the curtailing of food imports by the recently passed Corn laws, all contributed to provoking riots and political agitation. The financial situation was so serious that on March 15, 1816, the government ministers told the Prince Regent of the necessity for retrenchment and economy. For the Prince Regent's beloved Pavilion in Brighton, on which he had already spent lavish sums, there would not be "one shilling" appropriated by Parliament, as the ministers sternly phrased it.[1] The

Annual Register for 1816 records high unemployment, a bad harvest, and reduced wages. To the displeasure of the ministers and the Regent, a proposed property tax was defeated by pressure from merchants, bankers, and traders.[2] The bourgeoisie, however, was not the only group the government had to worry about. Agricultural laborers rioted in Norfolk, Suffolk, Huntingdon, and Cambridge; miners and iron workers rebelled in Staffordshire and South Wales;[3] there were numerous food riots and even "an organized insurrection in the Isle of Ely." The poor were "in danger of starving."[4] Despite all the disorder, the *Annual Register* remarks on the low level of violence, considering the conditions.[5] The Spa Fields riot, of December 2, 1816, however, coupled with the attack on the Prince Regent's coach in early 1817, alarmed the Tory ministers, precipitating a wave of repression, including the suspension of Habeas Corpus from February to the end of the year. Although the repression was by no means an unmitigated success for the government (which lost numerous jury trials and considerable prestige because of its use of spies and *agents provocateurs*), it seriously disrupted the radical movement. By autumn, ninety-six radicals in England and thirty-seven in Scotland awaited trial for treason.[6] Not since the 1790s had the government felt it necessary to wage such a war against the radicals.

In the Secret Report to the House of Lords the government states: "a traitorous conspiracy has been formed in the metropolis for the purpose of overthrowing, by means of a general insurrection, the established government, laws, and constitution of this kingdom, and of effecting a general plunder and division of property." The Spa Fields riot in particular is cited as an example of the insurrectionary spirit. After a peaceful demonstration in favor of reform, the "poorer classes," those "distressed manufacturers, mariners, artisans and others," contemplated liberating the prisons, employed pikes, tried to win the soldiers over to their side, attacked some bakeries and butcher shops, robbed some gun stores, and utilized the symbolism of the French Revolution (tricolor flags and the cockade).[7] The object of the agitators is to "infect" the populace "with a spirit of discontent and disaffection, of insubordination, and contempt of all law, religion, and morality, and to hold out to them the plunder and division of all property ... and the restoration of their natural rights."[8] What is especially disturbing about the revolutionaries is that they operate by word of mouth rather than writing, so it is difficult to penetrate their schemes.[9] The Secret

Report to the House of Commons notes perceptively that few rich or middle-class people, and hardly any agricultural laborers take part in the radical agitation; the disaffected—estimated in the several hundred thousands—are distinctly urban laborers and poor, without ties to parish, church, or lord.[10] The panic of property is caused by the emergence of a working class made desperate by hunger and bold by political consciousness.

William Cobbett, even more than the Spenceans, is responsible for the political awareness of the poor. Starting on November 2, 1816, Cobbett began to publish a two-penny version of the *Political Register*, a tactic which greatly increased his readership. An extremely influential essay which, by the end of 1817, had been read by hundreds of thousands of English laborers, was "To the Journeymen and Labourers of England, Wales, Scotland, and Ireland."[11] Samuel Bamford claims that Cobbett turned the workers away from rioting by converting them to the cause of parliamentary reform.[12] Since his essay influenced even Shelley, it is worth examining closely. After many years, it is still an eloquent political essay. One theme reiterated throughout and providing a unifying motif is class pride, the human dignity of the laborers and soldiers. Workers are not rabble, a swinish multitude (as Burke called them), but the source of all social values. Workers who are thrown out of work have a right to assistance because "there can exist no riches and no resources, which they [the workers] by their labour, have not *assisted to create*."[13] Moreover, Cobbett says, workers "create all that is an object of taxation; for even the *land* itself would be good for nothing without your labour."[14] However much he wishes to foster class pride, Cobbett wants to discourage class conflict, especially between the laborers and those directly above them—farmers, tradesmen, and employers. Low wages, unemployment, and high prices are not the fault of the "middling classes," because they are at the mercy of economic forces not of their own making. The real culprit is Corruption—taxes, the debt, paper money, sinecures and royal patronage, war, and a standing army. Since Corruption is caused by an unreformed Parliament, the solution is parliamentary reform. In this essay Cobbett favors moderate reform—suffrage limited to direct taxpayers—solely for practical reasons. He is afraid the rich will manipulate elections that are open to propertyless laborers and servants. Such reform is falsely libeled as disorderly and novel when in fact it is within the constitutional tradition of

England. Building on the libertarian achievements of the past, Cobbett says: "We want *great alteration,* but *nothing new.*"[15]

Acutely aware of the anti-reform propaganda which equates reform with revolution, and revolution with Jacobin violence, Cobbett offers his own analysis of the French Revolution. The violence of the revolution was not the fault of the people, who had been oppressed for centuries, but was caused by the obstinacy of the ruling elite, which would not grant any reforms. If there had been reform, there would not have been revolution.[16] The oppressors— the ministers, nobles, and priests—are entirely to blame for the violence.[17] Cobbett quotes Arthur Young's firsthand observations on the French Revolution published in the 1790s to make the point that the suffering of the poor was the real tragedy in France, not the lamentable but understandable "vengeance on their oppressors.[18] The quotation is clever because Young was then head of the Board of Agriculture, a highly influential and impeccably respectable organization. Cobbett also makes a direct link between the present suffering of the English poor and the wars of the past. Rather than grant parliamentary reform in the 1770s, the government waged war against the American colonies, borrowing money, taxing the populace to pay for the interest on the debt. Similarly, rather than reform Parliament, government prosecuted a war against French liberty, increasing the debt and putting more money into the pockets of the fundholders.[19] The war debt necessitated paper money which, in turn, generated inflation as well as high taxes on all the consumer items the laborers have to use. No war, no debt, no corruption. Cobbett's radical analysis still rejects revolution, using it more as a threat than a real possibility. He urges the workers to refrain from rioting and to take part instead in petitioning and meeting to promote reform.

Many workers heeded Cobbett's advise, but not everyone. After the Spa Fields riot the government found activity it considered seditious in Leicester, Loughborough, Nottingham, Manfield, Derby, Chesterfield, Sheffield, Blackburne, Manchester, Birmingham, Norwich, and Glasgow.[20] These trouble-spots are manufacturing districts, many of which were radical centers in the 1790s, some of which were Luddite centers as well. In March, the Manchester Blanketeers were dispersed by the military, and in June there was the abortive Derbyshire rebellion, which E. P. Thompson calls the very first wholly proletarian insurrection.[21] According to Samuel Bamford, not all the proponents of a "rising" were spies, even though Bamford himself was a firm constitutionalist.[22] It seems reasonable to infer from the evidence that some poor people in 1817 felt they had little to lose and much to gain by an armed rising. According to Thompson, however, the net effect of 1817 was to dissuade workers from revolution as an unworkable tactic. The constitutional approach championed by Cobbett and Bamford becomes the dominant tendency (briefly interrupted by Peterloo) until 1830-1832.[23]

Eighteen-seventeen was an unusually tumultuous year, but Shelley accepted almost all the ideas articulated in Cobbett's influential essay. Shelley himself was in London, the center of activity, most of December 1816, and all of January and February 1817. During these months the Liverpool ministry planned and began implementing its repressive program; but at the same time, members of the reform movement discussed, at meetings and in the press, what approach to take. The central question for the movement was whether to champion radical reform (annual parliaments, universal manhood suffrage) or moderate reform (triennial parliaments and suffrage limited to those who paid direct taxes, freeholders, and householders). The meeting of the Hampden Clubs in January 1817 declared for radical reform, against the wishes of Sir Francis Burdett and after William Cobbett had been converted to radical reform by Samuel Bamford. Despite Burdett's enormous prestige, the meeting ignored his preferences because of the pressure from "below," namely, from the laborers and journeymen Cobbett was appealing to. If the movement went leftwards, to keep the laborers away from Luddism, the Spenceans, and insurrectionary plots, it would alienate the supporters of reform in Parliament, both moderate Whigs and Burdettites, as well as the country gentlemen outside of Parliament who supported moderate reform. If the movement went rightwards, rejecting universal manhood suffrage, it would endanger its mass support among the laborers, who might turn to revolution. It is precisely this dilemma Shelley has in mind when he composes his first Hermit of Marlow pamphlet.

A PROPOSAL FOR PUTTING REFORM TO THE VOTE THROUGHOUT THE KINGDOM, BY THE HERMIT OF MARLOW

On February 3, 1817, the Prince Regent made his report on the public disorders, thus leading to the secret reports delivered to each house of Parliament. Following some debate on the merits of the repressive legislation, each house voted overwhelmingly to suspend Habeas Corpus later the same month. Shelley's essay had been written by February 22, and was published sometime before March 2 (Shelley alludes to it in a letter to Charles Ollier on February 22, and Hunt's *Examiner* quotes from it on March 2). Shelley had written the pamphlet shortly before the repressive legislation had become law, although already such legislation was imminent. One purpose is to combat the repression by placing the government, not the reform movement, on the defensive by holding a referendum to determine whether the nation wants reform. If the vote favors reform, then the government must begin a reform or have itself declared in rebellion against "the People" which has announced its "general will." If, however, the nation favors no reform, then the movement must mournfully accept its defeat.

Rhetorically clever and politically shrewd, the essay operates on two levels simultaneously. One message is moderate: it must be ascertained whether or not the nation wants reform. Shelley personally favors limiting the franchise to direct taxpayers, although he favors annual parliaments. Another message, however, is beneath the surface, just as in Cobbett's address to the journeymen and laborers: if there is no reform, then there will be revolution. There is no question in the author's mind as to what the outcome of the referendum will be. His tone is sarcastic: "Perhaps the People choose to be enslaved."[24] Shelley's confidence in the popularity of reform was probably well founded because in London, the Midlands, Lancashire, Yorkshire, Glasgow, and Dublin reform was surely popular, and might have been as popular elsewhere, even in the agricultural south. If the People express their general will in favor of reform, then reform is a constitutional fact; if the referendum for reform succeeds, then—no matter what the present members of Parliament think about it—*there will be a reform.* Fusing Rousseau's concepts with those of the Commonwealthmen and the French Revolution, Shelley was setting up a potentially revolutionary situation by means of an ostensibly moderate proposal. Shelley knew that it was such moderate, seemingly innocuous proposals that could lead to revolutionary upheavals, and that had done so in America and France.

Shelley says:

> If the majority of the adult population should solemnly state their desire to be, that the representatives whom they might appoint should constitute the Commons House of Parliament,

there is an end to the dispute. Parliament would then be required, not petitioned, to prepare some effectual plan for carrying the general will into effect; and if Parliament should then refuse, the consequences of the contest that might ensue would rest on its presumption and temerity. Parliament would have rebelled against the People then.[25]

The constitutional theory informing these statements assumes the prior achievements of revolutions: the Puritan revolution, 1689, 1776, 1789. There is even an allusion to civil war if Parliament fails to carry out the general will—a Rousseauian concept utilized by the French revolutionaries. (The most highly praised figure in the theological fragment was, of course, Rousseau.) The referendum, then, entirely usurps the prerogative of the Liverpool ministry—or anyone else in government—to determine policy on the issue of reform. The only legitimate law is that which accurately represents the general will.

The essay is not only threatening and bold in its theory of representation, but its practical features lay the foundations for an eventual seizure of power if Parliament refuses to grant a reform. The first step is to gather notable reformers from all over the kingdom in London, at the Crown and Anchor Tavern. Just such a meeting had indeed occurred in late January, when the Hampden Club delegates declared in favor of radical reform. Shelley's meeting will be more representative of the country and resembles, it seems to me, the revolutionary concept of the Convention. The meeting will organize the details of the referendum, such as dividing the country into three hundred electoral districts, "each to contain an equal number of inhabitants."[26] This in itself is a radical tactic because the unreformed Parliament contained gross inequities in representation, with some sparsely populated boroughs sending several M.P.s, while the industrial towns sent none. Revolutionary France had divided the population into equal districts. The one man–one vote concept is fundamentally antithetical to Old Corruption, which is based on virtual representation, not actual. Moreover, the Court and the landed interest viewed themselves as legitimate boroughmongers who had an unquestioned right to dominate politics. After all, were they not the rulers of their country? One man–one vote would also greatly increase the influence of the densely populated cities and towns, whose proreform sentiments were tumultuously apparent in 1817. There would be three hundred commissioners to ascertain the vote in their respective districts and to report the results to the meeting. In a revolutionary situation, these commissioners could become government officials. Indeed, Shelley's proposals, however moderate, have also generated a shadow government capable of challenging the legitimacy of the Liverpool ministry. Was Shelley serious?

By examining closely the names of those to whom Shelley wanted copies of the essay sent, one has to conclude that he was very serious. In a letter to Charles Ollier, his publisher, Shelley gives directions on how copies of the essay are to be disposed of. He gives a list of people and organizations to which he wants copies dispatched "*from the Author*, as soon as possible."[27] He wants generous advertisements and outlets at the radical booksellers, such as "Sherwood Neely & Co." (which published *Laon and Cythna* later in 1817),[28] William Hone, and Stockdale. "Send 20 or 30 copies to Messrs. Hookham & Co. Bond St. without explanation. I have arranged with them." Also: "Send 20 copies to me addressed to Mr. Hunt, who will know what to do with them if I am out of Town."[29] To say the very least, Shelley was eager to promote his pamphlet and did not take its circulation lightly.

The list of persons and organizations who are to receive the pamphlet directly from the author is illuminating for a number of reasons.[30] It is apparent that Shelley is appealing to a broad spectrum of reform sentiment, ideologically, geographically, and socially. Fourteen of the forty-two names are M.P.s, roughly half of whom are moderates like Grey, while the other half are Burdettites or left Whigs like Cochrane and Madocks. Of the extraparliamentary reformers, some of the radicals are represented (Cobbett and Cartwright), but some are not (Henry Hunt and Jonathan Wooler). Hunt's omission is surely deliberate, expressing Shelley's contempt for a man whom he and Leigh Hunt viewed as a violent demagogue, but Wooler's case is perhaps different; since the first issue of the *Black Dwarf* was published only on February 5, 1817, Shelley might not have been aware of Wooler's importance. The Burdettite papers, as well as the Whig paper, are to receive copies, as are the London Hampden Club (dominated by Burdett) and the Birmingham Hampden Club. From moderate Whigs who were lukewarm about even modest changes in electoral procedures, to radical republicans, Shelley's list is an incongruous one out of which he wanted to see a coalition emerge. Perhaps he hoped that fear of revolution, on the part of Whigs, coupled with a desire by the radicals to secure *some* change, would be motivation enough to stimulate a working coalition.

An interesting feature of the list is its geographical dimension, indicating that Shelley thought about the three hundred commissioners and electoral districts. From the southwest, there is William Peter (not "Peters," as it appears in the list) from Cornwall, a country gentleman and poet who authored a reform pamphlet in 1815 and was close to Samuel Romilly. From the east are the Taylors, father and son, from Norwich; this bourgeois Unitarian family had played a role in reform politics previously, in the 1790s. Ireland is represented by three men, George Ensor, John P. Curran, and William Bruce. Ensor (1769-1843) was a well-known Anglo-Irish radical author. Bruce (1757-1841) was a prominent Irish Presbyterian from Belfast who was a leader of Irish Unitarianism. Curran, a famous Irish lawyer, and Godwin's friend, had become much more moderate after the 1798 rebellion, and in 1817 was attending the "Meeting of Independent Gentlemen" for union and cooperation between the great landed interests and other classes to reduce military expenditures and promote constitutional reform of Commons.[31] The Scotch representatives were Robert Owen of Lanark and Andrew Duncan, a prominent academic. That the London-Westminster area is better represented than any other is appropriate since it was the center of radical agitation. Prominent reformers from there are: Robert Waithman, Francis Burdett's brother Jones, the Lord Mayor, Alderman Goodbehere, and Francis Place. Ten copies were sent the London Hampden Club, while a copy each went to the editors of three London papers—the *Statesman* (Burdettite), the *Morning Chronicle* (Whig), and the *Independent Whig* (Burdettite). Shelley did not ignore the provinces, however much he concentrated on London. From the north there is James Montgomery (1771-1854) of Sheffield, a famous poet and radical editor of the *Iris*. Manchester seems to be represented by "Mr. Walker (of Westminster)" because although this clearly alludes to Thomas Walker, Jr. (1784-1836), the Walker family was prominent in reform circles in Manchester. Five copies go to the Birmingham Hampden Club, an important radical center. In the west, in addition to Cornwall, are Berkshire (whose Mr. Hallet gets five copies, indicating the existence of a Hampden Club), and tiny Monmouthshire, on the Welsh border.

Although there is a fairly balanced representation of areas, there are some gaps. There is no one from Wales, except Madocks, the

M.P. Shelley knew so well in 1812-1814. There are no Irish Catholics, perhaps indicating Shelley's complete disillusionment with the Catholics he had worked with briefly in 1812. The only connection to Lancashire, a center of radical activity, is circuitous, through the Walker family (whose bourgeois and moderate credentials would be an obstacle to their having much contact with the working-class reformers like Samuel Bamford). Yorkshire is also not represented. One problem with Shelley's proposal is his lack of experience within the reform movement, because he knows hardly any radical or plebian reformers. Almost all his contacts are "respectable" and moderate. Even Burdett, who was considered too radical for the orthodox Whigs, was distancing himself quickly from plebian radicalism. Nevertheless, the Whigs were by no means completely cowed before the Tories. Their strength and resolve, such as they were, were fairly constant from May 21, 1810, onwards, when Thomas Brand's reform plan, which did not aspire to universal suffrage, but was substantial nevertheless (abolition of rotten and pocket boroughs; triennial parliaments; copyholder and householder suffrage), received 115 votes in favor, and 234 against.[32] Seven years later, on February 29, 1817, 105 Commons members voted against suspending Habeas Corpus.[33] Any coalition would have to be dominated by the parliamentary moderates who, however fearful of riot and disorder, were unwilling to endorse the encroachments on "English liberty" by the Tory repression.

Shelley's decision to appeal to the Whigs and moderates was a politically wise one. There was only one way a radical reform could be won in 1817: revolution. Because Shelley knew there was no support for manhood suffrage even among the Burdettites, he tried to bring the moderates and radicals together to effect at least some reform. Extrapolating from the essay, one can imagine a scenario like this. With moderate Whigs, Burdettites, and reforming country gentlemen and other "respectable" moderates in leadership, the referendum plan would go forward with the active cooperation of the radicals and plebian reformers. The Tory accusation of "revolution" would not be as persuasive with such an upper-class leadership. After the referendum results became public, then the ministers would be forced into an unhappy set of choices. They could abandon their principles and lead a reform of Commons, or they could resign, allowing the Whigs to take over—or, they could refuse to grant any concessions, and precipitate a confrontation, perhaps a civil war. Shelley's first choice was not revolution, so he must have imagined that the Tories would back down. Then, after the Whigs and Burdettites had enacted moderate reform, the field would be clear for more radical changes: annual parliaments, universal manhood suffrage, perhaps even a republic. Shelley believes in social evolution in gradual stages, each of which represents a certain development in public opinion. In the last paragraph of the essay, he agrees that universal suffrage is theoretically correct, but so is "a pure republic." The practical question is: what kind of progressive change can take place, given the present "state of public knowledge and feeling"?

Shelley's proposal is the most radical one with even a remote chance of success. The revolutionary hints are designed, like Cobbett's, more to frighten the Tories, than to provoke an actual revolution. If Shelley had made his proposal sooner—for example, at the Crown and Anchor meeting in late January held by the Hampden Clubs—then perhaps he might have had some success. The *Examiner* of March 2, 1817 reports a meeting of moderates at the Freemason Tavern which seems to have occurred just about the same time as Shelley's pamphlet was published. At the meeting are many of those on Shelley's list: Brand, Burdett, Kinnaird, Curran, Waithman, Goodbehere, Peter, and Phillips. If they had been able to discuss Shelley's proposal, then perhaps it might have gone somewhere. But by late February the machinery of repression was already in place and starting to bear down on the reform movement.

Shelley seems to have accepted the implications of an important idea in the theological fragment, namely, the necessity to tailor radical idealism to suit the conditions of society. The pamphlet is distant from the "Diogenes" approach to social change, but neither does it represent Platonic authoritarianism. Rather, it is an attempt to transform institutions to represent more accurately not Shelley's own perceptions of what is politically ideal, but the *public*'s. The referendum procedure is libertarian and thoroughly democratic, designed to force Parliament to reform and thereby avoid revolution. Lurking behind the proposal, however, is a clear threat of force. The difference between Shelley and other "respectable" reformers, like Brand, Holland, and Burdett, was that Shelley was willing to attach moderate demands to a popular movement of laborers and journeymen, but they were not. In the 1790s the Foxite Whigs could have made more extraparliamentary connections. For the Whigs, and even the Burdettites after the turmoil of 1816-1817, parliamentary reform was not a life-or-death issue. It was not until 1830-1832 that the Whigs actively pushed reform.

The level of social misery at this time cannot be exaggerated. Even the Prince Regent and other wealthy people found it necessary to dispense large sums for relief of the poor, thousands of whom were starving, according to a report in the *Examiner* of December 1, 1816. The first Spa Fields riot of November 16, 1816 had its violent moments, but it seems from the *Examiner* article of November 17, 1816 more like a traditional English food riot. The poor broke into bakeries and butcher shops, but spared the shop of one baker whose prices were low, thus displaying the "moral economy" of the English crowd. In the second, much more serious riot of December 2, the popular violence was precipitated, according to the *Examiner* of December 8, by the execution of four men at the North Bailey. Popular resistance to government policy had been expressed at executions in the eighteenth century, notably the Tyburn riots,[34] and in 1816 one can see why a hungry populace would resent executions. In a November 17, 1816 issue of the *Examiner*, it is reported that twenty-nine persons were sentenced to death at the last sessions at Old Bailey. Not a single one was sentenced for murder; every one was guilty of crimes against property, except "J. Winters," who had been convicted of "sacrilege." Over forty others were sentenced to transportation, some for life. It is certainly not surprising that on December 2 a politicized crowd should have turned to rioting after witnessing the hanging of four fellow sufferers. The poor had shown here and elsewhere that they could take direct action to express their displeasure at public policy and to relieve their distress; moreover, once they decided to act, they were far too numerous to be suppressed by the police or the army. If the poor were ever politicized in a revolutionary direction, then Tories, Whigs, and Burdettites had reason to tremble, because they could not have suppressed them; the repressive apparatus was too crude at the time. The social distress of this time created an explosive atmosphere within which Tories felt justified in suspending Habeas Corpus, Whigs feared stirring up the lower classes, and Shelley sought to bring the crisis to a resolution by institutionalizing popular support for moderate reform.

LAON AND CYTHNA

Laon and Cythna is a poem of 1817, another but different attempt to articulate a relevant politics. In the Hermit of Marlow pamphlet, Shelley suggests a tactic whereby reform consciousness could be effectively embodied in political institutions. In the poem, he addresses the leisure-class reformers and liberals, but does so in order to inspire them with revolutionary principles and ideals.

One possible influence on the genesis of the poem is the review of a *Coriolanus* production which appeared in the *Examiner*, December 15, 1816. Already well acquainted with Hunt by then, it is likely that Shelley read the review, written by William Hazlitt. Hazlitt makes the provocative point that although democracy is ethically correct, aristocracy and absolutist power are most susceptible to aesthetic representation. Echoing the Platonic argument against art, Hazlitt sees an inevitable antagonism between beauty and truth, because the essence of beauty is an intensity which is vivid and appealing to the senses, not necessarily consistent with the moral sensibility. The lesson of *Coriolanus* is that however morally odious he is, Coriolanus still receives the audience's sympathy, and the masses are despised. The natural tendency of poetry is to foster authoritarianism, a love for tyrannical power, and a contempt for the people. Written shortly after the Spa Fields riot of December 2, the review states unequivocally that poetry's logic leads far away from anything democratic or egalitarian. I want to suggest that Shelley read the review carefully, perhaps even discussed it with Hunt and Hazlitt, and then refuted its ideas by reversing the argument to equate the ideals of poetry with those of democracy. *Laon and Cythna* is a practical attempt to counter Hazlitt.

According to Hazlitt, one problem with a poetry that tries to be democratic is that it has to be rhetorical, didactic, and argumentative, so that "it presents no immediate or distant images to the mind." This could have influenced the antididactic statements in the Preface to *Laon and Cythna*, which declares the importance of feeling and sensation, sympathy and imagination, thus circumventing Hazlitt's objections. Hazlitt also says: "The language of poetry naturally falls in with the language of power."[35] Shelley's concept of the sympathetic imagination and his belief in the moral sense run counter to this idea. In the poem, Shelley tries to manipulate feelings so that readers sympathize with the revolutionaries, not the tyrants, and in this he is quite successful. Hazlitt separates the imagination and understanding, giving the imagination the following attributes: exaggeration, distortion, exclusion, intensity; it seeks the "greatest quantity of present excitement by inequality and disproportion."[36] As Socrates said in his dialogue against art, those who listen to and recite Homer's words on chariot driving are carried away by the beauty of the words, and never stop to wonder whether these words are good advice. Hazlitt's "understanding" is the "dividing and measuring faculty" which judges according to the relations between things, not the things themselves. It is also the "distributive faculty" which seeks "the greatest quantity of ultimate good, by justice and proportion." The imagination is aristocratic and Burkean; the understanding, democratic and Painite. Art and ethics, poetry and science, beauty and truth, exist only as unbridgeable dichotomies. The political implication for a democrat is that poetry can do nothing but harm to the egalitarian cause. Anticipating Peacock's *Four Ages of Poetry*, Hazlitt implies that poetry is inherently and unavoidably antidemocratic.

The emotional effect of poetry is carefully analyzed by Hazlitt. Poetry is "anti-levelling" because we sympathize with the domineering hero; "our vanity, or some other feeling, makes us disposed to place ourselves in the situation of the strongest party." Relying on Benthamite principles of self-interest, Hazlitt says: "We had rather be the oppressor than the oppressed. The love of power in ourselves, and the admiration of it in others, are both natural to man: the one makes him a tyrant, the other a slave." Moreover, there is an inevitable conflict between public and private feelings, with the latter always stronger than the former (Hume also made this point). History is a record of one tyranny after another, and is actually "Poetical Justice," because poetry sympathizes with the tyrant and loathes the oppressed.[37] Hazlitt's view of poetry is coherent and logical, at least assuming the premises it develops. That an intelligent liberal wrote it, and not a Tory, certainly would increase its significance in Shelley's eyes. Additionally, the *Examiner* was starting to attack the apostate poets who had influenced Shelley to an extraordinary degree: Southey, Coleridge, and Wordsworth. Hazlitt's attacks on Coleridge, motivated perhaps by concerns more personal than political, might have disturbed Shelley, since in 1816 he felt Coleridge was the best poet in England. Moreover, Byron had helped Coleridge to get *Christabel* published, a poem we know Shelley considered first-rate. From Mary Shelley's journal we also know that Shelley read Coleridge's political essay, *A Statesman's Manual*, shortly after it was published. Perhaps the essay stimulated Shelley to write on the relationship between Christianity and politics, as he did in the theological fragment. The *Coriolanus* review itself could have inspired the theological fragment, because one of the latter's major themes is metaphysical: divinity exists in people and nature, so that egoism is undermined structurally by the divinity

linking every individual to every other and to the natural world. If
one accepts the assumptions of Shelley's theological fragment, then
Hazlitt's argument must be rejected because it can account only for
self-love.

As early as *Alastor* Shelley was contemplating the sympathetic
functions of the imagination. Indeed, the tragedy of *Alastor* is that
the Visionary becomes a victim of the very dialectic Hazlitt de-
scribes: preferring intensity and vivid sensation to everything else,
the *Alastor* Visionary cannot adjust to the natural world and con-
demns himself to a premature death. He is, despite himself, an
aristocrat, spurning egalitarian relationships. In the Preface of *Laon
and Cythna*, as well as in the poem itself, Shelley argues for the
democratic tendencies of poetry.

The Preface begins by announcing its experimental intentions. In
some ways, Shelley's Preface is like Wordsworth's Preface to *Lyrical
Ballads*. Shelley's poem, like Wordsworth's ballads, is "an experi-
ment on the temper of the public mind." Like the *Lyrical Ballads,
Laon and Cythna* is "in contempt of all artificial opinions or in-
stitutions" and appeals instead to the "common sympathies of every
human breast." He draws a Rousseauian contrast between rule-
ridden artiface and the natural "moral sense."[38] Analogous to
Wordsworth's spontaneous overflow of powerful feelings is Shel-
ley's definition of what a poet should do: "communicate to others
the pleasure and the enthusiasm arising out of those images and
feelings, in the vivid presence of which within his own mind, consists
at once his inspiration and his reward."[39] As Wordsworth made
his appeal over the critics' heads directly to the readers, so Shelley
claims his poem was "fearlessly" written, without concern for the
critics. The "Public," he hopes, will use its own judgment and refuse
to fetter its imagination.[40] The emphasis on feeling, pleasure, social
community, and ethics is all Wordsworthian. Shelley's view of the
"essential attribute of Poetry" is hardly different from Words-
worth's: "the power of awakening in others sensations like those
which animate my own bosom."[41] The Wordsworthian dimension
refutes Hazlitt's ideas by stressing the sympathetic essence of the
feelings which poetry generates. Shelley finds a common human
nature, not Hazlitt's grim world of oppressor and oppressed. The
concept of self operating in Hazlitt's review is Lockian and Hobbes-
ian, and assumes a chaos of isolated egos struggling for scarce
resources. Atomistic individualism depicts society as an inevitable
struggle among competing egos who require the benevolent media-

tion of a powerful state or a liberal conscience (as Hazlitt recommends). For Wordsworth and Shelley, the self is organic and social, not atomistic but connected with nature, God, and humanity.

In some areas, however, the Preface and poem are distinctly un-Wordsworthian. Shelley does not, like Wordsworth, consider diction to be a major problem. He clothes his thoughts in "the most obvious and appropriate language." Such language as we find in the poem might be obvious and appropriate for Shelley, but would not suit readers outside the leisure class. Similarly, Shelley's use of Spenserian stanzas, allegory, gothicisms, and a narrative reminiscent of the sensationalist Alexandrian novel would hardly earn Wordsworth's approval. Shelley uses popular conventions, which Wordsworth abhors, to "clothe" and make more palatable his radical ideas.[42]

Another difference between the two poets is political. Wordsworth argues for an organic network of preindustrial people bound together by face-to-face contact and sympathy. Shelley, however, is an avant-garde poet who wants "to startle the reader from the trance of ordinary life" and "to break through the crust of those outworn opinions on which established institutions depend."[43] This is why, he explains, Laon and Cythna are brother and sister. Although Shelley appeals to a common human nature, organic connectedness, and even the moral sense, his ideological purpose is disruptive, not preservative. The tendency is almost Blanquist (although heavily leavened with nonviolence), because the poem itself and the poem's heroes assault the reader's preconceived notions. The poem is an avant-garde intervention, designed to shock the reader into accepting a new point of view.

Shelley wanted *Laon and Cythna* viewed as a political action. One should not despair at the French Revolution's failure; if one views events from the perspective of historical evolution, then one is encouraged by the advance of progress. Temporary defeats are simply a part of the process. Philosophical intellectuals, educated by poetry, love, and nature, should develop and express the full extent of their idealism because it will inspire the People (I am using "People" as Shelley does in the Hermit of Marlow pamphlet). When the People take part in revolution, the philosopher-poets should intervene to promote forgiveness and diminish violence. They have the responsibility of articulating a revolutionary culture capable of replacing the authoritarian culture of Christianity, aristocracy, and absolutism. One obstacle to social liberation is religious authoritarianism, which promotes self-hatred, resignation in the face of oppression, and an ascetic morality that worships pain. Especially critical of a Malthusian Christianity that tells laborers to limit their sensual desire, the poem celebrates the sexual love between Laon and Cythna. In the Preface Shelley says of love that it is "the sole law which should govern the moral world."[44] But even if the law of love cannot be actualized immediately or completely in the historical realm, the philosophers should still hold fast to it because it is the only reliable foundation for an ethically sound social order. The political ideal is still Godwinian anarchy, nonviolence, the "bloodless dethronement" of the oppressors, "universal toleration and benevolence of true philanthropy."[45] Intellectuals can work toward the ideal of perfectibility by being "liberal-minded, forebearing, and independent." The perfection philosophers seek is "the consequence of the habits of a state of society to be produced by resolute perseverance and indefatigable hope, and long-suffering and long believing courage, and the systematic efforts of generations of men of intellect and virtue."[46] In other words, even though Laon and Cythna are defeated, their example lives on after them, inspiring others and keeping alive the possibility of social liberation. Perhaps the next time the defeat will not be as complete, and someday there could even be victory. From *Laon and Cythna* to *Prometheus Unbound* and afterwards, Shelley is ambiguous on the question of time. Laon and Cythna act in the social world with the hope of succeeding, as does Prometheus. The implication seems to be this: the millennium could happen if there is a rapid transformation of social consciousness (more rapid than Shelley thought possible in his prose), but even if it does not occur, the philosopher-poet has to act in a millennial way.

There should be no confusion, however, between the Hermit of Marlow essay and *Laon and Cythna*. The former tries to embody the actual state of social consciousness in institutions, while the latter tries to *alter* that consciousness.[47] As a libertarian activist, Shelley does not want to alter institutions beyond the actual level of public opinion. But as a philosophical anarchist, he is not satisfied with moderate reforms and desires a radically new society, which *Laon and Cythna* is trying to promote.

Shelley was not writing *Laon and Cythna* for the followers of Cobbett or Wooler, but for the readers of the *Edinburgh Review*, the *Examiner*, the *Morning Chronicle*, and the *Independent Whig*. If the leisure-class liberals would undergo a cultural revolution, adopting Shelleyan principles and carrying them into practice, then they could lead a new movement that would go beyond merely parliamentary reform. However remote the poem appears from the realities of 1817 politics, it actually is an attempt to arouse the leisure-class liberals to lead a radical social transformation.

The poem recapitulates its theme in five separate ways. In the Dedication to Mary, Shelley depicts himself as a prototypical Laon, Mary as a Cythna, with allusions even to William Godwin and Mary Wollstonecraft. With recognizable echoes from "Hymn to Intellectual Beauty," the Dedication tells of a profound conversion experience during which Shelley had realized his true vocation and vowed to be "wise, / And just, and free, and mild" if "in me lies / Such power." Promising to oppose the selfish and tyrannical, Shelley devotes himself to acquiring knowlege useful for the struggle. The libertarian mission, however, is undermined when loneliness and disappointment in love lead to despair. Fortunately Mary came to rescue him as she defied "Custom" and strengthened him in his fight for justice. Their resolve is steeled by the prior examples of Mary's parents, ultraradicals in the 1790s. But even if Shelley is not successful in his libertarian project, at least he and Mary will be wholly themselves, undivided, and like "stars" that burn forever, inspiring other rebels.

The pattern, then, is this: conversion, disappointment in love, a loving relationship, libertarian struggle, defeat in the social world, ultimate victory as idealists. The pattern is repeated four other times: in Canto First, the allegorical section; Laon's story; Cythna's story; and in the concluding section of the poem, where the libertarian martyrs journey to the Temple of the spirits, thus inspiring the reader to practice high philosophical ideals.

Canto First opens with the narrator despairing over the failure of the French Revolution, so he is beginning where the poem actually ends, with the inadequacy of revolution. The poet wants to show that such failures are neither definitive nor complete, a source of inspiration rather than despair. The entire poem is designed to effect the narrator's conversion to hopeful libertarianism. Since he is alone and despairing, one presumes he is lonely and disappointed in love. When the strange woman arrives, she provides his erotic complement.[48] The social struggle is depicted by the battle between the serpent and the eagle. Although the serpent loses, the libertarians' ultimate victory is signified by all of them—serpent, woman, and narrator—journeying to the Temple of the Spirit, where the narrator will listen to the story of Laon and Cythna.

Laon's story begins with the conversion experience, by which he learns to love humanity and nature thanks to his Wordsworthian upbringing. His loving relationship with Cythna strengthens his commitment to change society. The disappointment in love occurs in Canto Third, where Cythna is taken away by soldiers, three of whom Laon kills before he is subdued. Suffering from madness and despair, he comes close to dying during his imprisonment until he is rescued by the Hermit, whose loving care brings Laon back to the social world. There is another conversion, this time to the principles of nonviolence and hope. Despair leads only to madness and death, whereas hope is a creative force, capable of sustaining life. The Hermit says in Canto Fourth, "men aspire to more / Than they have ever gained or ever lost of yore" (st. xii). Hopeful idealism is a revolutionary force, generating new social tendencies. The appropriate way to promote libertarian idealism is not with swashbuckling militarism, but by consistent pacifism: eloquence, unimpeachable virtue, hope, boldness, "soul-force" (as Gandhi called it). Laon then leads the rebels in revolution, intervening to prevent bloodshed and revenge. He is finally reunited with Cythna at the celebration of the revolution's victory, during which the new culture is ritually and festively represented. The success of the revolution is short-lived because soon afterwards the counterrevolution proceeds unabated. Laon is left with a small band of libertarians who fight valiantly but fruitlessly with pikes, "the instrument / Of those who war but on their native grounds / For natural rights" (Canto Sixth, st. xiii). Cythna, melodramatically rescuing Laon "in the nick of time," transports him to a secluded area outside the city; in this bower of bliss they make love. And so the defeat of the social revolution coincides with Laon's reunion with Cythna, prefiguring their "ultimate" victory after death.

Cythna, starting in Canto Sixth, tells her own story, which parallels Laon's. Forced to become Othman's concubine, she goes mad and is imprisoned on an island, where she is sustained by her pregnancy and the birth of the baby. But she is not fully converted to nonviolence until her cave becomes the "happy prison" of the creative imagination (VII, st. xxx-xxxvii). Liberated by an earthquake, then rescued by sailors, she practices her nonviolent ideals first with the sailors and then with the women of the society she rejoins. The revolution succeeds, then fails, and finally she is back in the narrative present, with Laon.

Although they contemplate separating—she to America, he to die—they cannot, and they die together, along with Cythna's child. Together they journey, as happened in Canto First, toward the Temple of the Spirit.

The way the poem is structured, defeat is never complete and is always mitigated by some sort of victory. The narrator, despairing the French Revolution, is encouraged by the woman's speech in Canto First. Although the serpent of Liberty is defeated in the allegory, it is not destroyed, and journeys to the Temple. Although Laon is in fact dead, he still is able to speak in his own voice in the Temple. Just as the revolution's defeat threatens the reader with despair, this despair is counteracted by both the lovemaking of Canto Sixth and Cythna's victorious story of conversion, liberation, and revolutionary success. The recapitulations and circular movements reinforce the theme of libertarian hope. This is an early version of *Adonais*: ethically correct behavior is justified not by immediate, worldly success, but by its ethical purity and ultimate significance. Another theme that this structure generates is the idea of historical flux. Stasis is an illusion, change permanent, and flux a primary feature of reality. Prefiguring "Ode to the West Wind," Canto Ninth draws the analogy between winter and counterrevolutionary terror. As winter puts to sleep seeds that will burst into life in spring, so terror puts to rest revolutionary possibilities which will also germinate in the future (st. XXI-XXIV). The poem and Preface have a progressive ideology, so that the dialectic of flux operates not as a meaningless eternal recurrence, but more as a Hegelian spiral.

The theme of hope within defeat reflects the political situation of 1817. Despite the triumph of reactionary governments throughout Europe after Napolean's fall, revolutions in Latin America were hopeful signs for the readers of the *Examiner*, which wrote enthusiastically of revolutions in Brazil and Chile.[49] Despite the repression, the government was losing jury trials when it tried to convict radicals. Disclosures of Sidmouth's system of spies and *agents provocateurs* outraged so many that even the Spenceans were acquitted in June. William Hone was acquitted three times, and Jonathan Wooler, acquitted on one charge, had the other charge dropped eventually. The repression by no means destroyed the reform movement, even though it did drive Cobbett to America.

This is only one way in which the poem discloses its historically specific character. Once it is accepted as a document of its times, then its historical nature becomes obvious. The principal obstacle to comprehending the poem historically is to see it only in relation to the French Revolution, which is actually a symbol for the English situation of 1816-1817. In the second Spa Fields riot, for example, the tricolored flag and cockade appeared, both French Revolution icons. One flag, reported in the *Examiner*, is especially interesting for its political symbolism. It read: "Nature—Feed the Hungry. Truth—Protect the Distressed. Justice—Punish Crime."[50] In Canto Fifth of *Laon and Cythna*, there is a trishaped sculpture symbolizing the revolution. Moreover, the celebration and ritual in that Canto are obviously patterned after the French revolutionary *fêtes*.[51] The *Annual Register* also reports that the Spa Fields rioters used the symbols of the French Revolution, even to the point of calling for a Committee of Public Safety.[52] This does not prove that the rioters, or Shelley, were simply imitating the French; rather, they were using the French Revolution as a symbol in their own, very different political situation.

Marx's words from *The Eighteenth Brumaire of Louis Bonaparte* are appropriate in this context:

> The tradition of all the dead generations weighs like a nightmare on the brain of the living. And just when they seem engaged in revolutionizing themselves and things, in creating something that has never yet existed . . . they anxiously conjure up the spirits of the past to their service and borrow from them names, battle cries and costumes in order to present the new scene of world history in this time-honoured disguise and this borrowed language.[53]

The French Revolution parallels and allusions are ways of trying to comprehend the present and shape the future. In 1816 Shelley urged Byron to write a grand epic on the French Revolution, but the motive was not historiographical, it was political: to make the Revolution relevant and alive for the present, as a means of guiding action and thought for the future. Similarly Cobbett, in "To the Journeymen and Labourers," offers an analysis of the French Revolution to bolster his own arguments concerning parliamentary reform.

The frame of reference for *Laon and Cythna* is primarily the insurrections and riots of 1816-1817. Although Shelley could dismiss some of them as merely food riots, famine-inspired,[54] he could not forget them, as the poem makes clear. The two Spa Fields riots, the march of the Blanketeers, the alleged plot in Manchester, and the June rebellions in Yorkshire, Nottinghamshire, and Derbyshire provide a context for the poet's imagination. All of them failed and were fairly easily crushed by the government, but they kept alive the possibility of revolution, especially if famine conditions had continued unabated (which they did not: 1818 was a much better year economically), and especially if no reforms were forthcoming. Cobbett, Wooler, and Shelley agreed on one thing at least: they all felt that if the Commons were not reformed soon, there would be violent revolution. The French Revolution is a point of reference because revolution seems imminent in England. In addition to the famine conditions depicted in *Laon and Cythna* (after the counterrevolution, in Canto Sixth) and actually found in the England of 1816-1817, there are other important parallels. In Shelley's poem, Laon argues against exacting revenge on the tyrant's soldiers because "We all are brethren—even the slaves who kill / For hire, are men" (Canto Fifth, st. XI). Cythna, in Canto Eighth, agitates among the sailors who have rescued her, winning them over to the libertarian side. Interestingly enough, one of the proposals Castlereagh wanted implemented in addition to suspension of Habeas Corpus was punishment of attempts by reformers to win over soldiers and sailors. Castlereagh attacked the "higher" ranks of people for creating a "revolutionary spirit" which was finding its way to the "lower orders."[55] The idea of forgiving the soldiers and befriending them was not original with Shelley; it was attempted in the Spa Fields riot. According to the *Examiner*, one flag read: "Be not afraid of the Soldiers, for they are our Brothers."[56] According to the *Annual Register*, another flag was inscribed: "The brave soldiers are our brothers; treat them kindly."[57]

Both Laon and Cythna are suddenly apprehended by soldiers, put in chains, and imprisoned. This violent process seems melodramatic, but represents what happened to many reformers in 1817; it also represented Shelley's own fear of arrest and imprisonment. Samuel Bamford, who was himself imprisoned in 1817, writes of that year: "it did sometimes happen, that . . . the father would be seized, chained, and torn from his family before he had time to bless them or to receive their blessings and tears. Such scenes were of frequent occurrence, and have thrown a melancholy retrospection over these days."[58] Shelley knew of such arrests, even of "respectable" moderates like John Wright, the Liverpool Unitarian minister, who was jailed for his religious opinions.⁵⁹ Shelley also expected to be arrested. Writing to Byron on April 23, 1817, he is still afraid of a criminal information being brought against *Queen Mab*.⁶⁰ And on September 24, after he has finished writing one version of *Laon and Cythna*, he speaks like someone who expects martyrdom in the near future.

> I am careless of the consequences as they regard myself. I only feel persecution bitterly, because I bitterly lament the depravity & mistake of those who persecute. As to me, I can but die, I can but be torn to pieces, or devoted to infamy most undeserved, & whether this is inflicted by the necessity of nature & circumstances, or thro a principle pregnant, as I believe, with important benefit to mankind is an alternative to which I cannot be indifferent.⁶¹

Laon and Cythna, then, can be seen as a spiritual exercise which prepares Shelley for martydom at the hands of a repressive government. While the poet was comparing his fate to that of Orpheus, there were over one hundred reformers in Scotland and England awaiting trail for treason, a capital offense.

The prominence Shelley gives to antiauthoritarianism and religious freethinking in the poem is not idiosyncratic. In addition to the Unitarian Wright, William Hone had to stand trial three different times for his antireligious "blasphemies." In the Secret Report to the House of Commons, the government ministers claim that the revolutionaries are opposed to gods and kings, and wish to undermine "habits of decent and regular subordination," as well as "principles of morality and religion."⁶² Robert Owen, in his well-publicized speeches in late 1817, shocked his respectable listeners by subscribing to freethinking principles. Cythna's speech to the sailors in Canto Eighth is the most antireligious and antiauthoritarian in the entire poem. In stanza VI, she has a pre-Feuerbachian analysis of anthropomorphism as a projection of human power onto a superior being of human invention. She says "we have one human heart" (st. XIX) which binds everyone together. Echoing the Diogenes speech of the theological fragment, she cautions against self-hatred, and urges the men: "but know thyself, / Nor hate another's crime, nor loathe thine own." It is the "dark idolatory of self" which generates the dynamic of self-hatred, guilt, and vindictive revenge and self-righteousness (st. XXII). Cythna makes her appeal for an antinomian religion of "love and joy," and mutual acceptance (st. XXII).

Antinomian pantheism is part of Shelley's preindustrial perspective, which also contains an agrarian mythology shared with other radicals, notably Cobbett and the Spenceans. In *Queen Mab* Shelley had already used the image of an earth mother giving sustenance to her children to signify the revolutionary society, and he does so again in *Laon and Cythna*. In Canto Second, Laon says that "we all were sons of one great mother" (st. XVII). In Canto Fifth, the earth is called "Maternal" (st. XXXIII); moreover, "Earth from her general womb / Pour forth her swarming sons" (st. XXXVIII), and "Earth" is "the general mother" (st. LV). The symbolic imagery for revolution in Canto Ninth is agricultural (the sleeping seeds), and the definitive symbol of counterrevolution is the famine produced by an unproductive land: "there was no corn" (Canto Tenth, st. XIX). In other words, *Laon and Cythna* identifies abundance with revolution, and famine with counterrevolution. The celebration marking the revolution's triumph is a vegetarian feast, a ritualistic representation of a nature fully capable of providing for everyone. Once the tyrants are victorious, however, scarcity returns. Cobbett's analysis is similar, because he assumes scarcity will be abolished by abolishing Corruption. The Spenceans, too, foresee a postscarcity society once laborers can return to the land previously monopolized by the aristocracy and gentry. The Spenceans are said to have viewed landholders as "stewards" of the public, not private owners (in this, they agree with *Political Justice*): "land is the people's farm; that landed monopoly is contrary to the spirit of christianity, and destructive of the independence and morality of mankind."[63] The agrarian myth of a generous earth mother corrupted and repressed by tyranny was not just a Shelleyan quirk, but a myth shared by many other reformers, especially from the lower classes. The antiagrarian radicalism of a James Mill or a Jeremy Bentham is foreign to both Shelley and Cobbett.[64]

Another feature which Cobbett and Shelley share is their hatred of Malthus. In "To the Journeymen and Labourers," Cobbett criticizes Malthus for mystifying the real problems by holding overpopulation to blame for poverty, whose real cause is an unreformed Parliament.[65] Shelley attacks Malthus in the Preface[66] and implicitly in the poem itself, which celebrates the beauty and joy of sensual love in Canto Sixth (st. XXIff.). Nature not only provides abundantly in spirit and food; she also wants her children to live a life of pleasure and joy. The virtues of ascetic self-denial are not Shelleyan. Cobbett, however, was not a feminist, as Shelley was. Feminism is perhaps the most atypical aspect of *Laon and Cythna*, but Jeremy Bentham was in favor of women voting, and Samuel Bamford reports that in 1817, at Lydgate, working-class women voted during reform meetings.[67]

Two other elements of the poem have contemporary resonance, the rebels' use of pikes to defend themselves, and Cythna's projected exile to America. According to the Secret Report to the House of Lords, the Spa Fields rioters used "pikes."[68] These were also the weapons of the Derbyshire insurrectionists. Such a crude instrument could only be effective during a mass rising in which the government's soldiers were vastly outnumbered. The reference to America in the poem would make readers think of Cobbett—and others— who fled to the States out of fear or desperation. Moreover, a typical reformer's tactic was to compare conditions in the United States with those in England to demonstrate the extent to which social improvement could be achieved with democratic reforms.

Were all the radicals of 1817 like Bentham, completely unsympathetic to poetry? Jonathan Wooler's *Black Dwarf*, a radical publication with a working-class readership, is filled with poetry, most of which is satirical, but some is lyrical. One can see the popular tradition out of which Shelley's *Peter Bell the Third* and *Swellfoot the Tyrant* come, because the most common kind of verse in the *Black Dwarf* is allegorical satire with topical references to contemporary events and people.[69] Another aspect of the poetry in the *Black Dwarf* is the fire imagery in lyrical poems which allegorically represent "Liberty" in its struggle against tyranny. In a poem entitled "Address to Parting Liberty," the poet uses the typical metaphor of fire to figure liberty: "Freedom's sacred fire."[70] Any close reader of Shelley knows how prevalent fire imagery is in the poetry and even the prose. It is interesting that such imagery, linked to reform politics, was commonplace, even though Shelley employed it with more skill than the anonymous poets of the *Black Dwarf*. It is worth remembering that poetry was not for all the reformers the anathema it was for Bentham. Samuel Bamford writes of singing the Union Hymn with his comrades in jail .[71] After being released from prison and returning home, he composed the "Lancashire Hymn," which has some parallels with Shelley's poetry. The "Hymn" utilizes an abstract "Liberty" and depicts a political course similar to that which Shelley portrays in "Ode to Liberty." The notion that poetry had nothing whatsoever to do with the struggle for reform in 1817 is simply not true.

Samuel Bamford did not think poetry was necessarily aristocratic, as Hazlitt did, but one has to ask how successfully *Laon and Cythna* overcomes Hazlitt's objections to a democratic poetry. The poem uses numerous literary conventions from traditional literature to produce an unconventional totality.[72] At strategic points in the narrative, Shelley's heroes do and say the unexpected: they practice nonviolence, rather than military heroism; their feast is vegetarian; Laon and Cythna are feminist, egalitarian, and freethinking; and so on. Shelley is attempting to redefine the heroic, but the poem is significantly "aristocratic." For one thing, the reader sees Laon, Cythna, and the Hermit, but "the People" remain a faceless abstraction. *Laon and Cythna* represents two revolutionaries, not the process of social revolution. Shelley wants to depict the democratic hero, not democracy itself, and democratic ideals and principles, not the actual speech and language of democrats.

As is well known, Shelley tried to publish *Laon and Cythna; or, The Revolution of the Golden City: A Vision of the Nineteenth Century*, but was prevented from doing so by Ollier, who was afraid of government repression. After Shelley suppressed, at Ollier's insistence, numerous passages that were considered too bold (on religion, monarchy, and incest), the poem was finally published— with a new title page—as *The Revolt of Islam, A Poem in Twelve Cantos.* Ollier's fear was by no means exaggerated, since at the time antireligious literature was subject to prosecutions.[73] The difference between the two poems is slight, and was obliterated in the mind of the public after the *Quarterly Review*, to which *Laon and Cythna* was sent, exposed the incest theme.[74] Shelley's poem did not provoke a cultural revolution, to say the least. The *Blackwood's* reviewer admired the author's skill as a poet, but would have nothing to do with his "principles," which were too democratic.[75] Shelley avoided prison in 1817, but he also failed to find an appreciative audience. If he, like Wooler, had found an audience, he probably would have been prosecuted, as Wooler was.

WE PITY THE PLUMAGE, BUT FORGET THE DYING BIRD. AN ADDRESS TO THE PEOPLE ON THE DEATH OF PRINCESS CHARLOTTE, BY THE HERMIT OF MARLOW

When the executions of the Derbyshire rebels—Brandreth, Ludlam, and Turner—came so soon after Princess Charlotte's death, the reform press naturally remarked on the coincidence, angry that the rebels had not been granted a reprieve. (Hunt's *Examiner* and Wooler's *Black Dwarf* both wrote on the conjunction of events.)[76] The official hypocrisy was disturbing because ostentatious mourning for Charlotte was immediately followed by a brutal execution of men whose guilt was in serious doubt. Before dying, Turner had said that "This is all Oliver and the Government." The reform movement was outraged that the Derbyshire rebels were not spared, because Oliver and other *agents provocateurs* had obviously had a part in the Derbyshire uprising. Shelley in his pamphlet makes an analogy between the French Revolution, as seen through Thomas Paine's eyes, and contemporary events; moreover, Shelley's analysis of the underlying causes of the economic distress mostly to blame for the Derbyshire rebellion is reminiscent of Cobbett's argument.

The title, *We Pity the Plumage, but Forget the Dying Bird*, is from Thomas Paine's *The Rights of Man*, Part One, written in answer to Burke. Specifically, Paine attacks Burke for a failure of sympathy and feeling, in that Burke sheds tears only for royalty and aristocrats but not for the People. The entire passage is worth quoting, especially in light of the Hazlitt review already discussed. That Shelley should pick this sentence indicates his preoccupation with the relations between power and art.

> Not one glance of compassion, not one commiserating reflection, that I can find throughout his book, has he bestowed on those who lingered out the most wretched of lives, a life without hope, in the most miserable of prisons.
>
> It is painful to behold a man employing his talents to corrupt himself. Nature has been kinder to Mr. Burke than he is to her. He is not affected by the reality of distress touching his heart, but by the showy resemblage of it striking his imagination. He pities the plumage, but forgets the dying bird.
>
> Accustomed to kiss the aristocratical hand that hath purloined him from himself, he degenerates into a composition of art, and the genuine soul of nature forsakes him. His hero or his heroine must be a tragedy victim expiring in show, and not the real prisoner of mystery, sinking into death in the silence of a dungeon.[77]

Here is an interesting reply to Hazlitt which depends on the nature-art dichotomy. Burke can sympathize with Queen Marie Antoinette, who is a tragic victim in the sublime mode, but because of his aristocratic bias and aesthetic blinders he cannot see "the real prisoner of mystery." Burke's aristocratic aesthetic has silenced his moral sense.

Shelley's pamphlet and the essays of many others at the time were important because, with little precedent in English history, the execution of working-class men was now important enough that people knew their names. It is worth comparing Shelley's response to the execution of the Yorkshire Luddites in 1813, when many more than three were killed. Although he was sufficiently upset and angry to pledge some money for a subscription to assist the families of the victims, he shortly thereafter withdrew the pledge in order to give the money to the Hunt brothers, who had just been convicted of libel and sentenced to prison. Neither Shelley nor anyone else wrote essays on the dead Luddites. But by late 1817, there is a new social environment within which working-class people cannot be dismissed; they have faces, names, and words. Shelley participates in this new cultural sensitivity, which Cobbett had pioneered in his "To the Journeymen and Labourers." One wonders whether Peterloo would have caused a nearly revolutionary situation if it had not been for the previous public outcry over the Derbyshire rebels.

The allusion to Paine and Burke raises the specter of the French Revolution and the English 1790s. In the third paragraph, Shelley refers to the Treason Trials of 1794, which almost led to the executions of Horne Tooke and Hardy. Shelley is suggesting that the English are in a prerevolutionary situation similar to France in 1789, although at this point there is a choice: "a despotism, a revolution, or reform."[78] Although he still wishes for reform, his tone throughout is anything but hopeful. Indeed, the last paragraph is apocalyptic.

The first point Shelley makes is that death is the great leveler, the one thing rich and poor have in common. Because of this, even the "poorest poor" must be included within the human family.[79] It is immoral that the sufferings and deaths of those at the bottom of society are not deemed important enough to lament. Shelley, however, is not practicing a new sentimentality, because the suffering he laments can be changed. The militarism of the "Kings and their ministers" has created an enormous war debt which has enriched a new aristocracy ("petty piddling slaves who have gained a right to the title of public creditors, either by gambling in the funds, or by subserviency to government, or some other villainous trade") while impoverishing the laborers. "The effect of this system is, that the day labourer gains no more now by working sixteen hours a day than he gained before by working eight." The new tyranny of the "double aristocracy" weighs heaviest on the worker. "Before, he supported the army and the pensioners, and the royal family, and the landholders," but now he must also support the fundholders. The chief evil of this system is this:

> one man is forced to labour for another in a degree not only not necessary to the support of the subsisting distinctions among mankind, but so as by the excess of the injustice to endanger the very foundations of all that is valuable in social order, and to provoke the anarchy which is at once the enemy of freedom, and the child and the chastiser of misrule.

A reform of Parliament, "a free representation of the people," is needed.[80]

Of all Shelley's writings, this one is the most aristocratically antibourgeois. Of the *nouveaux riches* generated by the war debt, Shelley says that these bourgeois "are not like the old aristocracy men of pride and honour." Trade is "villainous," and these bourgeois "are not 'Corinthian capital of polished society,' but the petty and creeping weeds which deface the rich tracery of its sculpture."[81] It is amusing to recall that Paine himself was a bourgeois who thought highly of trade and commerce. It is questionable whether the *nouveaux riches* of Shelley's day were any more immoral than the old aristocracy; the reverse is probably more accurate. What Donald Reiman calls Shelley's "reactionary agrarianism" is apparent here, but it is disconcerting to read that the laborer's support of the army, pensioners, royal family, and landholders is "a hard necessity to which it was well that he"—the laborer—"should submit."[82] Shelley is practicing that rhetorical duplicity he said was necessary in the *Essay on Christianity*. He heaps all the blame for the workers' suffering on the Debt, as Cobbett also did. Although Shelley anticipated a society in which laborers did not have to support an army, pensioners, and so on, he here adopts Cobbett's tactic of concentrating the public wrath on the fundholders.

The last paragraph of the essay is curious, because the first half is uncharacteristically sentimental while the second half is apocalyptic. In paragraph five Shelley had said that the Princess was nothing special, one of "thousands of others equally distinguished as she" who "had accomplished nothing, and aspired to nothing, and could understand nothing."[83] Shelley did not blame Charlotte, but criticized her superficial education. In the last paragraph, however, in extravagant rhetoric, he invites the reader to mourn for the Princess's death: "she who should have been the Queen of her beloved nation, and whose posterity should have ruled it for ever." Although Shelley himself was a republican, he is here utilizing Burdettite mythology, which invents a common interest between royality and the People. Moreover, Shelley is setting up the reader for a rhetorical reversal, when he identifies the dead Queen as the goddess of Liberty, who has been murdered by the execution of Turner, Ludlam, and Brandreth. Death has taken Charlotte, but *"man* has murdered Liberty." The prose changes abruptly to an allegorical mode in which tyranny is a spiritual force present everywhere in society. Shelley wants readers to mourn not just the Princess or the Derbyshire rebels, but "the corpse of British Liberty." Echoing *The Mask of Anarchy* and the 1819 sonnet beginning "An old, mad, blind, despised, and dying King," Shelley concludes: "if some glorious Phantom should appear, and make its throne of broken swords and sceptres and royal crowns trampled in the dust, let us say that the Spirit of Liberty has arisen from its grave and left all that was gross and mortal there, and kneel down and worship it as our Queen."[84] There is even a foreshadowing of *Adonais* in the dichotomy between "gross and mortal" and spiritual. There is an iconographic echo, too, from Wooler's *Black Dwarf*, whose frontispiece depicts a throne of broken swords, scepters, and crowns trampled into dust. Is it merely a reform of the Commons that Shelley wants here? The imagery and rhetoric are republican, not moderate. It is typical that as Shelley's language becomes more "poetic" and allegorical, the politics seem more radical.

The pamphlet, then, is a fusion of different voices, some of which are contradictory, not because Shelley was confused, but because he wished to reach a popular audience. As he said in the 1816-1817 fragment: "All reformers have been compelled to practise this misrepresentation of their own true feelings and opinions." Nevertheless, Shelley's "true" feelings can be discerned throughout the pamphlet. He attacks the aristocratic bias against sympathizing with laborers; he repeats Cobbett's critique of the new bourgeoisie; he calls for a "free representation" of Parliament; and in the last paragraph, in the allegorical language with which the pamphlet concludes, he suggests a revolutionary transformation of culture arising from the destroyed structures of aristocratic monarchy.

CONCLUSION

In 1818 the economy recovered, Habeas Corpus was restored, most of the radicals were out of jail, and Shelley left England. He tried unsuccessfully to make for himself an important position within the reform movement, but he remained only on the periphery. Bad timing may have undermined the effectiveness of the first Hermit of Marlow pamphlet. *Laon and Cythna*, however, could not have appealed to the leisure-class liberals because it was far too radical. The more bourgeois liberals were attracted to a Benthamite approach, hard-nosed and practical, and the more aristocratic liberals had no intention of uprooting class hierarchy. The only people who could have appreciated the politics of the poem were the laborers, for whom it was not even intended. There were no obstacles to the success of the second Hermit of Marlow pamphlet, but it did not procure for Shelley a Cobbett-like fame and following.

Pseudonyms are revealing; Shelley chose "the Hermit." The poet is ambivalent about political activism, wanting to intervene politically to promote libertarian ideals and work toward a millennial world, but the day-to-day realities of political action are remote from the idealism that inspires him in the first place.[85] He is an aristocratic rebel, a disinterested intellectual who has nothing personally to gain from social revolution. Russian aristocrats with an idealism similar to Shelley's, such as Herzen, Bakunin, Kropotkin, and Tolstoy, attached themselves to actual movements of peasants and workers, and thus avoided the hermitic fate. Those rebels, however, come out of a very different culture from Shelley's.

Nevertheless, despite the ambivalence which appears only in the second Hermit of Marlow pamphlet, Shelley's texts of 1817 follow the direction suggested by the theological fragment. The first pamphlet seeks to institutionalize the actual state of social consciousness already achieved, thus confirming the basic premise of philosophical anarchism: social institutions should reflect social consciousness at its most progressive point. Shelley uses the threat of force because the goal is rational, within reach, and has popular support—and also because, clearly, he feels the Tories would not precipitate a civil war (indeed, when a similar situation emerged in 1832, civil war was averted by many Tories preferring the lesser evil of moderate reform). The pamphlet does not contradict the "Diogenes" approach, because the third part of the theological fragment asserts only that complete equality must be the final result of institutional reform, preceded by the egalitarian reform of consciousness. The ethical idealism praised in the "Equality" section is expressed in *Laon and Cythna*, which tries to *alter* consciousness, not institutionalize its present state. The final Hermit of Marlow pamphlet is a political action in solidarity with the broad movement for reform, appearing at a time when radical culture was establishing the moral illegitimacy of the government's executions.

FIVE

Prometheus Unbound
in Context
(1818-1820)

INTRODUCTION

WHEN SHELLEY began composing the first act of *Prometheus Un-bound* in September 1818, he did not foresee that its last act would not be finished until December 1819, and that the entire lyrical drama, with other poems, would not be published until August 1820. Between the poem's beginning and end there occurred a political event of enormous importance for Shelley and England: Peterloo, the massacre at Manchester on August 16, 1819, when the Yeomanry attacked a crowd of unarmed demonstrators—men, women, and children. Shelley wrote the first three acts of *Prometheus Unbound* well before Peterloo, with the third act finished in April 1819, but the fourth act and probably most of the other poems in the *Prometheus Unbound* volume were composed after Peterloo. The massacre is important because it inspired a number of poetic and prose works, most of which were not published in Shelley's lifetime due to the repression; it also provided a test for his libertarian ideas, which were formulated prior to August 16, 1819. Something like Peterloo could have frightened the aristocratic Shelley out of his more radical tendencies, but it did not. Rather, it emboldened him to go as far as he ever went in a radical direction.

In the first part of this chapter I examine Acts I through III of *Prometheus Unbound* in a particular context of Shelley's literary development. Italy provides Shelley with a temporary sanctuary from the immediate influences of English politics. Although he follows events closely at secondhand, through newpapers and letters, he is more affected now by his Italian environment, including Byron.

Poems just prior to or simultaneous with the composition of *Prometheus Unbound*'s first act—*Rosalind and Helen*, "Lines written among the Euganean Hills"—redefine and reassert utopian ideals despite accumulating disappointments, personal and political. The first three acts of *Prometheus Unbound* restate more complexly the themes and concepts Shelley developed previously in *Queen Mab* and *Laon and Cythna*. Two other poems, *Julian and Maddalo*, and *The Cenci*, written before Peterloo, bear on *Prometheus Unbound* in certain ways because they test some Promethean concepts. It is ironic that just as Shelley puts the finishing touches to *The Cenci* he hears of Peterloo, the historical equivalent of the poem's rape and murder. Appropriately he quotes from his own play, telling his publisher Ollier how distressed he feels about the massacre: "Something must be done. . . . What yet I know not."[1] Shelley does, however, act in a literary way: *The Mask of Anarchy*, *Peter Bell the Third*, the Carlile letter to the *Examiner*, *A Philosophical View of Reform*, and *Popular Songs* were written between September 1819, and May 1820; not a single one of these was published in his lifetime. In the *Prometheus Unbound* volume he was able to publish some politically relevant poems, but even these were subject to alteration out of political fear. To see the *Prometheus Unbound* volume in its most meaningful context one must restore the dimension of the unpublished works.

ROSALIND AND HELEN

Rosalind and Helen,[2] a poem about the paradox of hope, has traditionally been slighted because Shelley himself did so, saying he finished it only to please Mary. Although it is not among his greatest poems, it deserves serious attention. The poem has four parts: an introduction (1-218), Rosalind's tale (219-593), Helen's tale (594-1274), and a conclusion (1275-1318). The style is interesting because its iambic tetrameter, with an irregular rime scheme and conversational diction, is quite remote from either the Spenserians of *Laon and Cythna* or the blank verse of *Queen Mab* and *Alastor*. In the Advertisement he locates the poem near the bottom of a hierarchy of "high" and "low" styles. If the poem amuses the "imagination" and awakens "a certain ideal melancholy favourable to the reception of more important impressions, it will produce in the reader all that the writer experienced in the composition."[3] As Shelley wrote those words in December 1818, he had already com-

141

pleted the first act of *Prometheus Unbound,* something in the "high" style.

The poem's subtitle is "A Modern Eclogue," suggesting the pastoral tradition of Theocritus and Vergil. Naming one character "Rosalind" recalls the Rosalind of *As You Like It,* especially since we know Shelley admired Shakespeare's women (in *Julian and Maddalo,* Maddalo's grown-up child is compared to "one of Shakespeare's women" [592]). The Rosalind-Helen relationship was intended to mirror (or idealize) the Isabel Baxter–Mary Shelley relationship, which had been severely strained by the quarrels between Shelley himself and Isabel's father and husband.[4] Since Isabel and Mary had been the best of friends before the elopement with Shelley, the poem represents Mary's desire for reconciliation with Isabel. At a literary level, Shelley's Helen and Rosalind are reminiscent of Shakespeare's Celia and Rosalind. Both pairs of women are in exile, residents of the pastoral world due to the disruptions of the urban world. As Shakespeare's two women are nobles "playing" the role of shepherds and rustics, so Shelley's women are rural solely by virtue of where they reside, not by virtue of their occupation. Neither woman tills the land or in any way lives the life of an agricultural laborer. In the eclogues of Theocritus and Vergil, the dialogue of rustics maintained the conceit, at least, that the speakers were in fact rustics, laborers on the land, but the conceit is dropped by Shelley. The pastoral antagonism between town and country is embodied in the role Shelley assigns "nature" as an ethical standard by which to judge the corrupt urban world, and as a regenerative power capable of healing the damaged spirit.[5]

Helen, with her young son Henry, meets her fellow outcast, Rosalind, at the shore of Lake Como. These tragic survivors try to comfort each other, and attempt to return to the friendship they enjoyed as children, even though they cannot return to childhood. The child is an important symbol. Helen's child, Henry, speaks with spontaneous generosity, and tries to bring Rosalind into their already existing network of affection. The child's natural innocence contrasts with adult suspicion and the brutal social world they have left. In Rosalind's story, her three children are a compensation for the loveless union with her husband. Moreover, Rosalind's husband wreaks his revenge on her by denying her custody of the children in the will (the parallel with Shelley's own life is obvious: he, too, was denied custody of his children by Harriet, on the grounds of his religious, social, and political opinions). Helen is saved from

142

suicidal insanity by her pregnancy, and later by mothering her child
(Cythna has a similar experience). And at the very end of the poem,
the children represent a promise of future happiness, since Rosa-
lind's child and Helen's fall in love and marry. The child symbolizes
natural innocence and libertarian hope, a counter to the forces of
tyranny and despair.

The child symbol is not the only Wordsworthian feature of the
poem; there is also a Wordsworthian "sacred spot" in the woods
where the speakers exchange their stories. This "stone seat" (106)
is part of a "roofless temple" (108) which is then compared to a
pagan religious shrine: "like the fane / Where, ere new creeds could
faith obtain, / Man's early race once knelt beneath / The overhang-
ing deity" (108-11). The spot is haunted by hellish shapes, ghosts,
demons, a naked child, and a fiend turning into a woman, all be-
cause an act of violence was once committed here. A brother and
sister went to this spot to live their life of incestuous love, but the
"multitude" discovered them, tore their child "limb from limb,"
"stabbed and trampled on its mother," and burned the young man
to death at the market place; this last atrocity was organized by a
Christian priest (146-66). A love blessed by nature is destroyed by
the values of the uncomprehending town, led by a bigoted priest.
This place is appropriate for the dialogue between Rosalind and
Helen for a number of reasons. Rosalind's passionate love ended
tragically because her father revealed at the wedding that the bride-
groom was in fact her half-brother. The youth died as a result of
the shock, and Rosalind, still traumatized, finally married a man
she did not love. The spot is sacred for Helen because her unmarried
union with Lionel was blessed only by nature, not social law. When
they were about to consummate their love, Helen said to Lionel:
" 'We will have rites our faith to bind, / But our church shall be
the starry night, / Our altar the grassy earth outspread, / And our
priest the muttering wind' " (851-54). Both women's allegiance is
to nature and its innocence; indeed, they are victims of a society
which rejects those values.

Rosalind's story starts with the burial of her husband, whose
death she guiltily welcomes. Her children feel no need to conceal
their feelings and express delight at the death of a tyrant, "a
man / Hard, selfish, loving only gold, / Yet full of guile" (248-50).
Her husband's last will and testament is a curse which has deprived
Rosalind of her children. Falsely accused of adultery and religious
infidelity, she is declared an unfit mother. If she does not leave the

children, then none of their father's money will go to them, leaving them in abject poverty. Shelley, however, was indeed "guilty" of adultery and religious unbelief, for which "crimes" he was deprived of his children after Harriet's death, which did not release him so much as haunt him. Rosalind is in a sense "guilty" because she loved another (her half-brother) and she possesses so many "natural," as opposed to intolerantly "Christian," qualities. Her husband was destroyed by his egotism, "bowed and bent with fears, / Pale with quenchless thirst of gold, / Which, like fierce fever, left him weak" (423-25). This is nature's revenge on the tyrant who represses his own natural instincts.

Nature cannot cure all ills, because Rosalind has no illusions concerning the poverty her children will suffer if she decides to defy her husband's will. Poverty is described as an unmitigated horror:

> 'Tis Crime, and Fear and Infamy,
> And houseless Want in frozen ways
> Wandering ungarmented, and Pain,
> And, worse than all, that inward stain
> Foul Self-contempt . . .
> (475-79)

The specter of poverty is an appropriate image from 1816-1817, when Shelley witnessed such unprecedented distress. Separated from her children, Rosalind wanders in a suicidal depression, reminiscent of the *Alastor* Visionary's journey, because she yearns to die into nature, achieving a peace denied her in life. Helen urges her to banish morbid thoughts and allow love and nature to restore her soul.

After Rosalind finishes her story, Helen begins hers, a distinctively and unmistakably Shelleyan story. Helen begins at the end, with "hope" being buried with Lionel, but there was a time when hope was alive in society. The French Revolution was a time when

> . . . men dreamed the agèd earth
> Was labouring in that mighty birth,
> Which many a poet and a sage
> Has aye foreseen—the happy age
> When truth and love shall dwell below
> Among the works and ways of men;
> Which on this world not power but will
> Even now is wanting to fulfil.
> (602-609)

Liberty is an organic process of birth, a natural process, which poet-prophets nevertheless can envision. Moreover, the French Revolution failed not because its ideals were impossible or unrealistic, but because desire and will were insufficient.

Lionel, a wealthy aristocrat, was a revolutionary enthusiast and poet whose "words could bind / Like music the lulled crowd" (636-37). He did not seek Fame or Power, but tried to move his auditors, even the tyrants in power, to feel emotions they were unaccustomed to feeling. His real power was in language because the "subtle witchcraft of his tongue / Unlocked the hearts of those who keep / Gold, the world's bond of slavery" (652-54). He communicated with their *human* nature, which is distinct from their merely social role as powerful men. The priests hated Lionel primarily because he wrote antireligious satires whose comic features were so popular. When the times change, the counterrevolution creates a new world from which Lionel feels estranged and to which he cannot adjust. He tries, unsuccessfully, to find a compensatory relief in love, which leaves him disillusioned. He finally triumphs over despair after falling in love with Helen. Perhaps Helen might have been able to restore Lionel, but the tyrants suddenly imprison him for "blasphemy." Here Shelley expresses his fear of imprisonment, while evoking the actual practice of repression in 1817. Lionel, despite his victimization, hurls at the tyrants an interesting lyric. " 'Fear not the tyrants shall rule for ever, / Or the priests of the bloody faith; / They stand on the brink of that mighty river, / Whose waves they have tainted with death' " (894-97). This, the Ozymandias theme, suggests that even tyrants are subject to a power greater than themselves, namely, historical change. This mighty river will sweep them away eventually, leaving their "swords" and "sceptres" floating like wrecks. Especially during counterrevolution, the inexorable power of history to move forward is grounds for hope.

Once released from jail, Lionel is wasting away physically, although spiritually he is still gentle and loving. Helen's love cannot reverse the deadly process initiated by the counterrevolution, because he is too exquisitely framed to survive in a world so antagonistic to his deepest desires.[6] Before he dies, they travel to his country estate where they visit a shrine dedicated to "Fidelity," a dog who saved Lionel's mother from drowning, although the dog itself perished. The "ancient steward" (992) weeps upon seeing his "master." Perhaps in no other poem is it so clear that Shelley was from the titled gentry, raised on semifeudal values. The selfless dog who sacrifices his own life for the life of his mistress evokes images of the ideal servant. Lionel spends his final days on the estate, where his very last day ends with Helen's wild harp-playing. The "life-dissolving" (1166) music, like the visionary music of *Alastor*, is an appropriate way to image Lionel's death, because he dies within an intense beauty he had spent his life trying to cultivate. He also dies with his lover, who subsequently goes mad but slowly recovers once she assumes the role of Henry's mother (Henry, of course, is Lionel's child). The poem concludes with Henry uniting with Rosalind's daughter, thus giving a hopeful ending to a tragic story.

The poem resolves the paradox of hope during a counterrevolutionary period by rooting hope in natural processes. A new generation once again thrusts forward a revolutionary innocence that could overwhelm the "outmoded creeds." Nature itself, in its woodland recesses, provides sanctuaries within which the damaged soul can restore itself and strengthen its determination to struggle for love and liberty. Time is a process of nature that will sweep aside the ephemeral products of tyranny, thus making possible a libertarian triumph. The most significant ground of hope is embodied in the poem's dialogic structure: feeling and sympathy. Helen, for example, tries to

> Unbind the knots of her friend's despair,
> Till her thoughts were free to float and flow;
> And from her labouring bosom now,
> Like the bursting of a prisoned flame,
> The voice of long pent sorrow came.
>
> (214-18)

Even though Rosalind, Helen, Lionel, and the murdered incestuous family are all defeated, their defeat is not total because of the redemptive magic of poetry. The outcasts, by exchanging their tales of woe and sharing their grief, are able to love and continue living, despite their social ostracism. Mutual aid and sympathy reconstitute the forces of utopia at a molecular level, thus defying the social forces which appear omnipotent. Contrary to what Byron was telling Shelley, hope is not simply self-destroying folly which leads inevitably to despair and madness; it is an active property that can withstand tyranny and initiate a movement toward liberty. Nevertheless, the aristocratic structure of the libertarian hope cannot be ignored. Residing in a nature accessible to the leisure-class intellectuals, libertarian hope is something "outside" society which the poet-prophet introduces.

"LINES WRITTEN AMONG THE EUGANEAN HILLS"

The poem is in rimed, euphonious tetrameters which are structured in a nearly symmetrical five parts.[7] The statement whose logic controls the poem is given at the beginning: "Many a green isle needs must be / In the deep wide sea of Misery, / Or the mariner . . . Never thus could voyage on." There have to be *many* moments of happiness in order to make life endurable, which ordinarily is not. As the mariner-voyage trope continues in the first part, a "sunless" sky is followed by a "tempest" which capsizes the vessel, thrusting the mariner into the sea and provoking a dilemma: is it better to drown, thus ending this death-in-life, or is it better to hope and survive by heading toward dry land? In a way parallel to Act I of *Prometheus Unbound*, the poem develops the equation of life in a fallen state and death. Although the mariner cannot know what biological death is, he already knows what death-in-life consists of: the absence of love and friendship (36-44). This is an existing misery compared to which the possible nothingness of death becomes a "haven." The true catastrophe, then, is not the cessation of biological life, but the destruction of life's joyful possibilities.

A theme which the poem develops is the redemptive power of poetry itself. At the poem's center, in the third part, is the great poet of Venice, Lord Byron (167-205).[8] The poets triumph over death as well as nature, and rise far above a society without liberty. The mere existence possible within tyranny is a social death-in-life to which Shelley unwaveringly refuses to grant any legitimacy whatever. A social order which does not nourish liberty does not deserve to exist and deserves instead to be annihilated, with society returned to a state of nature. Addressing Venice, Shelley says: "Perish—let there only be / Floating o'er thy hearthless sea, / . . . One remembrance, more sublime / Than the tattered pall of time" (166-72). The "biological" Venice can perish, leaving only Byron's poetic "remembrance," because a Venice without liberty is already dead, an uncreative nothingness that suppresses joyful potentialities. Only if "Freedom should awake" in Venice and the other city-states will they earn the right to exist. "If not, perish thou and they!" (160). If in life they have been uncreative, in death they may supply the substance for a renewal: "From your dust new nations spring / With more kindly blossoming" (165-66).

Poetry can transform the past into a form which is ultimately liberating. Just as Byron distills whatever is "poetic" and leaves behind the dross of Venice, so Shelley, in the poem's third paragraph, takes the last seven years of his own life and turns them into poetry. The old Shelley of 1811-1818 "dies," leaving "One white skull and seven dry bones" (49).[9] The event precipitating this revulsion for the past is probably the death of his daughter Clara, something that would trigger a remembrance of other deaths, Fanny Godwin's and his wife Harriet's. The destruction of the past is figured in a simile; the howling whirlwind as the only witness to the skull and bones is "like a slaughtered town, / When a King in glory rides / Through the pomp of fratricides" (57-59). The simile does not say that the king slaughtered the town (indeed, the fratricidal brothers seem to have done that), but he rides in triumph through what is now only a death-in-life. The king is the true symbol for the deity of death-in-life, while the poet is the deity of life in its creative, joyful possibilities. The dead, useless past is crystallized in a static symbol which is left permanently "On the beach of a northern sea" (45). Here is a death, a nothingness, and a kind of suicide that are not evaded, but realized in such a way as to make possible the ecstasy of the poem's later paragraphs.

There is a dramatic shift in the fourth paragraph to a scene and perception that are immediately at hand. The previous lines were not in the here and now, but in a hypothetical realm of symbols, figures, tropes, and subjunctive-conditional statements. The lyrical present is announced by the figure of the mariner's voyage. The "bark" of line 69 is a transparent metaphor because the speaker is " 'Mid the mountains Euganean" (70), not at sea. The legion of rooks hailing the sunrise contrasts favorably with the sea-mews of the previous paragraph, who watch over the ruins of a spent life. The beautiful sunrise introduces the sun symbol, which is a governing structure in the poem. Sunrise, noon, and sunset mark three important transitions, with the sunrise signifying the speaker's turn toward life in the here and now, the noon occasioning the speaker's ecstatic communion with divinity, and sunset revealing the Evening Star, Venus, the symbol of eternity. The sun gives not only light and warmth (to counteract the darkness and frigidity of death and death-in-life), but supplies fire, a powerful element in the poem.

The sun defines the lyrical present and demarcates a temporal progression during which the speaker achieves insight.

The absence of sun signifies death. The death-in-life of the first three paragraphs is ominously foreshadowed by the "sunless sky" of line 9. At the end of the third paragraph, the narrator says there is no lament for him who died on the shore; he is compared to "a sunless vapour dim / Who once clothed with life and thought / What nor moves nor murmurs not" (63-65). But the presence of the sun's element, fire, signifies life's potentiality, even when fire is turned against liberty. In the fifth paragraph, during the description of the sunrise, there is fire imagery related to Venice. From the speaker's vantage point on the mountain, he sees the sun radiating over the horizon of the sea, creating an illusion in which Venice seems to be within a fiery furnace:

> Column, tower, and dome, and spire,
> Shine like obelisks of fire,
> Pointing with inconstant motion
> From the altar of dark ocean
> To sapphire-tinted skies;
> As the flames of sacrifice
> From the marble shrines did rise,
> As to pierce the dome of gold
> Where Apollo spoke of old.
>   (106-14)

Although the imagery is visually brilliant, it also depicts immorality. The constructs of the city—the column, tower, dome, and spire—are fiery obelisks commemorating the dominion of Austria. The simile is especially revealing because the fiery obelisks are compared to the sacrificial fires dedicated to the god, Apollo, whose golden shrine was at Delphi. The alienation of human creativity, especially its prophetic-poetic aspect, is startlingly imaged by burning sacrifices to a golden idol; unable to accept their own creative fire, the idolators worship a god they have created, and one who continually impoverishes them. Similarly, the city's highest towers are paying symbolic tribute to the Austrian power which controls it. The "dome of gold" connotes the domination of wealth, the true deity of contemporary Venice. The long apostrophe to Venice in the subsequent paragraph articulates directly what the fire symbolism states indirectly here.

In the fourth part, dealing with Padua, there is another use of fire imagery. Where once there shone "the lamp of learning," there no longer is any philosophy at Padua. "Like a meteor," Padua's enlightenment burnt itself out, but "Now new fires from antique light / Spring beneath the wide world's might" (265-66). The "spark" of Padua has been trampled out by the tyrants. In a stunning series of lines, Shelley develops a simile that suggests a fiery social revolution, "sparked" by philosophy, but entailing a destructive power quite remote from scholarship.

> As the Norway woodman quells,
> In the depth of piny dells,
> One light flame among the brakes,
> While the boundless forest shakes,
> And its mighty trunks are torn
> By the fire thus lowly born:
> The spark beneath his feet is dead,
> He starts to see the flames it fed
> Howling through the darkened sky
> With a myriad tongues victoriously,
> And sinks down in fear: so thou,
> O tyranny, beholdst now
> Light around thee, and thou hearest
> The loud flames ascend, and fearest:
> Grovel on the earth; aye, hide
> In the dust thy purple pride!
> (269-84)

The confrontation with tyranny, mediated by the fire imagery, results in a complete victory for liberty. Fire, as an image of revolution, has this advantage: once the conflagration has consumed the old order, it has nothing more to burn, so it dies. The work of fire here is purely destructive, clearing the old so that the new can grow.

In the fourth part, there is an evocation of agrarian exploitation of the peasants near Padua (217-35). This is one of the few instances in Shelley's work, poetry or prose, where he depicts agrarian exploitation; the greater emphasis by far is on the oppression instituted by kings, priests, bourgeois, and the spirit of Mammon. The particular images of exploitation by the landlords and Austrian tyrants give way to a generalization which continues the agrarian trope of reaping and sowing: "Men must reap the things they sow, / Force from force must ever flow— / Or worse; but 'tis a bitter woe / That love or reason cannot change / The despot's rage, the slave's revenge" (231-35). This fatalistic conclusion precedes the revolutionary fire imagery and indeed lends it greater force than it would otherwise have. Act I, *Prometheus Unbound,* is consistent with these lines, even the last two, because in the poetic drama once a despot rages or a slave plots revenge, love and reason are powerless; despotism and slavery must follow their necessitarian courses. In *Prometheus Unbound,* Prometheus never convinces Jupiter that tyranny is immoral; rather, Demogorgon *by force* drags Jupiter from his throne and into the lowest regions where he is imprisoned. That despotism and slavery operate under necessity does not mean that Shelley admires revenge and violence. To break out of the cycle of oppression it is necessary to commence a creative process, which has nothing to do with hatred and violence. In other words, although all of Shelley's sympathy is with the rebelling slave who might hate and even inflict revenge on his oppressor, he never for once believes that liberty could be constructed by hate.

The destructive-creative dynamic is well illustrated by the following sequence: first comes the revolutionary fire passage, then the ecstatic communion with divinity. The fifth and final part begins with the sun's position at noon, when its rays are most direct. After some lovely description of the scenery, Shelley comes to the climax of the poem:

> And my spirit which so long
> Darkened this swift stream of song,
> Interpenetrated lie
> By the glory of the sky:
> Be it love, light, harmony,
> Odour, or the soul of all
> Which from heaven like dew doth fall,
> Or the mind which feeds this verse
> Peopling the lone universe.
> (311-19)

Divinity is an attribute of either nature or the self—an uncertainty which appears in the theological fragment of 1816-1817 and later in *A Defence of Poetry.* This unity of subject and object is a utopian image of what happens in the absence of tyranny. Once destruction has done its work, the forces of nature (or the mind, or both) can operate at full capacity to restore a paradise. Once death-in-life, which the poem identifies as the principal enemy of utopian hope, has been fully defeated, then creativity can reign.

In the last paragraph of the poem there is a utopian image of retreat and exemplary action, "a windless bower" the poet hopes to build for himself and those he loves. His rural retreat on the sea will permit a happiness so intense it may attract others to the "healing Paradise." The "polluting multitude" would be transformed, their rage subdued, and their strife healed by love. The moral regeneration would ultimately be followed by nature's renewal, according to the poem's last line: "And the earth grow young again."

The green isle has become a utopian outpost, a circle of creativity that can expand outwards in an organic, natural process of growth. The poem concludes as extremely as it began. If death-in-life can be sufficiently overcome to make suicide undesirable, then it can be triumphed over completely. Either the haven of biological death, or the liberation of joy in utopia; either the annihilation of Venice and Padua, or their libertarian redemption; these are the extreme alternatives that Shelley develops.

The poem is as aristocratic in structure as *Rosalind and Helen*, because social renewal is tied to the poet's fate. Even his retreat from society is the relocation of libertarian hope to a safer territory where nature and spirit can constitute an oppositional force. But Shelleyan nature interacts with poetic imagination to generate a specifically *social* creativity attached to an urban world, whose decadence is marked by the exile of art. We see here an early instance of Shelley's democratic Hellenism, which finds in the Athenian *demos* a model for libertarian democracy characterized by social creativity. The utopian retreat into nature can lead in different directions, toward either social reconstruction or merely personal salvation. Shelley cannot conceive of resolving the poet's crisis in terms other than social.

PROMETHEUS UNBOUND, ACT I

Begun in August of 1818 and not finished until, apparently, January 1819, the first act of *Prometheus Unbound* marks an important stage of Shelley's poetic development. In *Queen Mab* and *Laon and Cythna* he had tried to create myths, images, and dramatic situations using a revolutionary language purified of the debilitating faults which afflicted actual revolutionary movements. *Prometheus Unbound* is the third such attempt. The poem describes the process of breaking out of history and into utopia. There is a leap from a limited realm of existence to a realm where unnecessary and arbitrary restraints have been abolished. Focusing on the psychological preconditions for a utopian transition, Shelley explores the point at which consciousness finally ceases to be determined by the past and begins to determine itself under conditions of freedom. A belief that consciousness can eventually reach self-determination defines utopian hope, without which he feels he would, like Byron, sink into irony and resignation.

Contradiction seems to be an integral part of most utopian writing. Marie Louise Berneri, surveying utopian thought from Plato onwards, discloses a recurrent pattern. An initial humanitarian impulse to reduce human suffering becomes, as utopia, a blueprint for establishing a totalitarian regime.[10] Often using the metaphor of the diseased body, the utopist organizes his ideas in order to purify the unclean body-politic. Once the goal becomes purity, it is easy for the utopist to install himself as dictator of the new society, because he knows better than anyone else what should be cleaned up. In utopia, the sexual impulse is the most strictly regulated because, in the interests of unity and efficiency, the individual must have only one allegiance, to the perfect state. Plato tries to take the irrationality and passion out of sexual love; the Spartans make sure lovers do not become too attached to one another; Winstanley chooses the authoritarian family as the force to control sexuality; and Foigny finesses the problem by turning the ideal citizens into hermaphrodites. Utopian mobilization against potential sexual anarchy is part of the general war against nature's indeterminacy. Bacon's dream of a society ruled by scientists looks back to Plato's philosopher-kings and ahead to Skinner's behavior modifiers.

Adult sexuality also seems to be the one thing the paradise tradition cannot tolerate. Frank and Fritzie Manuel have written that sexuality "remains for centuries the forbidden fruit of maternal paradises, celestial and earthly."[11] Paradise, according to the Manuels, is basically an infantile fantasy of returning to the maternal breast or womb. The pleasures celebrated by paradise are oral, not genital, eating and drinking, not making love. Paradise is also, as its etymology suggests, a space within fortified boundaries, implying the need for protection, walls, defensive strategies. Although the Manuels say that when "plain belief in religious paradise became attentuated, utopia took over,"[12] they notice an important difference between the two. As the God-created paradise is replaced by the man-created utopia, it loses the "soft, maternal attributes" in favor of more aggressive, phallic heroism.[13]

153

While the Manuels and Berneri discuss literary fantasies, Norman Cohn's subject is actual millenarian movements that attempted to bring about the golden age. He traces the history of the millenarians from after the birth of Christ to the time of Cromwell. There is an interesting parallel between these mass movements of defrocked priests and impoverished peasants, and literary fantasies: both are antisexual. One of the most popular movements was that of the flagellants, for whom the flesh was to be mortified.[14] The millenarians, suffering from guilt for rebelling so radically on economic and religious matters, exorcised some of that guilt by punishing their sexual desires. Among the Anabaptists, like the Waldensians, the sexual code was stricter than even the official Catholic decrees.[15] The notable exception to the prohibition on sexual pleasure was the society of the Free Spirit, who were persecuted especially for their sexuality.[16]

> To have the Holy Spirit incarnated in oneself and to receive the revelation which that brought—that was to rise from the dead and to possess heaven. A man who had knowledge of God within himself carried his own heaven about with him. One had only to recognize one's own divinity and one was resurrected as a Spiritual, a denizen of heaven and earth.[17]

Sexual pleasure was pursued by the Free Spirit without regulations. Since they recognized no other authority "save their own experiences,"[18] they would not accept sexual restrictions. Although Cohn minimizes the free sexuality by emphasizing its "symbolic" value,[19] I think an opposite interpretation is feasible; the spiritual emancipation was a strategy for being able to enjoy pleasure without guilt. The Free Spirit were also pantheistic, saying that "Every created thing is divine."[20]

There are parallels between the Free Spirit and Shelley, who denied the transcendental existence of a God outside of and superior to man. Shelley also felt that heaven was something man himself could create on earth. And Shelley, like the Free Spirit, rejected authority constituted outside the subjective experience of the individual. In *Prometheus Unbound* sexual pleasure is celebrated as a triumph of liberated humanity, and pleasure itself, not ascetic purity, is the ruling idea of the poem. Although I do not want to press the similarities any further, because there is no evidence that Shelley knew about the Free Spirit, I want to emphasize nevertheless that both are fundamentally *atypical*. Anarchistic, libertarian, pleasure-oriented, not eager to dominate and control, Shelley's *Prometheus Unbound* avoids the unsavory aspects of both utopia and paradise in their traditional forms. Although the sexuality in Shelley's poem is adult, many of the soft qualities of maternal paradise are preserved. Despite the unequivocal statements on politics, economics, and social relations, Shelley's utopia does not have a ruling class, a philosopher-king who makes sure everyone is "free."

Inasmuch as *Prometheus Unbound* deals with paradise, it lacks the qualities which A. Bartlett Giamatti criticizes in the paradise tradition. He concludes that modern sensibilities are not attracted by the idea of paradise as people were before the Renaissance.[21] He cites Lionel Trilling's displeasure with the idea of paradise as an example confirming its obsolescence. Trilling's modern man is glad to be out of that dreadful and boring place, Eden. But the modern attitude, according to Giamatti, owes its distrust of paradise to the Renaissance epics which criticized it as false and deceptive. Tasso, Spenser, Ariosto, and Milton (authors, incidentally, whom Shelley knew well) all found fault with paradise on grounds that seem modern. In these epics, Giamatti continues,

> "peace" and "bliss" were found to be empty desires, unobtainable ends; it was precisely in the gardens of those massive works that the two words first revealed their elusiveness. It was the very knights seeking ease and pleasure who . . . in fact succumbed to a "state of virtually infantile passivity" as they lay motionless in the arms of the dominating female figure in the gardens. And it was this condition of soul, with its sterility and narcissism, which was so often the very "negation of the 'more life' " which those knights craved.[22]

The Giamatti-Trilling rejection of paradise is more absolute than Shelley's however. Shelley preserves a certain kind of narcissism, and although he rejects an infantile passivity, he just as firmly rejects a Faustian restlessness. Shelley does not, in *Prometheus Unbound*, dismiss ease and pleasure as illusory goals; however, he locates their realization, not in the static garden, but in the processes of play and lovemaking. He finds the potential for the "more life" the Renaissance knights were seeking in nature and man, not God. Herein lies the uniqueness of Shelley's achievement.

There have been useful suggestions as to what the characters in the poetic drama "represent," and it is inescapable as a reader not to ponder certain possibilities. The situation which the poem ad-

dresses is that critical moment when humanity abolishes the tyran-
nical *principle*—not just particular tyrannies, but tyranny alto-
gether. The poem investigates the preconditions and consequences
of this abolition. What must humanity do, think, feel, and imagine,
before it can free itself from hierarchy and domination in all their
guises? *Prometheus Unbound* argues for utopian hope by showing
that utopia is indeed possible; it illustrates a revolutionary process
in its ideal form; and it provides an experience by which the reader
can participate in this process. Thus it is an anarchist poem in that
it depicts a successful social anarchy, delineates an ideal objective
process for anarchist transformation, and puts the reader through
a process of discovery by which one can recognize an inner au-
thoritarianism that can be overcome.[23]

That Prometheus is the one who elevated Jupiter into a position
of power is an important assumption of Act I. Jupiter was created
by Prometheus at the moment the human soul divided itself, in-
stalling a powerful deity in heaven to worship and fear, but main-
taining hope in the eventual downfall of the tyrant. Prometheus
"bound" himself once he had alienated a part of himself as Jupiter,
who then imprisoned the liberator of humanity for uttering the
curse. The curse, however, is a self-fulfilling prophecy, so that what-
ever evils Prometheus "dares" Jupiter to inflict are in fact realized.[24]
From the perspective of "Earth" and others, the events do not
appear as they actually are. When Prometheus recalls his curse in
order to repudiate it, they interpret his moral transformation as a
surrender to Jupiter. According to Earth, first there was evil, and
then came Prometheus the savior (I, 157-62), but this version of
history is not accurate. Prometheus says to Jupiter in his curse that
he gave to the tyrant power over "all things but thyself . . . And
my own will" (I, 273-74). To Mercury, he makes the identical claim
for having installed Jupiter in power (I, 381-82). In Act II, Asia
within Demogorgon's realm relates the following: "Then Prome-
theus / Gave wisdom, which is strength, to Jupiter / And with this
law alone: 'Let man be free,' / Clothed him with the dominion of
wide Heaven" (II, iv, 43-46). If the evidence is clear that Prometheus
created Jupiter's tyranny, then how is it possible for Earth to so
misinterpret events? The primal division of the human soul into
tyrant and rebel is so archaic that the subsequent conflict has oc-
cluded its origins. Since for 3,000 years Prometheus has been bound
and tortured by Jupiter, the only sequence of events that seems

possible is that which Earth formulates: first came evil, then the rebel emerged to fight against it.

Why did Prometheus create Jupiter in the first place? The passage which best answers this question is Act II, scene iv, lines 32-125. I shall give a fairly speculative reading of the passage, and then take a more literal examination of the lines.

Shelley's evolutionary sequence occurs within two temporal realms, one historical and the other psychological. After a period of primitive communism (or childhood), there emerges a society capable of progressive advancement and self-determination (or responsible adulthood). Precisely at this point the human soul experiences alienation, fragmenting into several parts, one of which is an authoritarian deity over and above experience. Early civilization (and the adult) creates a powerful deity and lives by other hierarchical principles for a number of compelling reasons. Under conditions of scarcity society must wrest from a hostile nature an extremely difficult living, even under the most favorable circumstances. In order to dominate nature and transform it, there must be repression and delayed gratification. Between what is and what could be there is a wide gap filled by dream, hope, and a desire for a more fulfilling existence. The struggle for existence consumes most human energy, but some is left over to imagine what life could be under conditions of leisure.

The violence done to nature in the name of science and technology is necessary, but the price humanity pays for dominating nature is a high one, because people are parts of nature. Moreover, scarcity puts an enormous stress on the moral capacities, making ideals like liberty, equality, peace, and love difficult to practice. In a life dominated by misery, hard labor, little leisure, disease, and uncertainty, there is a logic in accepting otherworldly compensations. A supernatural heaven with a powerful but merciful dictator makes sense to someone whose everyday life is too impoverished to include a sphere of self-determined activity. In a situation where equality means universal poverty, scarcity provides an incentive to wage war and to engage in other conflicts, because the potential reward is an increase in one's own wealth and leisure.

Shelley believed, perhaps mistakenly, that the preconditions for complete human freedom existed in nineteenth-century Europe, so he concentrated his efforts on the *conditions* of freedom, mediating between the realm of anarchist ideals and authoritarian society. Although he felt that his own society was sufficiently developed for utopia, he did not think earlier societies had reached such an advanced stage. Shelley believed freedom had preconditions. For example, remarking on Tasso's madness around the time he was writing *Prometheus Unbound*, Shelley said that Tasso prayed to and feared an unjust tyrant because at that time it was impossbile to hope for anything else; hope, in that era, had to take a superstitious form or it could not exist.[25] Shelley, like Godwin, was aware of the revolutionary role of the printing press in greatly expanding the realm of philosophy. Hellenic culture, which Shelley loved more than any other, was marred, he realized, by slavery and the degradation of women.

One important factor in the origin of the divided soul is scarcity which, after 3,000 years, Shelley feels has been sufficiently overcome to permit human reunification within utopia. If nature is already tamed enough to permit extensive leisure and material security, if enough scientific knowledge has been accumulated to conquer scarcity, if, in short, repression and self-torture are no longer *rationally* necessary—then indeed the hour of liberation has arrived. This hour, however, could not have come sooner because the utopian preconditions did not exist.

I want now to take a more literal examination of Asia's speech. Asia asks Demogorgon a series of questions until she launches into an independent line of speculation on the question "Who reigns?" It is while answering this question that she gives a picture of human evolution (II, iv, 32-124). At first there is an elemental harmony, when the first society is overseen by Saturn, "from whose throne / Time fell, an envious shadow" (33-34). Saturn's reign was benign except that he prohibited freedom and knowledge. Edenic innocence is ignorance, blind obedience, and trust, a condition which corresponds to the Golden Age historically and childhood psychologically. The things Saturn refused to grant inspired discontent because people wanted

> knowledge, power
> The skill which wields the elements, the thought
> Which pierces the dim Universe like light,
> Self-empire and the majesty of love,
> For thirst of which they fainted.
> (39-43)

As a benevolent dictator, Saturn is similar to Milton's God who also oversees an Eden with certain limits on knowledge. The Saturnian age is unsatisfactory not for material but for psychological reasons.

At this point Prometheus enters. "Then Prometheus / Gave wisdom, which is strength, to Jupiter / And with this law alone: 'let man be free,' / Clothed him with the dominion of wide Heaven." His installing Jupiter in power is analogous to Milton's God creating Adam and Eve, but the irony is that Jupiter and Prometheus are both similar to Jehovah: Jupiter, by exercising his arbitrary power; Prometheus, by granting the power in the first place. The moment of freedom coincides with scarcity and the alienation of soul; the three follow so quickly in succession, it is hard to know which is prior to which: "And Jove now reigned; for on the race of man / First famine and then toil and then disease, / Strife, wounds, and ghastly death unseen before, / Fell" (49-52). The grammar suggests we know Jove reigned, "for" (i.e., because) famine "fell." Which came first, the famine or the deity? Whichever it was, the condition of freedom within scarcity is a "fall," poetically emphasized by the heavily enjambed "Fell" on line 52. Perhaps "Jupiter" was a necessary fiction for Prometheus, whose allegiance to "freedom" has entailed so much misery. Jupiter would take the blame for the sufferings actually caused by Prometheus's commitment to conquer nature and ignorance. The struggle for existence, then, has two different deities, one representing all the painful reality of labor and disease, the other standing for the promise of eventual deliverance. Moreover, the Saturnian age could be a myth Promethean man invents to make his painful life seem to be a noble form of rebellion rather than the consequence of necessity.

After the miseries of a scarcity-haunted existence, people are ready for the Promethean solace. "Prometheus saw, and waked the legioned hopes / . . . That they might hide . . . The shape of Death; and Love he sent to bind / The disunited tendrils of that vine / Which bears the wine of life, the human heart" (60-65). The misery created by Jupiter and the hope generated by Prometheus depend on each other; one without the other makes no sense. Indeed, the division of soul into Prometheus and Jupiter seems rational, considering the struggle for existence. But however rational the division in terms of the *telos* of an emancipated humanity, it is intolerable at the existential level without hope.

After hope and love, Prometheus gave to humanity a fire which "tortured to his will / Iron and gold, the slaves and signs of power, / And gems and poisons, and all subtlest forms / Hidden

159

beneath the mountains and the waves" (68-71). Had Shelley said only iron and emphasized only technology, then the reader would have had a much less ambiguous "fire" to interpret. As it is, this fire is as Jupiterian as it is Promethean. If any one word in Shelley's works has a consistently negative set of connotations, it is "gold," the symbol of Mammon, selfishness, and greed. How can science exercise power and create slaves without also, at the same time, reproducing political structures equally hierarchical? How can the search for scientific truth be disentangled from the search for particular power? This Promethean fire, which Shelley calls "Most terrible, but lovely" (67), is quite different from the erotic, creative "fire" he kindles in Acts I and II. The significance of Prometheus's conversion is particularly dramatic after reading lines like these because one realizes that Prometheus's liberating role had been for ages linked with domination, even though it was a tyranny exercised in the name of humanity's best interests. The process of "torturing to his will" the various useful elements is a violent act equivalent to Jupiter's torture of Prometheus. The gold symbolism proves that technological science is both Promethean and Jupiterian.

If wealth and science are morally ambiguous, other Promethean alleviations are less so: speech, thought, prophetic song, music, sculpture, medicine, astronomy, navigation, and cities. All are examples of self-determining power employed in an emancipatory way. Once Prometheus is unbound, he finds with Asia a home within a cave, where the reunited soul symbolizes boundless aesthetic power, forever making new forms of the beautiful. In the historical realm haunted by scarcity, however, creativity must divert a substantial portion of its energy to the useful, not only the beautiful: medicine, astronomy, navigation, and city-building are practical activities that have aesthetic components. The double nature of creativity is portrayed as power and beauty. Power: "And Science struck the thrones of Earth and Heaven / Which shook but fell not" (74-75). Beauty: "and the harmonious mind / Poured itself forth in all-prophetic song, / And music lifted up the listening spirit . . ." (75-77). The utopian impulse of art is suggested by some of the images. Music, for example, is depicted as walking "exempt from mortal care, / Godlike, o'er the clear billows of sweet sound" (78-79). Art yearns for a condition of complete self-determination, a state of autonomy within which it can enjoy complete freedom, including the freedom from what is "mortal" (scarcity, uncertainty, pain). Even as Promethean creativity tries to conquer the world of ignorance and scarcity—to lay the foundations of freedom's pre-conditions—it is also imaging forth the actual conditions of freedom.

After the long list of Promethean "alleviations," Asia has left human evolution in an advanced state, where the hostility of nature seems to be under control. Disease has been mastered, and death "grew like sleep" (86). The last image of nature that Asia leaves us is of the natural world turned into an object of aesthetic appreciation, complementing the human city: "Cities then / Were built, and through their snowlike columns flowed / The warm winds, and the azure aether shone, / And the blue sea and shadowy hills were seen . . ." (94-97). Despite such triumphs, an "immedicable plague" afflicts humanity, "The wreck of his own will, the scorn of Earth, / The outcast, the abandoned, the alone" (104-105). Although scientific technology has mastered nature, it has also divided humanity into estranged fragments which cannot reunite harmoniously. The psychological structures appropriate for bringing nature under control still remain after nature has been subdued.

Asia then realizes that "Jupiter" is not the "master" of domination itself. Indeed, as Demogorgon says, "All spirits are enslaved who serve things evil" (110). Even the tyrant is not free, because he must act as his hierarchical role demands; as a fragmented human power, he is not "free," but a slave to the necessity that inheres in structures of domination. When Asia asks, "Who is the master of the slave?" (114), Demogorgon answers indirectly, by saying everything is enslaved except "eternal Love." Only in the condition of love—free, unrestricted, unprivileged reciprocity—can the self enjoy freedom. Only if the self is whole, undivided, and harmonious can it freely love and play in a relationship which does not entail power and submission. With Roland Duerksen I agree that Demogorgon's statement, "the deep truth is imageless" (117), refers not to epistemological skepticism, but to love; that is, the deep truth which can overcome the master-slave relationship is love, which has no prescriptive language, no images.[26] Asia's counterpoint to the "deep truth" is her saying, "of such truths" (concerning ultimate reality), "Each to itself must be the oracle" (123-24). There is no ontological principle of domination in the universe, like an eternal Jupiter, nor is there a corresponding principle of love. Rather, these structures are products of human creativity, so that the self can create a Jupiter or a relationship of love. Only the individual can liberate itself from oppression, because oppression is a human construct, not something

161

existing eternally. As soon as the self withdraws the energy of Promethean hatred which sustains Jupiter, and as soon as Asia recognizes that Jupiter rules by means of human will, then the preconditions exist to permit the reunion of Prometheus and Asia and Jupiter's demise.

When Asia finally realizes that only the individual can liberate itself, she answers her own question: "Prometheus shall arise / Henceforth the Sun of this rejoicing world" (127). When will the "hour" arrive, she asks? Demogorgon then reveals the first signs of Promethean deliverance. Although Prometheus and Asia can create the preconditions of liberation, they cannot automatically produce liberation, because Jupiter, once created, is subject to the mortal processes of necessity. A tyrant, established in power, has to self-destruct. To hate and plot revenge against a tyrant is to keep breathing life into the tyrannical relationship. With the retraction of the curse, Prometheus has stopped giving life to Jupiter, thus allowing him to perish by means of his own inner contradictions. At a certain point these contradictions engender the tyrant's destruction, carried out by "necessity"—that is, Demogorgon.

Although Prometheus is a fragment, detached from the power he gave to Jupiter and separated from Asia's love, he is able to initiate a process which will lead eventually to his liberation. His first action is to cease hating and start pitying Jupiter. He welcomes, he says, the passage of each day, because each day brings the "hour" closer. The pivotal hour

> As some dark Priest hales the reluctant victim—
> Shall drag thee, cruel King, to kiss the blood
> From these pale feet, which then might trample thee
> If they disdained not such a prostrate slave.
> Disdain? Ah no! I pity thee.
> (I, 49-53)

Promethean hope had been based on hatred and revenge, knowing that Jupiter's reign was finite. Suddenly, however, Prometheus realizes that if Jupiter falls by means of Promethean hatred, then they will simply exchange roles. The sadistic image Prometheus evokes reproduces the torture Jupiter has always inflicted. To trample and enslave Jupiter is to resurrect tyranny in a new form, perpetuating the long history of hierarchical domination from the time of Saturn. What startles Prometheus out of his hatred is imaginative sympathy, putting himself in the place of Jupiter and identifying with his fate.

By imagining the future pain Jupiter will experience Prometheus frees himself from his hatred.

Hating tyrants has, up to now, sustained the hope of overcoming tyranny; without question such hatred is preferable to the submission practiced by Mercury, Jupiter's agent. Although hatred has been necessary for these many years, it has not been enough to extirpate tyranny itself. To break out of the cycle of hate, Prometheus has to perform a heroic deed of the imagination. From hate to pity is a movement away from privilege and certainty, because one is no longer in the role of totally innocent victim. As innocent victim, one can justify any act of retribution against the tyrant, who is defined solely by his tyrannical behavior. When hate turns into retributive action, however justifiable in ordinary terms, the victim turns victimizer, replacing the tyrant at the top of a hierarchy. Indeed, such an action is dramatically explored in *The Cenci*. Shelley wants to imagine a language and mode of perception capable of leading to the abolition of oppression itself.

No longer hating Jupiter, Prometheus wants to recall his curse because he no longer identifies with those words; he cannot even remember them. Needing assistance, he turns to Earth in order to bring back his own words. Earth is reluctant to resurrect the curse because she is afraid of what Jupiter might do. The spirits of nature "dare not" recall the curse which, for hopeful mortals, has been "a treasured spell. We meditate / In secret joy and hope those dreadful words / But dare not speak them" (I, 184-86). Perhaps Earth's cryptic utterance concerning Prometheus's incapacity to understand the language of "those who die" is a procrastination, a tactic to delay having to resurrect a curse which she feels will bring about Jupiter's retribution. It is ironic that the curse, marking the birth of the divided soul, is a sacred text too awe-inspiring to speak aloud. However useful the curse has been in sustaining hope, it has also perpetuated an idolatry of words and hierarchical reliance on an external deliverer. Negative connotations which cannot be ignored cling to certain words in Earth's speech: "Spell," "secret," "dreadful," and "dare not." This is the language of religious subjugation.

When Earth finally agrees to grant Prometheus's wish, she develops an interesting emblem of the divided soul: the two worlds of life and death. As she develops them, the two worlds are clearly the phenomenal world and the world of potentiality, where there exist "Dreams and the light imaginings of men / And all that faith creates, or love desires, / Terrible, strange, sublime and beauteous shapes" (200-202).[27] At death, one is reunited with one's other half, the phenomenal self collapsing into the unconscious self. Beings living in death-in-life are estranged from their deepest, most intense passions, which have only a shadowy, subterranean existence. Repressed, the ghosts of desire haunt a world of potentiality that has been excluded from the phenomenal world. One reason for having a ghost—the ghost of Jupiter—speak the curse is to prevent the speaker from being punished. Another, as critics have mentioned, is dramatic irony: to force Prometheus to recognize the "Jupiterian" aspects of the Promethean curse. And still another is to begin the process of uniting the two worlds of phenomenal and potential reality, because utopia is where the two worlds exist indistinguishably.

The curse, performed and enacted by the ghost, forces Prometheus into a moment of traumatic recognition, as he disowns his words. A self-fulfilling prophecy, the curse initiated the soul-division Prometheus is now trying to heal. He remembers his words in order to forget them, letting them die in the past so that they will no longer determine the present. He recalls in order to cancel and obliterate, to wipe the slate clean. "I wish no living thing to suffer pain" (I, 305) is the counterpoint to the curse. These are words that do not generate power and hierarchy because they are mostly negative, suggesting a creative void. The curse divides the soul and world into warring factions, but the anticurse is an unprivileged statement, a gift freely given to every living being, a symbolic and gratuitous action that is exemplary rather than definitive. The anticurse is not a "treasured spell" whose awe-inspiring content is too dreadful to speak; rather, it invites repetition and points to a change in feeling, a subjective restructuring that withdraws energy from the Jupiterian world.

Shelley was aware of the radical departure from the traditionally rebellious modes. After Prometheus announces his anticurse, Earth, Ione, and Panthea are anxious, thinking Prometheus has finally surrendered to Jupiter. If the only two alternatives are hate and submission, and if the anticurse contains no hatred, then it seems Prometheus has given up the struggle. To clarify the nature of Promethean resistance Shelley depicted the scene with Mercury, who offers a deal: in exchange for the "secret" Jupiter thinks Prometheus possesses, Jupiter will not only liberate Prometheus but will provide him with every imaginable sensual pleasure. What Prometheus must do in exchange is to subjugate his "will," something Mercury himself has done. The irony is that there is no secret Prometheus owns, because all he knows is that Jupiter's reign must end, that there is nothing Jupiter can do to save himself. (At an allegorical level the Mercury-Prometheus dialogue suggests something Kenneth Cameron has noticed, namely, the controversy among the liberal and conservative poet-intellectuals.)[28] Prometheus can reject Mercury's temptation because he knows that Jupiter will fall. Justice, when it comes, will not be a Jacobin terror: "For Justice when triumphant will weep down / Pity not punishment on her own wrongs, / Too much avenged by those who err" (I, 403-405). Echoing Book VII of *Political Justice*, Prometheus rejects the legal procedures of punishment, none of which, as Godwin illustrated, can change society in a lasting, salutary way. Only the greater, more expansive activity of reason can extend the realm of justice, according to Godwin. Will is important for rejecting the "necessity" of submission, for hoping, and for creating and imagining.

Surviving one temptation, Prometheus faces another, the temptation of despair. Perhaps, like Byron, Prometheus could reject Jupiter but remain convinced that the universe, however unjust, is nevertheless immutably fixed in its perverse arrangement. Shelley learned from Byron that defiance without hope was possible. The Furies present Prometheus with discouraging images of human incapacity, and evocations of historical efforts at libertarian reform that turned into tyrannical catastrophes. The Third Fury points to the propensity of self-torture, the "dread thought" and "foul desire" that vex "the self-content of wisest men" (I, 487-89). At this point, Prometheus's greatest fears concern the pain that humans inflict on themselves, not the enemies that threaten them from without. Prometheus cannot deny the potential for self-torture, but he says, "Yet am I king over myself, and rule / The torturing and conflicting throngs within / As Jove rules you when Hell grows mutinous" (I, 492-94). These lines point ahead to III, iv, 196, where the Spirit of the Hour speaks of liberated man as King over himself, ruling chance, death, and mutability as slaves. Prometheus rules over his self-torturing passions, whereas liberated man is not yet exempt from, even though he rules over, aspects of reality that cannot be dominated. Doubt and guilt, in the Spirit of the Hour's speech, are conquered by liberated humanity, but they are controlled by Prometheus. One has to infer a progressive development here, from ruling the self-torturing passions to conquering them.[29]

Although Prometheus endures the torture of the Furies, he nevertheless agonizes over the pictures of human folly: the self-hatred of the sense-enchanted youth; war; famine; the desire for knowledge exceeding the capacity to learn; Christ's liberating words turning into the poison of institutionalized religion; the failure of the French Revolution. All these, as well as other instances of cruelty and malice, torture Prometheus. Panthea remarks on Prometheus's torturing vision, saying that he sees "human death . . . wrought by human hands, / And some appeared the work of human hearts, / For men were slowly killed by frowns and smiles" (587-90). However terrible, all are *human* constructs, products of the will, not determinations of an external "Jupiter" who forces evil activity to take place. The liberating implication of the tortures is that if humanity created this tortured world, then it can un-create it. Indeed, perhaps all that Jupiter consists of is this "miscreative" principle that turns the human soul against itself.

The final torture (I, 618-31) is a portrait of the modern intellectual who cannot act, think, or feel beyond conventional parameters. The moral world is in fragments:

> The good want power, but to weep barren tears.
> The powerful goodness want: worse need for them.
> The wise want love, and those who love want wisdom;
> And all best things are thus confused to ill.

Good human qualities exist, but not in such a way as to generate a harmonious society. Pity once again delivers Prometheus from despair: "I pity those" who are not tortured by the malaise of human incapacity. Rather than define human evolution as finally fixed at a certain point, Prometheus continues to imagine the possibility of further growth by extending a gesture of sympathy to those more narrow than himself. After the last Fury vanishes, Prometheus contemplates death, the only thing that can bring a certain kind of "peace" (I, 634-45). Although Death can end the painful activity of idealistic hope, it also "hides all things beautiful and good." Death is "defeat," not "victory"—an escape, not a realization. Even if Prometheus could, he would not seek death.

Having survived Mercury and the Furies, Prometheus is offered the comforting spirits from the human mind. One of his final actions is to recognize in the historical world those utopian tendencies to sustain hope. The chorus of spirits assures him that someday human creativity can achieve complete self-determination. Each comforting image presents the mind with human agency overcoming determinate factors: the revolutionaries against the tyrant's party; the benevolent sailor; the disinterested sage; the idealistic poet; the forces of love and hope against despair and disappointment. If and when human agency reaches a point of self-determination, then Prometheus will be delivered.

The last words of Prometheus point to Asia and his desire for reunion. At this point it is necessary for him to withdraw fully from the phenomenal world in order to set the world of potentiality in motion.[30] He accomplishes this by desiring Asia, and inspiring Panthea's dream, which she relates in Act II. Prometheus's final deed is to desire so intensely that he provokes a dream of desire in Panthea, who then reenacts the dream for Asia. It is the subterranean, ghostly, unconscious world of dream and desire that must now perform the work of liberation.

ACT II

According to Frederick Pottle, Asia has her own heroic action to perform: she must descend into Demogorgon's realm and achieve self-knowledge.[31] Allegorically, wisdom (Prometheus) must learn to love, while love (Asia) must acquire wisdom; only thus can the moral chaos of fragmented humanity be reordered and overcome. Although Asia does indeed achieve wisdom in Demogorgon's cave, as I have already shown, her movement toward Demogorgon prefigures a utopian logic quite distinct from the movement of Act I. Will is a quality that Prometheus exhibits strongly in the first act, but relaxation of the will characterizes the second act. Asia and Panthea weaken their control over their perceptions, and are consequently sensitive to the voices of dream and desire. They descend into Demogorgon's volcano as if they are retracing their steps, unconsciously remembering an archaic path they once traveled but no longer recognize. The wisdom of self-determination that Asia acquires in the cave is a Platonic reminiscence, because she had to know, at one time, that love could replace Jupiter as an organizing principle; otherwise, it is difficult to see how she could have arrived at her conclusions. Allegorically, Asia is returning to the beginning of all things, the source, in order to remember an original state prior to the separation from Prometheus. She listens to the language of desire which leads her to Demogorgon's realm.

Act II depicts a faith in nature's benevolence, at the heart of which is an erotic exuberance that bursts and overflows boundaries.

This transfiguring love drives out winter and turns a barren valley into a lush one. It creates dreams, new desires, wordless feelings; fully unveiled, it is a blinding incandescence that annihilates lover and beloved in a fiery communion, but only so that reborn, they can burn again. The erotic dream Panthea remembers for Asia (II, i, 62ff.) suggests a new, exemplary pattern, another version of the Promethean ideal. In the dream, Prometheus undergoes a fiery transfiguration which induces Panthea to experience an orgasmic ecstasy. The trope used to conclude the lovemaking is the familiar water-cycle imagery (II, i, 83ff.), thus emphasizing the cyclic mode of being now typically Promethean. Ione, too, is affected by the "new" Prometheus, because she awakens, telling Panthea "I always knew what I desired before / Nor ever found delight to wish in vain. / But now I cannot tell thee what I seek" (95-97). A desire without a name is what Prometheus has created in others. This desire has to be explored, discovered, and created by beings liberated from the old, phenomenal world and fully engaged with the world of potentiality. Although Prometheus himself does not appear in the second act, his actions certainly do.

Near the opening of Demogorgon's cave Asia and Panthea pause. At the border between the phenomenal and potential worlds, Panthea likens the spot to a volcano whose "oracular vapour" is a maddening inspiration. If one follows the suggestion of G. M. Matthews, then Demogorgon's mountain itself is a volcano where the Oceanides, Panthea and Asia, enter and are transformed by the volcanic fire.[32] Moreover, the "vapour" has been maddening up to now only because the powerful life-force has been repressed. Allowed to function naturally, without restraint, nature's energy becomes a utopian element of liberation. This third scene of Act II also presents an interesting contrast with "Mont Blanc." Whereas in "Mont Blanc" the perspective is from the ground looking up, here Asia and Panthea are at the summit of the volcanic mountain, looking down, about to descend into Demogorgon's realm. The mountain peaks in the earlier poem represent the remoteness and amoral necessity of nature, but nature here is intimate and reassuring. Viewing the beautiful scene around her, Asia says she could "fall down and worship" nature (II, iii, 16). Before passing "through" phenomenal nature, they realize nature's beauty. By going to the Source of all things, they do not elevate the Source at the expense of things, but almost like the Free Spirit pantheists, they marvel at the divinity of nature. The scene Asia describes (II, iii, 19-42) is fluxional, in movement, a process, like "The Cloud." But this kind of mutability does not make Asia think of death, so dominant in "Mont Blanc." The vitality of nature, rather, is appreciated for its own sake. Even the violence of nature, which is so frightening in "Mont Blanc," becomes symbolic of human liberation.

> The vale is girdled with their walls—a howl
> Of cataracts from their thaw-cloven ravines
> Satiates the listening wind, continuous, vast,
> Awful as silence.—Hark! the rushing snow!
> The sun-awakened avalanche! whose mass,
> Thrice sifted by the storm, had gathered there
> Flake after flake, in Heaven-defying minds
> As thought by thought is piled, till some great truth
> Is loosened, and the nations echo round
> Shaken to their roots: as do the mountains now.
> (II, iii, 33-42)

In a deliberate confusion of tenor and vehicle, avalanche and social revolution seem to be one process, not two. The power of nature is now a useful force in human liberation, not something apart. The sun, again, is a libertarian force working in conjunction with Promethean consciousness, the heaven-defying minds.

As if to clarify the relationship between nature and consciousness, Spirits arise from the natural scene Asia and Panthea had been viewing and beckon them to penetrate phenomenal nature,

> To the Deep, to the Deep,
>   Down, down!
> Through the shade of Sleep,
> Through the cloudy strife
> Of death and of Life . . .
> (II, iii, 54-58)

In the printed version, the Spirits' song concludes scene iii, but in the draft manuscript, there is a fragment that probably followed the Spirits' song. Asia was to have said:

> The living frame which sustains my soul
> Is sinking beneath the fierce controul
> Down through the lampless deep of song
> I am drawn and driven along.[33]

169

This is an obvious anticipation of Act II, scene v, and it articulates a major theme of scene iii as well: control of self passes from the ego to more emotional powers. Asia and Panthea are *led* to the mountain top by listening to nature, by being responsive to their unconscious dreams. They get to a point at which it is necessary to go even further into the self, deeper down into the unconscious, closer to the Source of all things. The model for an experience like theirs is sexual intercourse; in lovemaking there is a responsiveness to the other within an atmosphere of trust, where the ego is sacrificed for the sake of pleasure.

The second act ends with a series of lyrics that carry to a conclusion the psychological process of descent and remembering. The duet between the Voice (probably of Prometheus)[34] and Asia occurs after she has gained "knowledge" in Demogorgon's cave. As in Panthea's account of Prometheus's transfiguration in her dream, the Voice's description of Asia's transfiguration presents an image of erotic fire which achieves a blinding incandescence. The Voice approaches loss of consciousness, entangled in the mazes of Asia's beauty. The Voice's tribute to Asia's power does not have the suggestion of enslavement, because the ego's dissolution is joyful and a phase in the cycle of love. The Voice loses himself in Asia's beauty in order to find himself; he "fails" in an orgasm of delight because he knows he will be reborn in her beauty.

The key image in the Voice's song is entanglement in the mazes of Asia's smiles. The principal strategy for foiling death and mutability is to create a web of beauty so intricate, and circles of love so expanding and profuse, that the self has, literally, no time to notice death and mutability. If death and mutability are not perceived, then according to Shelley's idealism, they do not exist. The eternity achieved by love is virtual eternity. In a note to *Queen Mab*, Shelley writes: "If, therefore, the human mind, by any future improvement of its sensibility, should become conscious of an infinite number of ideas in a minute, that minute would be eternity."[35] Virtual or not, the eternity Shelley proposes is so ambitious that he hopes we will forget our mortality when we listen to the beauty of his songs.

In Asia's song (II, v, 72-110), a mixed and extended metaphor links together the water cycle, music, sleep, and paradise. One does, indeed, get entangled in the mazes of the song, which turns in upon itself, then expands, only to return to where it started. The soul is a boat which, in turn, is likened to a sleeping swan. The verb, "doth float," applies equally to "soul," "boat," and "swan." The soul-boat-swan floats upon the "waves of thy sweet singing." The implied metaphor equates music with water. By the third line of Asia's song, tenor and vehicle are so thoroughly interwoven as to be interchangeable. The Voice's music is both the water on which the boat sails and the pilot directing the boat. The winding river emptying finally into the sea is a favorite image for the water cycle, a symbol for the mystery of the One and the Many. The prominence of the water cycle is also appropriate because Asia is one of the Oceanides and is identified with Aphrodite, who was born in the sea. Indeed, as Asia floats down to the sea on her song, she does achieve a rebirth, a "diviner day." The river winds between mountains and woods, creating a paradise of wildernesses. Wilderness is a paradise because it has no history, no past. The music that discovers the wildernesses creates them anew, as if they had never existed before. Since history no longer exists, the utopian concept of eternity can emerge as the imagination achieving full autonomy, and as fundamental perceptions no longer distorted by external determinations.

Asia's boat is borne to the ocean "like one in slumber bound," passing from the conscious to the unconscious, the willed to the unwilled. She floats "down, around, / Into a Sea profound, of ever-spreading sound." The image is one of descent and diffusion, as Asia continues her journey downwards, even after her dialogue with Demogorgon. She gives herself to the music, and allows it to carry her on a journey, going from multiplicity to unity, from river to ocean, from wakefulness to sleep. She loses herself in the music in order to find herself reborn, and sleeps in order to dream herself back to where she can awaken in a "diviner day." Lines 98 through 103, influenced no doubt by Plato or Neoplatonism,[36] also have a less esoteric meaning. The going backwards from Age to Infancy, through Death and Birth, is consonant with Asia's actions throughout the poem. She descends downwards and backwards, to the Source, retracing her existence and remembering what she has forgotten. In the first instance, she followed the dictates of Demogorgon's mighty law of natural love. In this instance, she descends further into herself and the Source of all things by following the beauty of music. The journey into the self is not complete unless it goes deeper than where nature alone can lead one.

In the first stanza, Asia's "I" sang to "thee," but in the second stanza, the "thou" has been subsumed into "we." Furthermore, they sail "Without a course—without a star— / But by the instinct of sweet Music driven." With the end of history, there are no longer any goals to strive for. They have nowhere to go because every place is equally blessed. That being so, they give up control of their egos to music. The prominence of music suggests that the aim of poetry is to become song. In Act IV, Earth says: "Language is a perpetual Orphic song, / Which rules with Daedal harmony a throng / Of thoughts and forms, which else senseless and shapeless were" (IV, 415-17). Because man has finally resolved his contradictions, he is able to make harmonious song, the only mode of speech appropriate to utopian conditions.

As they reach the end of their journey, they meet with images of hypostasis that characterize paradise: vaulted flowers, downward-gazing flowers, and watery paths. Critics like Giamatti and Trilling have found in paradise qualities of static permanence that leave one with feelings not of repose, but of claustrophobia. Shelley avoids this pitfall in the last three lines, where the "shapes" that inhabit paradise begin to "chaunt melodiously," thus commencing a whole new cycle of song and journey. The vaulted bowers and Narcissi are appropriate because they, too, are cyclic. The womblike bowers suggest an endless profusion of beauty and boundless fertility. Narcissus represents the cyclic nature of love, not solipsism, because Narcissus sees himself *in* the world; he perceives that intimate connection between subject and object that characterizes the fundamental unity that permeates the universe.

One almost forgets that Asia's entire song is a fabric of metaphors. As metaphor generates metaphor, and image gives birth to image, the poetry carries one deeper into an entangling beauty. Her song is fundamentally cyclical because its conclusion suggests another beginning. In utopia there is nowhere one needs to go, so one can go anywhere. The most compelling emblem for utopian song is the circle, which is the image Shelley uses to describe sympathetic love in *A Defence of Poetry*. As the circumference of love, beauty, and imagination expands, so expand the boundaries of utopia, and so contracts the territory of history. Utopian song takes place within a circle, and it also turns in upon itself in circles.

ACT III

The dramatic climax of this act is not Jupiter's downfall or the unbinding of Prometheus, but the Spirit of the Hour's speech announcing the liberation of humanity (III, iv, 131-204). Before examining these lines, one must look first at the Spirit of the Hour as a character. She first appears in Act II, scene iv, after Asia has interrogated Demogorgon. Actually, there are two "Spirits" of the Hour. One is a masculine "Ghastly charioteer" (144), who takes Demogorgon to Jupiter to remove him from power. Asia describes this grim Spirit thus: "A Spirit with a dreadful countenance / Checks its dark chariot by the craggy gulph" (142-43). Responding to Asia, he says,

> I am the shadow of a destiny
> More dread than is mine aspect—ere yon planet
> Has set, the Darkness which ascends with me
> Shall wrap in lasting night Heaven's kingless throne.
> (146-49)

This Spirit seems to be an allegorical representation of the revolutionary force necessary to "dethrone" the Jupiter-principle from society and consciousness; the Spirit is a power strong enough to keep Jupiter wrapped in everlasting night. Demogorgon must ride with this pre-utopian Spirit, while the other Spirit of the Hour, a very different creature, awaits Asia and Panthea. This Spirit of the Hour's chariot has "An ivory shell inlaid with crimson fire," while "the young Spirit / That guides it, has the dovelike eyes of hope!" (157, 159-60). The new Spirit, so unlike the previous one, is part of utopia. So swift is the Spirit's chariot that it can transport them around the earth and moon before "the cloud piled on Atlas can dwindle" (171). Each stanza ends with the refrain: "Then ascend with me, daughter of Ocean." Aphrodite being born in the sea is an image, evoked in line 157, which is reinforced by Asia's name—a daughter of Ocean. Moreover, the Aphrodite-sea allusion makes explicit the rebirth theme, preparing the way for Asia's transfiguration in the next scene and her ultimate reunion with Prometheus. This Spirit of the Hour, then, is associated with an erotic, aesthetic, utopian rebirth, not the revolutionary violence of her fellow Spirit who assists Demogorgon in dethroning Jupiter.

The Spirit of the Hour reappears in Act III, scene iii, where she bears Asia and Panthea to the spot of Prometheus's liberation. Prometheus, unbound by Hercules, assigns an important task to the Spirit of the Hour, who is to take a "curved shell which Proteus old / Made Asia's nuptial boon, breathing within it / A voice to be accomplished" (65-67). Again, the Spirit is linked with things of

173

the ocean (Proteus and a shell). With this shell she is to do the following: "Go, borne over the cities of mankind" and "breathe into the many-folded Shell, / Loosening its mighty music; it shall be / As thunder mingled with clear echoes" (76, 80-82). The first "breathing" was Proteus's, who created a "voice to be accomplished"; then Prometheus breathed the words to set the Spirit in motion, who will "breathe" into the prophetic shell her own voice, which will liberate the utopian music to usher in the millennium. Once this mystic music is released into society, then individual humans will "accomplish" the "voice" by speaking the new language and singing the lyrics of emancipation. Even Ione has a role in transmitting the prophetic music, because it is she who hid the shell (until a more propitious time) and who actually gives the Spirit the magical instrument. The complex chain of mediation—Proteus, Ione, Prometheus, the Spirit of the Hour, humanity—is not a gratuitous, but an important feature of the millennium itself. Utopian speech is new, uncreated, waiting to be given life by men and women finally emancipated from history. The language of utopia is not from a new dictionary, but a "voice to be accomplished," a process, something inchoate that can come into existence only by means of the individual "breath" which "loosens" potentiality into utopian actuality. Since the mystic shell of prophecy suggests the Aphrodite-like shell within which the Spirit of the Hour travels, this too evokes the theme of rebirth and social renewal.

One cannot, however, ignore the many critics who are disturbed by Prometheus's behavior once he is liberated by Hercules.[37] The actual liberation of humanity is not spoken of until line 64, where the Spirit of the Hour's task is described as a "toil." Before this, Prometheus lovingly describes the cave where he, Asia, and other spirits will reside for eternity. It strikes some readers as peculiar for the champion of humanity to retreat so quickly from a social orientation into a purely aesthetic repose. First, however, one has to recognize the dramatic and poetic tasks with which Shelley is faced in Act III, after Jupiter is deposed. If the poet were writing of a *coup d'état*, then the transition from the old to the new would be simple: Prometheus would take Jupiter's place on the throne, ruling in a "Promethean" way. Shelley, however, is writing an anarchist poem; he is concerned with the abolition of domination and hierarchy. Prometheus cannot "seize power," because power has been abolished and does not exist as something that can be seized. Therefore, Shelley has to create images and dramatic actions that embody authentically Promethean values, not a new code of laws. The long description of the cave is a static image representing the liberated imagination, now that Jupiter no longer represses and distorts consciousness. With hints of Coleridge's pleasure dome from *Kubla Khan*, Shelley's cave is a symbol for divine creativity, the process of making and unmaking language and meaning. It signifies a return to innocence and playfulness, the final healing of the tragic split between feeling and thinking.

Following the static image of the cave comes the announcement of the Spirit's "toil" to liberate humanity. If Prometheus were in fact liberated, and Jupiter deposed, the trumpet of prophecy would already have been blown. But as Earl Wasserman noted, what is simultaneous at the mythopoeic level must be rendered sequential in a human drama.[38] That the static image preceded the dramatic action is not in the least peculiar, because the former defines the "Promethean" qualities of the *process* individuals will undergo once they leave history and enter utopia.

In scene iv the Spirit of the Hour's climactic speech is preceded by the Spirit of the Earth's report on the liberation of humanity. Why two speeches instead of one? De Luca's article on "millennial announcement" provides the answer: the language announcing the millennium cannot be allowed to fix its qualities in a new code of imperatives which, in turn, will reify a new set of Jupiter-like commandments.[39] The Spirit of the Earth's speech, then, is one rendering of the millennium—actually, it is more than one, since different rhetorical techniques and tropes are utilized—and the Spirit of the Hour's is another. There could be, however, many other versions of the millennium which, by its very nature, is diverse, a multiplicity of creative activities that are ever changing.

What the Spirit of the Hour does—and what the Spirit of the Earth does not do—is to offer millennial images in a familiar political language. Many of these images are not, properly speaking, millennial, but transitional, midway between history and utopia. The many negative constructions bear witness to the process of historical transformation. Injustice negated becomes justice, but in utopia "justice" is meaningless, a relic from the historical past when domination and hierarchy still existed.

Immediately before the Spirit of the Hour's speech, Prometheus says: "We feel what thou hast heard and seen—yet speak" (97). In utopia feeling and language are so closely aligned as to be inseparable. The entire speech by the Spirit is superfluous because Prometheus already knows what transpired on earth. The "yet speak" is Prometheus's way of participating in utopian excess. In utopia, everything is gratuitous because the realm of necessity has been transcended. That Prometheus already knows what the Spirit will say helps explain, for one thing, the astonishing informality with which the Spirit announces the millennium. So casual is the Spirit that she digresses for thirteen lines (108-20) and must repeat herself ("I floated down" [106]; "As I said, I floated to the Earth" [124]). Such ease is appropriate under utopian conditions; under conditions operating in, say a realistic novel, such a tone would be unacceptable.

The Spirit of the Earth's descent into the social world is also gratuitous because she has already accomplished her task, blowing the trumpet of prophecy. She descends upon earth solely because she has been attracted there by its beauty: "Dizzy as with delight I floated down . . ." (106). Her "coursers," however, return to their birthplace, finally "exempt from toil" (109)—a condition enjoyed by all beings in utopia. As the Spirit floats down she "first was disappointed not to see / Such mighty change as I had felt within / Expressed in outward things" (127-30). The deflation emphasizes how radical the transformation of consciousness has been. Perception has altered far more than external reality, because the principal problems afflicting society at the time of Promethean deliverance were psychological and moral.

One series of lines describes the overcoming of a psychological condition peculiar to intellectuals, some of whose characteristics Shelley identified with Byron. "None wrought his lips in truth-entangling lines / Which smiled the lie his tongue disdained to speak" (142-43). The "none" with which this begins is the fifth such construction, and is not the last (there being two others). This negative construction embodies the qualities of both the pre- and post-millennial worlds. In this instance, the hypocrite fabricates a duplicitous language that no longer exists in utopia. The process of "truth-entangling" is not the same as the labyrinthine network of metaphors spun by Asia in her second-act duet with Prometheus's spirit, because a utopian verse is playful, at one with itself. The hypocrite's lips say one thing, while its tongue feels another. Consciousness and language are both divided in the Jupiter-world. The following lines seem to refer to Byron, or at least to a Byronic pose.[40]

None with firm sneer trod out in his own heart
The sparks of love and hope, till there remained
Those bitter ashes, a soul self-consumed,
And the wretch crept, a vampire among men,
Infecting all with his own hideous ill.
(144-48)

The fourth canto of *Childe Harold* upset and angered Shelley, pre-cipitating these remarks to Peacock: "The spirit in which [*Childe Harold*] is written is, the most wicked & mischevious insanity that ever was given forth. It is a kind of obstinate & selfwilled folly in which he hardens himself."[41] In "Lines written among the Euganean Hills," the "spark" of learning ignited a fiery revolution, while in "Ode to the West Wind" the poet offers himself as a fiery inspi-ration, whose "spark" has the same incendiary intent. The despair-ing intellectual, however, turns this creative fire against his own soul; he cannot hope and love because he has destroyed within himself the capacity to do so. The hopeless cynic is a "vampire" whose irony drains the vitality of those who try to live creatively.

Byron also seems to be alluded to in these lines:

None talked that common, false, cold, hollow talk
Which makes the heart deny the *yes* it breathes
Yet question that unmeant hypocrisy
With such a self-mistrust as has no name.
(149-52)

During the Genevan summer of 1816, Byron had adopted a panthe-ism reflected in *Childe Harold*, Canto Three. The fourth can-to, however, repudiates the Shelleyan strain and reasserts the By-ronic vision of lonely defiance in a world permanently unjust. By-ron's heart had first breathed, then denied a pantheistic *yes*. The convoluted introspection, the "self-mistrust" which "has no name," is the plague of self-consciousness, not just a Byronic malady, but a serious obstacle to wholeness at least since Descartes. Shelley knew that the mind's capacity to inflict pain upon itself was boundless. The hypocrite, the cynic, the ironist, and the self-conscious intel-lectual are all examples of consciousness divided against itself. The divided self elevates the intellectual will over natural spontaneity, thus reproducing a structure of consciousness appropriate for sci-entific mind dominating nature.

Among kingless thrones (131), "None fawned, none trampled"

(133); "None frowned, none trembled" (137). Domination of man by man, or woman by man (153-64), no longer exists because the individual finally possesses the self-esteem necessary to avoid a compensatory sadism or masochism within a power relationship. The icons of power—"Thrones, altars, judgement-seats, and prisons" (164)—"Stand, not o'erthrown, but unregarded now" (179) because once the psychological connection with power has been severed, then the things themselves become insignificant. As the utopian children in *Queen Mab* play in the abandoned prison, so the utopian beings in this poem feel no need to engage in actual iconoclasm since they have already been liberated by a psychological iconoclasm. The old Law, founded in oppression, lies in ruins, neglected and ignored, as new social relationships emerge to replace the static and hierarchical ones. Without the instruments of coercion—"swords and chains"—the "tomes / Of reasoned wrong glozed on by ignorance" (166-67) are incomprehensible curiosities, a perverse ordering of language into a brutal code long forgotten. Under conditions of scarcity, people flattered "the thing they feared" (188) and hoped to win concessions from Jupiter by submitting to his power. Now, however, these "shrines" are abandoned.

The final fourteen lines are an eloquent ode to the new anarchist society:

> The painted veil, by those who were, called life,
> Which mimicked, as with colours idly spread,
> All men believed and hoped, is torn aside—
> The loathesome mask has fallen, the man remains
> Sceptreless, free, uncircumscribed—but man:
> Equal, unclassed, tribeless and nationless,
> Exempt from awe, worship, degree,—the King
> Over himself; just, gentle, wise—but man:
> Passionless? no—yet free from guilt or pain
> Which were, for his will made, or suffered them.
> Nor yet exempt, though ruling them like slaves,
> From chance and death and mutability,
> The clogs of that which else might oversoar
> The loftiest star of unascended Heaven
> Pinnacled dim in the intense inane.
> (190-204)

Shelley has quickened the verse, since there are no static images or elaborate similes, and the casual, relaxed tone is dropped. Instead, the poetry hectically parallels the violent acts of revelation: tearing aside the veil; letting the mask fall; leaving the icons of power in ruins. The enjambment, dashes, and repeated words all hasten the language to its conclusion. The anarchist society is surmised at different levels, political and psychological, each of which previously marked a point of Jupiter-like stasis. Even the passions are now subject to the will. Chance, mutability, and death are the only things utopia cannot conquer, but even these are ruled like slaves. The final trope of the star is, as De Luca says, a utopian affirmation countering the deflating reminder of human limitations.[42] The millennial description concludes in a Promethean way, with human desire moving toward a seemingly remote object, an ideal. Shelley's utopian language achieves only moments of repose that lead to other moments of action and movement.

The Spirit of the Hour's speech is dramatically and philosophically appropriate. The static image of the sculptured dome (111-21) is the utopian counter to the icons of power. Although the speech begins casually, gratuitously, offhand—all tonally correct, since utopia has already been achieved—it concludes with the dramatic power one expects. The psychology of power and domination are dwelled upon, but the political forms which the Jupiter-world assumed are also figured, and negated by an anarchist society which does not have any "code" or set of definitive images. Indeed, Shelley is at pains to turn the poem back upon the reader where an anarchist process can take place. Most of the speech is a contradiction, one part Jupiter-world, one part utopia, so that the reader, while supposedly being offered a perfect world, is actually experiencing the world as it is. None fawned, none trampled, none live . . . as we actually do, here and now. The alternatives are imaged mostly as negations of existing conditions. What does "unclassed" mean, for example? Shelley leaves the process of definition up to the reader. A condition of being unclassed or tribeless or nationless is something one can, now, only imagine and work toward realizing. Indeed, that is precisely what Shelley wants readers to do: imagine and work toward realizing the ideals he has suggested. More positively, he does depict a dialogue of equals and lovers in Act II and later in Act IV. Beyond the lyrics of the "enchanted boat" and Act IV there is nothing more that is completely utopian because utopian blueprints would reconstitute Jupiter's code. Shelley remained true to his libertarian idealism by relying on negations, circular lyrics, and achieved coherences that deliberately collapse.

179

JULIAN AND MADDALO

Initially inspired by conversations with Byron in August 1818, and a desire to write a poem on Tasso, Shelley began *Julian and Maddalo* early in 1819 but did not complete it until August, after finishing *The Cenci*. He tried to make the date of composition appear earlier than it actually was because he wanted to obfuscate the personal origins of the Maniac's speeches. After William's death on June 7, 1819, a difficult estrangement with Mary ensued.[43] If in this poem Shelley pours out his melancholy feelings, he has more than enough unpleasant incidents to draw upon. The Shelleyan meliorist, Julian, tries to refute the pessimism of the Byronic fatalist, Count Maddalo, but surely some of the facts of Shelley's life thus far made pessimism a more likely perspective than optimism. His father had banished him from Field Place, making it impossible for him to see his mother and sisters, whom he loved very much; his soulmate Elizabeth Hitchener had become the detestable Brown Demon, just as his wife Harriet had become a burden until she killed herself; he had lost custody of his first two children; and there was no audience for his poems. Then in Italy Clara died, depressing and angering Mary because "Shelley's carelessness and unconcern had distinctly contributed" to the tragedy.[44] Then William died; his death provoked a stony silence in Mary's journal until August 4, Shelley's birthday. What must have frightened Shelley about Byron's sometimes flamboyant indulgence of guilt was that he had as much reason to feel guilty. He rarely acknowledged the way in which he harmed other people—not until 1821-1822. In the poetry, his heroes are passive victims, never unintentional victimizers.

A theme of considerable interest, especially since *Julian and Maddalo* was finished well after April 1819, when the third act of *Prometheus Unbound* was completed, is the difficulty of living a Promethean life. None of the major characters in *Julian and Maddalo* can live up to the standards of ethical idealism established by *Prometheus Unbound* and assumed in the later poem. Maddalo, cultivating despair, rejects the premise that utopia is even a goal worth pursuing. He speaks as a Prometheus who has been persuaded by the torturing Furies of Act I that fragmented humanity can never achieve harmony. Julian is a conscious Promethean, who resists the temptation of despair, but he fails the crucial test of experience, neglecting to assist the tortured Maniac. Another Prometheus who fails to be Promethean is the Maniac. As fortunate as the other two in upbringing and cultural education, he nevertheless cannot survive disappointment in love. Like the *Alastor* Visionary, the Maniac has erred not because of power or wealth, but because of a misguided idealism. The human capacity for self-torture lamented in *Prometheus Unbound* is a tragic fact in *Julian and Maddalo*. In Shelley's hierarchy, the devotees of Mammon are on the bottom; next come those who pursue fond illusions or who are not strong enough to endure life's disappointments; and at the top are the ethical idealists, like Prometheus, who are patient and learn through suffering to endure and hope. Although Shelley aspired to Promethean perfection, he encountered within himself—and struggled against—the qualities he projects onto his "weak" characters.

The poem opens with a description of the Lido, a scene especially conducive to idealistic speculation because it is so barren.[45] The natural scene, empty of objects, provides an infinite canvas on which Julian can paint his utopian desires: "we taste / The pleasure of believing what we see / Is boundless, as we wish our souls to be" (15-17). Once they arrive home, they discuss, like Milton's fallen angels, their prospects of regaining a paradise from which they have been exiled (41-42; 57). Julian maintains throughout the poem that paradise can be regained, while Maddalo, just as doggedly, disagrees because of his "pride."

The word "pride" is thematically central. According to the preface, Count Maddalo's weakness is "to be proud: he derives, from a comparison of his own extraordinary mind with the dwarfish intellects that surround him, an intense apprehension of the nothingness of human life."[46] In the opening scene, "one dwarf tree" stands on the shore with other insignificant flora, in symbolic contrast to the infinity of the universe and the mind. Whereas Julian absorbs the tree into his vision, Maddalo would allow the tree in the foreground to overshadow infinity. Julian's perspective incorporates objects into a vision of infinite possibility, whereas Maddalo proudly contrasts his own mind to the lesser ones he is acquainted with. In *Prometheus Unbound*, the Phantasm of Jupiter calls Prometheus "proud Sufferer" (I, 245), and Prometheus perceives his former self, the one who cursed Jupiter, in this way: "I see the curse on gestures proud and cold" (I, 258). Pride is a privileged stance toward the world in which the self is elevated above other beings.

In the poem's first part, there is another vision of nature that is a utopian emblem like the scene at the Lido. The sunset is a fiery apocalypse, the fusion of natural objects with a renewed and purified One Spirit.[47] As Maddalo uses his creative fire to belittle the world and extinguish hope, so Julian uses his own fire to engage the world in an apocalyptic dialogue. Since the "glow / Of Heaven descends upon" the landscape, heaven can unite with earth, restoring paradise and abolishing the difference between potentiality and actuality. They view "the flood / Which lay between the city and the shore / Paved with the image of the sky" (65-67). The water reflecting the sky implies their ultimate unity, whereas the word "flood" connotes a purgative deluge, drowning the old and the tyrannical, leaving behind only what belongs in utopia. The description of the sunset continues, with the fire imagery predominating.

> And then—as if the Earth and Sea had been
> Dissolved into one lake of fire, were seen
> Those mountains towering as from waves of flame
> Around the vaporous sun, from there came
> The inmost purple spirit of light, and made
> Their very peaks transparent.
>   (80-85)

Mountains, waves, sky, and sun "dissolve" into a fiery apocalypse, transforming the world into its potential unity and burning away those distracting features which make phenomena appear discrete and unrelated. Objects as things external to the mind and separate from each other are fused together in an apocalyptic vision.

Maddalo is unwilling to be moved by the sunset, and tries to negate the utopian images with images of his own. He interrupts contemplation of the sunset's beauty to use the fading light to visit the madhouse. This new object for contemplation blots out the apocalyptic vision: "I looked, and saw between us and the sun / A building on an island" (98-99). The sun, now, is discrete, not an element dispersed throughout the world. Maddalo's countervision is a distressing reminder of all that Julian wants transformed but which Maddalo believes is immutably fixed as human evil. Ironically, the sun sinks behind the madhouse tower, symbolizing the eclipse of creative fire by this Jupiterian mass of "miscreated" tyranny.

The bell ringing the inmates to their vespers speaks an authoritarian language; the bell's "hoarse and iron tongue" (104) invites the miserable victims to pray to a Power who, presumably, has seen fit to torture them for their sins. This grotesque irony is something that Shelley also perceived in the fate of Tasso, who wrote sycophantic poems to the tyrant Alfonso. Writing to Peacock, Shelley says, "to me there is much more to pity than to condemn in these entreaties and praises of Tasso. It is as a Christian prays to [and] praises his God whom he knows to [be] the most remorseless capricious & inflexible of tyrants, but whom he knows also to be omnipotent." If Jupiter is an omnipotent being, rather than a human construct, then prayer makes sense. In the letter to Peacock Shelley continues: "Tasso's situation was widely different from that of any persecuted being of the present day, for from the depth of dungeons public opinion might now at length be awakened to an echo that would startle the oppressor. But then there was no hope."[48] Without hope, Tasso understandably tries to assuage the arbitrary will of a tyrant, but Maddalo has no such excuse. With an irony that is not lost on Maddalo, Julian replies to the vespers: " 'As much skill as need to pray / In thanks or hope for their dark lot have they / To their stern maker' " (111-13). As they pray, they "make" their Maker, who in turn rewards them with self-contempt and fear.

Maddalo checks Julian's antireligious argument before it gets too far by developing some of the most eloquent antimeliorist lines in the poem.

> "And such,"—he cried, "is our mortality
> And this must be the emblem and the sign
> Of what should be eternal and divine!—
> And like that black and dreary bell, the soul,
> Hung in a heaven-illumined tower, must toll
> Our thoughts and our desires to meet below
> Round the rent heart and pray—as madmen do
> For what? They know not,—till the night of death
> As sunset that strange vision, severeth
> Our memory from itself, and us from all
> We sought and yet were baffled!"
>   (120-30)

The sun has completely set, making the belfry invisible, while they travel homeward in silence. Maddalo agrees that soul should be eternal and divine, but laments that it is not so; instead, soul aspires to a perfection sabotaged by the rent heart. Maddalo cites the sunset in its fading aspect, as it disappears, whereas Julian emphasizes just the opposite, its glorious beauty, however momentary. Julian perceives the bell in an antireligious way, while Maddalo uses it as a metaphor for the divided self, the irreconcilable conflict between desire and realization. Julian cannot dispute the reality of the divided soul and the uncertain fate of the dead; he only denies that such division has to be permanent or that such uncertainty is fatal to happiness.

In the second part Julian counters Maddalo in several ways. If "man be / The passive thing you say," then the lies of religion can do no harm because human nature would then be "teachless" (161-64). Julian, however, believes that the soul and heart can live harmoniously, that circumstances can be altered, that hope can create new conditions. He uses Maddalo's daughter as an emblem of innocence to disprove the fatalistic view. The child here, as in *Rosalind and Helen*, serves a symbolic purpose, of representing a living example of the utopian self, whole, undivided, and innocent. She is "A serious, subtle, wild, yet gentle being, / Graceful without design and unforeseeing" (145-46). He contrasts her unpremeditated happiness with the "sick thoughts" of last night (169), and proclaims that

> "it is our will
> That thus enchains us to permitted ill—
> We might be otherwise—we might be all
> We dream of happy, high, majestical.
> Where is the love, beauty and truth we seek
> But in our mind? and if we were not weak
> Should we be less in deed than in desire?"
> (170-76)

By exerting the will, mind can create all that it can imagine and hope. Permitted to exist, evil can be abolished by human creativity reassuming its full power.

Maddalo, unconvinced, cries "Utopia," making Julian respond in language that echoes *Prometheus Unbound*. Perhaps the chains which bind our spirit are as brittle as straw.

> "We are assured
> Much may be conquered, much may be endured
> Of what degrades and crushes us. We know
> That we have power over ourselves to do
> And suffer—what, we know not till we try."
> (181-86)

Prometheus unbinds his spirit's chains, conquering his hatred of Jupiter, enduring pain, and finally achieving power over himself after much suffering. Whatever humanity might accomplish if it tried, it would have to be "something nobler than to live and die— / So taught those kings of old philosophy / Who reigned, before Religion made men blind" (187-89). Socrates, Plato, and Diogenes were kings over themselves, ruling the mutiny within, serving the ideals of truth regardless of what those with political or religious power might say and do to the contrary. The anarchist philosopher, rejecting the ephemeral, illusory pleasures of an unjust society, dedicates himself to loving the truth, searching for it, and speaking it. Philosophy, however, was supplanted by Christianity, whose institutional authoritarianism has "blinded" humanity ever since.

Maddalo significantly ignores the substance of Julian's argument, completely neglecting the philosophy-religion dichotomy. He makes another division, this time between mere words and "reality." Utopianism might be true as far as logic and argument go, but the true test is "reality." He wants the Maniac to serve as a living refutation of utopianism because his idealism led to madness. Aspiring theories are vain because the self cannot go any higher than destiny has decreed. The soul may yearn for ideals, but the emotions are dominated by mundane experience, which disappoints our high expectations. That some men are driven to madness by misery neither surprises Julian nor creates any problems for him in his argument with Maddalo. Before they visit the Maniac, Julian has already won the debate, even though Maddalo will never be convinced of this.

The Maniac's speeches have no bearing on the "argument," which is over as soon as Maddalo refuses to debate logically. The Maniac, however, embodies a kind of pride that Shelley also analyzed in *Prometheus Unbound*, and his dramatic monologue provides an occasion for exercising sensibility and balancing the logical argument with emotional release.

In the final paragraphs of the monologue the Maniac comes closest to a Promethean position. He admits that his "writings" have only made him more wretched, increased the pain rather than diminished it. He begins with Promethean wisdom, " 'Those who inflict must suffer, for they see / The work of their own hearts and this must be / Our chastisement or recompense' " (482-84), but misinterprets it, because he, not his beloved, is the one who "inflicts." She rejected him, but he has cultivated the curse which binds him to his madness. Then, in the last paragraph, he seems again to achieve wisdom by refraining from suicide in order to prevent her from feeling more guilt.

> "Then, when thou speakest of me, never say,
> 'He could forgive not.' Here I cast away
> All human passions, all revenge, all pride;
> I think, speak, act no ill; I do but hide
> Under these words like embers, every spark
> Of that which has consumed me—quick and dark
> The grave is yawning . . ."
> (500-506)

He imitates the ancient philosophers, and speaks the Promethean words, but they are only words, underneath which exists the reality of a soul destroyed by its creative fire turned against itself. He still yearns for the "peace" of the grave rather than the endurance necessary for life (506-10). He has failed to effect a Promethean conversion, although he has tried. He cannot conquer the pride of his grief, which clings to him despite his protestations. He is a failed Prometheus, wedded to his curse, a devotee of death-in-life.

With the Maniac silent, Julian and Maddalo "Wept without shame in his society" (516). The Maniac displays so many admirable qualities which he undercuts at crucial points in the monologue. However sad and moving his speech, it nevertheless portrays unnecessary suffering. There is an irony, however, in that the monologue provokes Maddalo to speak lines he thinks support his own view but actually support Julian's: " 'Most wretched men / Are cradled into poetry by wrong, / They learn in suffering what they teach in song' " (544-46). Prometheus, too, was made wise by misery; misery is something Julian never tries to deny or evade, but he refuses to see it as definitive. And so when misery turns into song that teaches, the process conforms to the meliorist pattern, since good is being drawn from evil. Another irony is that Julian, the meliorist, does not stay in Venice to help the Maniac, but returns home to his friends and family.[49] His selfish decision has no bearing on the meliorist-fatalist argument, long ago won, but illustrates how even an idealist can fail to act in a manner sufficiently utopian.

The final part of the conclusion (583-617) ends in a most peculiar way that makes sense only if one understands the irony of the previous part. As Julian was guilty of not acting and feeling generously enough, so the reader, "the cold world" of the last line, is accused of shallowness as well. We are not told how the Maniac and his lover died because, in all probability, our interest is not sincere. Would *we* have stayed in Venice, trying with patience to "find / An entrance to the cavern of his mind," sacrificing ordinary pleasures for his sake? If we were Promethean, we would have stayed—but that is Shelley's point. We are not Prometheus. At best, we are unregenerate Prometheuses, with our curses and illusions. True, evil can be conquered, as Julian says, because meliorism corresponds to human potentiality. Julian is not a little facile in the way he assumes meliorism, as when he tells Maddalo, "for ever still / Is it not wise to make the best of ill?" (46-47). Maddalo is wrong, trounced badly in the argument, but he is the one who assists the Maniac, and he has an acute sense of the resistance "soul" encounters when it seeks to transform the world. For Julian—and the reader—to be truly Promethean, he must accept the difficulty of the task, perhaps the impossibility of ever achieving perfection, but be determined nevertheless to hope, endure, and suffer with as much power as possible. The final irony directed against Julian does not affect the poem's antagonist, Byronic fatalism. Maddalo is admirable, despite his fatalism, when he acts in opposition to its tenets; Julian is faulted for falling short of the standards of utopian behavior, not for being a meliorist advocate. The Maniac, like the *Alastor* Visionary, is superior to those who do not deeply feel and desire, far more admirable than those dedicated to wealth and power, but he is nevertheless mistaken. His tragedy is that of a Prometheus who fails to unbind himself.

THE CENCI

Begun in May 1819, after the first three acts of *Prometheus Unbound*, and finished in late July or early August of the same year, *The Cenci* is a historical, tragic treatment of the ethical problems that always concern Shelley. He chooses a story and historical epoch in neither of which can exist the ideal typology developed in *Prometheus Unbound* and suggested in *Julian and Maddalo*. An entirely different typology is at work in *The Cenci*, one that is designed specifically for a London audience and contemporary English readers. Perhaps there is a judgment here that only an ethical drama of the sixteenth century is primitive enough to approximate the moral condition of the Regency English. Shelley correctly believed that only a few readers would be persuaded by the beautiful idealisms of *Prometheus Unbound*, so that if he wanted a wider audience for his ideas, he had to adjust accordingly. *The Cenci*, then, does not provide "dreams of what ought to be, or may be," but a "sad reality"[50] which is developed in such a way as to produce in the audience a self-recognition. "Such a story, if told to present to the reader all the feelings of those who once acted it . . . would be as a light to make apparent some of the most dark and secret caverns of the human heart."[51] By experiencing the sad reality in all its complexity, the audience enters into a process of self-discovery. "The highest moral purpose aimed at in the highest species of drama, is the teaching of the human heart, through its sympathies and antipathies, the knowledge of itself; in proportion to the possession of which knowledge, every human being is wise, just, sincere, tolerant and kind."[52] The drama is a catalyst for precipitating another kind of drama in the spectator, whose moral capacities undergo an educational experience.

Shelley has little faith in a naive spontaneity supposedly existing underneath a layer of civilized pretenses. The moral capacities have to be engaged and made self-conscious, or, as he says: "It is in the restless and anatomizing casuistry with which men seek the justification of Beatrice, yet feel that she has done what needs justification; it is in the superstitious horror with which they contemplate alike her wrongs and their revenge, that the dramatic character of what she did and suffered, consists."[53] A self-division in the spectator is the split between mind and emotions. He hopes that his drama will effect a harmonizing of the two, thus removing the negative features of intellect, suggested by "restless and anatomizing," and of feeling, suggested by "superstitious horror." The drama forces the audience to face a series of dilemmas out of which there are no facile exits; indeed, the reader's sympathies are manipulated in disturbing ways so that one is transported out of the play's immediate frame of reference. This Brechtian kind of alienation effect is intentional, designed to teach self-knowledge of a very subversive nature to Shelley's audience. The spectator who sympathizes with Beatrice is deprived of simple pathos by the numerous instances when she delivers lines whose ethical meaning is ambiguous. We are trapped into believing Beatrice is spotlessly innocent, only to discover that we were mistaken.

There is not an ideal, but another kind of typology of characters at work in the drama. The two basic types are those who are naive, at one with their social role and self-concept, and those who are self-conscious, having undergone a process of doubling the self into knower and known, analyzer and analyzed. Beatrice, innocent before her doubling, reconstitutes herself as innocent. Count Cenci's self-consciousness led to his complete devotion to egoistic pleasure, extirpating all considerations of conscience. Orsino and Giacomo, after they reach a point of self-reflection, are neither completely innocent nor evil, although Orsino parallels the Count, while Giacomo, Hamlet-like, is torn between his identification with Beatrice and his father. Naive and self-conscious, innocent and evil, are the principal types Shelley is employing. The naive character would correspond to those who felt that English institutions required no alterations, or that even if flaws existed, they could not possibly be as serious as the reformers liked to claim. The innocent character would correspond to those in the reform movement who were convinced of the injustices perpetrated against them and who contemplated immediate action to rectify the situation. The self-divided Orsino and Giacomo might represent the intellectual, pulled one way by selfishness and fear, pulled another by sympathy and hope. However Shelley might have intended the process of identification, he also undermined the process by guaranteeing that any single identification could not carry the spectator through to the end of the play. Someone who is naive is forced to face the full extent of Cenci's and the society's evil. Reformers, convinced of their righteousness, witness their beloved "innocence" deconstructing before their eyes. The intellectual cannot retreat into irony, acquiesce in the status quo, or endorse a self-evident innocence. Shelley has created a labyrinth, the only way out of which is to distort the play's moral meaning or to achieve a self-awareness that transcends the consciousness of any particular character. Despite Shelley's protestations to the contrary, *The Cenci* is a didactic work—not only a "sad reality," but a tragedy whose unfolding, by both the characters and the audience, teaches a series of lessons. Since none of these is stated formulaically, they only exist as they are discovered by each spectator.

Camillo is the most damned naive character because, even though he is so close to power, he refuses to perceive its true nature. He has many opportunities to acquire self-consciousness, but misses every one of them. Dramatically, too, he is damned as the Pope's agent, who collects bribes and carries messages of death. As the Pope's mediator, he is like Mercury, without a will, ineffectually wishing for a better world while his actions make it worse. Camillo opens the play with an offer to the Count to exchange a third of his possessions for a Papal pardon for having committed murder. Without irony, Camillo says that "crimes like yours if once or twice compounded / Enriched the Church, and respite from hell / An erring soul which might repent and live" (I, i, 7-9). He never develops a cynical awareness of ecclesiastical politics, believing wholeheartedly in the rhetoric by which the church explains itself. The cash nexus, however, is so obviously the most essential component in Camillo's speech that one admires Cenci's honesty. While the church pursues its self-interest with ruthless brutality, it also practices a self-serving hypocrisy, pretending that whatever crimes it commits are done for noble purposes. Cenci, however, hides nothing: "I please my senses as I list" (I, i, 69). Although the Count reveals the full extent of his selfish desire, Camillo refuses to acknowledge it: "I thank my God that I believe you not" (I, i, 121). The irony here is that Camillo's God is a hypocritical deity who can accept bribes, ignore murder when it is convenient to do so, and pretend innocence.

Camillo, however weak, is unexceptional, as is demonstrated in Act I, scene iii, where the nobility reveals itself as cowardly. The Count grotesquely rejoices in the deaths of his two sons, and Beatrice challenges the guests to do something about his immoral tyranny, but they do nothing. A premise of the drama is that the Count, however evil as an individual, is tolerated by society, not just by the Pope, so that Beatrice cannot hope for any socially sanctioned relief. She tries, certainly, by petitioning the Pope and appealing directly to the nobles, but no one intervenes because the Count is too powerful (I, iii, 142-44). The good lack power, except to weep barren tears, and the powerful, to say the least, lack goodness.

The responsibility of the naive characters is indeed weighty, because if Camillo had fully acknowledged the Count's evil or if the banquet guests had challenged the Count, Beatrice would have been spared her later dilemma. Not to admit the full extent of evil and not to act ethically once confronted with it are naive in this sense: both allow the social actor to maintain his privileged status without questioning his role in the system of privilege. Evil must be a part of the system, or originate from an external source, or . . . be ignored. The banquet guests naively refuse to be implicated by the Count's moral affront, as if they could maintain their innocence by leaving the banquet and verbally chastising him. They do not see the evil which is systematic and which is within themselves; they do not see the evil of their cowardice. Camillo, for example, who knows both the Count and the Pope, is still able, by the play's end, to maintain his social role as Papal agent and his self-concept as a man of feeling and upright morality. When he finally does something, and attempts to persuade the Pope not to execute Beatrice, he is too late, playing his accustomed role as obedient but reluctant mediator of power. Camillo learns nothing from the tragedy he helped precipitate. He not only ignores his own guilt; he cannot bring himself to see the Pope and the entire patriarchical system as morally indefensible. When Beatrice is most brutal and deceptive, Camillo declares her to be the most innocent (V, ii, 61-62, 69).

One might argue that Camillo is not naive, just self-serving. He is self-serving, but he looks after himself by accepting his social role, never questioning it, or the system in which it plays a part. Unlike the Count or Orsino, he does not self-consciously advance his interests by manipulating the social system. He never subjects his own public "self" to analytical scrutiny, concealing and cultivating behind the mask another self which has to wrest from the social world the objects of desire. Rather, he contains contradictions within himself, absorbing and tolerating the excesses of power by rationalization. The Pope, as God's agent, can do no wrong, and even when Camillo disagrees with the Pope, he accepts his decision as harsh necessity.

The self-conscious characters—the Count, Orsino, Giacomo, and Beatrice—provide a sharp contrast with the naive characters, and represent a spectrum of types themselves. The Count is pure egoism, selfishness shorn of any other influences, the complete villain and Shelleyan antithesis. Orsino tries to manipulate the social world in a ruthless way, but he has only partial success, not simply because he lacks Cenci's power but also because his desire for Beatrice is humanizing, thus mitigating his nihilism to a certain extent. Giacomo, like Beatrice, achieves self-consciousness as a result of paternal oppression, but unlike hers, his self-concept is divided. When Beatrice is forced to examine herself, after Cenci has raped her, she reconstitutes her identity as someone who is as innocent as she was before the rape. The identity is conditional on implementing "justice," but it exists securely nevertheless, even after the Pope refuses to grant a pardon. At the two extremes of evil and innocence the characters are unified within themselves, but the middle two are divided.

The key passage announcing the theme of self-consciousness occurs in a soliloquy by Orsino, who has just been planting ideas of parricide in Giacomo Cenci's mind.

> It fortunately serves my close designs
> That 'tis a trick of this same family
> To analyse their own and other minds.
> Such self-anatomy shall teach the will
> Dangerous secrets: for it tempts our powers,
> Knowing what must be thought, and may be done,
> Into the depth of darkest purposes:
> So Cenci fell into the pit; even I,
> Since Beatrice unveiled me to myself,
> And made me shrink from what I cannot shun,
> Shew a poor figure to my own esteem,
> To which I grow half reconciled.
> (II, ii, 107-18)

The echoes from the preface are hardly accidental. The "secret" caverns of the heart are the intended objects of illumination by the play.[54] The "anatomizing" casuistry of the spectator confronting Beatrice's moral dilemmas is the essence of the dramatic interest.[55] The reader is invited to participate in this dangerous process of self-consciousness. From this passage alone, one would question the wisdom of self-examination, since it was from such a process that the Count discovered his evil and Orsino found himself in his own pit. The passage, however, echoes not only the preface, but a whole line of Shelleyan development from *Zastrozzi* to *Alastor*. *Zastrozzi* is an earlier, more benign version of the Count, whereas Orsino seems like Matilda. Orsino found his authentic identity, as opposed to his naive social role inherited without analysis, by means of trauma, that is, falling in love with Beatrice. Wanting her more than anything else, he subjugates older aspects of himself in order to possess her. Unlike the Count, Orsino still has remnants of conscience that are painful to repress; he has not achieved the unity within himself enjoyed by the Count.

Self-consciousness leads to a perception of power because the will becomes empowered. The Count, rooting his identity in sensual pleasure, uses the will not only to discover ever more delightful means of feeling, but to manipulate the social world and assume, if necessary, a false public role in order to safeguard his hedonism. Most members of the privileged class do not take advantage of their power to the extent possible if they were as ruthless and self-conscious as the Count. Others could be like the Count, if they dared. Orsino experiences power by repressing his conscience and manipulating events in a selfish way, effectively winning his escape from punishment in the end. Giacomo, tormented beyond endurance by a sadistic father, does not achieve self-consciousness until he confesses the desire and will to commit patricide. He dissipates his own power, however, by also identifying with the Count as a fellow father; thus weakened, he falls prey to Orsino and eventually the Pope. Beatrice is empowered by her self-consciousness, which ordains her as pure and innocent as long as her rapist-father is executed.

It is striking that in each instance of self-conscious empowering the resultant action is either morally or psychologically catastrophic. Although the naive characters are contemptible, the self-conscious ones are hardly ideal types. The preface and logic of the play present self-consciousness itself as the one process which can resolve the contradictions experienced by the spectator, but no act of self-consciousness depicted in the play is exemplary. There is something interfering with the vision of each character and determining the play's structure in such a perverse way that self-consciousness does not yield authentic knowledge. That "something" is patriarchy.[56]

Patriarchy, the dictatorship of the father, exists at many levels: familial, political, religious, and psychological. The naive characters accept patriarchy unquestioningly, whereas the self-conscious characters align themselves with patriarchy by an act of the will. With Giacomo, but especially Beatrice, the play illustrates how the patriarchal principle is reproduced in those very characters who have the least to gain from it. The lesson of anarchism is implied in *The Cenci*: if allegiance to the father-principle subverts the emancipatory intentions of rebellion, then only an outright rejection of patriarchy in all its forms can ground the project of liberation on a solid foundation.

The theme of partriarchy is developed in every act. The Count speaks of God as "the great father of all" (I, iii, 23) in the same way as Beatrice: "God, the father of all" (I, iii, 118). It is Beatrice who states the principle upon which the Count justifies his own tyranny: "great God, / Whose image upon earth a father is" (II, i, 16-17). The Pope, the Holy Father, who is God the Father's viceroy on earth, always identifies with and defends fathers against their children. Giacomo petitions the Pope for relief from his tyrannical father, the Count Cenci, but Camillo reports how the Pope reacts:

> "Children are disobedient, and they sting
> Their fathers' hearts to madness and despair
> Requiting years of care with contumely.
> I pity the Count Cenci from my heart;
> His outraged love perhaps awakened hate,
> And thus he is exasperated to ill.
> In the great war between the old and young
> I, who have white hairs and a tottering body,
> Will keep at least blameless neutrality."
>
> (II, ii, 32-40)

In a contest between father and children, such "neutrality" is of course pro-patriarchal. Camillo remarks that the Pope should favor Beatrice's petition, but the Pope is reluctant to side against fathers: "He holds it of most dangerous example / In aught to weaken the paternal power, / Being, as 'twere, the shadow of his own" (II, ii, 54-56).

In Act III, scene i, Beatrice recovers her sanity after being raped by the Count only by appealing to a powerful father, God. By punishing the bad father, Beatrice will vindicate the benevolence of the patriarchal system and reestablish her innocence. Giacomo, suffering from a new outrage at the hands of his father, comes storming into the Cenci palace, ready to throttle the Count. Like Beatrice, he justifies patricide by means of God the Father: "God can understand and pardon, / Why should I speak with man?" (III, i, 296-97). Giacomo, however, in the next scene, has a guilty conscience because he identifies with the Count as a fellow father: "and when my hairs are white, / My son will then perhaps be waiting thus, / Tortured between just hate and vain remorse" (III, ii, 25-27).

In the fourth act, the Count feels justified by God, who rewards his prayers and permits him to do as he wishes. Desiring to enslave not just Beatrice's body but her soul as well, the Count says, "The world's Father / Must grant a parent's prayer against his child" (IV, i, 106-107). When the assassins, Olimpio and Marzio, try to execute the sleeping Count, they are at first prevented from doing so by the taboo against harming the father. Olimpio projects onto the sleeping Count an image of the good, benevolent father (IV, ii, 9-13), and Marzio is frightened by the Count's words spoken in a dream:

" 'God! hear, O, hear, / A father's curse! What, art thou not our father?' " Marzio remarks: "I knew it was the ghost / Of my dead father speaking through his lips, / And could not kill him" (IV, iii, 18-23).

Apprehended by the authorities, Beatrice justifies herself in patriarchal terms (as being sanctioned by God who has worked out the justice of the Count's death) and defends the patriarchal concept of the family reputation, the "noble house," and stainless "name." Defending herself before the judges, Beatrice says, "my hate / Became the only worship I could lift / To our great father" (V, ii, 126-28). The Pope refuses to grant a stay of execution solely because he feels the patriarchy needs defending:

> "Parricide grows so rife
> That soon, for some just cause no doubt, the young
> Will strangle us all, dozing in our chairs.
> Authority, and power, and hoary hair
> Are grown crimes capital."
>   (V, iv, 20-24)

After hearing the sentence of death, with her faith in patriarchal justice shaken, Beatrice endures a nightmare vision in which her father's evil spirit rules even in death (V, iv, 60ff.).

The most compelling illustration of psychological enslavement to the father principle is Beatrice's "innocence." Before the rape she is innocent in that she tries to live the ideals of goodness put forth by patriarchy but rarely practiced. Comforting her stepmother, supportive of her brother, she follows the rules of society by turning down Orsino's proposals of marriage because he is now a cleric, legally bound to celibacy. She petitions the Pope, publicly rebukes her father's outrageous treatment of his children, and appeals to the nobility for aid. Her rape, however, drives her into temporary madness because if God exists and is just, he cannot permit such a violation of innocence. As an innocent, she *never imagined* incestuous rape, an act whose "shame" implicates even the victim under the patriarchal code. Driven to this extremity, Beatrice has few options: madness, rejection of patriarchy root and branch, or revenge. The second is hardly a plausible option because one cannot see where she could have acquired the materials for a thorough antiauthoritarianism. She has, really, two options: a madness in which she alternates between denying everything and accepting guilt and moral corruption; and a revenge in which God's justice will be done, the good father driving out the bad and reestablishing the good name of patriarchy. Before the rape her innocence seems innocuous enough, but afterwards she takes up the sword of justice, enforcing the patriarchal code. So convincing is her performance that Marzio prefers death to the accusing gaze of Beatrice, whose reconstituted "innocence" exacts pitiless judgment. Upon retrospective analysis, Beatrice's "innocence" is flawed from the beginning because it depends upon patriarchal concepts. It was framed within an arbitrary and externally constituted law, having an allegiance not to humanity but only to a circumscribed family, which is both patrilineal and patriarchal.

As is evident from the preface, Shelley admires and sympathizes with Beatrice, who is clearly the most distinguished character in the drama. She is as "innocent" as she can be, given the social situation that "violently thwarted" her "nature."[57] Unlike the Count or Orsino, her self-consciousness does not transform her into an egoistic sensualist; unlike Giacomo, she cannot suffer from a selfish identification with the father; and unlike the naive characters, she faces the implacable evil which is Count Cenci. She tries to be as innocent as her society permits. The spectator of the tragedy realizes that only a radically different society, based on principles that transcend patriarchy, could permit the emergence of an innocence which does not contradict itself.

PETERLOO

Peterloo intersects the *Prometheus Unbound* period at the midpoint between the composition of the first act and the publication of the entire volume of poetry. It signaled the intensification of the social crisis to a critical point, so that *something* would have to happen. For several months, Shelley thought England was on the verge of revolution, and he wrote accordingly, in a variety of genres, trying to make his own contribution. Most of the Peterloo-inspired works were never published in his lifetime because of the repression. As he was putting together the *Prometheus Unbound* volume, he was becoming aware that neither revolution nor reform but repression was on the political agenda. The volume as a whole is a defiant response to the repression, and expresses his bitterness toward it and his resentment over not being able to publish openly all his work.

In a carefully documented study of the Peterloo Massacre, Robert

Walmsley argues against what he calls the "radical myth" of Peterloo.[58] According to this myth, the government in London encouraged the Manchester magistrates to suppress the nonviolent protest that had gathered at St. Peter's Fields. The Hussars and Yeomanry cut down an unarmed crowd, causing eleven deaths and hundreds of injuries. Walmsley, however, proves that the London Home Office explicitly requested that the Manchester magistrates permit the August 16, 1819 demonstration in favor of parliamentary reform to take place; the Home Office did not want the protest suppressed. The magistrates acted contrary to the advice from London because they perceived the demonstration as a potential insurrection. The local authorities had been alarmed by the Sandy Brow episode at nearby Stockport on February 15, 1819 in which handloom weavers and other angry workers had held a reform demonstration where they had projected a far from nonviolent image to the Stockport authorities. As Walmsley reconstructs Peterloo, the sequence of events was thus: (1) the authorities were alarmed by the size of the crowd (between 80,000 and 100,000 men, women, and children from all over Lancashire), and by insurrectionary elements in the crowd (especially from Stockport), and so they prohibited the demonstration and had on hand the Yeomanry and Hussars to control the crowd in case there was an illegal demonstration; (2) despite the ban, thousands poured into St. Peter's Fields on August 16, so the authorities decided to arrest the main speakers, Henry "Orator" Hunt and others; (3) as the Yeomanry helped serve the arrest warrant on Hunt, parts of the crowd began to attack the Yeomanry with "sticks, stones, and brickbats"; (4) the Hussars were called in to defend the besieged Yeomanry, who were surrounded by a hostile and aggressive crowd; (5) the resulting massacre was a consequence, then, of the troops trying to defend themselves (this inference seems rather forced). The London government retroactively approved of Manchester's handling of the affair when it learned all the facts; the repressive legislation of December-January, 1819-1820, was a consequence of having acquired this new knowledge.

Although Walmsley's intentions are antileftist and based on a desire to vindicate William Hulton, the Manchester magistrate who orchestrated the official response to the demonstration, his interpretation of Peterloo is plausible. Stockport, a center of Luddite activity between 1811 and 1812, is a likely place for insurrectionary anger to have surfaced in the agitation for reform. That the crowd would be hostile to the Yeomanry arresting their leaders is hardly surprising. Walmsley presents us with a picture, not just of a passive crowd mowed down by the soldiers, but of an angry crowd, some of whom are willing to fight against the military. Our sense of Peterloo changes, then, from a police riot to class conflict. This view, however, is consistent with E. P. Thompson's. Even though the Home Office was originally permissive in its attitude to the Manchester demonstration, it was surely well prepared for the massacre that ensued, immediately endorsing the magistrates' actions and unleashing a repressive assault on the radical movement. The *Examiner* reports the government's fear of communism as a result of the demonstrations and protests.[59] Thompson suggests that if open, legal meetings had continued on the scale of 1819, England would have become ungovernable. Ironically, open meetings were considerably more "revolutionary" than secret plots to overthrow the government. The Liverpool regime would have to decide, sooner or later, to make concessions to the reform movement or to repress it. Peterloo forced the government to decide and, without hesitation, it opted for repression.[60]

What Luddism and even Peterloo suggest is that some workers were beginning to fight directly against their oppression. Malcolm Thomis and Peter Holt conclude that the Regency radicalism that culminated in Peterloo and immediately afterwards was not a revolutionary threat.[61] But both Luddism and other instances of insurrection suggest revolutionary tendencies that could have developed had conditions been more favorable. The severe political repression that was implemented between the 1790s and 1832 was not the consequence of Tory hysteria, but as Walmsley and Thompson agree, from their very different viewpoints, stemmed from prudent ruling-class strategy to *prevent* a revolution.

Shelley's immediate response to Peterloo is interesting, because in *The Mask of Anarchy* he encourages the poor to act. A poem, of course, is not a political essay, so that an imaginative "statement" is not the same as a prosaic one. A poetic response to Peterloo can be more uncompromising and militant than a prosaic response because a poem exists in a realm of symbolic reference. His militance is not without its qualifications and ambiguities, but what distinguishes Shelley's response is a desire to push the reform movement leftwards, to risk even revolution. At the time, most reformers tried to hold back the movement and keep it within a constitutionalist framework. However, before examining *The Mask of Anarchy* in detail, it is necessary to analyze Shelley's ambivalence toward the poor, and second, to establish the popular framework from which the poem derives its meaning.

It is not necessary to account for Shelley's distrust of the poor because he would have imbibed such a bias from virtually any source in radical and romantic culture. It was an unquestioned assumption that the poor were to be represented and led, not allowed to determine their own forms of struggle. This bias is reinforced in Shelley's case by the nature of his idealism, which elevates spirit over the bodily and terrestrial, and eternity over temporality. During the Luddite uprisings, he dismisses their significance because, according to Shelley, "hunger is the only excitement of our English riotings" which are "devoid of principle & method."[62] Assuming the rebellion possessed no spirituality at all, but only a kind of mindless response, he expressed a typically intellectual bias against both the workers and "hunger," as though having intense bodily needs disqualified one's self from also being rational. Spirit seems to exist only in those who do not hunger but who instead sympathize with those who do; he assumes that spiritual value can come only after disengaging one's self from the immediacy of experience, only after establishing a hierarchical superiority over the uncertain flux of human events.

Shelley, however, can also frankly accept the body and passionate feeling, and can see the degradation of the poor in physical terms, allowing for an aggressive response to events by the poor themselves. On the exploitation of the poor, Shelley has some of the most lucid statements ever formulated in the early nineteenth century. Unlike so many others who were active in the reform movement, Shelley did not share all its popular prejudices. Although he could not escape entirely from the movement's myths, he was usually able to transcend its limitations because of his position as an outsider. Distance gave him a freedom he could not have had in England. And so, paradoxically, a certain kind of insight is achieved at the price of exile, while at the same time that exile is also the source of contradiction.

Although *The Mask of Anarchy* is obviously a political allegory, the poem's meaning is not obvious.[63] For one thing, it has to be recognized as contradictory, at war with itself, not entirely resolved. The different elements making up the poem do not necessarily meld into a unity. At one level, this work shares the assumptions and configurations of the popular mythology and iconography; it is important to see to what extent Shelley shares in this culture and to what extent and how he differs from it. The poem takes ideas from the moderate reform movement, as well as its more radical wing, but also has ideas that come from neither.

I want to follow up and expand upon a suggestion made by the critics Stuart Curran and Karl Kroeber. Curran says that *The Mask of Anarchy* makes use of popular iconography, something which needs more study. He cites Kroeber's remark that the main figures in the procession of *The Mask of Anarchy* show "a marked, if independent, similarity to details of Cruikshank's designs for William Hone's *The Political Showman*."[64] If one carefully examines other Hone-Cruikshank works, then one starts to see some unmistakable patterns. In determining the nature of the popular mythology, I give a privileged treatment to three Hone-Cruikshank satires created between December 1819 and January 1820,[65] when Parliament was enacting repressive legislation as a response to Peterloo.

The first of the Hone-Cruikshank satires I will be discussing is *The Political House that Jack Built* (December 1819), which was inspired by the Peterloo Massacre and sold perhaps as many as 100,000 copies.[66] By March it was in its fifty-second edition.[67] The satire is written from the viewpoint of moderate reform, which pictures the ruling order as corrupt, while the printing press is imaged as a possible savior. The Liverpool administration, the Regent, spies, Peterloo, all are lampooned mercilessly, while the renovation of England is seen as possible only through Reform. "Reform" would signify here (1) freedom of the press and publication; (2) extension of the franchise to at least middle-class males; (3) parliamentary reforms such as abolition of the rotten boroughs, better representation for the urban areas, and abolition of the expensive patronage system; (4) financial reforms relating to the National Debt and the Bank of England; (5) a less reactionary foreign policy. The drawing of "Reform" in *The Political House* interestingly presents an abstract, disembodied image: on a flagstaff, against the sky, there is a banner on which "REFORM" is printed; at the very top, there is a wreath of laurel, and nowhere are there any people.[68] The reader is meant to try to forget, as a result of Peterloo, the disputes between radical and moderate reformers.

The second satire, *The Man in the Moon* (January 1820) was inspired by the Regent's speech to Paliament, when he asked for repressive measures to be taken against the reformers. When Par-

200

"Reform," from *The Political
House That Jack Built*

liament met on November 23, 1819, it did not investigate the Peterloo Massacre, as the reformers were urging, but passed instead the notoriously repressive "Six Acts" in an attempt to stifle reform even further. Hone turned to dream allegory in this satire, exploiting the conceit of having an "imaginary" Moon look exactly like Regency England. The satire consists mostly of the Moon-King's speech, which parodies the Regent's real speech.

The third, *The Political "A, Apple-Pie"* (January 1820) was produced at about the same time as the second. The villains and evils are the same, of course: the Liverpool administration, the Prince Regent, repression of the press, imprisonment of radical leaders, and so on. The subject of the satire is specifically the misuse of government money in the expensive patronage system. John Wade, an active reformer, published what he called *Black Book, or Corruption Unmasked*, in which he catalogued the placemen, pensioners, and other beneficiaries of government generosity. According to Wade, 2,344 people were annually receiving £2,474,805.[69] Utilizing Wade's research, Hone devises the political apple pie, symbolizing the government's handouts to the rich. As in a primer, he starts with "A" and goes through the alphabet, listing which aristocrats receive what amount of money.

What is so striking about the Hone-Cruikshank productions is the psychological representation of political conflict. At an unconscious level, this is what seems to be going on: the Nation should be maternal and nurturing, but instead it is both self-indulgent and aggressive. The second drawing of *The Political House* is entitled

"This is the house that Jack built,"[70] and portrays a three-columned, domed temple. On each pillar is the name of a different part of the nation: Commons, King, Lords. None has priority in the drawing, all being equal. But on top of the dome is a female figure, Britannia, draped like a Greek goddess, holding a staff with the Liberty cap on top of it.[71] The popular icon for the nation was not paternal, to say the least. Britannia does not appear again in *The Political House*, but she is in *The Man in the Moon* twice. In the first instance,[72] she is being burned to death on top of a printing press, and around her dance, all holding hands, the symbolic representatives of the Quadruple Alliance (of which England was a member). In another drawing,[73] she tries to protect the printing press from three male figures, whose weapons include a hatchet, a hangman's noose, a dagger, and chains. The printing press was, of course, an important libertarian symbol under the political repression. The maternal figure, however, is what interests me here. In *The Political House*, the representation of the Peterloo Massacre is especially important for its depiction of motherhood and the family.[74] In the background, the Yeomanry on horseback, with sabres drawn high, are slashing away at the crowd. The most prominent victim is a young woman with a child at her breast, and there is another child, obviously dead, lying on the ground next to hers. (In fact, one of the first Peterloo victims was a child who was trampled by a soldier's

"This is the House that Jack
Built," from *The Political House
That Jack Built*

HOLY COMPACT AND ALLIANCE,
The purposes of which
I need not mention—
You that have brains can guess
at the intention.

"Holy Compact and Alliance,"
from *The Man in the Moon*

THESE ARE
THE PEOPLE
all tatter'd and torn,
Who curse the day
wherein they were born,

"The People," from *The Political
House That Jack Built*

horse. The *Examiner* reports of Elizabeth Farren, a mother with a child who was attacked by the Yeomanry at Peterloo.)[75] In the foreground there is also a mother with an infant at her breast. She is sitting on the ground, in obvious despair, covering her face. Next to her is a man without wife or child, also in despair, wearing tattered workman's clothes, staring vacantly into space. But next to him is a man, presumably a father, in a more hopeful pose, chin in hand, pondering what to do; clinging to his knee is a child looking up into the man's face. What Peterloo violated most, then, was the family, especially the nurturing mother. Children were being threatened and fathers did not know how to protect them. The nation should protect the family, but instead it destroyed this basic unit and attacked the mother.

The corrupted nation was represented in one of two ways: by images of self-indulgent gluttony or of aggression. The Prince Regent is always portrayed with a prominent paunch, but the most vivid imagery of self-indulgence is in *The Political "A, Apple-Pie."* In this satire, the economic abuses of the ruling order are symbolized by having various figures consume parts of the national wealth; by the end, there is no pie left for John Bull, the people.[76] The most startling drawing, from a psychoanalytic viewpoint, is of the bishops.[77] They are on all fours, with piglike features protruding from their ecclesiastical robes. They are eating the pie like dogs or pigs, lapping it up with their tongues. There is an unmistakable cunnilingus image: a bishop's eager tongue is inside the V-shaped slice of pie. The nation, rather than nurturing the people, turns the whole issue of nurture into a travesty. Cunnilingus can be an important symbol of degradation for a powerless group because the act can represent the failure of the phallus; the equation seems to be that powerful phallus equals political and economic power. So Cruikshank was representing both the decadent self-indulgence of the ruling class and their "impotence."

To understand the phallic imagery, one has to understand the double meaning of the word "thing." As Edgell Rickword says, " 'Thing' in popular diction stood for the (male or female) genital organ."[78] When Ferdinand of Spain gave the Regent an enormous cannon as a token of his gratitude for helping defeat Napoleon, popular journalists called it "The Thing." One satire was entitled: *A Representation of the Regent's Tremendous Thing Erected in the Park.*[79] The phallic symbolism of weaponry would be obvious to Cruikshank's audience. There is an imposing cannon representing "Lawless Power" in *The Political House.*[80] The most important phallic imagery appears in *The Man in the Moon*, where Peterloo has another symbolic representation;[81] here, the foot soldiers thrust bayonets and sabres into the mouths of the demonstrators. Instead of giving maternal nurture, the corrupted nation sends soldiers who commit a kind of fellatio-rape of the people. Instead of the maternal breast, the nation offers "steel lozenges," as Hone calls them. The destructive and humiliating phallus is the most critical symbol with which to indict the ruling order.

"Bishops," from *The Political "A, Apple-Pie"*

STEEL LOZENGES

will stop their pain,
And set the Constitution
right again.

"Steel Lozenges," from *The Man
in the Moon*

Perhaps one reason for the psychological configurations of the reform movement's mythology is the ambivalence the democratic forces felt toward "independence."[82] By 1819 paternalism was a hypocritical pretense behind which the wealthy exploited the rest of the population, but as an ideal it was difficult to repudiate completely. According to Francis Hearn, the norm of class reciprocity was a strong belief among the poor, who revolted only when their "betters" violated the norm, rejecting the ideal of paternalism with great reluctance.[83] Paternalism subverted by bad fathers might generate the kind of psychosexual symbolism one finds in the popular iconography.

Shelley's *Mask of Anarchy* shares in this popular mythology. Stanzas thirty-seven to ninety-one, the long speech comprising most of the poem, are spoken by a maternal spirit, probably Britannia, who is introduced thus:

These words of joy and fear arose

As if their Own indignant Earth
Which gave the sons of England birth
Had felt their blood upon her brow,
And shuddering with a mother's throe

Had turned every drop of blood
. . . To an accent unwithstood . . .
(138-45)

Earth, mother, liberty, seem to fuse into a libertarian *spiritus mundi*, a univocal symbol of both nurture and power. So compelling was the maternal icon that Sir Francis Burdett also invoked it in his *Examiner* letter protesting the Peterloo Massacre. A major source of the poem is Burdett's letter, in which "tyrants" are imaged as eager to "rip open their mother's womb."[84] The bad father threatens maternal liberty in Burdett, Shelley, and the popular mythology of Hone-Cruikshank. A rejected stanza from "Ode to the Assertors of Liberty," written in October and directly concerned with Peterloo, represents social liberation and evokes the millennium by symbolizing a former tyrant playing with a child: "For fangless Power grown tame and mild / Is at play with Freedom's fearless child— / The dove and the serpent reconciled!"[85] Without "fangs," Power is harmless.

The aggressive and self-indulgent father of the iconography is present too in Shelley's *Mask*. The maternal spirit tells the assembled people not to resist the attacks of the soldiers.

> "Let the fixed bayonet
> Gleam with sharp desire to wet
> Its bright point in English blood
> Looking keen as one for food."
> (311-14)

Here gluttony is fused with aggression. In the next stanza, there is a similar psychosexual configuration.

> "Let the horsemen's scimitars
> Wheel and flash, like sphereless stars
> Thirsting to eclipse their burning
> In a sea of death and mourning."
> (315-18)

The star imagery, especially the "Thirsting to eclipse their burning," is a typically Shelleyan way to express desire, usually sexual desire; one finds this kind of imagery in both *Prometheus Unbound* (IV, 450) and *Epipsychidion* (567). In the early stanzas of the *Mask*, the symbols for the Liverpool government are depicted as indulgent. Castlereagh has "Seven blood-hounds," all "fat," to whom he gives "human hearts to chew" (9-13). The Anarchy procession enters London "Drunk as with intoxication / Of the wine of desolation" (48-49). The economic extravagance of the ruling class is a form of gluttony. An instance of conspicuous and unnecessary consumption is the Regent's so-called "education" which "Had cost ten millions to the Nation" (76-77).

One problem the popular mythology presents is finding a viable way to resist the bad father. Shelley has another female figure, the "maniac maid" whose name is "Hope," who is actually the one who instigates the revolution in the *Mask*. She commits the courageous act which her ineffectual father never could: "she lay down in the street" impeding the progress of "Murder, Fraud, and Anarchy" (98-101). Instead of resulting in her death, this act of apparent self-sacrifice produces "A mist, a light, an image" (103) which grows into a "Shape"; this Shape not only liberates the minds of the enslaved people but somehow has also destroyed the procession of tyranny. Symbolized here by "Hope" is Shelley's idea of massive nonviolent resistance, which is the most original and contradictory idea he presents in the poem. But before exploring that, we must retrace our steps somewhat and review the actual historical events, in order to put Shelley's response into a context.

The response of the radical leadership to Peterloo was surprisingly timid, and one has to agree with E. P. Thompson that the leaders must have been more alarmed than inspired by the revolutionary situation. Henry Hunt and Jonathan Wooler recommended the following: passive resistance, remonstrance, legal action against the perpetrators of the Massacre, and abstinence from taxed items.[86] Others called for parliamentary investigation of the Massacre (which was ironic, because when Parliament did meet on November 23, it started to pass the "Six Acts"). The only adequate radical proposals came from Dr. Watson, the Spencean leader, and Richard Carlile, the Painite journalist; they recommended, three months after Peterloo, "meetings . . . throughout the Kingdom on one and the same day." Going beyond the 1790s tactic of the convention, this was a call for a general strike, which was sabotaged from the start by Henry Hunt, who spoke against the plan.[87] The general strike of December never materialized, the "Six Acts" were passed, and "by the end of December 1819 the movement was in virtual state of collapse," with almost every radical leader in jail or awaiting trial.[88] The collapse, however, was only temporary, as the movement survived and continued throughout 1820.

Although Shelley repeats some of the moderate proposals in *The Mask of Anarchy*, such as trusting the courts (327-35) and refraining from violence, the main direction of *The Mask of Anarchy* is more radical than even what the Spenceans were saying, and anticipates by several months the call for a general strike. The key to understanding the uniqueness of Shelley's poem is his proposal for massive nonviolent resistance.

Even before the maternal spirit delivers her speech, there is an allegorical enactment of aggression against the tyrants. The maniac maid, Hope, through her nonviolent resistance, produces richly ambiguous consequences. At first the result of her passive opposition is delicately spiritual:

> When between her and her foes
> A mist, a light, an image rose,
> Small at first, and weak, and frail
> Like a vapour of a vale:
> (102-105)

But then the imagery becomes more aggressive.

> Till as clouds grew on the blast,
> Like tower-crowned giants striding fast,
> And glare with lightnings as they fly,
> And speak in thunder to the sky, . . .
> (106-109)

The organic metaphor of the storm introduces the idea of striding giants and natural violence. The movement toward violence continues in the next stanza.

> It grew—a Shape arrayed in mail
> Brighter than the Viper's scale,
> And upborne on wings whose grain
> Was as the light of sunny rain.
> (110-14)

The medieval "mail" is incongruous, but it is a way to signify an allegorical struggle between good and evil, which finally culminates in stanza thirty-three.

> And Anarchy, the ghastly birth,
> Lay dead earth upon earth
> The Horse of Death tameless as wind
> Fled, and with his hoofs did grind
> To dust the murderers thronged behind.
> (130-34)

Did "Anarchy" die before or after the Horse of Death fled? The most unforced reading would say before, and if so, who killed "Anarchy"? By implication, the constantly metamorphosing spirit unleashed by nonviolent resistance killed Anarchy and incited the Horse of Death to trample the other tyrants. What is interesting here is the denial of direct responsibility for taking *aggressive* action against the tyrants. Although they are in fact killed, even ground to dust, it is not clear who is responsible for having done it. Shelley's nonviolence here softens aggression and relieves Oedipal anxiety over killing the evil father. Allegorically, stanza thirty-three depicts the self-destruction of tyranny as a result of nonviolent action, despite the violent imagery.

A similar kind of ambivalence is apparent in the popular iconography, in which Britannia is always portrayed holding a staff surmounted by the liberty cap; the visual image suggests a spear. Although this liberty icon was intended primarily to project maternal benevolence, it also projects aggression. The stanza that concludes the poem and is the only one to be repeated is a curious one to signify nonviolence.

> "Rise like Lions after slumber
> In unvanquishable number
> Shake your chains to Earth like dew
> Which in sleep had fallen on you—
> Ye are many—they are few."
> (151-54 and 369-72)

What is foremost here is struggle, unity, and revolutionary consciousness; this is not moral argument, but political exhortation, an appeal to *physical* superiority. The contrast between this unambiguous assertiveness and stanza eighty-four (340-44) is jarring:

> "And if then the tyrants dare
> Let them ride among you there,
> Slash, and stab, and maim, and hew,—
> What they like, let them do."

In effect, however, Shelley's analysis of the political problem and his main proposal for a "great Assembly" go far beyond the confines of the moderate reform movement. Unlike anything one would find in Cobbett or the other popular journalists, Shelley provides an economic analysis in lines 160 to 204 that anticipates socialism. The workers "are made" for the benefit of the rich; they nourish

209

the rich who give in turn mere subsistence, if even that. The "Ghost of Gold," the paper money decried so often by Cobbett, is a force of reification that robs the worker of his or her subjective will as well as the material wealth that he or she produces. The worker is not an individual, with a unique subjectivity, but is "All that others make of" him or her (187). Liberty is not just political rights, but real benefits such as bread, clothes, food, and shelter. By rooting "liberty" in the rights of the poor, Shelley is much closer to the socialistic Chartists than to the political forces which finally succeeded in passing the 1832 Reform Bill.

In the proposal for a great assembly (262-372), *fraternité* is expressed with great power. The maternal spirit invokes *all* her "children," from the poorest to the richest, "From every hut, village, and town / Where those who live and suffer moan / For others' misery or their own" (272-74). Going beyond the narrow focus of electoral rights, the spirit invites to the assembly the inhabitants of the workhouse and the prison, as well as "Women, children, young and old" (277). The political implications of the assembly are anarchist in the complete negation of artificial distinctions among people. Once assembled, the people are asked to be passive when attacked, to allow the laws, "The old laws of England," to be their protection, to practice restraint even if their tyrants do not; and yet at the end, they are asked to be aggressive Lions rising in great number. Ambivalence is the only word adequate to describe Shelley's attitude toward social revolution. The idea of massive nonviolent resistance, in the context of a general strike and an egalitarian assembly, is a way for Shelley to express his revolutionary vision while at the same time relieving some of the anxiety this vision produced in him.

A PHILOSOPHICAL VIEW OF REFORM

When Shelley begins A *Philosophical View of Reform*, he expects a revolution in England, although it will not occur until a financial crisis precipitates it. As he tells Peacock on September 9, there will be "no coming to close quarters until financial affairs decidedly bring the oppressors & the oppressed together."[89] Announcing his intention to begin the essay on November 6, he says, "the people are nearly in a state of insurrection" and that "Every thing is preparing for a bloody struggle."[90] By December 15, he tells his publisher he is preparing an octavo on reform which "now that I see the passion of party will postpone the great struggle till another year, I shall not trouble myself to finish for this season."[91] But only eight days later, to Leigh Hunt, he says: "I suppose we shall soon have to fight in England."[92] He begins the essay expecting a decisive contest between the government and the reform movement which is delayed temporarily—but only temporarily—by traditional party loyalties. After the Six Acts were passed by Parliament in late December and early January, he probably put aside *A Philosophical View of Reform* because he felt the government had triumphed over the reform movement. I surmise this from indirect evidence, Mary Shelley's letter of February 24, 1820. Writing to Marianne Hunt, Mary says she would not want to be in England now, however much she dislikes the Pisans.

> I am too much depressed by its [England's] enslaved state, my inutility; the little chance there is for freedom; & the great chance there is for tyranny to wish to be witness of its degradation step by step & to feel all the sensations of indignation & horror which I know I shd experience were I to hear daily the talk of the subjects or rather the slaves of King Cant whose dominion I fear is of wider extent in England than anywhere else.[93]

If Mary was feeling this way, I believe Shelley was as well; indeed, I suspect Shelley himself was the one who exclaimed most vociferously about his "inutility" with the passage of the Six Acts. Once he realized the reform movement was not dead, but alive and struggling, he regained hope for his political writing, urging Leigh Hunt to find a publisher for his reform essay (May 26) as well as his popular songs (May 1).[94] With Donald Reiman, I believe Shelley worked on *A Philosophical View of Reform* from November to possibly January, but the essay was "finished" by then—as finished as it would ever be.[95] He probably wrote most or all the popular songs in this period—or earlier—because they refer so immediately to Peterloo. Shelley stops work on the political material sometime in January because he does not think he has a chance of publishing it, so he turns to writing some of the poems which will be included in the *Prometheus Unbound* volume. Then, in May, he regains hope of finding an audience for his political work.

A Philosophical View of Reform develops a theory of history which it applies to the specific conditions of post-Peterloo England. The essay assumes that some kind of English reform will occur, so that the only questions are what kind of reform, when, and how. He argues against revolution and civil war by developing a bold "Promethean" strategy of nonviolent resistance, education of the poor, and perpetual but moderate contestation, thus moving society along a path of gradual reforms. Examining the characteristic work of Bentham and Owen will help illustrate what is distinctive in Shelley's essay. Bentham, in his *Plan of Parliamentary Reform, in the Form of a Catechism . . .*,[96] concentrates on the particularities of reform, arguing for their practical utility. When he cites historical evidence, he does so to make debater's points, especially to show that democracy, since it is practiced in the United States, is not just a utopian dream. He tries to allay the fears of the rich by saying that democracy will not cause any redistribution of wealth; communism, he claims, is impossible since it would lead to universal starvation. Bentham wants "good government," by which he means one that is efficient and "rational." He so distrusts anything resembling direct democracy or popular assemblies that he wants a secret ballot, since even speeches on the hustings are conducive to violence and irresponsibility.[97] Bentham envisions a rule of experts who will administer the state according to a utilitarian code that ignores region, vested interests, and momentary passions. As a negation of "Old Corruption," Bentham's program was gaining adherents until the 1832 Reform Bill put the Benthamites in a position to influence government policy, especially Poor Law reform.[98] Owen, however, was not as fortunate, at least not in this period. Appealing to the wealthy and powerful, Owen argued for the establishment of planned communities in which the poor would work in humane factories. Since poor people could not have supplied the capital necessary for starting these communities, Owen was correct in trying to persuade the powerful to finance Owenite settlements, but naive in thinking he would succeed. Owen, too, emphasizes the practicality of his scheme, which he does not situate historically.[99]

Shelley's essay is distinctive not only for the historical context in which he puts the issue of reform, but also for the libertarian nature of the reform itself. He develops a theory of history, culture, and social change, locating England's present crisis in a theoretical context.[100] History is a process of dialectical conflict, a succession of moments in which "liberty" and "tyranny" achieve varying states of equilibrium. By liberty he means a social condition approaching self-determination, with the political ideal a rational anarchy, and the cultural ideal a fully creative artist. Tyranny is hierarchical

212

domination, the external determination of existence by a tyrannical idea ("God," "law," "nation") or by any variety of tyrants inhabiting the economic, religious, political, judicial, sexual, or social realms. The ideal of complete liberty, the anarchist self-determination depicted by the Spirit of the Hour in the third act of *Prometheus Unbound*, entails complete equality, the obliteration of class hierarchy. This ideal, according to Shelley, cannot be achieved except as the last stage of social evolution. "Equality in possessions must be the last result of the utmost refinements of civilization; it is one of the conditions of that system of society, towards which with whatever hope of ultimate success, it is our duty to tend."[101] As he argued earlier in the theological fragment, a premature equality cannot maintain itself because hierarchical modes of thinking will ultimately reproduce themselves in the form of classes.

Democracy permits rich cultural development because it so highly values self-determination. The Italian republics and municipal governments which opposed the Pope and Roman Empire generated an aesthetic culture of monumental significance.[102] Like the anarchists Peter Kropotkin and Rudolf Rocker, Shelley sees in the small, decentralized city-states Sismondi wrote about an exemplary political form of participatory democracy.[103] Democratic city-states encourage diverse modes of free expression, whereas the centralized, imperial nation-state is hostile to unfettered creativity. An indirect consequence of the Italian Renaissance, according to Shelley, is the libertarian inspiration which animated Chaucer, the "father" of English literature. Liberty is a fire whose sparks fly unpredictably, igniting new and unforeseen conflagrations. Chaucer appropriated from Italy "the generous disdain of submission which burned in the bosoms of men who filled a distant generation & inhabited another land."[104] Part of the English Reformation, the flowering of literature in the age of Shakespeare was a cultural acme at once "caused" by the social libertarianism but also "the causes of its more complete developement."[105] Shelley also implies a connection between the aesthetic creativity of the Elizabethans and the political revolution undertaken by Milton and the Puritans, who brought to "public justice one of those chiefs of a conspiracy of priveledged murderers & robbers"[106]—that is, Charles the First.

History is dialectical not only because effect becomes cause (culture influencing society which influences culture), but because history is cumulative. One generation stands on the shoulders of the next, inheriting their libertarian victories. For example, the Puritan

Revolution established the principle that the People's will has the right to grant or withhold legitimacy to established government.[107] Cultural activity is also cumulative since, as Shelley says, without Lord Bacon, Montaigne, and Spinoza, the revolutionary writers of the eighteenth and nineteenth centuries would not have been able to write as they did.[108] Progress is not inevitable or evenly distributed throughout every sphere. Athenian liberty perished, and so may the libertarian dialectic begun by the Italian republics. The extinction of hope that for ages has characterized China and India, a torpid resignation in the face of tyranny, is a possibility for even the West.[109] However sensitive Shelley was to the power of "objective" conditions, he emphasized that liberty depended on human agency. Rejecting the pessimistic fatalism of Byron, he did not therefore countenance a naively optimistic determinism, as though progress were automatic. Moreover, progress in one realm does not mean progress everywhere. As advanced as the Athenians were, they still held slaves and subordinated women.

History is a dialectical struggle between liberty and tyranny (in all their different forms), but liberty can grow only by being practiced more often by more people. Shelley does not believe in Hegel's "cunning" of History by which ostensible retreats from liberty are paradoxically advances. Citizens learn to be free by practicing freedom, exercising the will, imagination, intelligence, and capacity to love. He admires a law (which does not, of course, exist) that permits the citizens to revise the United States Constitution every ten years.[110] No code, enacted by one group living under specific, unique conditions, should completely determine the society of a later group. Although there is libertarian progress in the movement from absolutist monarchy to representative democracy, such democracy is not the final realization of freedom because the human will cannot be "represented." The political ideal is a condition under which complete self-determination can take place: a "self governing Society."[111] Because he favors rational anarchy, Shelley opposes one of Bentham's dearest proposals, the secret ballot.[112] He also favors, on anarchist grounds, acquainting the poor with all their rights, educating them in every aspect of their exploited condition.[113] The risk of violent revolution is necessary because the poor, like the intellectuals, have to learn the libertarian virtues by practicing them. The only safeguard against demagogic manipulation is enlightenment, so that the poor will not be "masses" guided by

214

leaders, but independent citizens, rationally deciding policy in conjunction with their fellows.

With his historical theory, Shelley locates the context within which he discusses the problem of English reform. By a subtle, dialectical analysis he shows that the real contest is no longer, as it was in the seventeenth century, between the libertarian parliament and the tyrannical crown, but between the people, especially the poor, and the rich. The nobility used the people in their struggle against the crown, but once this victory over absolutism was achieved, the nobility used the crown to advance their own concerns. After the truly representative Long Parliament was succeeded by the narrowly representative parliaments of the merchants and landowners, all branches of government—Commons, Lords, and monarchy—represented only the rich. After 1688, then, the "power which has increased therefore is the power of the rich."[114] Beginning in the eighteenth century we can see the emergence and development of the "double" aristocracy, the addition of a new class of rich created by the public credit system. To finance the wars of the eighteenth century, especially the expensive campaigns against the American colonies and revolutionary France, the government had to borrow money from a bourgeoisie which enriched itself by accumulating the interest. The traditional aristocracy did not use their own money to pay back the bourgeoisie, but taxed mercilessly the consumer items used by the poor and "middling classes," who actually financed the debt. The wars, bad enough themselves, also created a new aristocracy and substantially increased the misery of the population.[115] The essay's analysis closely parallels Cobbett's, from whom Shelley derived most of the "double aristocracy" concepts.

By increasing taxes and turning to inflationary paper money, which the credit system necessitated, the government made life unbearable for poor people. Real wages could not keep up with prices, so that it took a manufacturer sixteen hours to earn what he previously made working only eight hours.[116] Children were forced to work, turned "into lifeless & bloodless machines";[117] the old and feeble, under penalty of starvation, must also work and contribute to the so-called national prosperity. The industrial revolution has inaugurated an economic order worse than the previous one, whose aristocracy was not nearly as materialistic and selfish as the new aristocracy of "attornies & excisemen, & directors, & government pensioners usurers, stock jobbers, country bankers."[118] Shelley identifies the forces of liberty as the poor and those members of the "middling classes" whose property is legitimate because it is the product of their own effort.[119] He sees in small property a check against the rich and powerful. Libertarians and anarchists have frequently identified the small property owner as a force for progressive social change. It was French artisans and tradesmen, not industrial workers, who carried out 1793, 1848, and 1871. Proudhon's ideal, like Henry George's, entailed the decentralizing of land into small holdings, not collective farms. The populist movement in the United States between 1880 and 1900 was led by the small farmer, whose challenge to big capital was perhaps as powerful as anything mounted by the industrial proletariat. Although the Marxian tradition has been consistently hostile to what it contemptuously labels the petty bourgeoisie, the anarchist tradition has been much more friendly to those whose independence and initiative suggest they will contribute to a participatory democracy. Shelley, however, did not envision the libertarian ideal as being fully realized by small property, since this is only a temporary stage liberty passes through on its way to complete equality and classlessness.

At the juncture defined by the ascendancy of the double aristocracy, Shelley proposes the following: abolition of the national debt; disbanding the standing army; abolishing tithes and sinecures; permitting complete freedom of thought in religion; reform the judicial system.[120] Abolishing sinecures and forcing one part of the wealthy class to pay back the other is a means of decreasing taxes on the poor and increasing their real wages. The standing army was not only expensive to maintain, but was used principally to suppress strikes and demonstrations. Shelley's *bête noire*, the established church, is undermined by another reform, which will permit more freedom for philosophy to contest religious superstition for the allegiance of the population. Judicial reform is essential for a libertarian transformation because, as Godwin showed in minute detail, citizens cannot be self-determining as long as an externally constituted and bureaucratically administered legal code takes precedence over democratically practiced philosophy. In a fragment perhaps related to this essay, entitled "On a System of Government by Juries," Shelley follows Godwin in assuming that law, properly understood, is merely opinion. If opinions are to be as enlightened as possible, people have to acquire public wisdom by practicing it. "When law is once understood to be no more than the recorded opinion of men, no more than the apprehensions of individuals on the reasoning of a particular case, we may expect that the sanguinary or stupid mistakes which disgrace the civil and criminal jurisprudence of civilized nations will speedily disappear." Public opinion must be liberated from its stagnation, since it is at present "fenced about and frozen over by forms and superstitions."[121] Shelley's concept is to strengthen social forces at the expense of institutional power.

His other comments on the English situation are equally informed by a libertarian logic. For libertarian reasons, he wants a moderate, nonviolent approach to reform, not civil war or violent revolution. Once the political conflict becomes a civil war, the reform movement ceases to be governed solely by liberty, because militarization has its own logic which is hostile to liberty. The "pageantry of arms & badges corrupts the imagination."[122] The soldier, even for a libertarian cause, is still a soldier, who is trained to be obedient, "habitual," and "mechanical." "The person who has been accustomed to subdue men by force, will be less inclined to the trouble of convincing or persuading them."[123] There should be a nonviolent but persistent challenge to the established order, which will be contested on many fronts. Shelley wants "open confederations" of reformers, not "secret associations," which is a proposal reminiscent of his 1812 plan for an association.[124] Popular assemblies small enough to permit participation by everyone could replace the demonstrations in which people are passive recipients of speeches by a few.[125] If there is a large assembly, such as the one in Manchester on August 16, then the reformers should stand firm when the military attack because nonviolent resistance might convert the soldiers to the side of reform; such conversions would be enduring victories for reform because the soldiers would act from deeply felt conviction rather than out of fear and instinctive obedience. The reformers should "publish the boldest truths in the most fearless manner, yet without the slightest tincture of personal malignity." The latter qualification seems aimed at Cobbett, although reform journalism in general was not noted for philosophical disinterestedness. Despising imprisonment and persecution, the reformers would engage the government in a "perpetual contest & opposition."[126] Rejecting sectarian divisions,[127] the reformers will unite and systematically defy the government, withholding taxes, writing petitions, and pressing the issue of reform at every opportunity.[128] Demogorgon's concluding speech, which was written about the same time as the essay, seems to capture the essence of Shelley's message to the reform movement:

To suffer woes which Hope thinks infinite;
To forgive wrongs darker than Death or Night;
 To defy Power which seems Omnipotent;
To love, and bear; to hope, till Hope creates
From its own wreck the thing it contemplates;
 Neither to change nor falter nor repent . . .
(IV, 570-75)

Unless there was some kind of libertarian intervention resembling the measures Shelley proposed, he believed that a revolutionary conflict, with all its attendant problems, would be inevitable. At times, he seems to think the moment has passed when a gradual reform is feasible ("Two years ago it might still have been possible to have commenced a system of gradual reform").[129] But even if an English civil war begins, only a "Promethean" process of libertarian education can lead society toward self-determination. As in the theological fragment, he depicts the role of mediator between ideals of perfection and a world in need of transformation: "our present business is with the difficult and unbending realities of actual life, & when we have drawn inspiration from the great object of our hope [complete equality, rational anarchy] it becomes us with patience & resolution, to apply ourselves to accommodating our theories to immediate practise."[130] No matter which way England moves, his theory can accommodate the new developments. If the conflict wanes to the point of quiescence, then he would emphasize militance; if the danger is civil war, he would counsel moderation.

PETER BELL THE THIRD

In *A Philosophical View of Reform*, Shelley dialectically links society and literature. Always following or preceding "a great & free developement of the national will," English literature is the "most unfailing herald" or "follower" or "companion" of English liberty.[131] The essence of art and social liberty is self-determination, so that poetry is both a cause of, and caused by, social liberty. In an age like Shelley's, even the poets who are not reformers "actually advance the interests of Liberty" because they are "compelled to serve, that which is seated in the throne of their own soul." Great poets do not express their own narrow ideas, but "measure the circumference or sound the depths of human nature with an comprehensive & all-penetrating spirit, at which they are themselves

218

perhaps most sincerely astonished for it [is] less their own spirit than the spirit of their age." The creative poet, then, draws his inspiration from a suprapersonal—or better, transpersonal—spirit, a *Zeitgeist* which influences all the poets. Since they are so sensitive to this spirit, which actually affects the entire society, "Poets & philosophers are the unacknowledged legislators of the world."[132] They do not proclaim laws from a privileged realm or with an idiosyncratic perception; rather, they allow themselves to be the vehicles through which the future discloses itself. As poets discover—uncover, unveil—the spirit which lies within them, they are also revealing to society its innermost truths which, sooner or later, it must confront.

Peter Bell III is interesting in this context because Shelley shows a poet who once unveiled the *Zeitgeist*, but now represses his creativity and serves the forces of tyranny. There are many reasons why he would satirize Wordsworth, especially after Peterloo. The *Examiner* had been having some fun with Wordsworth's *Peter Bell* even before it was published, since Keats, on April 25, 1819, reviewed Reynolds' brief parody, *Peter Bell*, which satirized Wordsworth's style. After Wordsworth's poem was published, Hunt wrote a caustic review on May 2, 1819. If, however, the Reynolds-Hunt-Keats satirizing was Shelley's only source, then it is hard to explain why he wrote the poem in October rather than immediately after reading the *Examiner* material in June. But Shelley also was aware that Wordsworth had in 1818 intervened on behalf of the Lowthers against the liberal Brougham in the Westmorland election, an important contest for the reformers. Wordsworth did not simply cast his vote for the Lowthers, his patrons and benefactors, but penned an antireform pamphlet, *Two Addresses to the Freeholders of Westmorland*, wrote letters to the local newspapers, and assisted the Lowthers in every way he could.[133] Shelley followed the election closely from Italy, remarking to Peacock—after he learned of Brougham's narrow defeat—"What a beastly and pitiful wretch that Wordsworth! That such a man should be such a poet!"[134] Even this irate comment acknowledges the twofold nature of Wordsworth, the man and the poet, the one despicable, the other admirable.

Peter Bell III is a Peterloo-inspired poem not simply because the massacre is directly alluded to (645-52), but also because there would be considerable interest in a "party squib"[135] like this in the polarized, agitated state of English society. Although it is certainly a party squib in the battle of the books between right (*Quarterly Review*) and left (*Examiner*), it is also a serious poem, one of the longest Shelley ever wrote, and unfairly neglected by critics. The five-line stanzas have an *abaab* rime scheme, like a Spenserian cut off after the fifth line, but the iambic tetrameters are anything but stately, and resemble more the *ottava rima* lines of Byron's *Don Juan* and *Beppo*. This, the most Byronic of Shelley's poems, has moments of comic brilliance, especially in the third part, that make one wish he had written in this mode more often. But despite its many Byronic features, *Peter Bell III* is distinctly Shelleyan because it expresses a profound admiration for the earlier poetry of Wordsworth and presents a coherent argument for the utopian imagination.

Shelley read Wordsworth's *Peter Bell* before writing his own poem,[136] so one must turn to Wordsworth, whose poem was published April 7, 1819, a time when it makes sense to speak of published literature in terms of politics. As political action, Wordsworth's *Peter Bell* is as "ultra-legitimate" as Shelley's is in favor of reform. The poem is dedicated to Robert Southey, Poet Laureate and Tory apologist, and author, so Shelley erroneously thought, of the *Quarterly*'s vicious attack on Shelley and his *The Revolt of Islam*. The Prologue contains a conservative argument against imagination, something that must have impressed Shelley as especially objectionable. The poem itself is a story of Peter Bell, potter, who has married twelve different women and who has led, Wordsworth tells us, "a lawless life." While trying to steal a donkey, Peter discovers a dead man and experiences a series of terrifying adventures that culminate in his desire to "reform." Peter hears a "fervent Methodist" urging sinners to repent, which, by the poem's end, he does.

Although the poem might be interesting in other ways, as a political document it is thoroughly reactionary. The only organization with a plebian following that congratulated the authorities on their handling of the Peterloo Massacre was the Methodists, a group of religious "fanatics" regularly criticized in the *Examiner*. Methodism has long been considered as a form of social control over the poor, even though, as E. P. Thompson has shown, workers often manipulated Methodism for their own uses and were not simply passive dupes.[137] Isaac Ludlam, one of the workers executed for his part in the Pentridge Rebellion of 1817, was in fact a Methodist preacher.[138] But the general direction of Methodism ran counter to radical pol-

itics and class conflict. If radicalism survived a Methodist conver-
sion, the survival was despite the religion, not because of it. Meth-
odism encouraged quietism and cultivated asceticism and guilt, as
does Wordsworth's *Peter Bell.*

Shelley's *Peter Bell* is designed to overturn the religious mysticism
of Wordsworth's poem. The different parts, "Death," "The Devil,"
"Hell," "Sin," "Grace," "Damnation," and "Double Damnation,"
are pointed and intentional demystifications of Christian concepts,
as well as being a parody of sorts of the seven sacraments. Shelley
is poking iconoclastic fun at the assumptions of Methodism, while
Wordsworth directly and indirectly grants them validity. There is
nothing new in Shelley's attack on Christianity, but in *Peter Bell
III* he links this with a critique of the apostate poet, who has turned
away from liberty.

Peter Bell—really Wordsworth—begins with a flawed but creative
imagination which he eventually destroys to satisfy the reactionary
reviewers. Peter's inadequacies are passivity and narrowness. Uniting
with the external world (278-79), he exercised an imagination which
lacked active power. "Nothing went ever out, although / Something
did ever enter" (296-97). Despite this "wise passiveness," as Words-
worth more positively named it, Peter's mind is "individual" and
"new created all he saw" (303-307). Nevertheless, he could not
"Fancy another situation . . . Than that wherein he stood" (299-
302). Peter is also a hired poet, employed by the "Devil," who is
clearly supposed to represent the *nouveaux riches* whose wealth is
acquired by "fraud." The Devil pursues wealth at the expense of
everything else, even pleasure, which "Nature" defends in a satirical
speech directed at puritanical Peter (320-32). The true logic of
nature is unbounded, unconditional joy and the liberation of sex-
uality from artificial constraints. Peter wrote poetry under these
unfavorable conditions and nevertheless came into contact with the
creative fire of liberty, the spirit of the age:

> But Peter's verse was clear, and came
>   Announcing from the frozen hearth
> Of a cold age, that none might tame
> The soul of that diviner flame
>   It augured to the Earth . . .
>   (433-37)

Once he wrote this poetry, libertarian despite itself, the critics were
outraged by its originality and abused these deviations from Pope.

221

Unable to withstand the negative criticism, Peter turns against himself, destroying the creative faculties within. He becomes even more puritanical, imitating the creed of Calvin and Dominic: happiness is wrong (573-74). Hating pleasure, he deserts his "Soul," which is likened to a dying fawn wounded and moaning in a cave (605-607). As the Calvinist and Dominican mind represses the body, so does Peter Bell repress his imagination. The next logical step in "dullness" is political tyranny, repressing the poor in their struggle for liberty. He discovers that apostasy "sells," so he continues to write "odes to the Devil." The imagination repressed, the soul destroyed, Peter sinks to the lowest possible moral level by participating in the denial of nurture that was so indignantly protested in the popular iconography. After alluding to Peterloo, the poem makes reference to the child-eating Moloch that Peter Bell worshiped in his pseudo-poetry (650-51). Sexual repression, political repression, sadism, and "dull" poetry are linked together in a chain of consequences following from the failure of imagination.

The two poles are creative imagination and the cash nexus. The imagination is boundless, overflowing, joyful, pleasurable, freely giving of itself, actively shaping a world of love. The cash nexus, like Godwin's stasis, is a force of death, repression, denial, destruction, and selfish narrowness. A poet can cease serving liberty only after ceasing to be a poet, only after destroying the imagination. Afterwards, the shadow of a poet merely serves Mammon, but does not—cannot—*create* anything. The "damned" world of part three is a London governed solely by isolated egos pursuing personal gain. People, not fate or "God," damn each other by robbing and cheating one another in an attempt to get ahead. Only a few escape this hierarchical dialectic of oppression because they believe "their minds are given / To make this ugly Hell a Heaven" (244-45); they "weep to see what others / Smile to inflict" (254-55). Those few with imagination, however, are unable to alter the chaos of domination, within which:

> All are damned—they breathe an air
> Thick, infected, joy-dispelling:
> Each pursues what seems most fair,
> Mining like moles, through mind, and there
> Scoop palace-caverns vast, where Care
> In throned state is ever dwelling.
> (256-62)

Rather than turn hell into heaven, each mind turns in upon itself, creating an inner world which grants no peace or tranquility. In short, no one is happy, since the only enduring happiness is a product of imagination, the outward activity of spirit reshaping the world.

As in *A Philosophical View of Reform*, the most common target of abuse is the high bourgeoisie rather than the aristocrats. Indeed, the poem is not without its share of social snobbery, since both rustic and bourgeois life are ridiculed from an aristocratic stance. It seems merely cruel to poke fun at Peter's "nasal twang" and cheap hair oil (since he could not afford the expensive brand) (7-8). Some of the antibourgeois allusions also seem to be sneers, for example the jibes at Grosvenor Square and the slop-merchant from Wapping. (Once again, Shelley the "agrarian reactionary" rears his head.) Moreover, Cobbett is attacked in the body of the poem (239) and in a footnote[139] for encouraging class revenge, something *A Philosophical View of Reform* strenuously argues against. At this time, September 1819, Cobbett was fair game for someone like Shelley because: (1) he was in America, separated from the reform movement; (2) in the Westminster election of 1818 he had supported Orator Hunt, instead of Burdett and Kinnaird, both endorsed by the *Examiner*; and (3) his writing style, as analyzed by E. P. Thompson, did indeed appeal to class feelings, although Cobbett never called for class revenge. Comparing Cobbett and Hazlitt, Thompson shows that Hazlitt, however "left" his opinions, stays nevertheless within a discourse of cultured gentlemen, while Cobbett is well beyond the pale. He relies on "we-them" assumptions of class, and employs concrete illustrations and imagery rather than allusions to an intellectual tradition.[140] In support of Thompson's analysis I want to look at a passage from the *Political Register*. Parliament passed a new banking act which Cobbett hated, and which he analyzed to show how it would harm the interests of the laborers. He then begins to sneer at Parliament: "These are the '*noble lords*' and Sir Francis's 'gentlemen of the country'! These are the pupils of the great Universities! These are the big-wigged, long-robed, and high-blooded men, who lift their heads, half-shut their eyes, draw up their upper lip, open their nostrils, and talk of the '*Lower Orders*'!"[141] Cobbett was unique not in discovering class—the rich had done that long ago—but in developing a language of class *for* the so-called "lower orders."

As in all the Peterloo-inspired writings, Shelley wants to steer society between "Cobbett's snuff, revenge" (239) and the tyranny of the rich, aristocratic, and bourgeois, who are "damned beyond all cure" (232). The principal focus of the poem is on the deformation of a poet whose imagination promises so much that its repression constitutes a tragedy. Poets are important because they make up that small group between the rich and the poor who can escape class hatred long enough to formulate a peaceful resolution of the social conflict. If imagination is able to grow, then it will increase at the expense of tyranny and revenge, the products of class antagonism. The death of a poet and the birth of a tyrant-serving "rhymester" make more possible the advent of civil war and less likely the multifaceted movement toward rational anarchy depicted hopefully in *A Philosophical View of Reform*.

THE CARLILE LETTER AND *POPULAR SONGS*

An eyewitness to Peterloo, Richard Carlile, inspired another of Shelley's unpublishable works, the open letter to Hunt's *Examiner* protesting Carlile's trial. That Shelley chose to defend Richard Carlile publicly is interesting because Carlile, whose persecution by the government the *Examiner* followed closely from early 1819 onwards, represented the most progressive aspects of English radicalism. Carlile was a former tinner, a follower of Paine, an enemy of Christianity, and an advocate of Enlightenment and radical reform. He attacked many of the prejudices that other reform leaders like Cobbett and Henry Hunt opportunistically reinforced. Carlile was also a fearlessly defiant journalist and bookseller, who refused to be intimidated by repression. Factors that might have led Shelley to defend Carlile are Carlile's heroic defiance and their personal relations. Carlile read *Queen Mab* while he was in prison for the first time, and afterwards asked Shelley for permission to publish it; Shelley refused. In December 1819, Carlile's journal *The Republican* published Shelley's old pamphlet, *A Declaration of Rights*, anonymously. It is tempting to speculate as to how Carlile found a copy of one of the pamphlets for which Dan Healy was imprisoned. Perhaps Shelley sent Carlile a copy?

Carlile began his radical career in 1817 by selling William Hone's satirical *Parodies*, for which he received a short prison sentence (August 14 to December 20, 1817). After Sherwin was frightened away from publishing his *Weekly Political Register* by government repression, Carlile took over the operation and changed the title to the more provocative *The Republican*, in 1819. In addition to publishing the journal, Carlile published and sold radical literature which the courts deemed blasphemous and seditious. Early in 1819 he was arrested for publishing Paine's *The Age of Reason* and Palmer's *Principles of Nature*, but he was not tried in court until after Peterloo, when numerous other radicals were being prosecuted. Carlile's trials resulted in convictions, of course; for publishing Paine, he was fined £1,000 and sentenced to two years in Dorchester jail; for publishing Palmer, he was fined £500 and sentenced to one year in jail; he was also to remain in jail until he paid the fines, and furthermore, he had to give a security of £1,200 to insure good behavior for life. In other words, Carlile received what amounted to an indeterminate life sentence because there was no possibility of his ever obtaining such a large sum of money. He did not leave prison until November 18, 1825, after he had served six years. He was released because of popular pressure, not because he had paid the fines.

Carlile, however, was undaunted. During the trial for publishing Paine, he read into the court transcript large segments of *The Age of Reason*; after the trial, his wife published the trial transcript, which was technically legal, although the technicality did not deter the authorities from also prosecuting his wife. At the time Shelley was composing his protest letter, the other reformers, led by Henry Hunt, were criticizing Carlile as too radical; Hunt identified himself as a law-abiding, God-fearing, Christian reformer who was as horrified by Carlile's outrages as the government. Hunt's opportunistic backstabbing did not persuade everyone of Carlile's depravity, because after Carlile was imprisoned there was a spontaneous effort to continue publishing and selling the radical literature for which he had been prosecuted. From October 1819, when he was convicted, to 1825, when he was released, over one-hundred-fifty men and women also went to jail in the effort to keep open Carlile's radical bookshop. The heroic defiance of these radicals helped create freedom of the press and enriched radical culture with a tradition of nonviolent resistance.[142]

Shelley's protest letter parallels Carlile's own defense in court, where he represented himself. Carlile, too, establishes the contradiction between the letter and the spirit of the law by arguing that if Deism is illegal, then so too Unitarianism, whose theological principles are similar. And if Christianity is the only legal religion,

225

it is inconsistent to allow so many sects. But Shelley goes beyond this kind of defense in his letter.

Shelley's letter begins by protesting the court's hypocrisy in not prosecuting the butchers of Peterloo but instead convicting a Deist for blasphemy. At this point, the language starts to break down and becomes overwhelmed by the popular mythology; he condemns the Yeomanry who "cut off women's breasts & dash the heads of infants against the stones."[143] Once again, the corrupt society is imaged as a violator of maternal nurture and children. Shortly after this outburst, Shelley expresses his willingness to go to prison, because he admits he is as much a "blasphemer" as Carlile.[144] This is the only time he ever expresses a willingness to go to jail in defiance of the repression, and it significantly occurs in the Carlile letter, protesting someone else's imprisonment. Seeing in Carlile someone rather like himself, Shelley is able to feel the injustice as if it were his own. He attacks, next, the hypocrisy of legal procedure which supposedly guarantees a trial by one's peers, who in Carlile's case could only have been Deists. Declaring the irrationality of the blasphemy laws themselves, Shelley argues that at the very least Carlile should have a new trial.

The worst hypocrisy, however, is the double standard: while Deists of the leisured class are published and read with impunity, only the lower-class freethinkers are prosecuted. Hume, Gibbon, Drummond, Godwin, and Bentham can doubt the existence of God, but when Carlile or his philosophical mentor, Paine, engage in the same activity, they become "blasphemers." It is not just class, Shelley says, but class politics that generates the double standard, because religion is "the mask & garment" for political conflict. By prosecuting Carlile, they strike at a political opponent and "in his person at all their political enemies." Religion is an ideological means of social control which is designed to prevent reform. If religion were recognized as the superstition it really is, "the government would be reformed, & . . . the people would receive a just price for their labours."[145] But without reform, England faces "the alternative of despotism or revolution."[146] Shelley bases his hope for social emancipation on psychological liberation, freedom from the distortions of hierarchical religion. Political rights alone are meaningless if the spiritual tyranny of Christianity continues. Although some reform leaders openly attacked Carlile as a liability to the movement, Shelley does not, and instead declares himself in solidarity with the most enduringly radical aspects of the reform movement.

Another of Shelley's efforts to affect the reform movement was a volume of poems to have been entitled *Popular Songs*. According to Richard Holmes, the volume was to include, along with *The Mask of Anarchy*: "Lines Written During the Castlereagh Administration," "Song to the Men of England," "Similes for Two Political Characters," "What Men Gain Fairly," "A New National Anthem," "Sonnet: England 1819," "Ballad of the Starving Mother," and probably "Ode to Liberty," and "Ode to the West Wind."[147] I also think "An Ode written October, 1819," whose original title was "Ode to the Assertors of Liberty," would have been included. Of these eleven titles, only three were published in Shelley's lifetime.

One cannot know for certain which poems would have gone into *Popular Songs*, nor can we be certain that all the poems so intended have survived the uncertain and not always honest transmission from Mary Shelley, Leigh Hunt, Thomas Medwin, and other editors. There have been curious, to say the least, alterations, omissions, and outright suppressions. Medwin, for example, by altering Shelley's title from "England" to "Lines Written During the Castlereagh Administration," distances the political meaning of the poem for the 1832 audience.[148] Transcribing it, he also made so many changes in the punctuation and capitalization, that Medwin's is a corrupt text—yet this is the one printed in the Oxford *Poetical Works*. Medwin also changed the title of another "song" from "To S——th and C———gh" to "Similes."[149] Shelley's title is immediate, *to* Sidmouth, Home Secretary, and Castlereagh, Foreign Secretary, whereas Medwin's accents the historical distance from 1832 and suppresses the specific references. In 1862 Dr. Garnett published in his *Relics of Shelley* a seven-line fragment beginning "People of England, ye who toil and groan."[150] In fact, however, the Shelley notebook from which Garnett got these lines contains a total of forty-one lines, which are drafts of what seems to be a lengthy "song" addressed to the "people" of England.[151] Perhaps Shelley completed the song which has since been lost. Mary Shelley published a song called "What Men Gain Fairly,"[152] but she omitted to transcribe the seventh line, an omission that seriously damages the poem's integrity and distorts its meaning.[153] What additional suppressions or distortions Mary practiced with "Song to the Men of England" or "A New National Anthem" one can only guess; both are printed in the Oxford *Poetical Works*. Perhaps most disturbing has been the fate of "Ballad of the Starving Mother," which is not even included in the Oxford edition and which was not adequately edited until 1969.[154] The only songs to have come to us relatively unscathed are *The Mask of Anarchy*, "Ode to the Assertors of Liberty" (whose title was changed in the *Prometheus Unbound* volume to circumvent the repression, but also to call attention to the parallel between Spain and England) and—assuming that they would have been included as songs—"Ode to Liberty" and "Ode to the West Wind."

The same themes developed in *The Mask of Anarchy* are present in the other songs: labor, nurture, the maternal icon, necessity, religion, Peterloo, aggression, rebirth, and anarchism. "England,"[155] for example, alludes to Peterloo, then evokes the maternal icon:

> Corpses are cold in the tomb—
> Stones on the pavement are dumb—
> Abortions are dead in the womb—
> And their mothers look pale like the death-white shore
> Of Albion, free no more!

The violated mother was about to give birth to "Liberty," which has been slaughtered. The "Oppressor" is ironically told to celebrate his victory because, like Jupiter's, it will be brief, erased eventually by the processes of necessity. "Wealth" is the one who cries "Havock!", thus blaming the rich for England's disorder. The tyrant is also ironically invited to have "God" for his "guide" as he marries "Ruin," thus identifying the God of Christianity with the tyrannical principle. Another poem, "A New National Anthem," also develops the theme of the maternal icon. Liberty is figured as a "queen" who has been "murdered," but the only way the song suggests of resurrecting her is to create her. The anarchist theme is expressed thus:

> She is Thine own pure soul
> Moulding the might whole,—
> God save the Queen!
> She is Thine own deep love
> Rained down from Heaven above,—
> Wherever she rest or move,
> God save our Queen!
>   (15-21)

and

> Be her eternal throne
> Built in our hearts alone—
>   God save the Queen!
> Let the oppressor hold
> Canopied seats of gold;
> She sits enthroned of old
>   O'er our hearts Queen.
>   (29-35)

A hierarchical concept, like the queen, is subverted to encourage self-determination; a narrow nationalism is invoked in order to be destroyed and replaced by a universal and disinterested benevolence. Patriotic worship of royalty is a misguided idealism Shelley tries to redirect.

The maternal icon and the issue of nurture dominate the forty-one line fragment, "People of England."[156] The "people" are chastised for nurturing their oppressors, creating everything they have, while getting in return nothing, and worse than nothing. The labor necessary to sustain a decent life has increased because of economic developments caused by the selfish rich.

> People of England . . . men whose manly brow
> Scarce earns with sweat, the food
> Mothers, who from yr flaccid bosoms, feed
> Men with the drainings of your pallid need.

The tyrants at Peterloo attacked an unarmed crowd, including "women in whose wombs the infant leapt / Who if it shall survive may yet be strong / To do what I will ye to do." In the latter lines, the maternal icon fuses with the rebirth theme, suggesting, as does the end of "Sonnet: England in 1819," that the Peterloo deaths are graves, "from which a glorious Phantom may / Burst, to illumine our tempestuous day." The necessity of Demogorgon will destroy the self-destroying tyrants, but only the fully creative people can construct a libertarian society.

The maternal icon occurs most prominently in the "Ballad of a Starving Mother."[157] The narrator introduces Parson Richards who is at his gate with his hound, to whom he gives bread. A woman approaches the Parson and begs for food in a speech that comprises most of the poem. With "a babe at her breast" (5), she tells her sad story: how she was seduced, impregnated, and abandoned by a minister who, by the poem's end, we realize is Parson Richards

229

himself. She is so starved that her breasts no longer give milk (9) and the baby sucks in vain. Her body is so ravaged she is not attractive enough to be a successful prostitute. The starving mother, however, does not simply suffer in a passive way, thus provoking only a sentimental response. She tells the Priest, "consider that God who created us / Meant this for a world of love" (45-46), and she also says, "upon my soul, I begin to think / 'Twere a joy beyond all pleasure / To sit up in Heaven, and see you drink / In Hell, of your own true measure" (49-53). Hardly a humble Christian, this starving mother; unlike Wordsworth's Peter Bell, she laments the destruction of pleasure and joy. She indirectly attacks Malthus by showing a contradiction between Biblical "word" and political economy.

> "O God! this poor dear child did I
>   At thy command bear and cherish!
> Thou bads't us increase and multiply—
>   And tyrants bid us perish!"
>   (65-69)

The woman, after her speech, collapses with her dead child, while the Parson never offers a word. The last stanza captures the essence of the Parson's crime: a failure of feeling.

> He turned from the bosom whose heart was broke—
>   Once it pillowed him as he slept—
> He turned from the lips that no longer spoke,
>   From the eyes that no longer wept.
>   (81-84)

What greater sin in the popular mythology than refusing to help a starving mother? The corrupt ruling elite once again threatens the mother, while the elite itself is self-indulgent, feeding its hounds but not the poor.

The gluttony and aggression of the ruling class are prominent features in "To S——th and C———gh." First, there are two ravens about to attack "fresh human carrion"; the poem also has a shark and dogfish about to consume the Africans thrown overboard from a slave-ship. There are, in addition, other kinds of destructive creatures, such as vultures, wolves, crows, and vipers. Killing the nurturing mother, the ruling class is a cruel inversion of nurture because it acquires its own sustenance by "eating" the people whom it should feed. The second stanza of "Song to the Men of England" addresses the question of nurture: "Wherefore feed . . . Those ungrateful drones who would / Drain your sweat—nay, drink your blood?" (5-9). Shelley, in this poem, gives the popular mythology a socially radical interpretation by introducing the issue of labor. The workers are exhorted to seize what is really their own, the product of their labor, and not to allow the "drones" to exploit them.

The theme of labor is developed in another song, which defends small property:

> What men gain fairly, that they should possess
> And children may inherit idleness
> From him who earns it . . . this is understood—
> Private injustice may be general good

These first four lines suggest a legitimate kind of property that overrules even the anarchist criterion of utility, since one who "gains fairly" his wealth can, without penalty, pass it on to his children. The intended audience for this would be the shopkeepers, artisans, farmers, and men of small property who read the *Examiner* and comprised, along with the "manufacturing mob" (as he called the followers of Cobbett and Orator Hunt in *Peter Bell III*), the political base of the reform movement. The poem's other six lines, however, justify expropriation:

> But he who gains by base & armed wrong
> Or guilty fraud, or base compliances
> With those whom force or falshood has made strong
> May be despoiled; even as a stolen dress
> Is stript from a convicted thief & he
> Left in the nakedness of infamy[158]

As I read these lines, they deem illegitimate all forms of aristocratic property: land seized by the barons or taken from the Church; wealth acquired from the "fraud" of war-incurred government debt and contracts; those who live off the government "dole"—placemen, sinecurists, and churchmen. The farmer, artisan, and shopkeeper are invited to view as thieves the men of wealth, who rule the economy and the government. One has to go to the Spenceans to get such an insurrectionary perspective on property.

The "Song to the Men of England," already briefly discussed, concerns itself with laborers, not small property owners. The workers create the world of objects—food, clothing, shelter, weapons—

and they should control them, recover them as their own. Just as "Jupiter" is the projected power of a miscreating imagination, so the wealth created by workers is an identical form of alienation. One will look in vain through the works of Cobbett or any other radical author to find such an uncompromising view on labor alienation. In Hunt's *Examiner*, however, Shelley could have read in 1818 and 1819 numerous articles dealing with industrial laborers and the problems of the poor. When Peel proposed his Cotton Manufacturers Bill limiting hours to 10½ per diem, factory owners used the arguments of laissez faire to counter it.[159] When a bill was finally passed in 1819, children under nine were forbidden to work in the cotton factories and hours limited to 13½ for "those between nine and sixteen."[160] Robert Owen argued against the abuses of child labor in the columns of the *Examiner* on March 29 and April 5, 1818. But a Poor Law amendment was passed in the spring of 1818 which placed pauper children in houses of industry, Dickensian institutions that outraged the liberals. In the May 31, 1818 issue of the *Examiner* there is a moving letter, "Workhouse Discipline," describing in simple, understated language the terrible fate of· an aged couple who had worked hard all their lives, only to suffer the indignity of applying for relief and being forced into a workhouse, where they were separated and endured individually the tortures of the penitentiary regimen. When workers and employers waged a conflict in Manchester in 1818, Leigh Hunt was not neutral but came out unequivocally against the owners, who were contemptuously viewed as uncultured *nouveaux riches* whose only skill was exploiting the poor.[161] During this strike involving 200,000 workers, the Hunts urged the Bounderbys of Manchester to increase wages, decrease hours, and improve working conditions.[162] After Peterloo, the August 29, 1819 issue of the *Examiner* has a vivid description of the Manchester slums, depicted with the moral indignation of an Engels or Dickens or Carlyle.[163] Although Shelley could not have derived his justification for expropriation from Owen or Hunt, he would have learned from them a fine moral outrage at the degradation of the poor by their so-called "betters."

Another context of *Popular Songs* is interesting. In Barry Gordon's study, *Political Economy in Parliament 1819-1823*, he shows the prominence and influence of Ricardo, Mill, and McCulloch— the authors of political economy. "Laissez faire" was the only response to the more than 1,200 petitions to Parliament for relief of agricultural distress.[164] As an M.P., Ricardo promoted laissez faire by arguing against the numerous proposals to aid the poor and regulate the economy to benefit the poor. None of these proposals even came close to passing, so the fault is hardly Ricardo's. But what Ricardo and his supporters tried to do is worth noting in this context: at a time of extraordinary social uncertainty and rapid change, which entailed great suffering and anxiety, the political economists offered a *scientific* explanation for the workings of the economy, as though it were an autonomous organism, and shifted the center of discussion from ethics and social responsibility to the "natural" and scientific laws of economics. Although the political economists supported repeal of the Combination Acts and a radical solution to the National Debt problem, the Ricardians were banishing ethics from economics. Shelley, however, is investing the labor theory of value with utopian possibilities, and supplementing the moral outrage of Hunt and Owen with a radical analysis. "What men gain fairly—that they should possess," but the rich "May be despoiled." Shelley tries to direct attention away from a narrow concern for merely political rights, and to broaden "reform" to include an analysis of estranged labor.

> Sow seed,—but let no tyrant reap;
> Find wealth,—let no impostor heap;
> Weave robes,—let not the idle wear;
> Forge arms,—in your defence to bear.

Neither *Popular Songs*, nor the Carlile letter, nor *A Philosophical View of Reform*, was published in Shelley's lifetime. If Shelley had lived in London rather than Italy at the time, perhaps he would have found a way to publish them, but that is something we will never know. These works, as a whole, represent an extraordinarily creative response to the English crisis following Peterloo and illustrate Shelley's ability to mediate his ideas in different genres and for different occasions.

THE *PROMETHEUS UNBOUND* VOLUME AND ACT IV

If the *Examiner* can be believed, then the *Prometheus Unbound* volume was published August 14, 1820, almost a year to the day after Peterloo, almost two years since Shelley had first begun work on the lyrical drama. Entering Charles Ollier's shop to purchase *Prometheus Unbound . . . With Other Poems*, one would have encountered the poems in the following order. The dates of composition, approximate and sometimes problematic, are within parentheses.

> *Prometheus Unbound*: Preface (April, Oct.–Dec. 1819).
> I (Sept. 1818–Jan. 1819).
> II-III (March–April, 1819).
> IV (Dec. 1819).
> The Sensitive Plant (March 1820).
> A Vision of the Sea (Summer 1819).
> Ode to Heaven (Dec. 1819).
> An Exhortation (Oct. 1819).
> Ode to the West Wind (Oct. 1819).
> An Ode, written October, 1819, before the Spaniards
>   had recovered their Liberty (Oct. 1819).
> The Cloud (Spring 1820).
> To a Sky-Lark (June 1820).
> Ode to Liberty (March–July 1820).[165]

Considered as a volume, the book of poems has a coherence and unity organized around three themes: ontology, the libertarian poet, and liberty. The title poem, of course, deals with all three themes, whereas the nine other poems break down into three different groups. Poems concerned mostly with ontological questions are "The Sensitive Plant," "A Vision of the Sea," and "Ode to Heaven." "An Exhortation," "Ode to the West Wind," and "To a Sky-Lark" deal with the libertarian poet, while liberty as such is the theme of "An Ode, written October, 1819, before the Spaniards had recovered their Liberty," "The Cloud," and "Ode to Liberty." The order in which the poems appear corresponds to the thematic grouping, with the exception of "To a Sky-Lark" which, like "Ode to Liberty," was added to the volume shortly before it was published.

The ontological theme proceeds on the assumption that "Jupiter" does not exist. By "Jupiter" Shelley means an ontological principle of evil determining human endeavor. The first three acts of the lyrical drama describe the abolition of Jupiter by means of a Promethean-Asian process of recovery, remembrance, and reunification. In a Promethean world, then, the ontologically oriented poems question the status of mutability, death, and ultimate reality.

"The Sensitive Plant" depicts the horror of material decay, as a beautiful garden suffers the ravages of winter after its equally beautiful gardener dies. The poem has three distinct moments, the "paradise" of harmonious unity and ecstatic love, the process of decay after the "Lady" dies, and contemplation of a paradise that has been lost. Richard Caldwell, in a psychoanalytic reading, sees the poem symbolizing a fantasy of infant-mother symbiosis which is destroyed by the process of individuation. The experience of a discrete identity, separate from the mother, is felt as the death of the mother, and selfhood is a nightmare worse than death, which at least is a possible route back to the maternal paradise. The desire in the poem is not for the lost maternal object but for the lost state of symbiosis, a condition in which desire is not even felt as desire. Mutability destroys the perfect subject-object relationship.[166]

The garden paradise with its maternal protector could represent many things, including the child-mother symbiosis. At the social level, tyranny's denial of nurture is something the third part could be representing. The death of the Lady is the death of liberty, slain at Peterloo, and also by the passage of the Six Acts. At the personal level, the Lady could be Shelley's own mother, the dead Harriet, or his wife Mary; the Sensitive Plant could be Shelley himself, his childhood, or his dead children. Perhaps the mother-child paradise was brought to the poet's mind by the infant Percy Florence, born on November 12, 1819. Perhaps it was a growing sense of his own mortality that inspired the poem. The philosophical question raised by the death of the Lady and the demise of the garden is the dualism of matter and spirit. Without question matter dies, decays, turns into forms that the third part describes with a fascinated revulsion, symbolically equating death with excrement. If spirit does not exist here, where does it exist? What is the ontological status of "love, and beauty, and delight" in a mutable world? His "modest creed" is that, within an epistemological skepticism so lucidly explicated by Earl Wasserman, spirit is eternal, existing independently of decaying matter.[167] The nightmare of mutability, then, is endured as Prometheus endures the Furies. The Promethean response is also to focus on the moment of beauty, the world of parts one and two, and consign the nightmare world of part three to the necessitarian processes immune to spirit's activity.

"A Vision of the Sea"[168] also raises the question of death. The mother, on the verge of drowning with her child, asks desperately:

> Alas! what is life, what is death, what are we,
> That when the ship sinks we no longer may be?
> What! to see thee no more, and to feel thee no more?
>
> (82-84)

The poem ends inconclusively as a deliberate fragment, before the moment of revelation. Although it contains vivid descriptions of the sea, ship, storm, and shipwreck, it also has numerous echoes from Coleridge's *Rime of the Ancient Mariner* and Byron's *Don Juan* (Canto II), exploits the popular interest in shipwrecks (not for nothing was this inferior poem the favorite of Shelley's contemporaries), and reminds one of the Shelleyan trope of the vessel at sea. "Lines written among the Euganean Hills" is the most apt parallel because there the "mariner" is also poised between life and death, wondering whether death could be any worse than death-in-life. That "A Vision of the Sea" has a mother and child at its center, as does "The Sensitive Plant" (although in a more symbolic way), cannot be accidental, evoking as it does both the sociopolitical icon of the maternal figure threatened with destruction and Shelley's own preoccupation with dead children.

"Ode to Heaven" is another poem whose point of view is skeptical since the reader is offered three different but equally plausible perspectives on what "heaven" is—that is, ultimate reality. Regardless of whether ultimate reality conforms to the ideas of the deists or Platonists, there is no ontological principle of evil in the universe, so that it is the responsibility of free consciousness to create meanings during life. The first voice sounds Holbachian, and harks back to the *Queen Mab* period, because the spirit of nature can provide guidance to errant "man." The second voice is Platonic, even suggesting that death will provide a path to a reality far more glorious than mere life. The third voice is also reminiscent of *Queen Mab*, as well as of "Ozymandias," in its deflation of anthropocentric pride, as though it were "presumptuous" to think that the universe is principally concerned with insignificant "man." This view, while discouraging to the utopian who seeks in nature a model for emancipation, nevertheless poses no insuperable obstacles to the idealistic project of social amelioration. If the universe is not anthropocentric, then it will not bother to interfere with human liberation, something entirely in the hands of humanity. Indeed, taken together, these three poems delineate a humanism that follows from a Promethean metaphysics. The decay of matter cannot negate the eternity of spirit, nor is the uncertainty with which one has to approach the question of death fatal to the utopian project.

The poems concerned with the libertarian poet approach the utopian project from three different angles. "An Exhortation" seems to be directed toward Southey, Wordsworth, and Coleridge, urging them to reject the flattery of "wealth and power" and assume their true roles as authentic poets. "Ode to the West Wind" has an ontological counter to "The Sensitive Plant" because here the violent transition to winter is celebrated as revolutionary energy ultimately beneficial, not morbid. Moreover, the poet can so position himself in relation to this powerful force that he can overcome death and isolation. The utopian promise of beauty is symbolized by the sky-lark, and this poem illustrates the poet's impossible task of capturing beauty in language. Mediating between ideals of perfection and the human world is the theme of "To a Sky-Lark." The bird's unpremeditated, wordless beauty has an effect on the auditor that is so immediate—without mediation—that the bird seems to be without a body. Even the most lyrical poet is condemned to the material world of decay and contradiction: "Our sincerest laughter / With some pain is fraught— / Our sweetest songs are those that tell of saddest thought" (89-90). The concluding stanza echoes the final words of "Ode to the West Wind" by being in the form of a prayer, by sacrificing his own, merely personal identity to the greater power of beauty. Addressing the bird, the poet says:

> Teach me half the gladness
>   That thy brain must know,
> Such harmonious madness
>   From my lips would flow
> The world should listen then—as I am listening now.

Inspiration entails destruction of the poet's merely human self so that in "Ode to the West Wind" he becomes a fiery apocalypse and in "To a Sky-Lark" he achieves madness. Ordinary states of consciousness cannot produce poetry because of the dualistic nature of the poet's situation. The world of actuality is dominated by "Jupiter"—domination, hierarchy, death, decay, misery, loss, toil, hatred, and pain. The poet, as a human, exists in this world, and lives in another dimension, of potentiality, the ought-to-be, that is present to some extent in the actual world, but fully present only in the imagination. Mediating between these two worlds is the poet who lives *as a poet* only in the imagination, but who cannot escape the human condition. The poet's condition is inescapably contradictory, but it must be endured, and endured joyfully, because the poets—and in this category Shelley includes everyone who is imaginative, experiencing potentiality in any of its forms—transform the world, moving it toward utopia.

Moving toward utopia is a theme of the poems concerned with liberty. Peterloo is the subject of one poem, which urges upon the people the nonviolent anarchist lesson of nonretaliation and Promethean self-determination, refusing to perpetuate the cycle of oppression and generating instead a dialectic of creativity, leading toward utopia. Although "The Cloud" is apolitical, it is a poem of liberty in the sense that it fully embodies the utopian concept of play, for which the cloud's processes provide a natural model. The volume's final poem, "Ode to Liberty," is a major effort, situating Peterloo in a broad historical and philosophical context, giving the doctrines of *Prometheus Unbound* a historically specific reference.

When "An Ode, written October, 1819, before the Spaniards had recovered their Liberty" was written, it was probably one of the many Peterloo-inspired "songs" Shelley was to have collected and published. The original title, "An Ode to the Assertors of Liberty," speaks even more directly to the Peterloo incident, but any English reader of 1820 would immediately recognize the allusions to the massacre. The "Ode" is a *Mask of Anarchy* in miniature, with even some verbal echoes (arise, chains shaken). The reform movement is asked to rise and awaken, to engage in "holy combat" (14), which is not civil war. Rather, the assertors of liberty are to break out of the dialectic of oppression, imaged in line 9: "The slave and the tyrant are twin-born foes." "Freedom" is now "riding to conquest" by means of "Famine and Toil"—that is, Necessity, or in the language of *Prometheus Unbound*, Demogorgon. The people are told: "Lift not your hands in the banded war, / But in her [Freedom's] defence whose children ye are." Clarifying what "holy combat" means is the fourth stanza:

Glory, glory, glory,
  To those who have greatly suffered and done!
    Never name in story
Was greater than that which ye shall have won.
Conquerors have conquered their foes alone,
Whose revenge, pride, and power they have overthrown:
Ride ye, more victorious, over your own.

The extraordinary feat is not vanquishing a foe, a single set of tyrants, but conquering the very principle of oppression, tyranny itself—which is the subject, of course, of *Prometheus Unbound*.

"The Cloud" negates tyranny itself by example rather than argument; the processes it depicts try to *be* utopia. The water cycle has been a favorite Shelleyan trope, like fire imagery, to figure libertarian transformation (cf. the "sun-awakened avalanche" of *Prometheus Unbound*, II, iii). "The Cloud" celebrates the changes of the water cycle, from vapor, to cloud, to rain or snow, and back again to vapor. The activities of the cloud, its makings and un-makings, are an emblem, too, of the poet who mediates between "heaven" and "earth."[169] The anarchist poet cannot allow any images to become sacred that might turn into an authoritarian code, thus merely replacing a Jupiterian with a Promethean tyranny. Therefore, the authentically Promethean image is one that, in the language of Daniel J. Hughes, collapses after it achieves coherence, dwindles after it kindles, is unmade after it is made. It is the process of creation, not the created products themselves, that are exemplary in a libertarian way.

The process of making and unmaking is illustrated in the beginning and ending of "Ode to Liberty." The first stanza describes how a "voice"—not the poet's own—emerges from a process of inspiration ignited by the Spanish Revolution. The poet merely "records" what the voice says. At the end of the poem the voice ceases, giving rise to images and metaphors of sudden extinction. The inspired poet depends on ephemeral moments of rapture which cannot be willed into being and which point toward a utopian potentiality. The poem is an ambitious tracing of liberty from its origins to the present, *A Philosophical View of Reform* in verse.

The Spanish Revolution which inspires the poem and which is alluded to in the title of the Peterloo "Ode" was carefully followed in the *Examiner*, which kept an attentive eye on all international events, from the revolutions in South America to the student movement in Germany. Although the Spanish Revolution did not bring about utopia, it did effect radical changes without much violence: suffrage for all literate males; biennial parliaments; no representative allowed to serve two consecutive terms; representation by population; freedom of the press; abolition of the Inquisition.[170] Precisely such a liberal revolution was needed in England, Shelley believed, if violent revolution or a far worse tyrannical stagnation were to be avoided. Even though Peterloo did not result in sweeping reforms, the Spaniards demonstrated for Shelley that liberty can indeed be wrested from a tyrant.

The evolution of liberty sketched in the poem is a familiar trajectory: from Athenian democracy to the Roman republic; the catastrophe of the "Galilean serpent," institutionalized Christianity;

the emergence of Saxon liberty and the Italian communes and city-states; the Reformation and Enlightenment; the French Revolution, the Jacobin Terror, Napoleon, and the Bourbon restoration. The attack on religion in stanza XVI is not simply anticlerical, but anarchist, because the goal of overcoming superstition is the complete liberation of mind, until "human thoughts might kneel alone, / Each before the judgement-throne, / Of its own aweless soul, or of the power unknown!" (231-33). No longer breathing life into kings, priests, or other Jupiterian fictions, Promethean mind can recover its power, assume responsibility for its deeds, and determine its own destiny. Stanza XVII, echoing Asia's speech in Demogorgon's cave, devalues the achievements of technology, art, and science if these other aspects of progress do not coexist with liberty. The burden for overcoming the tyrannical principle rests with the individual, who has willed the master-slave relationship into existence and can therefore abolish it. The volume ends, then, with an appeal to the reader to "dethrone" tyranny, psychologically and institutionally, since only individuals can effect the kind of libertarian revolution Shelley imagines as the realization of potentiality.

Potentiality being realized is the theme of Act IV, which Shelley added in December 1819, seven months after *Prometheus Unbound* was supposedly completed. One reason for adding the new act might be the nature of Act III's climax, which is a utopian negation of actuality, so that utopia is pointed to rather than embodied in the language. Act IV, like "The Cloud," *is* utopia, not a representation of it, and provides a positive vision of realized idealism to inspire the post-Peterloo reform movement. Shelley's muse here is not the "misery" of *Julian and Maddalo*, but the joy of the sky-lark. The fourth act develops an integral aspect of his utopian vision, and its social significance is rooted in its defense of play and pleasure, as opposed to estranged labor and factory (or religious) discipline. Liberated humanity is not confined within an enclosed garden, or regulated by a utopian dictator, but is free to develop as *homo ludens*.

Social historians tell us that popular forms of play have always been suspect in the eyes of political authority. Robert Malcolmson observes that civil "and ecclesiastical discipline, it is clear, often had to be defended against the counter-morality of popular sports and festivities."[171] Discipline is the key word. Medieval priests, Puritan moralists, and factory owners were some of those who were worried that play encouraged a kind of sensibility which was an-

240

tiauthoritarian and insubordinate. Beginning in the mid-eighteenth century, opposition to popular recreations was starting to be effective. Eighteenth-century moralists were disturbed because laborers, if given the chance, preferred leisure to extra work. To increase productivity, leisure had to be forcibly diminished. The proposed strategy was to decrease wages, increase prices, and make employment uncertain; thus the employer could have an "economic necessity" to stimulate as much "productivity" as he wanted. Meanwhile, enclosures were eliminating the fields where workers used to play, and factories were enforcing a kind of discipline at odds with the work-play rhythm of rural life. Malcolmson concludes that "many customary rights were forcibly undermined, and . . . their dissolution was often effected by men of property in order to enhance their own interests."[172]

In his article, "Towards a Critical Theory of Play," Francis Hearn defines play:

> Play is a context, a set of principles for organizing experience, constituted by any activity that is voluntary and open-ended (i.e., free from both external and internal compulsions), noninstrumental (in the sense that it is pursued for its own sake and has at its center of interest process rather than goal), and transcendent of ordinary states of being and consciousness.[173]

While the industrial revolution was promoting factory discipline, while Methodists and other evangelists were trying to root out all forms of play and pleasure, and while "economic necessity" was increasing the amount of labor necessary to maintain a worker's existence, Shelley was celebrating play, a noninstrumental use of language pursued for its own sake, with its center of interest on process, not goal. Leigh Hunt too defended play in the pages of the *Examiner*. He looked back fondly to the heathen spirit of games and celebrations and tried to revive this spirit for Christmas and Mayday.[174] Resolving mutability by means of play, then, was a strategy pregnant with social implications.

The most elaborate celebration of *Spieltrieb* is in Act IV of *Prometheus Unbound*. The first movement of Act IV (1-184) is the death of linear time, making possible the liberation of the Spirits. As long as the temporal focus was progressive—looking for freedom in the future, weighted down by injuries of the past, unable to enjoy the scarcity-haunted present—then one's spiritual possibilities were bound up and repressed. Now that love's eternity has replaced Time, the Spirits are free to celebrate the water cycle (40-47) and the dominion of music (48-55). Another theme from Asia's song is spoken by the Semichorus of Hours, who say that the voice of the Spirits "Has drawn back the figured curtain of sleep / Which covered our being and darkened our birth / In the deep" (IV, 58-60). Sleep protected the dream from harsh reality, but also darkened it with repression.

In the third quatrain of the song by the Chorus, the Spirits celebrate the death of Time and the power of utopian song.

> But now—oh weave the mystic measure
>   Of music and dance and shapes of light,
> Let the Hours, and the Spirits of might and pleasure
>   Like the clouds and sunbeams unite.
>   (IV, 77-80)

The mystic measure and the new concept of time point back to Asia's song in Act II. In utopia, language is song, movement is dance, and the sun's light can be woven into the fabric as well. The unity underlying the interaction of clouds and sun is the same kind of cyclical unity that can now inform utopian time. The mystic measure also weaves itself a pantheistic universe. As Asia says in Act II, "Common as light is love. . . . It makes the reptile equal to the God (II, v, 40 and 43). With the downfall of Jupiter and the abolition of hierarchical domination, the sacred permeates all living things. Prometheus himself began the consecration of all objects when he said, "I wish no living thing to suffer pain."

As is clear in this first movement, the appropriate activities in utopia are singing, dancing, and playing. Like Schiller, Shelley pictures the liberation from tyranny as an opportunity for the full development of "play." The Spirits are "free to dive, or soar, or run" (IV, 139) anywhere they please. The mystic measure turns all endeavors, including even science (116; 141-57), into aesthetic activities because there is no longer any external compulsion. As Asia said in her song, one sails without a course, without a star. One sails in order to sail. Utopia means, literally, no where, and in utopia that is precisely where one goes because, strictly speaking, there is no *place* to go. The Spirits define Paradise as all that human love gazes on (IV, 127-28). Paradise, then, is not so much a place as it is the erotic power to transform mere place into love's residence. The first movement, like Asia's song, blurs one's discrete associations with water, music, light, and dance. The mystic measure, like the song of Orpheus, tames all things with a power that does not dominate, but that subdues with its beauty. The new concept of eternity receives further illustration after the Spirits leave. Panthea and Ione dwell briefly on the paradox that although the music has ceased, the beauty of the songs can be recaptured by remembering them. The song merely assumes another form, but it does not die in the memory (IV, 180-81).

The second movement (185-318) has received a great deal of attention. Although it is clearly an introduction to the Moon-Earth duet, its clarity seems to stop there. Panthea's description of the Earth's "Aeolian modulations" (186-88), which are accompanied by Moon's "undernotes" (189-93), leads me to guess that Shelley is describing the music of the spheres. The difficulty of the verse comes partially from the elusiveness of the music. As the two spheres of music emerge from the forest, Panthea says that they part as lovers only to increase the pleasure of coming together again. The power of love dispels anxiety with oxymorons: "dear disunion," "lovely grief," and "sweet sad thoughts." Individuality is not cursed by loneliness, but is a blessing that heightens the pleasure of communion.

Ione's description of the Moon's sphere of music (206-35) contains familiar images, such as the water cycle, infancy, music, heat, and cold. The whiteness that is so prominent seems related to phases of the water cycle associated with the moon; thus, the whiteness implies that the moon is about to renew itself and dissolve its frigidity. Later (424-30), the association of death with white is made explicit. After Ione's description of the moon symbol comes Panthea's picture of the earth symbol. The music and light that flow, spin, whirl, and roll with furious precision grind and knead objects into elemental subtlety. The "self-conflicting speed" and "self-destroying swiftness" are aspects of the orb's wildness and sense-drowning intensity. This intoxicating sensuality reminds one of Shelleyan inspiration, where the vitality and destructiveness of poetic creativity are inextricable. The multitudinous orb seems on the verge of exploding, but instead of bursting into fragments violently, it maintains itself at a white heat. It is startling to come upon, at this point, the sleeping Spirit of the Earth, "Pillowed upon its alabaster arms, / Like to a child o'er wearied with sweet toil." Once again, Shelley uses the image of the child to symbolize libertarian innocence (cf. IV, 388-94).

Panthea's second speech (270-318) modulates once again back

to the jagged rhythms that preceded the image of the child. The harsh poetry, paradoxically enough, begins from a star on the child's forehead. Earth abolishes its past and abandons its history, so that it can become a paradise of wildernesses. Just as Prometheus and Asia had to move backwards in order to realize themselves, so does earth, which has to acknowledge the past that tormented it, and then cleanse itself in rebirth. The violent images (shoot, swords, spears, tyrant-quelling, etc.) are necessary because the past is not easy to abolish. The secrets of the earth's heart are "deep" and need to be penetrated. This is a marvelous image for un-earthing repressed memories. Earth needs to confront "the melancholy ruins / Of cancelled cycles" in order to make a fresh beginning. The orb within orb is a picture of vitality and erotic exuberance, but history is imaged as "ruin within ruin." Earth has a vision of the destruction that once afflicted its surface. By bringing the buried past to the surface, Earth is able to say, "Be not!" and "they were no more." The goal of remembering, in this instance, is to forget and let go of the past in order to have a present.

The duet of Moon and Earth (319-502), the real center of the fourth act, shares many of the characteristics we have already seen in Asia's song and other lyrics. But what becomes distinctive in the duet is the dialectic of repression. With the liberation of Prometheus, Earth's volcanoes are comic with "inextinguishable laughter" (IV, 334), whereas before, the volcano was an emblem of repression because so much energy was compressed and contained by Jupiter's tyranny. With liberation, Earth's erotic power can flow freely: "The boundless, overflowing, bursting gladness, / The vaporous exulta- tion not to be confined!" (IV, 320-21). When Jupiter put bonds on boundless energy, he created a poison that afflicted Earth. Jupiter's hatred, which is repression, turned "our green and azure universe" into "black destruction," splintering and battering the forces of nature "into a lifeless mire" (IV, 338-55). The repression of the life-force produced the forces of destruction. Now that Jupiter no longer frustrates natural power, nature once again enjoys its equi- librium in a healthy exuberance.

In Act II, Panthea speaks of a volcano just before they descend into Demogorgon's own volcano. The enchanting sound, she says, has carried them to the realm of Demogorgon,

> Like a volcano's meteor-breathing chasm,
> Whence the oracular vapour is hurled up

Which lonely men drink wandering in their youth
And call truth, virtue, love, genius or joy—
That maddening wine of life, whose dregs they drain
To deep intoxication, and uplift
Like Maenads who cry loud, Evoe! Evoe!
The voice which is contagion to the world.
(II, iii, 4-10)

The qualities that have seeped through the apparatus of repression act as an intoxicant, inspiring philosophers and libertarians. But the ambiguity of inspiration is also obvious. That the energy *is* repressed is not insignificant, just as the wine of life is also maddening. Since Jupiter, the sceptred curse, dominates the world, libertarian inspiration is also madness. The Maenads cry "Evoe! Evoe!" and they also—which Shelley does not have to mention—tear apart the flesh of animals and the limbs of the poet Orpheus. Hope is contagion when it leads to self-destruction and violence.

The duet implies that Jupiter derived what power he had only from *repressing* natural energy.[175] Once Jupiter falls, he becomes the epitome of nothingness, a "thirsty nothing," and "void annihilation" (IV, 350-55). Unrepressed love is, on the other hand, a plenitude, a fertility, and an encircling melody. The intensity and potential violence of the multitudinous orb make more sense when one considers the importance of repression. The effects of trying to frustrate the furious and awesome power of the multitudinous orb will be cataclysmic. The duet celebrates the deliverance of erotic delight from the bonds of repression. The Earth sings of "a storm bursting its cloudy prison," and praises the potentiality released "Out of the lampless caves of unimagined being" (IV, 370-423). Even the Moon, as she circles the Earth, suggests the destructive power that ensues from repressing love (IV, 450-92). She uses the Maenad image in such a way as to remind us that violence is both the means and the consequence of thwarting natural desire (IV, 470-75).

The response of Panthea and Ione to the duet is a continuation of erotic celebration (IV, 503-509). They are washed by the waters of music and arise reborn. To Ione, Panthea's own words are "clear, soft dew." At this point, it seems that the symphony of love could continue indefinitely, and at this precise moment, Shelley has Demogorgon reappear. The effect is jolting. Demogorgon resurrects a whole set of issues one had thought were disposed of long ago.

Chapter Five

Shelley bids goodbye to the lyrics of love in a way analogous to the role of Prospero who, threatened by Caliban, had to banish the idyllic dream. Shelley, unlike Prospero, is under no external compulsion to introduce the element of irony. In the final speech, we are carried back to actuality which is not, alas, the world of our dreams. Jupiter still rules. Demogorgon returns us to ourselves where we must begin the processes depicted by the poem, "to hope, till Hope creates / From its own wreck the thing it contemplates."

The *Prometheus Unbound* volume, without the unpublished texts composed after Peterloo, gives an incomplete, even false picture of Shelley's literary project. The image of Shelley as an ineffectual angel too pure for this corrupt world cannot be sustained in light of *The Mask of Anarchy, A Philosophical View of Reform*, and *Popular Songs*. The poet's fate, lamented so prominently in this volume, is not the consequence of thwarted otherworldly idealism, but is primarily the result of political radicalism frustrated by the repression. The unpublished texts are a necessary complement to the *Prometheus Unbound* volume, which acquires its full meaning only once the context is restored.

SIX

Defending
the Imagination

(1820-1821)

INTRODUCTION

WERE IT NOT for Peterloo, it is unlikely that *A Philosophical View of Reform* would have been written; similarly, without the stimulus of Thomas Love Peacock's *The Four Ages of Poetry*, Shelley probably would never have composed *A Defence of Poetry*, his greatest prose work. His earlier ideas on the imagination are scattered throughout numerous and usually fragmentary essays, so that it is fortunate that Peacock provided an occasion for Shelley's definitive statement. As a document in the history of aesthetics, the *Defence* has long been considered a major text, but it also announces a social and political aesthetic. Indeed, there is a line of progressive development from Godwin's *Political Justice* to Shelley's Irish pamphlets, *Queen Mab*, theological fragment of 1816-1817, *A Philosophical View of Reform*, and finally *A Defence of Poetry*. The philosophical anarchism of Shelley's *Defence* does not contradict Godwin's *Political Justice* so much as it supersedes it with ideas he has been developing over a decade.

Although one readily accepts Godwin's influence in a work like *Queen Mab*, one rarely thinks of Godwin influencing *A Defence of Poetry*. There is, however, a striking prefiguration of the *Defence* in Godwin's *Letter of Advice to a Young American . . .* (1818). Godwin advises a student on the most appropriate course of study to follow in order to acquire a philosophical education. The imagination, he writes, is a primary moral agent, so that one ought to cultivate "moral sentiments" at the expense of learning dry facts.[1] There is a historical overview of Western culture from the Greeks and Romans to modern times (as there is in the *Defence* and Schlegel's *Lectures on Dramatic Literature*, which Godwin recommends, and which Shelley read); in this overview, Godwin praises the poetry of chivalry for advancing the position of women, as the *Defence* also does.[2] Almost all the philosophers and poets Godwin praises, Shelley too praises; even the *Defence*'s admiration for Dante might be traced back to Godwin's Chaucer study. In addition to these superficial similarities, Godwin's essay insists upon the primary importance of literature and the creative imagination in education.

Although Godwin and Wollstonecraft were novelists, they had only high praise for poetry. The most morally impeccable character in *Caleb Williams* is a poet, and according to Wollstonecraft, "I am more and more convinced, that poetry is the first effervescence of the imagination, and the forerunner of civilization."[3] In Godwin's anti-Johnsonian *Life of Geoffrey Chaucer* (1803-1804), he substitutes the "romantic" geniuses (Chaucer, Spencer, Shakespeare) for the neoclassical men of taste (Cowley, Dryden, Pope). Adumbrating Shelley's own *Defence of Poetry*, Godwin says:

> It is easy to perceive, and has been verified in the example of all ages and climates, that poetry has been the genuine associate of the earlier stages of literature. There is then a freshness in language admirably adapted to those emotions which poetry delights to produce. Our words are then the images of things, the representatives of visible and audible impressions: after a while, too many of our words become cold and scientific, perfectly suited to topics of reasoning, but unfitted for imagery and passion; and dealing in abstractions and generalities, instead of presenting to us afresh the impressions of sense.[4]

For both Wollstonecraft and Godwin, poetry is closer to the body, the senses, the origins of civilization than any other mode of discourse. The cold and scientific words seem to be suitable for reasoning, but one wonders what kind of reasoning could be done with such a language. There is surely a tension in these statements between the assumptions of progressive enlightenment and the implications of poetry. The vitality of poetry contradicts an instrumental view of language that seems implicit in both Wollstonecraft and Godwin. Either essential reality exists separately and apart from words, so that even cold words can adequately manipulate categories and concepts, or essential reality is linked inextricably with a certain kind of language—poetry. Although they praise poetry, their praise implies the superiority of philosophy.

Godwin was not unfamiliar with another view of language. In a letter to Godwin, Coleridge writes in 1800:

> I wish you to write a book on the power of the words, and the processes by which the human feelings form affinities with them. . . . Are not words, etc., parts and germinations of the plant? And what is the law of their growth? In something of this sort I would endeavour to destroy the old antithesis of Words and Things; elevating, as it were, Words into Things, and living things too.[5]

Words as things: that is, rather than act as an instrumental language that manipulates already known categories in the objective world, poetry will use an organic language-for-itself. Coleridge's view follows logically from visionary radicalism, because if the objective world is ideological, so is its language; and if the words signify falsehoods, whatever "reasoning" is done with them must also be false. Coleridge is more astute here than Godwin in drawing out the radical implications of poetry—implications that Shelley fully develops in his *Defence*.

Shelley wrote the *Defence* during February and March, 1821, intending it for publication in Ollier's *Literary Miscellany*. This journal had published Peacock's *Four Ages of Poetry*, but it folded after just one number. Shelley was left again with an unpublished piece of writing that he probably would have included in *The Liberal* if he had not drowned in 1822. The *Defence* illuminates the poetry of this period because so many of these poems are primarily concerned with writing poetry or defending the values of the imagination. *Letter to Maria Gisborne* (June-July, 1820), although not a public poem, has a self-portrait of the poet in relation to society that is comprehensible in terms of the *Defence*, which also helps explain the two very different poems of August 1820, *Swellfoot the Tyrant* and *The Witch of Atlas*. Both *Epipsychidion* (January-February, 1821) and *Adonais* (May-June, 1821) have long been recognized as poems about poetry and the imagination, but they are also about utopia. Even after Peterloo failed to occasion the fatal social crisis Shelley thought inevitable, he continued to assume that such a crisis was imminent, so that *Swellfoot the Tyrant* and, later, *Hellas*, are written under this assumption. Had Shelley lived longer, he undoubtedly would have continued to address himself in appropriate ways to the fate of the English reform movement. But he is also concerned, in the *Defence* and the poems of this period, to explore the imagination and poetry from a utopian perspective.

A DEFENCE OF POETRY

At one level, Shelley is refuting Peacock by redefining poetry in such a way that utilitarian science is subsumed within and becomes inferior to "Poetry." Opposed to Peacock's demystifying ironies, such as calling poetry a "trade" like every "commodity" on the "market,"[6] Shelley argues for the poet as prophet and legislator. For Peacock, poetry is "ornamental and figurative language,"[7] but for Shelley it is a primary instrument of knowledge. All the great poems have been written already, according to Peacock, so the contemporary task for creative people is to improve society in practical ways. Shelley, however, claims that social amelioration can proceed only if it is guided by an ethical sensibility educated by poetry. Shelley's debate with Peacock is prophetic of later critiques of science by twentieth-century philosophers (Lukács, Husserl, Heidegger, Sartre, Dewey, Marcuse, and others). Instrumental reason—the rationality by which the objects of nature are dominated and controlled—cannot give a moral purpose to human society. When such reason masquerades as ethics, the consequence is moral disaster, deifying physical force as an insuperable "objective" power. Some modern thinkers have insisted, as Shelley did, that only the human subject can determine a world of ethical meanings, regardless of technological science or of any other supposedly "objective" force. Shelley prophetically recognized the course scientific thinking would take, and offered a thorough and rigorous alternative.

Poetry is so important because corrupt language can distort the perception which, according to Shelley's idealism, determines reality. Poetry defamiliarizes existence to reveal its essential features, as they appear instinctively to the child and the "savage."[8] After the primitive connection with existence has been lost, one can reexperience it through Poetry, or lose contact with it because of superstition, error, and dead language. Rational discourse, in its properly subordinate role, represents the relations between poetic thoughts and enumerates the discoveries of poetry in a distanced, abstract way.[9] When "reason" exceeds its bounds and usurps Poetry's role, it generates a tyrannical code, a dead language that will obscure existence. In the fragmentary "On Life," probably written in late 1819, Shelley says: "The mist of familiarity obscures from us the wonder of our being."[10] Life is "the great miracle" and a perpetual "astonishment" which, as children, we experienced naturally;[11] as adults, we only occasionally overcome the "mechanical and habitual" modes of perception in "reverie," during which we enjoy "an unusually intense and vivid apprehension of life."[12]

Shelley writes in the fragmentary "Speculations on Metaphysics": "we do not attend sufficiently to what passes within ourselves. We combine words, combined a thousand times before. In our minds we assume entire opinions; and in the expression of those opinions, entire phrases, when we would philosophise."[13] If language is never defamiliarized, then it is never Poetry, wholly belonging to the subject who uses it. From borrowed words one derives borrowed opinions, or "Superstition," which is the condition of being subjugated by a fictional reality of someone else's making. A precondition for Poetry, then, is the relaxing of superstition long enough to permit original perception. The *Defence* argues that after the instinctively poetic stage of children and primitive people, the civilized, potentially more pleasurable, stage begins.[14] But, "if no new poets should arise to create afresh the associations which have been thus disorganized, language will be dead to all the nobler purposes of human intercourse."[15] The most favorable conditions for cultivating Poetry are to be found within democratic and self-governing societies.

Sociological criticism, like Peacock's, asks how society affects literature, but Shelley reverses the terms, showing how imagination creates the "liberty" by which society progresses. The way in which Shelley connects liberty and imagination is one of his most original achievements. Society is either creative or static, libertarian or tyrannical, tending toward utopia or death. Creativity is contagious and boundless, overflowing with a desire to propagate itself, so that creativity in one sphere tends to inspire the whole society. His favorite trope for expanding creativity is the widening circle, encompassing and assimilating more as it moves outward. Since the active imagination is making and unmaking perceptions, disclosing the wonder of life beneath the veil of familiarity, it erodes the constructs of superstition. Like Godwin's fluxional reason, Shelley's imagination is its own authority, refusing to be hedged in by predictable boundaries. In the fragmentary "On the Revival of Literature," Shelley echoes *Prometheus Unbound* (III, iv, 202): "Super-

251

stition, of whatever kind, whether earthly or divine, has hitherto been the weight which clogged man to earth, and prevented his genius from soaring aloft amid its native skies."[16] Tyranny is static and contracting, trying to control the indeterminacy of life, but liberty is expansive, like the imagination.

Poetry is the source of social creativity. Since every epoch "has deified its peculiar errors," Poets cannot escape the contamination of the *Zeitgeist*, although all progressive advances in morality are the result of Poetry.[17] "Ethical science arranges the elements which Poetry has created," and merely "propounds schemes and proposes examples" and offers "admirable doctrines." Poetry is superior because it "awakens and enlarges the mind itself by rendering it the receptacle of a thousand unapprehended combinations of thought. Poetry lifts the veil from the hidden beauty of the world, and makes familiar objects be as if they were not familiar."[18] Ethical science is rational discourse, important within its own secondary sphere, but Poetry acts on the very instrument of moral experience, the imagination. "The great secret of morals is Love; or a going out of our own nature, and an identification of ourselves with the beautiful which exists in thought, action, or person, not our own."[19] By educating the imagination, Poetry combats egoism and counteracts the calculating principle, encouraging instead community and mutual aid.

> A man, to be greatly good, must imagine intensely and comprehensively; he must put himself in the place of another and of many others; the pains and pleasures of his species must become his own. The great instrument of moral good is the imagination; and poetry administers to the effect by acting upon the cause.[20]

As the circumference of society—genuine association, a living network of culturally diversified interactions—expands, the domain of arbitrary power and superstitions contracts; the one grows at the expense of the other. For society not to sink back into frozen forms— dead language—it has to renew continually its imaginative process. Liberty has to be practiced, or it will be lost. In the fragmentary "The Elysian Fields," Shelley has a character say: "Public opinion rather than positive institution maintains [freedom] in whatever portion it may now possess, which is in truth the acquirement of their incessant struggles. And yet the gradations by which freedom has advanced have been contested step by step."[21] Imagination, as it works through public opinion, wrests victories from tyranny, but institutions *per se* are secondary to the living presence of liberty in the public mind. "Public opinion would never long stagnate in error, were it not fenced about and frozen over by forms and superstitions."[22]

Shelley chooses as an example of Poetry's libertarian influence on society the role of drama in Athenian democracy, an imperfect but nevertheless exemplary society in history: "never at any other period has so much energy, beauty, and virtue, been developed."[23] The Athenians "employed language, action, music, painting, the dance, and religious institutions"[24] to produce tragedies, which are "as mirrors in which the spectator beholds himself . . . stript of all but that ideal perfection and energy which everyone feels to be the internal type of all that he loves, admires, and would become. The imagination is enlarged by sympathy," and the "good affections are strengthened,"[25] so that the drama "teaches . . . self-knowledge and self-respect."[26] The highest form of art is not the lyrical self-expression of the isolated poet, but a socially integrated drama which educates an audience of democratic citizens. The education is didactic, but experiential, touching the imagination, not the reason. Poetry is connected with the social good because "the highest perfection of human society has ever corresponded with the highest dramatic excellence."[27]

As society declines into corruption and tyranny, so do the arts. Poetry expresses the most pleasure a particular society can experience, so libertarian societies enjoy a wider spectrum of aesthetic delight than tyrannical ones.[28] As time proceeds, it retains the Poetry and rejects the errors of historical creativity, preserving what is best and providing steps from which to advance. A literary masterpiece, for example, is "an inexhaustible fountain" that can provide pleasure during different historical epochs.[29] Poetic ideas, as soon as they are born, are indestructible, even if it takes centuries for them to influence social practices. The idea of equality, for example, starts with Plato's and Christ's "poetry," continues to influence history in a decisive way, and results eventually (and in conjunction with other events) in the abolition of personal slavery and the (relative) emancipation of women.[30] Courtly love poetry advanced woman's cause immeasurably;[31] Dante "announced" the birth of Italian liberty;[32] and Milton helped to demystify Christianity because *Paradise Lost* "contains within itself a philosophical refutation of that system of which, by a strange and natural antithesis, it has been a chief popular support."[33] Poetry, then, in however contradictory or imperfect a manner, does battle against tyranny. Despotism and superstition make progress with "the extinction of the poetical principle" because people become "insensible and selfish: their own will" becomes "feeble," resulting in their enslavement to the will of others.[34] Liberty, imagination, and Poetry depend on one another, supporting and sustaining each other in a cultural interaction. Whatever moral progress has been made by civilization has been owing to Poetry, according to Shelley.

In *A Philosophical View of Reform*, Shelley identifies "the principle of Utility as the substance, and liberty and equality as the forms according to which the concerns of human life ought to be administered."[35] The meaning that Peacock and a whole school of thinkers attach to the concept "utility," however, is more circumscribed than Shelley's concept. According to Shelley, Peacock's utility signifies conquering scarcity by increasing material security, eliminating "the grosser delusions of superstition," and promoting a degree of tolerance to permit the rational pursuit of self-interest.[36] Indeed, Shelley has identified the essence of what will become nineteenth-century Liberalism, developed by Bentham, Ricardo, James Mill, Cobden, and Bright, and significantly modified by John Stuart Mill and the Fabians. What disturbs Shelley about this kind of utility is the promotion of science at the expense of ethics and the redefinition of ethics as calculating self-interest. The advances of science, technology, and political economy have increased wealth, but have also increased the misery of the laborers, exacerbating "the extremes of luxury and want." Because of the "unmitigated exercise of the calculating faculty," the "rich have become richer, and the poor have become poorer."[37] Only the imagination, educated by Poetry, can generate the first principles by which to structure society in an ethically advanced way. Free trade and laissez faire are policies designed to liberate the productive capacities of society on the threshold of an industrial revolution, but their moral assumptions, if one can call them that, deify the selfishness of the individuals who do what they want with their own.

For Shelley, it is not urgent that the quantity of useful knowledge be increased, because so much of it already exists in an undigested form. "We want the creative faculty to imagine that which we know; we want the generous impulse to act that which we imagine; we want the poetry of life."[38] The imagination has to provide a means of organizing the "facts" so that genuine social amelioration can take place. Science, divorced from Poetry, has intensified inequality and increased the burden of labor which the poor must bear. "Poetry, and the principle of Self, of which money is the visible incarnation, are the God and the Mammon of the world."[39] Poetry unfolds a different kind of utility, one that subsumes and subordinates science. Poetry, unveiling the wonder of life in its infinite complexity, is superior to science because imagination, not reason, is the great teacher. The creative poet does not "produce" verse by means of the will and intellect, but situates the imagination so that the poetry discloses itself. The inspirational model of composition is Shelley's solution to the problem of how the imagination acquires reliable knowledge. The process of inspiration, like "reverie," defamiliarizes the world and uncovers "the wonder of our being" which has been hidden from us.[40] As imagination educates sensibility, it enables society to act with ethical wisdom, fostering an expanding circle of mutual aid and sympathy rather than a chaos of isolated and competing egos pursuing their own self-interest.

The social implications of an inspirational model for the poet are developed by a contemporary critic, Eleanor Wilner, who discusses the romantic bard's mediating relationship to society, which she relates to the experience of the primitive shaman. Distinguishing between societies more or less stable, she concentrates on cultures suffering from extreme disruption and crisis. The shaman characteristically responds with a "vision," a radical departure from tradition that will make possible the regeneration of society. The revitalization process initiated by the shaman involves "the return to origins, the awakening of primal and powerful emotions freed of the inhibitors of past social prohibition, and the resultant reempowering of a renewed self."[41] By virtue of the shaman's special place in society, he is a sensitive barometer of social distress, which he experiences as an individual; his crisis and vision, however, are social because he wants to disrupt the norm only in order to reestablish social equilibrium. Wilner draws a parallel between the visionary shaman and visionary romantic poets like Blake, Beddoes, and Yeats. The romantic visionary, although highly individualistic, is responding to social instability and seeks a new social order. Wilner has offered a way to account for the romantic visionary in social terms. The difference between the shaman and the romantic poet, however, is that primitive societies acknowledge the importance and function of the shaman, while modern society sees poetry as a sphere of activity separate from the hard realities of politics and economics.

A libertarian society has to be creative in order to remain libertarian, just as creativity in any society will tend in a libertarian direction. Language requires perpetual renewal and revision in order to destroy an emergent "code" that will acquire independence from the subjects who originally created it. The social model appropriate for Shelley's imagination is, of course, the Athenian democracy, a decentralized city-state small enough to permit direct participation, but diversified enough to allow healthy conflicts and variety. What Shelley saw on the horizon, however, was the industrial state and unbridled selfishness. As he says in the fragmentary "Speculations on Morals": "The only distinction between the selfish man, and the virtuous man, is that the imagination of the former is confined within a narrow limit, whilst that of the latter embraces a comprehensive circumference." There are, however, no certain or easy methods to combat selfishness since "disinterested benevolence is the product of a cultivated imagination"[42] and only a democratic society can properly cultivate imagination. It is some consolation to Shelley that even if his own society "decays," his poetry and that of others will survive as carriers of the libertarian spirit to influence the future.

1820 POEMS

Letter to Maria Gisborne prefigures *Adonais* to an extent because it deals with the problem of a poet's public existence. The first fourteen lines are an introductory trope comparing Shelley to a spider and silkworm, one who spins a net of poetry not to win immediate acclaim from the "idle buzzers of the day," but to gain immortality in the hearts of those who remember him through his poetry. The *Letter* is somewhat similar in structure to Coleridge's "This Lime-Tree Bower My Prison" because both have a circular movement which passes through an imaginative reconstruction of a scene from which the poet is unwillingly excluded. In the poem's first part Shelley describes simultaneously his external surroundings and his inner state, mingling "objective" imagery with highly subjective digressions. He then turns to Maria Gisborne and reminisces about their pleasant times together. Next, he imagines what London is like for the Gisbornes and reviews the people they will meet and some of the sights they will see. The poem concludes with the poet's insisting the Gisbornes return by winter, hopefully with their other friends, so that Shelley will be surrounded by all those he cares for.

In terms of the *Defence*, the most interesting section is the second paragraph, where he makes some witty digressions on the room in which he is writing. The tone of the paragraph is playful, with no overt hostility to Henry Reveley's mechanical devices and gadgets scattered throughout the room. In fact, Shelley provided financial assistance for Henry's projected steamboat. Nevertheless, the digressive similes and allusions consistently equate machines with torture.[43] The instruments hanging on the wall are "dread engines, such / As Vulcan never wrought for Jove to clutch / Ixion or the Titan" (22-24). These victims of arbitrary power that Shelley has chosen to evoke suggest at the very least the ambiguity of technology, its power to oppress as well as liberate. The following allusions are even more explicitly antiauthoritarian:

> —or the quick
> Wit of that man of God, St. Dominic,
> To convince Atheist, Turk or Heretic
> Or those in philanthropic council met,
> Who thought to pay some interest for the debt
> They owed to Jesus Christ for their salvation,
> By giving a faint foretaste of damnation
> To Shakespeare, Sidney, Spenser and the rest
> Who made our land an island of the blest,
> When lamp-like Spain, who now relumes her fire
> On Freedom's hearth, grew dim with Empire:—
> With thumbscrews, wheels, with tooth and spike and jag,
> . . . and other strange and dread
> Magical forms . . .
> (24-44)

The tortures of the Inquisition, which was abolished in the Spanish Revolution of 1820, are brought to mind in conjunction with the English poets "damned" by the Catholic Church. The *Defence* deals with the opposition between the pleasures of Poetry and joylessness of despotism, which in *Letter to Maria Gisborne* is associated with the mechanical. As a contrast to the implements of torture, Shelley describes the comic "gnomes" who feed from quicksilver underneath the earth (58-65). Their friends, the earthquake demons, participate in a joyful play reminiscent of *Prometheus Unbound*, Act IV. Shelley seems to emphasize "play" by apologizing for a paper

257

boat he has been playing with (75), and by earlier describing the completed steamboat as a vessel that would "sport" in the sea (21).

Another contrast in the poem is between the natural and artificial, the country and the city. The spider-silkworm who is figured as the poet is a being who creates organically out of itself fine threads of poetry. A machine, however, seems to defy spiritualization, as Shelley speaks of trying to breathe "a soul into the iron heart / Of some machine" (18-19). He uses mechanical metaphors when dismissing the abusive reviewers, but employs a natural scene as the spell by which he completely banishes that unpleasant world (106-31). Nature, at peace with itself, provides Shelley with a sanctuary from the "worms" and "carrion jays" who attack his poetry and reject his libertarian ideas. The imaginative reconstruction of the Gisbornes in London contrasts friendship with the unhappy urban setting, with its prostitutes and political graffiti. The urban scene is then contrasted with Shelley's pastoral residence (274-91), which is harmonious and beautiful, untainted by the city's corruptions. Shelley's agrarian bias is evident as he renders picturesque the peasant's song, which is "Rude, but made sweet by distance." The poem, however, is remote from any kind of primitivism because in the concluding paragraph, which sketches out a kind of utopian community for Shelley, the most prominent activities are urbane conversation and learned reading.[44] Nature, then, is at once a pleasant backdrop for the imagination, and a symbol for the imagination in its most creative moments.

One last comment on the *Letter*: it is interesting that William Godwin is described as the "foremost" of living Englishmen who will stand "Before the dread Tribunal to come" (200), yet Shelley does not include his father-in-law in the ideal community he imagines for himself at the poem's end. Although his personal relations with the anarchist philosopher were as low as they could be, with Godwin angrily demanding more money, Shelley could still appreciate the past achievements from which he learned so much.

A few months later, in August, Shelley wrote two very different poems that nevertheless relate coherently to the *Defence*. The *Witch of Atlas*, composed in only three days, is not just a poem about poetry and the poet, but—despite its irony—a poem about utopian poetry and the apocalyptic imagination. *Oedipus Tyrannus, or Swellfoot the Tyrant* has a connection with the ideas of the *Defence* because the satire's coherence derives from a libertarian anti-Malthusianism. The two poems illustrate the diversity of Shelley's imagination which can, with equal ease, create *ottava rima* stanzas about a mythopoeic witch in the "high" style of *Prometheus Unbound*, and a raucous satire in familiar diction, with numerous and outrageous puns and classical allusions. The one poem has no specific social reference, but the other exploits the Queen Caroline affair of 1820, when the Peterloo-inspired movement for reform, suffering badly from repression, rallied behind the beleaguered Queen. The latter poem shows that Shelley's disappointment over not having published his Peterloo works did not prevent him from trying again to write for the reform movement.

The Witch of Atlas is framed by irony at the beginning and end. The stanzas dedicated "To Mary" are an ironic apology for writing a poem displeasing to his wife, who preferred his less ideal writings, like *The Cenci* and *Rosalind and Helen*. Although the dedication is light, it must have struck a raw nerve, because Mary Shelley omitted to publish it when she included *The Witch of Atlas* in *Posthumous Poems*. In the first stanza Mary is accused of being "critic-bitten"—that is, affected by the judgments of those writing for such periodicals as the *Quarterly Review*, whose attack on *The Revolt of Islam* is alluded to in stanza III. The 1817 poem, also dedicated to Mary, was composed in great hopefulness, as an "experiment" on the public mind, but the experiment failed, leading Shelley to question either his own poetic ability or the actual prospects for libertarian social change. Rather than support Shelley in his utopianism, Mary echoes the hostile critics, so that his visionary power is now completely unconnected with his love for her; in the 1817 dedication, her love gave him strength and inspiration to pursue his vision, but now "that is dead." The present poem tells "no story," which is a literary weakness according to Mary, but the *Defence* has a low opinion of mere stories, unpoetic sequences of unrelated "facts." He defends himself in the last three stanzas by ridiculing Wordsworth and *Peter Bell*, which represent the failure of imagination to transcend the mere particulars of actuality. Moreover, Shelley's witch took only three days to create, while Wordsworth's *Peter Bell* took an appalling nineteen years. The dedication, then, criticizes Mary, the hostile critic of the *Quarterly Review*, Wordsworth, and the "public" for being so unsympathetic to the visionary imagination, whose spirit is playful like a kitten (st. I), and loving (st. VI), but also capable of a self-deprecating irony. The irony continues into the first stanza of the poem itself where the poet laments philosophy's antipoetic effects because "Error and

Truth" have "hunted from the earth" the products of the mytho-poeic imagination, leaving us "nothing to believe in." The kind of philosophy alluded to, however, is the scientific-mechanical ration-ality criticized in the *Defence* and *Letter to Maria Gisborne*.

After the introductory ironies, the poem launches a series of creations, always emblematic of the poet's imagination. The Witch is created by the gods and the elements to remind the reader that her real creator is the poet—or rather, the poetic imagination. As a vapor, cloud, meteor, and star (st. III), she assumes the meta-morphic shapes of the water cycle and fire, and symbolizes imag-ination, love, and utopia. She grows into a female shape while she is in a "cave" (st. IV), a favorite symbol of the imagination (cf. "the cave of the witch Poesy" in "Mont Blanc," and Prometheus's cave in *Prometheus Unbound*). At first her beauty is so powerful that it subdues, like Orpheus's song, the predatory ferocity of animals. Beauty transforming nature, also a millennial symbol in *Queen Mab* and *Prometheus Unbound*, suggests the immense power of the imag-ination when it is fully liberated. In the cave of imagination the Witch weaves "a subtle veil" (st. XIII) and tends the magic scrolls and potions over which she has control. The texts sacred to the imagination speak a language that will deliver humanity from its oppression, restoring the paradise long ago lost and vanquishing "the earth-consuming rage / Of gold and blood" (st. XVIII). The tend-ency of imagination is not static but prolific and always changing, so the Witch continues to metamorphose, bidding adieu to the mortal creatures who lack her immortality (st. XXIV), creating a child (an "Image"), taking a voyage with Hermaphroditus in her boat, and finally intervening in the lives of imperfect humanity. The Witch, then, is a product of imagination, a poet and creator of beautiful images, and a poet-prophet who mediates between utopian ideals and the human world. As a poet, the Witch resembles the spider-silkworm weaver of *Letter to Maria Gisborne*, and even one of her poems, Hermaphroditus, suggests the androgynous features of the poet if one combines the female spider with the male silkworm.[45]

The last quarter of the poem describes the Witch in her role as mediator and libertarian troublemaker. Like Prometheus, she per-ceives in human dreams "Distortions foul of supernatural awe, / And pale imaginings of visioned wrong / And all the code of custom's lawless law / Written upon the brows of old and young" (st. LXII). She wants to "write" something different, a utopian poem that will release people from their Jupiterian bondage. With the equanimity of Queen Mab,, she is not disturbed by human folly because she sees through mere personality and social role to the living human soul (st. LXVI), the libertarian potentiality beneath the tyrannical actuality. With a potion she rewards some of her favorites with a kind of immortality that defeats the worst consequences of decay. The Witch also rights wrongs, chastising the miser, correcting the lying "scribe," subverting the authoritarian intentions of priests, making kings mock their own power, turning soldiers into blacksmiths (beating the swords into millennial plowshares), urging jailors to release victims of political repression, bringing timid lovers together, and making couples and friends happy. The Witch, as poem, as poet, as symbol of the imagination, can accomplish these utopian tasks by acting directly on the potentiality veiled by custom and superstition. Her actions are not "revolutionary" in the commonly understood sense of the word, but anarchically subversive of arbitrary power, sexual repression, and egoism.

The poem ends abruptly, with the speaker promising a continuation later, in the winter, when imagination is less skeptical than in "these garish summer days." The reader is brought full circle back to stanza I and the dedication, to the fate of imagination in an "unpoetic" age.

Reading the *Examiner* from Peterloo to August of 1820, one sees a social-political conflict with many battles and numerous confrontations, but no decisive conflict powerful enough to topple the Liverpool government or silence the reform movement. The level of struggle was serious and violent. A group of Spenceans attempted a *coup d'état*, but were apprehended, tried, and executed. Even "respectable" reformers were brought to trial and convicted. James George Bruce, a reformer, but not a famous one (although he might have been chosen by Shelley to receive the 1817 *Proposal For Putting Reform to the Vote*),[46] was the unfortunate victim of a court that decided to punish someone for the murder of a Chester constable; it just so happened that Bruce was chosen, transported for life.[47] In Oldham the military rioted upon hearing a "Peterloo" song, attacking civilians with considerable brutality.[48] Glasgow, after a successful general strike, was in a state of insurrection for some weeks before the forces of repression could restore "order."[49] And with the Queen's "progress" through the country, on her way to Parliament, there were large demonstrations in support of her and "Liberty." At Dover a crowd rioted while trying to prevent Italian witnesses, hostile to the Queen, from entering the country.[50]

From Mary Shelley we learn that the inspiration for *Oedipus Tyrannus* was accidental and somewhat ludicrous, as a group of squealing pigs interrupted Shelley's recitation to friends of the sublime "Ode to Liberty." After George III's death, George IV wanted to divorce Caroline, from whom he had been separated for years, and who had lived in Europe. In preparation for the divorce proceedings he had hired spies—the Milan Commission—to gather evidence of her "adulterous" behavior to bolster a case against her. Caroline, however, wanted to be Queen, resisted George's plans to push her aside, formed an alliance with the Whigs, and won the support of the democratic populace in her fight to retain her position. Parliament would decide her fate. Shelley exploits many of the comic possibilities of the affair, but also develops from it an anti-Malthusian argument in favor of libertarian reform.

The conceit of ironically figuring the democratic "people" as pigs, hogs, and swine was first developed by radicals in the 1790s after Edmund Burke's infamous phrase, "the swinish multitude." By Shelley's time it was a satirical convention employed, for example, in an *Examiner* burlesque of August 30, 1818 entitled "A new Catechism, For the Use of the Natives of Hampshire; Necessary to be had in all sties."[51] Raucous political satire is unusual for the *Examiner* but common in the *Black Dwarf*, which often would have at least one comic assault on Old Corruption. Hone's parodies and the satires produced in conjunction with Cruikshank were, as I have already discussed, enormously popular. Comic political satire like that of Hone and the *Black Dwarf* makes certain assumptions about the predispositions of the audience that give the satirist a range of possible targets and shared values. Radical satire would already assume the venality of the Tory government, the arrogance of the rich, the justice of parliamentary reform, and the dignity of the so-called "lower orders." In short, social and political conflict are already assumed in this kind of satire, so that its principal purpose is not to argue novel ideas, but to give to accepted notions an artistic shape in which the audience can take delight, understanding the clever rearrangement of shared values and perceptions.

Shelley operates within these satirical conventions, but also provides a set of allusions that only a classicist—and not a popular audience—could fully appreciate. More importantly, he introduces a line of thinking not commonly assumed in the reform movement. He takes the Queen Caroline affair as the plot material which he transforms into an argument against Malthus and in favor of libertarian reform. Although Cobbett, Hazlitt, Shelley, and Godwin (whose critique of Malthus was published in 1820) identified Malthus as the archenemy of reform, not everyone in the reform movement did so. Malthusian ideas were shared by the Tories and Whigs, as well as the reformers of the Benthamite school, and even Carlile. The reformist Brougham, who defended the Queen in the House of Commons, was a Malthusian, while the Queen's most strenuous supporter in print, William Cobbett, was just as vehemently against Malthus. The critics C. E. Pulos and Kenneth Cameron have already identified the play's anti-Malthusian elements, upon which I will be expanding.[52] For a utopian anarchist like Shelley, Malthus's ideas could not be more odious because, according to the principle of population, social amelioration must inevitably lead to an increase of population to levels higher than the economy can support, thus leading to a battle for scarce resources, and eventuating in the social inequality that preceded the reforms. Malthus gave a scientific imprimatur to the idea that inequality was inevitable, permanent, and immutable. But not all anti-Malthusians were for equality; Hazlitt liked to scoff at utopian ideas of perfectibility and Cobbett insisted on maintaining a social hierarchy, despite reforms.

I think it is plausible, especially in light of *Oedipus Tyrannus*, that, as Pulos argues, the "fatal child" that Jupiter expects will insure his continued reign in Act III of *Prometheus Unbound* is Malthusian necessity.[53] If population increases render futile every effort at social amelioration, then Jupiter will indeed remain in power indefinitely. Another dialectic, suggested by *Oedipus Tyrannus*, can emerge: out of ruling-class complacency and refusal to grant reforms (because of Malthusian assumptions), the poor rise up from their exploitation and remove the rich from power, but refuse to install a new ruling elite and instead equalize power and property.

The play begins within the Temple of Famine, the society's most sacred dwelling. The religion of Famine—Malthusianism—insists that social inequality cannot be altered, so the privileged members enjoy themselves and do not even try to better the conditions of those "under" them. Swellfoot, who stands for George IV, opens the poem with a homage to Malthusian ideas, addressing the society's spiritual divinity, Famine.

> Thou supreme Goddess! by whose power divine
> These graceful limbs are clothed in proud array

263

[He contemplates himself with satisfaction.]
Of gold and purple, and this kingly paunch
Swells like a sail before a favouring breeze . . .[54]

His brain is "untroubled" because the scientific Necessity of the Famine religion excuses his luxury and domination; he can indulge himself without restraint because his power is impregnable. His paunch and his fat behind (his "most sacred nether promontories") comically allude to immoral gluttony, while the "swine" nearly starve. The psychology of nurture is evoked in the controversy between the swine and the privileged elite over living conditions. The Chorus of Swine reminds Swellfoot that in previous reigns "pity was a royal thing" (38), evoking the ideal of reciprocity between monarchy and the people; but with the monarchy neglecting the people's welfare, the "swine" cannot even "nurture" their own children. One "sow" complains her teats are empty of milk (49); another says, "I could almost eat my litter" (50); and one pig says, "I suck, but no milk will come from the dug"(51). The physical starvation mirrors and is conditioned by the denial of nurture by the ruling elite, whose laissez-faire Malthusianism is a departure from previous state policies. After the swine petition the king for relief—"You ought to give us hog-wash and clean straw, / And sties well thatched; besides it is the law!" (65-66)—Swellfoot labels their words seditious and blasphemous, and calls in the agents of Malthusian doctrine, "Solomon the court porkman, / Moses the sow-gelder, and Zephaniah / The hog-butcher"(69-71). Swellfoot directs Moses: "Out with your knife, old Moses, and spay those Sows / That load the earth with Pigs; cut close and deep" (72-73). Swellfoot continues to Moses:

> Moral restraint I see has no effect,
> Nor prostitution, nor our own example,
> Starvation, typhus-fever, war, nor prison—
> This was the art which the arch-priest of Famine
> Hinted at in his charge to the Theban clergy—
> Cut close and deep, good Moses.
> (74-77)

The arch-priest speaks the language of Malthus, who did indeed recommend what Swellfoot attributes to him, and who even called for the abolition of poor relief. The philosopher Dugald Stewart, using Malthusian logic, justified child labor.[55] Disease, famine, war, and prison have not thinned the population sufficiently, and there-fore more drastic measures are required—so argues Swellfoot, whose sterilization idea was not, however, in the Malthusian mainstream (yet). Shelley illustrates the terrifying logic of Malthusian ideas by suggesting castration.

Swellfoot and other members of the elite are disturbed by the prophecy, whose key words are "choose reform or civil war!" With good reason Shelley believes that the social crisis is so severe that unless there is some kind of reform, a revolution will erupt. Ac-ceptance of Malthusian ideas blocks any contemplation of reform because social amelioration will only increase population and give false hopes; ironically, the religion of Famine is paving the way for an insurrectionary conflict. The elite believes that Malthusianism guarantees its perpetual success, but just the opposite is the case.

Malthus is by no means the only target of *Oedipus Tyrannus*, which also identifies the established order with murder and paper money. Mammon, the arch-priest of Famine, who stands for Liv-erpool, speaks of disinheriting his eldest son in favor of his daughter Banknotina, who will marry the gallows (I, i, 195-204). The sites of public executions are then alluded to (Hounslow Heath, Tyburn, New Drop) in order to suggest a contemporary reality, namely, the many unfortunates who were actually executed for "fraud" and "forgery," crimes made possible by the paper money system. The *Examiner* of February 22, 1818, for example, reports on the exe-cutions of four people, three for forgery; Hunt protests against the mercantile interest that is actually behind these executions.[56] In a symbolic way, then, paper money kills people by leading to the executions of those who try to take illegal advantage of the system. Economic tyranny is also satirized by the way the government con-sumes so much money in the form of "patronage, and pensions, and by-payments," while at the same time it neglects to treat the poor humanely (II, i, 13). A response to the increasing poor rates ("Lean-Pig rates") (II, i, 4) was to skimp on poor relief rather than force the wealthy to pay more taxes (increasing poor rates usually hurt the men of small property, like the farmer, and had little effect on the great landowners). The rich consume the nation's wealth in a selfish, extravagant way, while the poor suffer lives of deprivation. As Mammon says of the King's feast, "The price and pains which its ingredients cost / Might have maintained some dozen families / A winter or two—" (II, ii, 25-27).

Before the trial of the Green Bag (which was the much satirized container of evidence against Queen Caroline), the Chorus of Swine sing to "Famine," but for reasons very different than the ruling elite's. Famine, for the swine, is the force of Necessity that will eventuate in revolution: "dividing possessions . . . Uprooting oppressions . . . Till all be made level again!" (II, ii, 52-60). The fear of the revolutionary "leveling" is a constant theme of government spokesmen who justify the brutal repression on these grounds, while the reform movement emphasized the constitutional and reformist nature of the changes they wanted. Shelley is showing the two sides of the Malthusian religion: if the elite will not grant concessions to the reform movement, then there will be a revolutionary leveling which the elite fears more than anything else. If the elite wants to spare itself the worst fate, it should grant reforms, not increase repression.

To announce Shelley's libertarian message he needs a "deity" quite independent from Famine. The goddess "Liberty" intervenes immediately before Queen Iona pours the contents of the Green Bag on her accusers, transforming them into "*a number of filthy and ugly animals.*" Liberty pleads with the goddess of Famine thus:

> I charge thee! when thou wake the multitude,
> Thou lead them not upon the paths of blood.
> The earth did never mean her foison
> For those who crown life's cup with poison
> Of fanatic rage and meaningless revenge—
>   But for those radiant spirits, who are still
> The standard-bearers in the van of Change.
>   Be they th' appointed stewards, to fill
> The lap of Pain, and Toil, and Age!—
> Remit, O Queen! thy accustomed rage!—
> Be what thou art not! In voice faint and low
> FREEDOM calls *Famine*,—her eternal foe,
> To brief alliance, hollow truce.—Rise now!
>   (II, ii, 90-102)

The religion of Famine has provoked so much disorder that a revolution is at hand, but "Liberty" asks that the insurrection be as nonviolent as possible. Famine is similar to the Demogorgon that dethrones Jupiter, whereas Liberty speaks for the Promethean philosophy of forebearance, forgiveness, and imagination. The vanguard of libertarians which Liberty asks to lead the revolution is similar to the associations of philanthropists that Shelley tried to organize in 1812, and to the role that Laon and Prometheus play in their respective poems of anarchist revolution. It is clear by now that Shelley believes such a vanguard is necessary to prevent a Jacobin or Napoleonic kind of authoritarianism, because only libertarians are trained in the philosophy of disinterested benevolence.

The poem's final words do not evoke philosophical pensiveness, but laughter. Iona Taurina, sitting on the Minotaur, is about to chase the bestiary of the metamorphosed ruling class in a manner that suggests the country squire at the hunt. Imagining Iona Taurina on top of the bull, shouting "tallyho," dissolves the Queen Caroline affair into the farce that it actually was. Nevertheless, it is astonishing to see how much distinctively Shelleyan material Shelley managed to fashion into a mode so bound by convention.

Shortly after *Oedipus Tyrannus* was published in London, some members of the Society for the Suppression of Vice examined a copy and threatened the bookseller with prosecution for libel if he did not immediately consign all remaining copies of the offending poem to the fire, where Shelley's satirical farce expired.

1821 POEMS

Epipsychidion, composed shortly before *A Defence of Poetry*, is an eloquent defense of the imagination. The "Emily" of the poem was Teresa Viviani, the daughter of the governor of Pisa, who kept her in a convent until her arranged marriage. Shelley, Mary, and Claire started visiting Teresa in November of 1820 when she was nineteen years old. Shelley seems to have fallen in love with her, an event commemorated by the poem, composed in January-February, 1821. Familiarity bred its proverbial contempt because by 1822 he was disillusioned with Teresa, married since September 8, 1821. Writing to John Gisborne, Shelley says of *Epipsychidion*:

> I cannot look at it; the person whom it celebrates was a cloud instead of a Juno; and poor Ixion starts from the centaur that was the offspring of his own embrace. If you are anxious, however, to hear what I am and have been, it will tell you something thereof. It is an idealized history of my life and feelings. I think one is always in love with something or other; the error, and I confess it is not easy for spirits cased in flesh and blood to avoid it, consists in seeking in a mortal image the likeness of what is perhaps eternal.[57]

The voice of the final sentence is not entirely absent from *Epipsychidion* because the "editor" of the "Advertisement" speaks with skepticism; he suggests that the poet, now dead, who wrote the poem, believed in "a scheme of life, suited perhaps to that happier and better world of which he is now an inhabitant, but hardly practicable in this."[58]

The subtitle is provocative and raises the theme of unjust imprisonment: "Verses Addressed to the Noble and Unfortunate Lady, Emilia V——, Now Imprisoned in the Convent of ——." At one level the poem is a feminist protest against the repression of women, who pass from father to husband as pieces of property. Emily is not the only victim of imprisonment, which is fully criticized in the free love section (149-89). There is an absolute conflict between two ways of living, one of which is repressive, ultimately imprisoning, and the other loving and imaginative. To concentrate one's love on one or two objects only and consign the rest of humanity "To cold oblivion" is in accordance with "the code / Of modern morals" which governs "those poor slaves" who "travel to their home among the dead / By the broad highway of the world, and so / With one chained friend, perhaps a jealous foe, / The dreariest and longest journey go" (156-59). The consciousness which imprisons others is idolatrous in the sense of being fixated by power. "True Love" (in the draft version, "Free Love") is like imagination, which "fills / The Universe with glorious beams, and kills / Error, the worm, with many a sun-like arrow / Of its reverberated lightning" (166-69). Only the profusion and fluxional multiplicity that is free love—and imagination—can expand the circle of genuine communion so that "Error" can be vanquished. Imprisoning structures, psychological and social, cannot create but, like Jupiter, can only destroy by constructing boundaries and codes to limit the natural exuberance of life. Love and hope, however, are truly creative, limited only by the will, the capacity to "dare" something beyond what was previously considered possible. By the activity of loving (or imagining, or creating) humanity can regain a lost paradise. Imprisonment is an act of violence, setting life-destroying and wholly artificial and rigid curbs on what desire can accomplish. Ultimately prison is a "sepulchre," a coffin within which life, unable to grow, is turned in upon itself as a destructive force.

Prison is a structure also overcome by the poem's self-reflexive language. The poem's inscription, taken from Emily's own words, can be translated thus: "The loving soul launches beyond creation, and creates for itself in the infinite a world all its own, far different from this dark and terrifying gulf."[59] The soul that loves transcends actuality and creates in another sphere a "world" lacking the restrictions of the imprisoning world. The language appropriate for Emily's "created" world cannot be referential, tied to the prison world, but must be a language that is self-generating, spinning out of itself—like the spider-silkworm of *Letter to Maria Gisborne*—a utopian poetry. During the invocation to Emily, the poetry tries to find metaphors and images adequate to capture her essence, but the task is necessarily impossible because the Ideal cannot be fixed by words. For Shelley "Emily" is not just a beautiful young woman he is attracted to, but the vessel in which he perceives the Ideal he has been searching for his entire life. Her mortal form is a veil behind which exists an impersonal divinity: she is depicted as "Veiling beneath that radiant form of Woman / All that is insupportable in thee / Of light, and love, and immortality!" (22-24). She is the "Veiled Glory of this lampless Universe!" (26), lampless because it is not animated by the Ideal. Emily is like the transfigured Asia, someone in whom the Ideal lives a natural existence. But she herself is not the Ideal which, rather, appears and discloses itself through her mortal form. The second part makes it clear that the Ideal cannot be "imprisoned" in one body because its essence is Protean. Poetry tries to trace the operations of the Ideal by imitating the fading coal of inspiration: to achieve coherences that of necessity must collapse, to reach fiery kindlings which must "dwindle."[60] Poetry, by falling back into its own sources, can "represent" the overcoming of prison because it has refused to allow itself to be imprisoned by static images from the world of actuality. The code of the social world is the antithesis of the prolific imagination, which generates one metaphor after another in an attempt to represent what cannot be represented.

The Intellectual Beauty or Ideal that Shelley is celebrating is imaged as a "Being" in the second part, after the invocation. Paralleling other autobiographical allegories in Shelley's work, this one pictures divinity as a presence in nature, poetry, and philosophy, a pantheistic Being he can pursue as a child and youth with effortless ease. There is a crisis once he leaves "dreamy youth" because the Being escapes and he cannot recall her. "Wither 'twas fled, this soul out of my soul?" (238). As in Wordsworth's poems of loss, Shelley has lost an instinctive access to divinity, which he now has to pursue actively. Thereafter the quest for divinity becomes an erotic quest, looking for the Ideal in human form, in the way that love is depicted in Plato's *Symposium* by Diotima. "In many mortal forms I rashly sought / The shadow of that idol of my thought" (267-68). After numerous disappointments he achieves a certain equilibrium with the Moon and the Sun, both of whom rule the poem's speaker, a passive recipient of their light and warmth. One Platonically loves what one lacks, so this passivity is an accurately imaged condition. But, as Daniel Hughes points out, the fluxional Comet collapses this static coherence, introducing a dynamic image of fire, and disturbing the equilibrium enough to permit the third section.[61]

The flight to the paradisal island with Emily is, at one level, an attempt to figure in language the Ideal embodied naturalistically in a hostile world. Since it is taken for granted that the Ideal cannot, as in *Prometheus Unbound*, transform the entire world, the poet imagines the subject-object unity in a realm just beyond the reaches of civilization. Emily, the island, and his relationship to both of them are as perfect as mortals can make them, a utopian refuge for unrepressed desire. Emily and the island are representations of the Ideal, like the Witch of Atlas or the Witch's Hermaphroditus, or even like the many metaphors of *Epipsychidion*'s first part. Part three is distinguished by a suspension of disbelief, so that the poet allows himself to imagine words that could depict the union of subject and object—a union the first part repeatedly represents as impossible. The flight to the island is a utopian fiction, another "daring" act of the will, another contradiction of what is possible. Far from naive, this part begins with a complete awareness of the boundaries it is violating (388-407), since "true love" is pictured as overleaping "all fence," "with invisible violence" and powerful strength. If Love can "make free / The limbs in chains, the heart in agony, / The soul in dust and chaos," it is a force that has to overcome resistance and transcend the world of actuality (405-407).

As the images of the paradise island unfold, the theme of subject-object unity becomes dominant. The island, which has avoided the corruption of history, is where "the last spirit of the age of gold" still lives (428). The divinity which *is* the island "is a soul within the soul" (455), a mirror of the poet's deepest desire, "Like echoes of an antenatal dream" (456), joining together the most archaic intensities of desire. Scarcity has spared the island its terrible evils, "Famine or Blight, / Pestilence, War and Earthquake" (461-62), so that for the inhabitants nature was never a hostile power that had to be subdued. The island is so fortunate that even its ancient kings were benevolent, leaving constructs, like the tower, that blend with nature and serve utopian purposes. So complete is the union of subject and object that:

the Earth and Ocean seem
To sleep in one another's arms, and dream
Of waves, flowers, clouds, woods, rocks, and all that we
Read in their smiles, and call reality.
(509-12)

Another dimension of this utopia is its agrarian and aristocratic features. "This isle and house are mine" (513), he tells Emily, and they will establish a household in the tower abandoned by a king. The island natives are "Simple and spirited; innocent and bold" (429), and will provide a pleasant air of the picturesque for the speaker and his "lady." On their country estate they will have "books and music," but not the objects of "luxury" which are not in "true taste." There will be no need for the speaker to acquire money through rents or cash crops or any other means because, presumably, they will pluck meals from the trees like Adam and Eve. The Advertisement, however, states that the poet "has bought" one of the Sporades islands, and "had fitted up the ruins of an old building."[62] This particular estate fuses the best features of nature and civilization without the evils of either, because there is no scarcity to necessitate a struggle against nature. These aristocratic features demonstrate how hard it is to "clothe" the Ideal in terrestrial images; they pull the poetry back to an actuality it wants to transcend.

At another level the island is also a hypostasis where the imagination stops on its quest for the Ideal. A favorite Shelleyan symbol is the boat of the soul floating on the sea in search of a harbor. The island is where the soul can rest and release the imagination to perform its activities freely and joyously. This hypostasis is, however, a fiction created by the suspension of disbelief, so that it necessarily collapses. When the speaker says "I pant, I sink, I tremble, I expire!" (591), he is not expressing a sexual swoon, but announcing the inevitable collapse of the poetic fictions fabricated in part three.[63] Only in the imagination can the Ideal build a retreat; only in a fiction can the Ideal be represented. The voice of the epilogue comes from the world of actuality, not utopia, well after the coal of inspiration has faded. The poet again expresses a fear of being misinterpreted, as he did in the Dantean prologue, by the "dull" who will read lust for love, adultery and promiscuity for "true love," unlawful sexuality for free imagination. The tone of the epilogue suggests that Shelley accepts this mistreatment as inevitable and derives comfort from the awareness that at least a few will understand. He has defended the imagination in *Epipsychidion* as a Platonic Eros which compels the soul beyond itself and its prisons. Love of nature, sexual love, the writing of poetry, the acts of imagination, are all participations in the divinity called Intellectual Beauty or the Ideal, and are all activities by which utopia can be constructed. Utopia exists as poetry, the imperfect and contradictory attempt to embody the Ideal. Whether or not the potentiality within the poem can ever be released into society and history is something the poet cannot know. He does what he can by expressing desire to the fullest extent possible, and expanding the circumference of his own imagination to form the widest possible circle. The poet's struggle "Tills for the promise of a later birth / The wilderness of this Elysian earth" (188-89).

Some critics have suggested that the trajectory of Shelley's development can be charted as veering away from politics, society, even life itself, and toward a Platonic mysticism, an asocial spirituality, a *contemptus mundi* akin to that of the medieval ascetics. Earl Wasserman, for example, points to *Adonais* as the poem where Shelley finally gives up his earthly hopes and locates the Ideal in the afterlife.[64] Milton Wilson, drawing a distinction between a political millennium and a Platonic apocalypse, sees *Adonais* declaring an "uncompromising Platonism which Shelley could not accept wholeheartedly elsewhere." Shelley the radical is eclipsed by the Platonist who sees human life itself as an evil from which death delivers us.[65] Ross Woodman, who calls *Adonais* Shelley's most "Shelleyan" poem, reads it in terms of an absolute conflict between life and death, matter and spirit, so that the triumph of spirit is identical with spirit's release from the body after death.[66] Although each of these critics offers many valuable insights, I nevertheless think that the dualism operating in the poem is not new, is consistent with Shelley's previous poetry, and in no way contradicts his utopianism. First, however, one must distinguish between poems and prose, because Shelley always permits himself more hope in poetry than in prose, where he is much more skeptical. One can scan the entire corpus of Shelley's prose for his statements concerning death and immortality without finding a single dogmatic sentence affirming immortality. Without question, Shelley wanted death to provide

272

what life had not, but he unwaveringly maintained his skepticism on the issue. Desire for immortality is clearly present in *Adonais*, particularly in the third part, but the Neoplatonic One to which the postmortal spirit returns is a metaphor, a symbol, and must be understood as a poetically useful fiction, like the flight with Emily to the island in *Epipsychidion*.

Adonais is yet another defense of imagination, an angry protest against the mistreatment of Keats at the hands of hostile critics, especially one in particular, the author of a review in the *Quarterly* which attacked Keat's *Endymion* volume. Shelley assumes the murdering critic is Southey, whom he suspected of writing the negative review of *The Revolt of Islam* which also appeared in the *Quarterly*.[67] At one level *Adonais* accuses the forces of cultural reaction of murderous insensitivity, of actually killing John Keats who, unlike Shelley, could not sustain the abuse with which his creations were met. Keats's death and the myth of his murder (a myth without any foundation in fact because Keats died, of course, from tuberculosis) provided Shelley with an opportunity for publicly attacking his own detractors. Ever since the publication of the *Quarterly Review*'s essay on *The Revolt of Islam*, he had wanted to fight back, but had been restrained by a sense of decorum and a Promethean conviction that it was inappropriate to combat one's enemies using their tactics. *Peter Bell the Third* assaults a member of the apostate Lake poets, Wordsworth, who is briefly criticized in *The Witch of Atlas* too, but Southey is never mentioned by name, not even in *Adonais*. Indeed, Wordsworth would not have been so openly criticized if he had not intervened so vigorously on the side of the Tories, especially in publishing the infamous lines on "carnage." Shelley did not, however, put his name to *Peter Bell the Third*, which is comic and, moreover, tempered by praise for Wordsworth, and the three stanzas of anti-Wordsworthian jest in *The Witch of Atlas* are lightly satirical. *Adonais*, however, launches a thoroughly serious and uncompromising attack on the cultural Toryism that Shelley identified with Southey.

Like so many of Shelley's poems, this one falls into three parts: part one (stanzas 1-17) is a lamentation; part two (18-38) offers several consolations to the mourners; part three (39-55) is the triumphant celebration of Adonais's spirit immortally reborn in the living imagination as his spirit returns to the "One." The murderous Critic, who is first attacked in the Preface, is implicitly criticized throughout the lamentations, since Adonais is portrayed as such an invaluable member of the human community. Moreover, the first part concludes with a curse: "the curse of Cain / Light on his head who pierced thy innocent breast, / And scared the angel soul that was its earthly guest!" (st. 17). The second part also concludes with a curse on the Critic (st. 36-38), which identifies his worst fate as to continue living, being himself and knowing himself because "Remorse and Self-contempt shall cling to thee" (st. 37). While the pure spirit of Adonais "shall flow / Back to the burning fountain whence it came" (st. 38), the Critic's "cold embers choke the sordid hearth of shame" (st. 38). Like Jupiter, the Critic will self-destruct from his own evil which can destroy, but not create. In the triumphant third part, the Critic is left far behind as an insignificant cipher while Adonais becomes one with the universe of beauty and spirit.

One theme I want to develop is the existential situation of the utopian poet. The pain and stress so evident in *Adonais*'s portrait of the utopian poet can be traced back to the shamanistic or prophetic role Shelley assigned to the true poet. Existing wholly in neither actuality nor potentiality, his inspiration destroys his mortality, and he is in the unique position of being able to cultivate libertarian images that are not "tainted" by self-interest. The Godwinian ideal of disinterested benevolence finds its most reliable exponent in the utopian poet, who appeals to an Ideal that claims universality, while most political ideals are partial and vitiated by class interests (of course, in reality, Shelley's own Ideal is far from pure). *Adonais*, then, records the living situation experienced by the disinterested mediator between utopian ideals and an interest-ridden actuality. As in "Lines written among the Euganean Hills" and Act I of *Prometheus Unbound*, whatever pain the utopian endures is necessary and justified by the moments of beauty.

In one movement of the poem, Adonais starts as a "broken lily" (st. 6), and becomes flowers "exhaling" from the corpse (st. 20). The speaker consoles himself by realizing that "death feeds life" and, as Wasserman says, "the impersonal sum total of animation persists even though individualized matter disintergrates."[68] The theme of nature's cyclicity is apparent, but after the speaker consoles himself with "Nought we know, dies," he asks himself the question which sabotages the consolation: "Shall that alone which knows / Be as a sword consumed before the sheath / By sightless lightning?" The movement from broken lily to corpse-flowers is a remarkable consolation which, however, depends on the angle of perception.

Viewed within a massive scheme of cyclical time and immense space, the death of Adonais is a passage from one mode of life to another. Nothing, in fact, *dies*. Viewed from the ordinary perspective of a living person, the passage still represents loss because the unique presence—the mind, the soul—is no longer alive.

The transition that begins midway in stanza 38 depends upon a new perspective on the immortality of the soul. In the preceding stanza, the soulless Critic, living as he lives, has no life, but "lives" a death-in-life, a self-destructive prolongation of sterility, an invulnerable nothing. In fact, only in death will the Critic be creative, because his corpse will renew nature and make possible a new beginning. The loss of mere existence, the poem now sees, is not as lamentable as the death of a creative poet, because what matters most is beauty, not mere existence. The dead Adonais has a fate more enviable than the live Critic, whose life, without beauty, is not worth living.

If an eternity is possible through the activities of memory, then Adonais lives on through his poetry as it is reborn in the living imagination. In this case, memory is unequivocally a blessing, but if one changes focus slightly, memory becomes a curse. What it is that feeds the memory, and the identity of the rememberer, are crucial variables. "Loss" and "regain" define the ambiguity of paradise. As long as one forgets the harsh reality that is the actual context in which memory occurs, then one can dwell in beauty. Beauty, however, is vulnerable. The soft tenderness of beauty requires protection and necessitates struggle. The struggle itself to create beauty in an ugly world is so wearying that to forget is also to escape from pain, and so there is a kinship between death and paradise. One sleeps and dreams of pleasure, but awakens to a world of pain. And if paradise is only a memory, why continue to endure the torturing discrepancy between predatory reality and the paradise of dream? This question draws one to Keats's "Ode to a Nightingale," where the speaker is half in love with easeful death because living is so painful. Pleasure is escape, but death is the ultimate escape. Just as "the snake Memory" (st. 22) can be a blessing or a curse, so can "Paradise" shift its allegiance to life or death. Paradise exists in *Adonais*, unlike utopia in *Prometheus Unbound*, as a limited potentiality, coexisting with a dominant actuality which is the very negation of paradise.

Urania's "Paradise" is a familiar Shelleyan place. "With veiled eyes, / 'Mid listening Echoes, in her Paradise / She sate, while one

with soft enamoured breath, / Rekindled all the fading melodies"
(st. 2). Shelley locates an intense aesthetic moment in the process
of reviving songs of beauty, reliving the creative process. *Fading*
beauty is echoed and rekindled: thus, memory is eternity.[69] The
erotic playfulness that characterized utopia in *Prometheus Unbound*
reappears here too. The breath is soft and enamoured, and like
Panthea and Ione, Urania and her attendants are able to maintain
the cyclicity of beauty and pleasure by remembering, and thus reen-
acting, the past. However, because Urania's paradise does not exist
absolutely, but only as a green isle in a sea of misery, it is ambiguous.
First, Urania was unable to protect her son, Adonais, because she
was in *her* paradise. Also, Urania is told to *awaken*, "wake and
weep!" (st. 3).

In stanza 22, the ambiguities of sleep and death, dream and
paradise, come into fullest expression.

> *He* will awake no more, oh, never more!
> "Wake thou," cried Misery, "childless Mother, rise
> Out of thy sleep, and slake, in thy heart's core,
> A wound more fierce than his with tears and sighs."
> And all the Dreams that watched Urania's eyes,
> And all the Echoes whom their sister's song
> Had held in holy silence, cried: "Arise!"
> Swift as a Thought by the snake Memory stung,
> From her ambrosial rest the fading Splendour sprung.

This stanza pictures paradise as a sleep from which one awakens
only to grieve. In Keats's words, it is "Where but to think is to be
full of sorrow / And leaden-eyed despairs, / Where Beauty cannot
keep her lustrous eyes, / Or new Love pine at them beyond to-
morrow." It is, aptly enough, *Misery* who tells Urania to awaken.
The Dreams and Echoes of paradise behave uncharacteristically,
and urge Urania to go out into the world. Here, Memory is a stinging
snake, because to remember Adonais is to awaken into a nightmare-
world. The implication here and elsewhere is that being unable to
awaken is not nearly as bad a fate as one had thought at first;
indeed, it is similar to paradise itself.

Stanza 24 makes explicit a number of themes only partially de-
veloped before.

> Out of her secret Paradise she sped,
> Through camps and cities rough with stone, and steel,

And human hearts, which to her aery tread
Yielding not, wounded the invisible
Palms of her tender feet where'er they fell:
And barbed tongues, and thoughts more sharp then they,
Rent the soft Form they never could repel,
Whose sacred blood, like the young tears of May,
Paved with eternal flowers that undeserving way.

One recalls *Prometheus Unbound*, Act I, where the Sixth Spirit sings, "Desolation is a delicate thing" (772-79). This song has its source in Agathon's speech in the *Symposium*, where Agathon pictures Love, instead of Homer's Ate, delicately inhabiting the soft places of men and gods. Shelley's innovation is to equate desolation with "the monster, Love." The first line of the song speaks appropriately to the stanza at hand: "[The best and gentlest dream visions of joy] And wake, and find the shadow Pain. . . ." The hardness of actuality pierces and cuts the soft places where tenderness lives in Urania. In this stanza, her paradise is "secret," thus implying a need for secrecy. The verb "wounded" sets in motion important reverberations. Beauty, love, pleasure, tenderness—that is, the qualities of paradise—are soft and vulnerable, whereas ugliness and hate are piercing, cutting, like stone and steel, sharp but invulnerable. Adonais was killed by a piercing shaft of poisonous hate to which he was vulnerable because he was a creator of beauty and dreamer of paradise.

A struggle between softness and hardness takes place throughout the poem. Adonais is "pierced" (st. 3 and 17), "broken" (st. 6), and defenseless, lacking a shield or spear (st. 27). The road to Fame is "thorny" (st. 5). In a reversal, the beauty of Adonais's song is said to "pierce the guarded wit, / And pass into the panting heart beneath / With lightning and with music" (st. 12). In stanza 20, the image of sword and sheath suggests that creative beauty has to wage war with its opponents, even though the essence of beauty is the antithesis of battle. In stanza 39, in a mad trance we "strike with our spirit's knife / Invulnerable nothings." Whether struggle is thought to be futile or necessary, the softness of paradise must penetrate a resisting hardness, or defend itself, or suffer inevitable wounds at the hands of harsh reality. For these reasons, the poem's speaker says: "From the world's bitter wind / Seek shelter in the shadow of the tomb" (st. 51).

The first two lines in the twenty-fourth stanza have rich associations. From Urania's wounds fertilizing blood flows and paves her way with eternal flowers. As in "Ode to the West Wind," the poet must fall upon the thorns of life in order to create beauty: blood is creative fire.[70] As in "Orpheus," the wounded poet indulges his grief and creates exquisite beauty, for which he must pay the price of destruction. In a historical, rather than millennial world, the effort to expand the circumference of beauty, pleasure, sympathy, love, and the other utopian attributes, necessitates wounding. Urania survives the ordeal of bleeding, but Adonais does not.

Shelley's alleged self-portrait in stanzas 31 through 34 makes sense in this context. The frail Form is somewhere between Adonais's weakness and the strength of Urania, who cannot die. The Form is an oxymoron of strength and weakness: frail, but like a leopard; like a storm, but feeble; expiring, but beautiful and swift. Unlike Adonais, the Form survives, but only *just* survives. The Actaeon image unites the predatory theme with the memory theme. The ugly brutality of the world is predatory and orally destructive. Wolves, ravens, vultures and cannibalism characterize the sadistic power of the Jupiter-world. When the Form gazes on nature's pure beauty, he glimpses paradise, which, instead of becoming his residence, becomes his haunting demon. He experiences Paradise as something lost and inaccessible. Not the promise, but the impossibility of happiness, has been the consequence of the Form's communion with beauty. The other poets keep their distance because he indeed represents a dangerous possibility. Whereas Adonais was killed by the direct attack of reality, the Form tortures himself with the memory of a beauty that is inconstant and powerless to overthrow the Jupiter-world. In stanza 33, the Form, as Carlos Baker has said, wears the apparel of a devotee of Bacchus.[71] If a poet is dressed like a Maenad, then the implication seems clear enough: the poet calls into existence his own destruction; the Form creates beauty for others, but for himself creates only pain; inspiration and creativity lead to death because remembering Paradise while still in the historical world is to create hell.

The eternity Adonais achieves is the work of memory, and so forgetting is another kind of death. The Critic is a "nameless worm" (st. 36) contrasted with Adonais, who is a "remembered name" (st. 37); the "nameless" is also a reference to the poem's inscription from Moschus, who will not "name" the poisoner of Bion, just as Shelley will not grant immortality to Keats's murderer. In stanza 44, the "dead live" as living poems. The poet lives on through the survival of poetry, and as the world remembers the poetry, so it breathes life into the dead, and keeps alive the hope of utopian transformation. But the poem's speaker does not rest content with his consolation after he discovers that Adonais, in death, is closer to Paradise than the living who must suffer.

"Fear and grief / Convulse us and consume us day by day, / And cold hopes swarm like worms within our living clay" (st. 39). If life is a bad dream, then it is a nightmare made even more unbearable by hope. As in the case of Actaeon, the image of something better makes endurance that much more wearying. The struggle to create beauty is, in some ways, antithetical to the essence of Paradise, which is erotic play and unity. In death at least there is an end to alienation: Adonais "is made one with Nature" (st. 42). Within Nature's cycle, where all things "pant with life's sacred thirst; / Diffuse themselves; and spend in love's delight / The beauty and the joy of their renewed might" (st. 19), Adonais can participate in the cyclicity of love. During the climax of the speaker's triumphant rhapsody on death, he says, "Die, / If thou wouldst be with that which thou dost seek! / Follow where all is fled!" (st. 52). The last words remind one of the injunction in Act II, *Prometheus Unbound*: in order to liberate the world's potentiality, one must descend and retrace one's steps back to the source; as in Asia's song, one must go as far back as death and birth. Existence and nature, at their origin, are fundamentally pure, and in death, one returns to the source.

Here is Shelley's grimmest portrait of hope. But one must also put this in its poetic context because Adonais's death came after and as a result of a life of poetic creativity. The yearning for purity expressed in the poem is also the desire for peacefulness by someone who has struggled and endured. Could anyone deny that there are situations in which to continue living is by no means the only reasonable way to affirm life in all its utopian possibilities? The crucial question is whether, in Shelley's praise of death, he is transforming what used to be political and psychological categories into metaphysical ones.

Shelley is not, I believe, making a metaphysical defense of suicide. For example, when he says, "what still is dear / Attracts to crush, repels to make thee wither" (st. 53), he is not arguing against desire itself, only its frustration; there is still the feeling that desire *ought* to be satisfied. I interpret the last stanzas to mean that Shelley is carried toward suicide, which he nevertheless refuses to accept. I emphasize the fact that he is driven there by forces outside his control. The "low wind" that "whispers" in stanza 53 becomes the "breath whose might I have invoked in song" in the last stanza. The West Wind, destroyer and preserver, *descends* upon the speaker. He has not willed himself to the brink, but has found himself there anyway. If the possibility of utopia is to be maintained from the position of the inspired poet-prophet, then the poet must accept his social isolation and esteem poetry as a spiritual activity which has been ostracized. Poetry and society also divide into their separate spheres in *A Defence of Poetry*; but in the essay poetry returns to society in the form of unacknowledged legislation, while in *Adonais* the split seems permanent. Despite these consequences, Shelley remains committed to poetry, whether it leads to self-destruction or new possibility.

The difference between the divinity of *Adonais* and that of earlier poems is not its location in a dualism but its inability to make existence more bearable for the utopian poet. Although in stanza 43, a pantheistic presence is "bursting in its beauty and its might / From trees and beasts and men into Heaven's light," the living utopian poet is "far from the trembling throng," and is "borne darkly, fearfully, afar" (st. 55). When Shelley feels actuality might be transformed by the Ideal, he is capable of responding with a wide range of literary projects, but when he perceives actuality as a resistant surface, impermeable to Spirit, he returns then to potentiality as it exists in its purer states. The divinity celebrated in *Adonais*'s third part is alternately human and natural, the product of past and present Poets, but it is not anything even close to the "heaven" of Christian mythology. If the poem's speaker does decide to die, he has no hope in a *personal* immortality; rather, he hopes to return to the One from which his spirit came initially. The primary meaning of immortality in the poem is the entirely naturalistic process by which dead poets live by being read creatively by successive generations. As to whether the Neoplatonic One is simply a metaphorical symbol for this process, or is to be understood more literally, the poem is characteristically unclear. Adonais, as in stanza 38, "wakes or sleeps with the enduring dead," and the poem refuses to erase the ambiguous "or."

The poem is skeptical concerning the nature of a postmortal existence, but there is no skepticism over the imagination, whose values Shelley asserts unequivocally. Although individual poets might be lured toward death by the anguish of utopian creativity, poetry itself, represented by Urania, is "chained to Time" (st. 26), and cannot escape into a postmortal One. To win a place in Fame among the distinguished poets, one has to walk the thorny road of struggle, desire, will, endurance, hope—the Promethean virtues. In Act I of *Prometheus Unbound* the Titan knows that "Peace is in the grave," but death "hides all things beautiful and good," and it would be "defeat . . . not victory" (638-42).

SEVEN

An Ethical Idealism

(1821-1822)

INTRODUCTION

CRITICS DIFFER sharply about Shelley's final phase, some finding him mystically transcendent or even suicidal, others perceiving in his positions more continuity. There is unquestionably something distinctive about the poems and letters of his last months, but I do not believe Shelley was near suicide, or cultivating a thoroughly mystical transcendence of everything earthly (especially politics), or ready to repudiate a decade of libertarian hope. He was, however, bitterly discouraged about the unpopularity of his writings, and sometimes despaired of ever writing again when he conceived of himself as a Demosthenes who spoke only to the waves.[1] As a public author, whose poetry and prose were intended to educate a living audience, he resorted to the hope of posterity's appreciation as a defense against feeling utter futility. Considering the poor reception his works encountered, his isolated situation in Italy, and his avant-garde ideas, it is actually remarkable that he did *not* turn to mysticism and despair. Indeed, he subjected himself to a painful self-examination, and reformulated his libertarian politics accordingly.

To pursue the Ideal as if it were a personalized Absolute, as if it could be possessed by the individual, is to be self-destructive, to lead oneself to despair, false hope, and irresponsible actions. Much earlier in *Alastor*, and more recently in *Epipsychidion*, Shelley realizes that the Ideal cannot be possessed by the individual, that the quest for the Absolute is both quixotic and doomed to failure. In November of 1819, during his most prolific period of socially oriented writing, he tells John Gisborne how important and difficult is the task of self-awareness:

all of us who are worth any thing spend our manhood in unlearning the follies, or expiating the mistakes of our youth; we are stuffed full of prejudices, & our natural passions are so managed that if we restrain them we grow intolerant & precise because we restrain them not according to reason but according to error, & if we do not restrain them we do all sorts of mischief to ourselves & others. Our imagination & understanding are alike subjected to rules the most absurd.[2]

This is Shelley speaking in one of his most rational moments, not the Shelley who sympathizes with those misguided idealists in his poems who follow where passion leads, nor the Shelley who pursued the Ideal as embodied in various women in his personal life. According to Donald Reiman, the most dramatic change in Shelley's intellectual life was in the area of love: from a narcissistic concept of love as communion with a self-created Ideal for which one tries to find mortal embodiment, to a more Platonic concept of love as going out of the self and identifying with the beauty existing outside the self.[3] After his disillusionment with Teresa Viviani, Shelley admits his error in trying to find flesh and blood incarnations of the Ideal. On August 15, 1821, he writes to Mary that "love far more than hatred—has been to me, except as you have been it's object, the source of all sort[s] of mischief."[4] It would seem Mary might agree because in a March 20, 1822 letter, she lists "Emilia" as one of her life's worst disasters, on the same plane as the deaths of her children.[5] In Shelley's final months, he gives more emphasis than before to the necessity of controlling the "passions within" as a prerequisite for moral autonomy. In *Prometheus Unbound* the millennium was precipitated by conquering self-generated evils, but none of them was identified with love. Shelley had always been generous with the follies and excesses of love, simultaneously criticizing and forgiving the *Alastor* Visionary, celebrating and declaring impossible a personal ownership of absolute beauty in *Epipsychidion*. By the time he writes his last poems, however, he can see that love can cause as much suffering as hate.

A letter to John Gisborne of April 10, 1822 illustrates the process of self-examination that is reflected in the poetry. Reading *Faust*, Shelley tells Gisborne, is painful and irresistible at the same time because although it awakens "the reproaches of memory, & the delusions of an imagination not to be restrained," it nevertheless provides a rare pleasure. At issue is the scope of desire, whether to be content with "the narrow good we can attain in our present state." Comparing the admirers of *Faust* to Wordsworth, for whom the earth is the place where "We find our happiness or not at all," he clearly prefers the Faustians. However, there is a chain of association in the letter, critical of Faustian desire, linking *Faust*, himself, Wordsworth, Plato, Calderon's *El Magico Prodigioso*, and Rousseau's *La Nouvelle Héloïse*. He is drawn to *Faust*, which gives him some discomfort because he "is prey to the reproaches of memory, & the delusions of an imagination not to be restrained." What reproaches and delusions is he referring to? One can see, starting with *Faust*, a pattern of consistent allusions to the follies of love, especially in its most passionate forms. Faust's love for Margaret, Saint-Preux's for Julie, Cypriano's for Justina—all are examples of uncontrollable passion that casts over desire a veil of romantic idealism which, once torn aside, reveals tragedy. Margaret's ruin is perhaps the most poignant, the one that seems to affect Shelley most strongly.[6] Although one cannot ascertain all the details of Shelley's love life, one can see where the "reproaches" and "delusions" might come from: Harriet, the inspiring presence behind *Queen Mab*, who is abandoned by Shelley and who commits suicide; Elizabeth Hitchener, who joins the libertarian commune, but who becomes the detestable Brown Demon, a hermaphroditical beast, and whose reputation is ruined by her association with Shelley; Claire Clairmont (did Shelley have an affair with her?); the Neapolitan child (whose child was it?); Teresa Viviani; Jane Williams.

Despite the painful recollections *Faust* evokes, Shelley reads the poem repeatedly to enjoy the pleasure of sympathizing with a rare form of idealism, one that rejects the satisfactions of desire available within temporal existence and points toward an unrealizable Ideal. When Shelley admires "Faust," he means the poem, not the character, because what affects him so much about Goethe's play is the *tragedy* of desire. The idealist, impatient with the opportunities for modest social change, pursues the Ideal, and brings only tragedy to himself and others. Faced with the choice between extinguishing the idealism, which is the message he reads in Wordsworth's lines, or retaining it, even as it is tempered by tragic self-awareness, Shelley readily endorses the latter. Although this has been his position since *Alastor*, the tone now is sadder, the awareness more subtle, and the perspective more complex.

Romantic love ceases to be the crucial experience whose passionate intensity can point toward utopia. The only reliable guide now is a severely chastened ethical idealism. Shelley tries to mediate carefully between the Ideal in its absolute form (symbolized in the poetry by the planet Venus, Vesper, or Hesperus) and imperfect actuality. He has always recognized the need to mediate the Ideal, but the emphasis in earlier poems was far more on the Ideal than on mediation. Romantic love is a utopian paradigm in his earlier work, where sexual love is both a communion with the Ideal and an emblem of utopian Eros which has other forms—social, literary, political. The tragedy in *Julian and Maddalo* is a result of *unrequited* love, not of love's fulfillment or development through time.

While Shelley feels compelled to defend his Faustian idealism against Wordsworthian positivism, he also cultivates, in his final months, a very Wordsworthian attitude toward the everyday pleasures available to time-bound mortals. The "Jane Williams" poems and other late lyrics have a constant theme of appreciating the present moment for what happiness it can offer, while forgetting the past and future. Accepting the temporal for what it is, impermanent but sometimes joyful, requires a suspension of utopian hope. Reconciling desire to the temporal and limited does not mean, however, that Shelley has *rejected* hope; rather, he has discovered that the rigors of hopeful idealism need to be balanced with ordinary pleasure, that visions of the Absolute must not eclipse the wonders of the sublunary world.

With a greater appreciation of transient pleasures comes an equally acute respect for history. The Ideal, as far as the practicing author is concerned, exists only insofar as it is mediated through actual human beings and societies, so that even though it is necessary to keep one's eye on Hesperus, the symbol for the Ideal, one cannot lose sight of the ways in which actuality can be changed according to ethical ideas. Shelley's commitment to actuality differs from what he interprets as the Wordsworthian position in this: while Wordsworth (or so Shelley thinks) wants to establish the horizon of desire with the satisfactions currently available within the field of actuality, and Shelley also wants as much happiness created within actuality as possible, the latter refuses to draw the horizon of desire at the point where actuality ceases. Shelley believes in hope, the possibility of immortality, the creative idealism of potentiality, the Faustian striving after the Ideal. Just as Goethe's *Faust* is to be understood not moralistically, but tragically, as the complex and contradictory workings of desire, so are actual historical conflicts to be viewed

285

in this dialectical way. Even if the Ideal can never be realized in history, the poet's duty is to maintain faith in social improvement, to refrain from despair or pursuit of a private quest for the Ideal (a quest doomed to failure and unfortunate consequences), and to keep alive and refine those ethical values created by generations of poets and creative societies. While Shelley has always protested against domination by political, economic, religious, and social powers, he is now equally sensitive to the ways in which moral autonomy can be undermined by the passions. It is curious. Godwin's rationalism was tempered by a later romanticism, while Shelley's romanticism becomes tempered by a later rationalism; from different starting points, they seem to converge (although I think Shelley's mature perspective is much more encompassing than Godwin's).

HELLAS

A number of streams fed the inspiration which ultimately produced *Hellas*, a lyrical drama composed in the first three weeks of October 1821. One source is Shelley's Hellenism, which is a love not simply for Plato and Homer, but for an entire democratic culture. The high praise for Athenian drama in *A Defence of Poetry* was no passing enthusiasm, as this tribute to the Greeks in a letter of November 16, 1819, indicates:

Were not the Greeks a glorious people? . . . If the army of Nicias had not been defeated under the walls of Syracuse, if the Athenians had, acquiring Sicily held the balance between Rome & Carthage, sent garrisons to the Greek colonies in the south of Italy, Rome might have been all that its intellectual condition entitled it to be, a tributary not the conqueror of Greece; the Macedonian power would never have attained to the dictatorship of the civilized states of the world. Who knows whether under the steady progress which philosophy & social institutions would have made, (for in the age to which I refer their progress was both rapid & secure,) among a people of the most perfect physical organization, whether a Christian Religion would have arisen, or the barbarians have overwhelmed the wrecks of civilization which had survived the conquests & tyranny of the Romans.—What then should we have been?[7]

It was a tragic misfortune that military and diplomatic events perversely resulted in the destruction of Hellas and the rise of Alexander, the Roman Empire, and Christianity. Although the spirit of this past Hellas can be revived by contemporary democrats, and although it can serve as an inspiring ideal for present movements, Shelley's greatest concern remains the historical events of his own time. Some critics have read *Hellas* as an essentially transcendent poem whose passionate center is in the postmortal realm, where the vagaries of history are meaningless. But I agree with other critics who see the poem as a political action designed to promote the Greek war for independence by rallying English public opinion around the Greek cause.[8] While Shelley had always been an avid Hellenist, the Greek rebellion provided him with an opportunity to assist the cause of Greek liberty in a direct way. Greece provided, in fact, the third revolution (following the Spanish and Neapolitan revolutions) to give the Quadruple Alliance anxiety. Shelley sympathized with these revolutions in the same wholehearted way as he tried to assist the English reform movement, and identified these European rebellions as libertarian. Another factor in the composition of *Hellas*, it seems to me, is Shelley's determination to restrain his narcissistic idealism and mediate carefully between utopian ideals and historical possibilities. He would try again to reach a sympathetic audience in order to educate it effectively, but without compromising his ethical idealism.

The historical context of *Hellas* is a Europe dominated by the Quadruple Alliance (England, Austria, Prussia, and Russia). These powers differed among themselves on various issues, but more or less agreed on suppressing or containing any revolutionary threats to the status quo. When Spain had its revolution in 1820, Castlereagh was concerned, as were Metternich and Czar Alexander, but nothing was done because Spain was politically isolated and strategically unimportant; the revolution did not affect the balance of power.[9] When, however, Naples revolted on July 2, 1820, inspired by Spain, this did indeed present a direct challenge to the Alliance, one of whose members, Austria, controlled Lombardy, Venetia, and other Italian states along the Adriatic. If Naples were to become a constitutional monarchy, it would send a revolutionary signal throughout post-Napoleonic Italy. Austrian troops did, in fact, invade Naples and suppress the revolution, occupying the city on March 23, 1821. Shelley followed the Neapolitan revolution with an enthusiasm expressed in his "Ode to Naples" and also evident in letters. One letter of September 1, 1820, describes favorably the revolutionaries' use of violence in threatening the royal family with execution if Austria should make war on Naples; such threats, according to Shelley, are "A necessary, & most just measure when the forces of the combatants as well as the merits of their respective causes are so unequal. That kings should be every where hostages for liberty were admirable!"[10] On February 18, 1821, he speaks of the Neapolitan peasantry who, he hoped, would become "citizens & men." Perhaps even the libertarian Lombard League could be revived, thus inaugurating a new age of decentralist democracies federated against empires.[11] When Austria triumphed, Shelley was bitter: "This attempt in Italy has certainly been a most unfortunate business. With no strong personal reasons to interest me, my disappointment on public grounds has been excessive. But I cling to moral and political hope, like a drowner to a plank."[12]

The struggle for "liberty" had its international dimension, but even more international was the fight against it. Writing to Metternich, Castlereagh comments on post-Peterloo England: "Although we have made an immense progress against radicalism, the monster still lives, and shows himself in new shapes; but we do not despair of crushing him by time and perseverance."[13] The monster in England was more democratic than in most of the other countries, which were nationalistic or experiencing antimonarchical revolutions. The revolution in Naples revealed the class differences among the rebels after the Constitutional government of Naples, backed by the landed proprietors who were the backbone of the Carbonari, sent troops to Sicily to suppress the armed peasants and urban poor who wanted a more democratic constitution.[14] To pursue its interests, however, the Quadruple Alliance made few distinctions between revolutionaries, all of whom were dangerous. Thus Castlereagh, explaining why the four nation-states must work together to suppress the monster of radicalism: "the existing concert [i.e., the Quadruple Alliance] is their only perfect security against the revolutionary embers more or less existing in Europe."[15]

Living in exile near the Shelleys in Pisa was Prince Mavrocordato, one of the most prominent Greek leaders, who was especially fond of Mary, and to whom *Hellas* is dedicated. In the spring of 1821 good news came from Greece: Ipsilanti had declared a war of independence against the Turks, thus launching Greece into a long, bloody, but ultimately successful war of liberation. Despite an initial loss, the Greeks had been consistently successful in their battles against the Turks during 1821. The international situation was complicated because Turkey was an old enemy of Russia, who considered aiding the Greeks. Castlereagh advocated and followed a policy of nonintervention because he hoped Turkey would defeat the revolution, thus maintaining the balance of power. Turkish military forces were far superior to those of the Greeks, but several years later, in 1827, England, Russia, and France finally did assist the Greeks and helped them win their independence in 1829. In 1821, however, the nonintervention policy was supported vigorously by Metternich and Castlereagh, and a little more reluctantly by Alexander. A sober political analyst in 1821 would not have given the Greeks much of a chance unless Russia made war on the Turkish Empire; and if Russia intervened, it undoubtedly would try to subjugate Greece as the Turks had done. The Greek revolution, as the Spanish and Neapolitan revolutions before it, became a focal point for the left. The *Examiner* set up a subscription for arms and ridiculed the Castlereagh policy of nonintervention,[16] while Byron eventually went to fight and die in Greece, and Shelley wrote *Hellas*.

Although *Hellas* was composed in a moment of inspiration, as Shelley tells John Gisborne,[17] that inspiration seems to have been conditioned by a number of prior experiences, all of which tended to make him temper his radical ideas to the expectations of his audience. Peacock had been telling him that poetry was irrelevant to social progress. In June of 1821, while the Greek revolution is under way, Shelley learns of the Clark piracy of *Queen Mab*, a poem now "better fitted to injure than to serve the cause which it advocates," says the poet, because of its bad poetry. He is less upset than amused by the poem's publication, and thankful to be in Italy at the present moment rather than near an English prison.[18] In a letter to the *Examiner* he absolves himself of responsibility for publishing *Queen Mab* but also protests against the repression.[19] Shortly after the *Queen Mab* controversy he learns from Leigh Hunt that William Hazlitt has attacked him in print.[20] Perhaps Shelley already knew of Hazlitt's critique in "On Paradox and Commonplace," but after receiving Hunt's letter, one assumes he read the essay. By January 25, 1822, Shelley puts Hazlitt together with Gifford as an enemy from whom he expects only abuse.[21] Although Hazlitt's criticism is far more extreme than anything Shelley could accept, it nevertheless raises some issues that Shelley himself was recently contemplating. The gist of the critique is that Shelley, so preoccupied with his fantasies and own imagination, does the cause of reform actual harm by his extravagant utopianism.[22] The net result of all these developments—Peacock's utilitarian jibes, Shelley's despair over not reaching the public, his awareness of narcissism's unfortunate consequences, the *Queen Mab* controversy, and the Hazlitt criticism—seems to be this: he sets out again to write poetry that will serve the interests of a specific political cause without either compromising his ethical idealism or tainting the cause with an unnecessary ultraradicalism. By 1821 Shelley had a public reputation, even if it was more infamous than distinguished, which he tried to exploit for the benefit of the Greeks.

An emphatic mediation of the Ideal is not new, because as early as the Irish pamphlets Shelley fully realizes that utopia cannot be built in a single day. Peacock, Hazlitt, Keats, and others speak to a part of Shelley that has long existed, that has even produced such mediating works as the two Hermit of Marlow pamphlets. *Hellas*, nevertheless, reflects a scrupulous repression of the merely personal and autobiographical. There are no instances of shocking incest or provocatively phrased statements on atheism; romantic love, insofar as it exists in the poem at all, is satirized. As the Peterloo-inspired poems were acutely aware of audience expectations, so is *Hellas*, which tries to practice the injunction of the theological fragment: to accommodate one's truths to the predilections of the audience.

That the Greeks are Christian, not Islamic, and belong to the Western, not Eastern, tradition, are two facts Shelley does not allow his audience to forget. At no point in the play does Shelley actually misrepresent his views on religion or culture, but he presents these views in a way designed to make an English audience identify with the Greeks and their cause. The East-West dichotomy appears in the Preface with criticism of China and Japan as stagnant societies, and in the poem itself by contrasting the Greek captive women, who are libertarians, with the Indian slave, who is romantically attached to her tyrant. Since it was *Queen Mab*'s "atheism" that made the poem so notorious, perhaps Shelley's Christian emphasis is a way to show the public he is not a dogmatic atheist. A careful reader, however, can see that Shelley is not even remotely close to joining the Anglican or any other church. In a note he explains: "The popular notions of Christianity are represented in this chorus as true in their relation to the worship they superseded, and that which in all probability they will supersede, without considering their merits in a relation more universal."[23] And in another note

290

he expresses skepticism on other metaphysical issues.[24] Those critics who seem to think *Hellas* takes a dogmatic position on a postmortal existence have to ignore the contents of these notes, which are as philosophically rigorous in a skeptical direction as anything Shelley ever wrote. Perhaps he hoped the reader would sympathize with the plight of the Greeks and then subject the Christian bias to a more philosophical examination.

Mediation is not misrepresentation. One paragraph of the Preface was so militantly radical that Ollier suppressed it, and it was not restored until 1892.[25] *Hellas* is a poem unequivocal in its commitment to "liberty," that is, the various nationalist, antimonarchical, and democratic movements in Europe and elsewhere. These movements had limited goals, far short of Shelley's libertarian utopia, but they were the historical vehicles through which the spirit of Liberty actualized itself. Wasserman is certainly correct to show the parallel between Hegel's and Shelley's evolutionary historicism, but I think Shelley is even more dialectical than Wasserman acknowledges.[26] The interaction is not between a universal Spirit and a historical world (nor does Shelley desire to transcend, rather than change the world); instead, living historical agents revive and refine libertarian ideas by modifying a historical reality which, although conditioned by Necessity, is capable of being reshaped by Liberty. Creative, imaginative human beings have to breathe life into the libertarian ideals which otherwise would not exist. The process of change is cumulative and somewhat progressive, as Shelley argues in *A Philosophical View of Reform* and *A Defence of Poetry*, but each generation must revise—"see again"—the truth of Liberty. *Hellas* tries to engage the reader in a process of libertarian revision, perceiving the cultural past, the historical present, and the future in new ways.

Since there has been some question about *Hellas*'s views on violence and nonviolence, it might be useful to see how "Ode to Naples" resolved this problem, because the Neapolitan revolution raised the same issues as the Greek insurrection. The first stanza of the "Ode" (as reedited by Judith Chernaik)[27] depicts a Naples which has won its freedom nonviolently, as actually was the case: the Neapolitans forced the king to proclaim the Constitution. Also prominent in this stanza is the idea of libertarian reform as "reform," "formed again," resurrected from the past: "Metropolis of a ruined Paradise / Long lost, late won, and yet but half regained" (57-58); and "Thou which wert once, and then didst cease to be, / Now art, and henceforth ever shall be free" (62-63). In the second stanza military imagery is evoked in order to be qualified in a nonviolent way because the "Giant" which is Naples is arrayed "in Wisdom's mail" and asked to "Lift thy lightning-lance in mirth," not revenge, even though the Austrians might invade. Similarly in the next stanza, we see a philosophically confident upholder of Liberty and oppressors who cannot win if the Neapolitans maintain their integrity. The shield of Naples will be a mirror in which the Austrian troops perceive themselves in a true light, and they will turn against Austrian despotism rather than mechanically attack Neopolitan Liberty. Naples should conquer its foe "with unapparent wounds" (84), not violence. The other stanzas develop these ideas further, identifying Naples with a cultural renaissance and Austria with a destructive, Jupiterian repression, "Like Chaos o'er creation, uncreating" (138). Like Alexander Pope's Dullness, Austrian tyranny represents everything which negates imagination and beauty. The conflict is not merely a military one; in fact it is primarily a philosophical and cultural contest. If Naples wins *and* maintains all its libertarian virtues, then it is a true victory. The implication is that even if the Neapolitans use force, they can hope to triumph over Austrian despotism only by cultivating the non-militaristic virtues of imagination.

Hellas presents the same argument, translating the conflict between Greece and the Turkish Empire into the philosophical language of liberty and despotism. Virtue, not physical force, will assist the Greeks in their revolution. In the first choral movement three battles are associated with "Freedom's splendour": Thermopylae, Marathon, and Philippi (54-57). Greek democracy triumphed at Marathon, but at Thermopylae the Greeks were defeated by the Persians and at Philippi Roman republicanism was defeated by Roman imperialism. These battles are significant to libertarians not because of the military prowess displayed by the democratic generals but by the heroic way the soldiers of "freedom" fought, even in defeat. It is a matter of consequence whether one side wins or loses, but even more critical is the way the libertarians uphold their ideals. Mere military success is irrelevant if there is no democratic culture. Mary Shelley had just finished writing a novel, *Valperga*, in which an idealistic man, Castruccio, liberates his city from tyranny, but then reimposes a despotism, installing himself as the ruler.[28] As soon as Castruccio ceases to live as libertarian, his military victory becomes meaningless. Similarly, the one poem Shelley added to *Hellas* when it was published is critical of Napoleon who, despite his military victories, did not advance freedom, and instead: " 'Napoleon's fierce spirit rolled, / In terror, and blood, and gold, / A torrent of ruin to death from his birth' " (34-36, "Written on Hearing the News of the Death of Napoleon").

The instances of heroism depicted in *Hellas* are reminiscent of *The Mask of Anarchy*. Hassan describes to Mahmud a battle in which the Greeks are hopelessly outnumbered, yet one soldier defiantly kills himself in Roman republican style rather than be taken prisoner (388-89). Two others also commit suicide, preferring death and fidelity to their ideals over mere survival as slaves. After the Turks slaughter a large number of unarmed Greeks, a voice delivers a stirring libertarian speech, in much the same way as the maniac maid, Hope, and the maternal spirit of the Earth, deliver their speeches in *The Mask of Anarchy*. The speech (412-51) is a kind of *Adonais* for the dead Greeks who choose freedom over despotism and will enjoy an immortality not allowed to tyranny. Every tyranny goes the way of Ozymandias and returns to dust, but libertarian ideals can be resurrected by successive generations who communicate with the Ideal, which exists as a pantheistic presence in nature and as a cultural heritage. Venus, the symbol for the Ideal, appears a number of times in the poem, thus serving as a point of orientation for the Greek captives. *There* is the Ideal toward which they are moving, which inspires them and sustains hope, whose values they try to live by.

There is no question that Shelley wanted the Greeks to defeat the Turks in the revolutionary war; this is the primary reason he wrote *Hellas*. But the Greek side is to be admired only insofar as it is libertarian and democratic, actually a rebirth of the Athenian *demos*. The idealism of the poem is, I believe, frequently misinterpreted as metaphysical, identifying evil with temporality and mortality. Rather, Shelley's vision stems from his ethical idealism, a strategy for mediating between the Hesperus of unattainable perfection and the historical world dominated by Necessity, the eyeless charioteer. The principal question is not whether *Hellas* endorses violence or nonviolence; the important problem is maintaining an *ethical idealism*. *Hellas* advocates using enough force to conquer the Turks but at the same time opposes a degree of violence that would turn the Greeks into tyrants. Precisely how this balance might be achieved in practice Shelley cannot say, but that is not his task.

The chorus articulates an idealism which is just the opposite of mystical:

> But Greece and her foundations are
> Built below the tide of war,
> Based on the chrystalline sea
> Of thought and its eternity;
> Her citizens, imperial spirits,
>   Rule the present from the past,
> On all this world of men inherits
>   Their seal is set—
>   (696-703)

The Athenian democracy built Western civilization's foundations, which are "eternal" for as long as that civilization exists. Those foundations are "below the tide of war" in this sense: although the Greeks lose at Thermopylae, and their ideals are defeated at Philippi, their contributions to culture as Poetry live on long afterwards and cannot be defeated militarily. Thought and its eternity are the living spirit of humanity which creates, imagines, and loves; eternity is not a postmortal realm of ultimate perfection to which the dead are transported. When the "world's eyeless charioteer, / Destiny" (711-12) passes by, old tyrannies and religions not founded on enduring principles will perish, but whether liberty or new tyrannies will follow is entirely the consequence of free will, not Necessity. Change is certain: if revolutionary energy is repressed, there will be earthquakes or volcanoes, but no tyrannical repression can be permanent since its stasis is contrary to the real nature of existence. If the Greeks defeat their enemy and also exact revenge and indulge in needless murder, then they will lose by winning. Wisdom, Pity, Conscience, Love: without these, the Greeks cannot create liberty, even if they manage to win militarily (711-37).

The dramatic climax of the poem is the appearance of Ahasuerus, whose speeches recapitulate the themes already developed by the chorus. The Wandering Jew was a character in Shelley's gothic novel, as well as in *Queen Mab*, but this 1821 character is closest to the Diogenes of the theological fragment of 1816-1817. The earlier Diogenes articulates an ethically austere anarchism that declares moral autonomy as the arduous task of the individual. The expansive eroticism of *Prometheus Unbound* and *Epipsychidion* is no longer the mode for liberation. Ahasuerus has achieved his wisdom by retreating from the world of illusions and conquering his own passions. He is not, however, an ascetic saint hierarchically situated above mortals and eager to dictate a new, more stringent code of morals to a slothful humanity. Rather, he is a pantheist, more like Saint Francis than Saint Dominic. Nor does he argue in favor of a *contemptus mundi*, even though he exists at the margins of society. The mutable world is not to be despised—even the worm beneath Mahmud's feet is instinct with spirit—but the determining spiritual factor is thought, not matter. The spheres ruled by power, "blood and gold," are subject to decay, and are, from the perspective of the Ideal, ephemeral, while the authentic creations of human spirit are eternal and rule forever, as Athenian culture still affects Western civilization. "Thought / Alone, and its quick elements, Will, Passion, / Reason, Imagination, cannot die" (795-97), but "what was born in blood must die" (811). In terms of *Hellas*, then, Mahmud and his Turkish empire will perish, giving way to new forms of either liberty or tyranny, but the ideals of libertarians and Poets will live on forever, even if they do not "succeed" in the historical realm. At some point in the future, Prometheus will be unbound, Jupiter deposed, and a millennium of utopian joy inaugurated, but until that point—which may never be reached completely—is approximated, the virtuous and the idealistic must expect to suffer. The final choral movement does not celebrate a postmortal "Hellas" accessible only to those no longer "oppressed" by time and mortal existence, but asserts the beauty of the Ideal that is worth dying for. Perhaps the Greeks, like the Neapolitans, will not prosper on the battlefield, but if so, libertarian ideals must be kept alive for a more fortunate day.

The chorus says:

> If Greece must be
> A wreck, yet shall its fragments reassemble
> And build themselves again impregnably
>   In a diviner clime
> To Amphionic music on some cape sublime
> Which frowns above the idle foam of Time.
>   (1002-1007)

The statement here is a reformulation of Demogorgon's final words: "to hope, till Hope creates / From its own wreck the thing it contemplates." The allusion to Amphion does not illustrate mysticism, but creativity, because Amphion "built the walls of Thebes simply by playing the lyre."[29] The foam of Time is idle because it cannot create what thought can: love, beauty, virtue, all that deserves to be eternal, symbolized by Venus. There are no fewer than three separate allusions to Venus in the last choral movement where the speakers try to be hopeful but are prepared for the worst—a Turkish victory. The point of this, however, is not the irrelevance of defeat, but the superiority of the libertarian side, because even if victory eludes the Greeks at this particular moment, they achieve a victory nevertheless by remaining true to their ideals. Moreover, the struggle for liberty is not limited by geography, because America ("young Atlantis") will challenge the permanence of "Power"; the folding-star of Love shines for the young American republic as well as for the beleaguered Greeks. The "brighter Hellas" of which the final chorus speaks is not mystical, but altogether social in the sense that the new Hellas will be a genuine perception of the living imagination, thus necessarily different and better than the old Hellas. In the millennial tradition of Vergil and Isaiah, the chorus boldly prophesies the victory of the Greeks over the Turks and the establishment of a new culture, but even if this new Hellas is not able to succeed in the historical realm, it can serve as an inspiring ideal for later generations who may be more fortunate in their struggle with despotism.

I have been concentrating on the chorus and Ahasuerus, who articulate the poem's libertarian vision, but the play's dramatic center is the tyrant, Mahmud. He is a familiar Shelleyan figure in his greed, sadism, violence, and other despotic qualities. Mahmud, however, is pessimistic, tortured by the uncertainty of the war and his fear of defeat. As he seeks assurances of victory, he can think of nothing but defeat. The process of Mahmud's self-awareness is assisted by Ahasuerus, and includes a self-confrontation with a ghost who speaks the forgotten curse. The past, through the phantom of Mahomet the Second, tells Mahmud that his empire is destined for decay when "wolfish Change" precipitates a "greener faith" (870-73). The only genuine rule, the ghost suggests, is over the "mutinous passions," the control of which is truly kingly, while to dominate others by means of power is trivial, at least philosophically. The moment of self-awareness comes when Mahmud adopts a tragic attitude toward history, "woe to all!", because neither oppressor nor oppressed gains anything from the dominion of power. He is convinced that Islam is "dying," and his final words bear witness to his pessimistic resignation. While his supporters cry "Victory!", he responds, "Victory? poor slaves!" (930). They are poor and slavish because they do not perceive history in its true, dialectical light, as an ever-changing process that dooms whatever is not based on eternal foundations. As the tyrant acquires self-knowledge, he increases his misery, thus acting out one of Shelley's important ideas, the self-destructive nature of tyranny. Despotism destroys itself with its contradictions, and *then* the forces of liberty can move effectively. *Hellas* is optimistic because it identifies Mahmud in the final stages of moral deterioration, losing his sense of ethical justification. As despotism disintegrates, it permits a less militaristic response by the libertarian movement. Mythically, Prometheus cannot be reunited with Asia until Demogorgon removes Jupiter from power. *Hellas*, like *Prometheus Unbound*, separates revolution into two phases, one destructive (whose deity is Necessity), the other creative (whose symbol is the Evening Star). A Demogorgon within Mahmud is on its way to bringing down an internal Jupiter.

CHARLES THE FIRST

The eight-hundred or so lines of *Charles the First* that are extant indicate that Shelley continued to be preoccupied with mediation of the Ideal after *Hellas*. He contemplated writing a play on Charles I as early as July 20, 1820, but did not compose a substantial number of lines, apparently, until January 1822.[30] There has been considerable speculation about why Shelley did not finish *Charles the First*,[31] but I think there are two main reasons. First, as a dramatic play in the Shakespearean tradition, not a lyrical drama, it required public performance, which Shelley deemed unlikely as long as he was so unpopular with the English public. Therefore, whenever he was acutely conscious of his reputation, he felt discouraged from writing.[32] Second, writing a historical drama is difficult and time-consuming, necessitating research, the collation of facts, and the orchestration of numerous characters and events. One sees how Shelley might not eagerly try to finish the play as long as he felt that his reputation was, at best, notorious.[33] Had Shelley not drowned, however, I think *Charles the First* would eventually have been finished.

From the first four scenes of Act I—all that Shelley completed, or nearly completed—one can surmise the general direction of the play. One clearly prominent theme is the way political tyranny self-destructs as tyrants pursue policies that are correct in terms of a normative role, but politically disastrous and imprudent. Because the king needs money to pay for armies to enforce his will in Scotland and Ireland, he decides to call a Parliament (against the advice of Strafford) and tries to collect ship-money (which leads to Hampden's tax resistance, a crucial escalation of the republican resistance). The republican leaders are about to set sail for America, but rather than let these "troublemakers" emigrate, the king chooses to assert his will. Charles could have spared himself the political miseries of dealing with Hampden, Pym, Cromwell, and Vane if he had allowed them to leave England, but by so doing he would also have been forced to admit his own diminishing power. The torture and imprisonment of the religious radicals, like Prynne, Bastwick, and Leighton, are expressions of both kingly power and powerlessness, because although he has the power to torture the rebels, he lacks the ability to win their allegiance as subjects. Moreover, the Puritans who are victimized by Laud and Charles are powerful symbols that actually discredit the hierarchy, not strengthen it. A moderate toleration of the Puritans, such as recommended by David Hume in his history,[34] would have been more expedient, even though such latitudinarianism would also have been a declaration that neither church nor crown possessed absolute power. Shelley's point, then, is that no matter what Charles does, he cannot any longer retain absolute control. If he is flexible, he in fact undermines the royal prerogative and grants reforms. If he is as inflexible as he was, he precipitates revolution.

The point at which power can no longer defend itself is the historical moment in which Shelley is interested. Mahmud and Charles are similar to each other, and also, Shelley perceived, to monarchs of his own day, those—as he called them in the *Hellas* Preface— "ringleaders of the privileged gangs of murderers and swindlers, called Sovereigns."[35] He was an accurate prophet; in the nineteenth century few monarchies survived the age of revolutions, and almost none retained absolute power. Shelley believed that England, and indeed all of Europe, had reached a stage of development where significant reforms had to be forthcoming or there would be revolution. He was correct in this, because England avoided revolution in 1832 only by granting significant reform, while other European countries fluctuated between revolution and reform. Like *Hellas*, *Charles the First* displays a growing awareness of historical specificity, which permits a certain range of libertarian responses to events determined by Necessity. Ethical idealism is not rejected for an amoral historicism, but this idealism is now rooted in the social evolution of history.

As despotic power self-destructs, the Ideal has a problematic existence because it cannot appear purely and completely, but only as it is mediated through living—and imperfect—human beings limited by the particular errors of the *Zeitgeist*. The dome of many-coloured glass refracts the Ideal into not a few ephemeral images. Achieving self-knowledge and mediating the Ideal as ethically as possible are activities as essential as they are difficult. It is impossible to determine with certainty what political issues the play intended to analyze, but Shelley probably would have praised the Long Parliament as he did in *A Philosophical View of Reform*, and criticized Cromwell as a Napoleon. We do know, however, that the play is preoccupied with the issue of art and power, especially language and power. The most closely examined cultural mediation between the Ideal and history is how words and other symbols relate to political power, the "illusions" by which people maintain their ignorance, and the truths behind the appearances.

Scene i depicts and comments on not just a masque, but a specific masque that raised the issue of power and art in a dramatic way. William Prynne, a lawyer, wrote in 1633 a Puritan attack on plays and other forms of neo-Papist idolatry called *Historio Mastix*, which the king would have tolerated except for the intervention of Laud, who wanted Prynne prosecuted for his views on religious questions. Proceedings then were initiated against Prynne, after which the court let it be known that it would appreciate some display of loyalty from the other lawyers, who then eagerly planned and carried through an elaborate, expensive masque. Shelley's source for this information describes it this way:

> About *Allholantide*, several of the principal Members of the societies of the four Inns of Court, amongst whom some were servants to the King, had a design that the Inns of Court should present their service to the King and Queen, and testify their affections to them, by the outward and splendid visible testimony of a Royal Masque of all the four societies joyning together, to be by them brought to the Court, as an expression of their love, and duty to their Majesties.
>
> This was hinted at in the Court and by them Intimated to the chief of those Societies, that it would be well taken from them, and some held it the more seasonable, because this action

299

would manifest the difference of their opinion, from Mr. *Prynne*'s new learning, and serve to confute his *Historio Mastix* against enterludes.[36]

Whitelocke goes on to describe the masque in all its ornate splendor, including the Roman-style chariots, and reports the total cost of the presentation as an astounding twenty-one thousand pounds. The king and queen were so pleased with the masque that they ordered and watched a repeat performance.[37] Shortly afterwards, William Prynne was tried, convicted, and tortured, losing his ears, and thus becoming a Puritan martyr.

A more modern account of the masque by a contemporary scholar says that the crown demanded the masque from the Inns of Court, whose production, *The Triumph of Peace*, was more ambiguous than Whitelocke's account might indicate because the lawyers asserted the ideal of joint, not dictatorial, political responsibility. The king misinterpreted the masque so badly that he wanted a repeat performance.[38] Although Shelley did not know more about the masque than what he learned from Whitelocke's limited account, he knew the close relationship which existed in the masque tradition between art and power. The masque procession had triumphal chariots, an ostentatious display of wealth (a spectacle which was expected and praised, the more lavish the better), a celebration of power, and a dissonant (but conventional) antimasque of beggars, cripples, and clowns. The parallel in Shelley's last poem with the triumphant chariot of "Life," with its grotesque procession of victims, is fairly obvious. The masque referred to in scene i, then, is a Jupiterian art, beauty being used to affirm power and luxury rather than educate the public.

In the opening dialogue a Puritan, "Second Citizen," disagrees forcefully with a younger man who takes delight in the beautiful surface of the procession. Where the Youth sees beauty, the Puritan sees luxury and deception, while both speak a familiarly Shelleyan language. For the Youth, the masque is a delightful escape from a dreary existence, thus superficially echoing Shelley's typical praise for the ephemeral and inconstant visitations of Intellectual Beauty. The Youth's ideas, however, are ironically undermined, especially when he calls the masque "innocent" (16). Although the Puritan does not appreciate the surface beauty of the masque, which Shelley himself clearly does (see the speech by the Youth, 137-49), he does something far more important by demystifying and esteeming it for what it is worth ethically. Behind the external beauty is an elaborate symbolic celebration of injustice, which the Puritan describes thus:

> Ay, there they are—
> Nobles, and sons of nobles, patentees,
> Monopolists, and stewards of this poor farm,
> On whose lean sheep sit the prophetic crows,
> Here is the pomp that strips the houseless orphan,
> Here is the pride that breaks the desolate heart.
> These are the lilies glorious as Solomon,
> Who toil not, neither do they spin,—unless
> It be the webs they catch poor rogues withal.
> Here is the surfeit which to them who earn
> The niggard wages of the earth, scarce leaves
> The tithe that will support them till they crawl
> Back to her cold hard bosom. Here is wealth
> Followed by grim disease. . . .
> And as the effect pursues the cause foregone,
> Lo, giving substance to my words, behold
> At once the sign and the thing signified—
> A troop of cripples, beggars, and lean outcasts
> . . . to point the moral
> Of this presentment, and bring up the rear
> Of painted pomp with misery!
> (150-74)

To the uncritical Youth, the antimasque is a necessary complement which makes us appreciate the masque's beauty even more: "Who would love May flowers / If they succeeded not to Winter's flaw?" asks the Youth (176-77). To the Puritan, the antimasque is what the masque's beauty tries to "mask" and what, in fact, the masque's aesthetic values generate. To celebrate "pomp" is to appropriate immorally the surplus wealth created by the laborers. Aristocratic art celebrates the idleness of the rich who reap what others sow, and thus the masque upholds the values of "luxury." Like Godwin, Shelley perceives luxury as the unjust monopolization of wealth which, in turn, impoverishes the laborers who must toil not only for their own meager subsistence, but to provide the privileges of the rich. The masque, then, is not "innocent," a beautiful illusion that gives pleasure but causes no harm because, as Shelley read in Whitelocke's account, it cost twenty-one thousand pounds and, even worse, legitimized social inequality.

As a dramatic contrast to the masque and its values, Shelley introduces into scene i Leighton, the Puritan victim of torture, whose face has been branded. He tells onlookers that although his appearance has been altered, his "mind" is "unchanged" (90-91). The presence of Leighton foreshadows Prynne's torture after the masque, and is also an ironic comment on the masque's ideological purpose of distancing the lawyers from their Puritan colleague. The masque tries to "mask" the ugly reality of the brutality of power, or, as one Citizen says, "When lawyers masque 'tis time for honest men / To strip the vizor from their purposes" (76-77). The notion of art being used as an ideological tool is prominent in Peacock's *The Four Ages of Poetry*, but alluded to as well in Shelley's *Defence*, which identifies the drama during the Restoration period as: "When all forms in which poetry had been accustomed to be expressed became hymns to the triumph of kingly power over liberty and virtue." Moreover, in such periods "the calculating principle pervades all the forms of dramatic exhibition, and poetry ceases to be expressed upon them."[39] Distinguishing between authentic poetry and art corrupted by power and the calculating principle, Shelley identifies the masque as a specimen of the latter; the masque is an artfully constructed "appearance" that tries to overwhelm the "reality" of social conflict.

It is a tribute to Shelley's realism that he does not idealize the Puritan rebels, who oppose not only aristocratic masques but the "heathenish custom / Of dancing round a pole dressed up with wreaths / On May-day" (98-100). (Leigh Hunt wrote an *Examiner* article defending May Day celebrations [May 10, 1818], and Shelley and his circle always admired the heathenish spirit of playfulness and lamented the sour effects of a joyless Christianity.) The Puritans of the play are also violent, dogmatic, and revenge-minded, all being qualities Shelley despised. The rebels depicted without moral blemishes are Hampden and Vane, who are more political than religious opponents of the regime. Perhaps Shelley intended to distinguish between a Puritan fanaticism, which mixed truth with error, and a more unequivocally virtuous republican idealism, embodied in someone like Hampden. That he wanted to distinguish between kinds of rebellion is indicated in a notebook, where he sketches the outlines of the first two acts and at one point contrasts Hampden's "rational & logical" reasons for resistance to Vane's "impetuous & enthusiastic" rationale.[40]

The second scene discloses the power to which the art of the masque is connected. This scene has many instances of dramatic irony illustrating the theme of power's self-destruction. The king, to finance his military domination of Ireland and Scotland, where his "word" no longer rules, orders taxation policies and wants to call a Parliament, both of which will generate more social unrest. In fact, Hampden, the principal speaker of scene iv, will resist paying these taxes, thereby helping to create the culture of resistance which will turn into revolution. Moreover, the king prevents Hampden and other rebels from fleeing to America because he will not act out of unkingly fear (381-84). Laud thinks that if the king calls a Parliament, then "A word dissolves" it (344), but he incorrectly overestimates the power of the king's word. Because the king no longer speaks a language which can effect the allegiance of the people, he has to resort to repressive measures which only exacerbate social unrest. The less real power the king has, the more violent power he has to exert. The king is under the illusion, as are his advisors, that he has a divine right, that God works his will through him (134-40). Just as Jupiter has the false confidence he will reign forever, so Charles believes he is safe and protected by an omnipotent God, when in fact Necessity is operating in ways that will dethrone him. Another irony is the king's extravagant praise of Strafford, who is called "perfect, just, and honourable" (310); but later in the play, Shelley planned to dramatize the king's betrayal of his "beloved" minister, since the conclusion of the second act would apparently be "Strafford's death."[41]

Exerting a strong presence in the second scene is Archy, the royal fool, into whose mouth Shelley puts effective satire and prophecy. Like Ahasuerus, Archy speaks truth to power which, however, cannot accept it and prefers instead to entertain self-serving illusions. If Archy's truths were taken seriously, then the king would have to grant reforms he is clearly unwilling to allow. In a subsequent scene Shelley would probably have portrayed Archy's dismissal, on the advice of Laud, thus creating another instance of dramatic irony: by expelling Archy's truthfulness, the king drives out his best, most reliable advisor, while retaining Laud, whose fanaticism will draw him into civil war. There is an interesting parallel suggested in this scene between the poet and the fool. As long as the fool or poet speaks words which power can tolerate, he is accepted as a pleasant diversion, a harmless source of entertainment:

> He lives in his own world; and, like a parrot
> Hung in his gilded prison from the window

Of a queen's bower over the public way,
Blasphemes with a bird's mind . . .
(98-101)

As someone directly under the king, the fool's prophecies and sat-
ires, like the conventional antimasque, are safely bounded—a "gilded
prison"—to permit a truthfulness unacceptable in courtiers. If, how-
ever, the fool (or the poet) goes too far and tells power what it
cannot afford to hear, then power dispenses with this kind of art,
relying instead on the flattery of masques.

Art as escape is another theme of scene ii, since whenever the
queen is especially distressed she turns to music (442-45) or painting
(464ff.). After Archy has uttered some especially distasteful proph-
ecies, she tells the king:

Your brain is overwrought with these deep thoughts.
Come, I will sing to you; let us go try
These airs from Italy; and, as we pass
The gallery, we'll decide where that Correggio
Shall hang . . .
(461-65)

When art is most intensely itself, according to Shelley, it speaks the
disturbing language of Archy and provokes "deep thoughts." As
art becomes less and less itself and more amenable to power, it
tends to become escapist and illusory, an attractive "mask" con-
cealing the truth underneath.

The third scene is just barely developed, but its point seems ob-
vious enough: to show Laud and Strafford torturing the condemned
Prynne and other rebels, thereby creating ironically their own de-
struction, since these acts of repression merely assist the growth of
a rebellion which eventually claims the lives of both men, both
victims of executions. When Juxon pleads with Laud for some
moderation in the treatment of rebels, Laud says: "I / Could suffer
what I would inflict" (43-44). He wants to demonstrate how "tough"
he is, but the irony is that he announces his own fate in the future,
when the torturer is in turn tortured. The rebel Bastwick, in con-
trast, welcomes the judicial violence on religious grounds because
he has faith in the millennium which will soon sweep away the
unjust persecutors of the Puritans. Although Bastwick speaks the
familiarly Shelleyan words of social apocalypse, his words may be
undermined by later events, since it is unlikely Shelley perceived

304

even the best years of the Commonwealth as an achieved millennium (28-32). Moreover, Bastwick sounds like an unregenerate Prometheus, self-righteous and eager to turn power against the oppressor. Perhaps later in the scene, had Shelley finished it, Bishop Williams or Prynne would have countered Bastwick's extravagant claims.

The next scene depicts the rebels about to leave for America, before they receive the king's order to remain in England.[42] Hampden wants to emigrate, while Vane is reluctant, although the particular focus of the scene is not absolutely clear. One theme introduced here and certain to be developed throughout the play is the Venus symbolism. Vane speaks of the "evening star" (9) which is then addressed by Hampden as "thou, / Fair star, whose beam lies on the wide Atlantic" (18-19). It is also invoked to guide them to America where "Power's poor dupes and victims yet have never / Propitiated the savage fear of kings / With purest blood of noblest hearts" (26-28). Vane seems to be alluding to the star when he says the soul that owns no master and "the eagle spirits of the free" should "scorn the storm / Of time, and gaze upon the light of truth, / Return to brood on thoughts that cannot die" (52-54). Perhaps the scene will be an argument against emigrating, since the Ideal knows no geography and shines equally on England and America. Dramatically, the scene is ironic because Hampden, most eager to leave England, will lead the battle for tax resistance; in Act II, Hampden's trial was to have been a centerpiece. The king, who should have let Hampden leave, refuses permission and helps destroy himself; Hampden, who wants to leave, is prevented from doing so and later plays a heroic role in the contest against royal privilege. Necessity, here and everywhere in the extant *Charles the First*, seems to be a force so powerful that it belongs in the list of characters.

What we have, then, of *Charles the First* indicates that Shelley's literary development is following a pattern established by *Hellas*. He has a renewed respect for Necessity and at the same time a scrupulous regard for the Ideal and its mediations. He is fascinated with the ironies and paradoxes that arise from art's relationship to power. Charles is to be portrayed as a king losing power because his words no longer master reality; he is a failed poet, who cannot quell the mutiny he finds within or without. As the king flounders in his illusions, resorting to violence and repression, he creates his own destruction, while prosperity blesses the republicans and Puritans, who tame their passions, mediate the Ideal, and exert a moral authority.

THE TRIUMPH OF LIFE

There is not only more disagreement among critics on Shelley's last poem than on any other, but the kind of disagreement that exists makes a synthetic reconciliation impossible. One rather large group of critics sees *The Triumph of Life,* even in its fragmentary form, as an antiutopian palinode, announcing a definitive break with Shelley's past radicalism and formulating instead a rigorous idealism which equates mortal existence and evil; only after death is there any hope of communing with the Ideal. Another group sees the poem as continuing along the path Shelley has been traveling for some time, affirming a certain kind of radicalism, but criticizing numerous errors idealists are prone to commit. It is the latter group of critics with whom I agree. Although *The Triumph of Life* is a complex poem, difficult to interpret, it develops coherently a set of themes which announces not a *contemptus mundi* but an ethical idealism.[43]

The introductory section distinguishes between the poem's speaker and other natural objects by means of the sun-star symbolism. As dawn emerges, the sun brings the natural world to life as nature joyously greets the sun. The speaker, however, is estranged from natural processes because he has a consciousness which is capable of keeping him awake all night with "thoughts which must remain untold" (21). An estranged, perturbed protagonist is not new in Shelley's poetry: the narrator of Canto I, *Laon and Cythna,* is in despair until the French Revolution is put in its proper perspective; Prometheus in Act I is tortured by the Furies who depict instances of human perversity when consciousness is turned against human happiness. Whereas nature is ruled by a natural Necessity, the human is a being with consciousness and will, able to create and imagine. The nature-consciousness dichotomy is not new either; it is present even in parts of *Queen Mab.* Although divinity is in nature and provides joy to the human being who is able to appreciate it, nature alone is not enough. Moreover, a certain kind of romantic naturalism is a dangerous folly. While the sun is the symbol for natural existence in its divine aspect, the stars—in particular, the planet Venus, or the Evening Star—symbolize another realm, that of the Ideal as it relates to human consciousness. The irony of daybreak is that the sun's brightness hides Venus, the Ideal, which is visible only at night, when nature is symbolically asleep. The poem's speaker is ironically awake during the night, but falls into a visionary sleep when the sun rises and everyone else awakens.

In his visionary trance he sees a procession of Life's captives who are enslaved by their errors, not simply because of their humanness. If the captives are enslaved by the immutable nature of existence, then questions of psychology and ethics, not to mention history and politics, are irrelevant. The captives, however, are tormented by their mistakes. For example, one group is so "weary with vain toil and faint for thirst" that they

> Heard not the fountains whose melodious dew
>
> > Out of their mossy cells forever burst
> > Nor felt the breeze which from the forest told
> > Of grassy paths, and lawns interspersed
>
> With overarching elms and caverns cold,
> > And violent banks where sweet dreams brood, but they
> > Pursued their serious folly as of old. . . .
> > (67-73)

Rather than appreciate the reality of nature's beauty, the captives chase after shadows and illusions, missing opportunities to experience joy.

A simile forcefully introduces the poem's political theme whereby people enslave themselves and celebrate it as though they were victorious. Like the masque of *Charles the First*, the triumph of Life's chariot is a "triumph of kingly power over liberty and virtue."[44] The poem's speaker sees the chariot of Life with the monster in the seat of power thronged by a wild crowd of captives

> > with fierce song and maniac dance
> > Raging around; such seemed the jubilee
> > As when to greet some conqueror's advance
>
> Imperial Rome poured forth her living sea
> > From senatehouse and prison and theatre
> > When Freedom left those who upon the free
>
> Had bound a yoke which soon they stooped to bear.
> > (110-16)

307

When the slaves are released from servitude on the day of jubilee, they merely join the general self-enslavement.[45] Roman "freedom," which Shelley identifies with the republican period, and which perished at Philippi (a battle mentioned in *Hellas*), became Roman imperialism not only because of greedy tyrants but because people permitted and helped create the tyranny. A counterpoint to the self-enslavement of the Romans is the "sacred few" who are not simply the sacred two, Socrates and Christ.[46] Free from the chariot of Life are those

> who could not tame
> Their spirits to the Conqueror, but as soon
> As they had touched the world with living flame
>
> Fled back like eagles to their native noon,
> Or those who put aside the diadem
> Of earthly thrones or gems, till the last one
>
> Were there; for they of Athens and Jerusalem
> Were neither mid the mightly captives seen
> Nor mid the ribald crowd that followed them
>
> Or fled before. . . .
>   (128-37)

One group, like "Adonais," Chatterton, Lucan, and Sidney, is not enslaved, because their creative spirits waged a premature battle with the forces of destruction and were dispatched to death before they could be corrupted. Another group rejects political and economic power for the only valuable power, wisdom. "They of Athens and Jerusalem" refers not only to Socrates and Christ, but to the very best of "Hellenic and Hebraic" culture,[47] as Shelley again shows his love for the self-governing city-state by identifying the highest ethical idealism with two cities. Shelley is continuing to esteem the Diogenes style of rebellion epitomized earlier with *Hellas*'s Ahasuerus, the Puritans and republicans of seventeenth-century England, and Archy the Fool. It is significant that it is the philosophical rebels whom Shelley most admires and deems exemplary, not the "Adonais" types who are not strong enough to survive.

One particularly dangerous error the poem elaborates is depicted immediately after the evocation of philosophical rebellion. The rhythm of the poem is a point-counterpoint, thesis-antithesis kind of dialectical revelation. So, the acme of ethical idealism is followed by the depths of sensual enslavement. This particular passage represents Shelley's most explicit rejection of a Dionysian-Maenadic eroticism, about which he had been ambivalent before. That all forms of sexual desire are not consistent with ethical idealism is something Shelley learned the hard way, and was reinforced for him by Goethe's *Faust*, Caleron's *El Magico Prodigioso*, and by his revised perspective on Rousseau's *La Nouvelle Héloïse*. The portrait of mere lust (137-75) assumes a dualism which it is important not to misunderstand. Neither Shelley nor the poem rejects sexuality as such; what is rejected is a desire that is only sexual, without any other human qualities. The enslavement by lust serves as an interesting contrast to Rousseau's principal error depicted later in the poem, which consists in being enslaved by personalizing the Ideal and pursuing it as though it were possible to possess the Ideal in the natural world. The poem distinguishes carefully between the Ideal in its most absolute aspect, symbolized by Venus, and its temporal existence, which has a natural but limited divinity which, however, cannot eliminate the necessity of ethically mediating the Ideal. The Ideal cannot be experienced in its absolute form, and to think that it can is to commit the error of Rousseau and the *Alastor* Visionary. As an error, this is more forgivable than the selfish, unimaginative modes of error, but it is still an error.

After the portrait of lust Rousseau makes his appearance as a metamorphic chestnut tree who plays his role of Vergil to the Dantean speaker.[48] As a Vergil, Rousseau is an able guide whose commentary on the procession of captives and allegorical self-portrait comprise the rest of the poem. As a recent study of Rousseau's reputation in England has shown, after the attack on him and on the French Revolution by Burke, Rousseau's personal failings, revealed in his autobiographical works and documented by contemporaries, became identified with the errors of the French Revolution. As Rousseau lacked judgment, so did his followers such as Robespierre; as the one was a hypocritical sensualist, so were the French revolutionaries, supposedly idealistic but in fact violent and self-serving.[49] From *The Triumph of Life* one can extrapolate the following analysis: the failure of the French Revolution was due to the inability of true wisdom to emerge from the Enlightenment, in which power and knowledge were too closely linked, and adequate scope was not given to imagination; the failure of Rousseau was not the result of an excess of lust for political or economic power, but of an idealism that overreaches itself. Rousseau was creative, if also imperfect, and left a valuable heritage of libertarian "beacons," the truly useful results of the Enlightenment and French Revolution. The analysis is subtle and dialectical: Rousseau is more heroic than the captives, but is not as exemplary as the philosophical idealists numbered among the "sacred few"; the French Revolution was by no means perfect, but neither was it empty of value.

First we see Rousseau, then Napoleon, then the Enlightenment figures, thus comprising a thematic cluster around the specific event, the French Revolution, and the general concept, power and knowledge. If one cannot "repress the mutiny within" (213) and achieve self-knowledge, then one is victimized by Life, a slave of illusions and incapable of moral autonomy. Napoleon possessed power, but only the power to destroy. Like Ozymandias, Napoleon tried to control a world he could only dominate temporarily. Like Charles I, he could employ social violence but could not create a lasting culture. Whereas Rousseau left a "thousand beacons" of Liberty after his death, Napoleon fell to disgrace like "a thousand climbers" before him. Shelley's point is that Napoleon, representing the most degraded aspect of the French Revolution, is not a revolutionary at all, but merely a recent avatar of the proud tyrant; he is not a product of creative ideas but a wielder of destructive power. After the Napoleon evocation, the poem's speaker suffers the torture of the Promethean Furies, grieving "how power and will / In opposition rule our mortal day," and asking "why God made irreconcilable / Good and the means of good" (228-31). The speaker is nearly overwhelmed with despair until Rousseau clarifies some of the issues. Knowledge connected with power (Voltaire and Kant[50] with the benevolent despots, Frederic, Catherine, and Leopold) cannot lead to true wisdom, nor can passionate idealism lead to wisdom if the passion is misdirected as Rousseau's was. Nevertheless, it is folly to think that one can or should retreat from society because the Ideal is so feebly reflected in the historical world (248-51).

The subsequent captives are victimized by either lust (like Plato) or power (like Alexander and Aristotle). The example of Plato is interesting because it reveals a fine distinction between the eternal spirit and mortality: Plato's spirit informs the entire poem, but "All that is mortal of great Plato" is enslaved to the boy Aster. Socrates could control his sexuality, but his disciple Plato could not. Similarly, "the great bards of old" quelled the passions which they sang about, but Rousseau "suffered what I wrote." At this point the speaker intervenes to help distinguish between Rousseau's *creative*

310

errors, and the merely destructive errors of kings, popes, and other instruments of wealth and power (281). A figure describing religious tyranny suggests that Shelley's concern with the radical Protestants of the seventeenth century was far from a shallow one; popes and other divine intercessors

>rose like shadows between Man and god
>Till that eclipse, still hanging under Heaven,
>Was worshipped by the world o'er which they strode

>For the true Sun it quenched.
>(289-92)

Like the radical Protestants, "Rousseau" wants an unmediated relationship to the divinity—a theme prominent in the theological fragment.

The poem has thus far dealt extensively with the political theme of power's corruption, but the theme of misguided idealism remains to be developed by Rousseau's allegorical self-portrait. At the allegorical level, this is what seems to happen: after birth, Rousseau becomes aware of a divinity that passes away but which he searches for, ultimately finding it in the form of a self-created Ideal he tries to possess. Like the *Alastor* Visionary, he tries to embrace his dream, and like Faust, he tries to know the unknowable. When he attempts to possess the Ideal in the form of a female, the Ideal passes away, leading Rousseau to despair and sensualism. After the shock of disappointment, he slowly becomes aware of the Ideal as something that has to be mediated rather than pursued as a personalized absolute.

The experience with the pantheistic spirit is rendered thus:

>"for a space
>The scene of woods and waters seemed to keep,

>Though it was now broad day, a gentle trace
>Of light diviner than the common Sun
>Sheds on the common Earth, but all the place

>Was filled with many sounds woven into one
>Oblivious melody, confusing sense
>Amid the gliding waves and shadows dun."
>(335-42)

311

Rousseau's losing contact with divinity is parallel to the lines quoted earlier (66-73), where adults are so diverted by various tasks that they lose the once instinctive appreciation of nature. When he reacquires the ability to perceive divinity, the "shape all light," he commits the error of confusing the two elements, one pure and the other mediating. The shape all light, Iris, and the rainbow are all combinations of light (which, in its pure form, is invisible) and moisture (which reflects and refracts light); there is the One and the dome of many-coloured glass. Rousseau's error is to think he can possess the One by seizing the many-coloured glass which can only stain the white radiance of eternity. He personalizes divinity in the form of a female figure who offers him a potion of nepenthe. Like the *Alastor* Visionary's dream woman, Rousseau's woman is also beautiful, even if she is sinister, since the more he gazes on her brilliance the dimmer his real visionary power becomes, just as day blots out the stars of the Ideal. Gazing on her is not enough, so "between desire and shame / Suspended" he wants to possess her in a double sense, of physical union (symbolized by drinking the potion—that is, mingling with her substance) and intellectual knowledge (symbolized by his questions in line 398). By possessing the Ideal he hopes to gain not only ineffable happiness but equally powerful knowledge about himself.

After he drinks the potion, symbolically uniting with the Ideal, he loses his visionary capacity to be in contact with the divine (405-409), and sees instead a new kind of reality after the Ideal "wanes" and retreats (412-33). The Ideal, symbolized by Venus, does not disappear:

> "the presence of that fairest planet
> Although unseen is felt by one who hopes
>
> That his day's path may end as he began it
> In that star's smile, whose light is like the scent
> Of a jonquil when evening breezes fan it. . . ."
> (416-20)

The Ideal, though lost as a constant presence or a personalized absolute, " 'Glimmers, forever sought, forever lost' " (431). The new reality Rousseau perceives after losing the Ideal and experiencing the shock of disappointment (" 'So did that shape its obscure tenour keep / Beside my path, as silent as a ghost' " [432-33]) is the Triumph of Life, in particular the triumph of sensuality (" 'savage, stunning music' " [435]). Unable to appreciate nature (" 'me sweetest flowers delayed not long' " [461]), or solitude (462), he engages in a pursuit of sensual pleasure (465-68).

At precisely this point, where Rousseau's disappointed idealism has led to a loveless sexuality, the poem evokes Dante, whose song told

> "the wondrous story
> How all things are transfigured, except Love;
> For deaf as is a sea which wrath makes hoary
>
> The world can hear not the sweet notes that move
> The sphere whose light is melody to lovers—"
> (475-79)

The kind of love referred to is obviously not like Rousseau's failed romantic quest or merely sensual desire, but is rather the proper human mediation of the Ideal, enabling "lovers" to hear the subtle music. There is an appropriate way to experience divinity, to "love," and it is possible to commune in however a mediated way with the Ideal.

The evocation of Dante leads to Rousseau's grimmest account of hell, a procession of bestialized humans who worship power:

> "Some made a cradle of the ermined capes
>
> Of kingly mantles, some upon the tiar
> Of pontiffs sate like vultures, others played
> Within the crown which girt with empire
>
> A baby's or an idiot's brow, and made
> Their nests in it; the old anatomies
> Sate hatching their bare brood under the shade
>
> Of demon wings, and laughed from their dead eyes
> To reassume the delegated power
> Arrayed in which these worms did monarchize
>
> Who make this earth their charnel.— Others more
> Humble, like falcons sate upon the fist
> Of common men, and round their heads did soar,
>
> Or like small gnats and flies, as thick as mist
> On evening marshes, thronged about the brow
> Of lawyer, statesman, priest and theorist. . . ."
> (495-510)

Rather than pursue the true path of wisdom by quelling the mutiny within and ruling the passions to become king over the self, the deluded captives of Life worship power and its symbols, dominating other people when they do not possess self-knowledge. The others more "humble" are tools of power, like falcons who do the bidding of a hunter. Contrary to Yeats, Shelley's image of falcon and falconer is not symbolic of order but of authoritarianism. The intellect can also be at the service of power, a theme too of *Charles the First*. To pursue lust, like Rousseau, or power, like the bestial captives, is to deform the human spirit and obliterate the true beauty which is possible: " 'From every form the beauty slowly waned' " (519).

Rousseau, however, at the moment of his speeches to the poem's narrator, is not part of the procession, but someone who has dropped out, more spectator than participant. As such, Rousseau's purgatorial significance seems clear: he was a captive, ruined by a misguided and disappointed idealism, but upon acquiring self-awareness after much suffering, he is still one who worships the Ideal. He failed in his own quest, but by educating the speaker he has redeemed his error so that he seems finally liberated from the chariot of Life "which now had rolled / Onward, as if that look must be the last" (545-46). The speaker (like the narrator educated in *Laon and Cythna*, like Prometheus who is educated in Act I) has an opportunity to avoid the errors of despair, misguided idealism, and loveless sexuality. He has the privilege of witnessing a historical panorama, such as Queen Mab presented to Ianthe's spirit, from which he can learn ethical idealism. The direction of the poem at the point it breaks off, interrupted by Shelley's death, is toward clarifying even more finely the precise ways in which the Ideal should be mediated.

CONCLUSION

As is evident from my interpretation of *The Triumph of Life*, I disagree with those who take the poem as a dramatic renunciation of Shelley's radicalism and faith in social improvement. At its center is an ethical idealism dedicated to creating a society within which the Ideal can prosper to the widest possible extent. The poem shows a profound respect for history and historical dialectic and appreciates the difficulty of living an ethically ideal existence. Exposed to the temptations of lust, misguided idealism, and power in all its distorting guises, the human soul has an arduous path to virture. If virtue is far more difficult to pursue in 1822 than in 1812, this does not mean Shelley has given up on utopianism, but that he has come to realize all the obstacles to utopian desire and social improvement. Having learned from his painful mistakes, which enable him to sympathize with Rousseau—and Faust, and Cypriano, and Saint-Preux—Shelley refuses to imitate Byron and indulge his guilt to the extent that it cripples the capacity to hope for the Ideal. Rather, he maintains control over those thoughts which must remain untold, and situates his own problem within a literary-cultural-historical context where it can be philosophically comprehended. In Shelley's most mature phase he puts ethics at the center of his project without sacrificing psychology (the task of self-knowledge), politics, or history. To approach a condition of moral autonomy, of freedom from the compulsions of power or passions, one must be a philosopher in the ancient sense of loving wisdom more than anything else.

The kind of politics that follows from these assumptions is complex. Balanced between a respect for historical Necessity and a moral imperative not to be corrupted by the errors of the *Zeitgeist*, the ethical idealist tries to be in the vanguard of social change without actually leading any particular movement. In a letter written shortly before his death on June 29, 1822, to Horace Smith, Shelley's style of anarchist rebellion is eloquently depicted.

> It seems to me that things have now arrived at such a crisis as requires every man plainly to utter his sentiments on the inefficacy of the existing religions no less than political systems for restraining & guiding mankind. Let us see the truth whatever that may be.— The destiny of man can scarcely be so degraded that he was born only to die: and if such should be the case, delusions, especially the gross & preposterous ones of the existing religion, can scarcely be supposed to exalt it.— if every man said what he thought, it could not subsist a day. But all, more or less, subdue themselves to the element that surrounds them, & contribute to the evils they lament by the hypocrisy that springs from them.—

Shelley then alludes to the political situation in Ireland and England, commenting that certain concessions must be granted or there will be revolution. He then continues:

> I once thought to study these affairs & write or act in them—
> I am glad that my good genius said *refrain*. I see little public
> virtue, & I foresee that the contest will be one of blood & gold

two elements, which however much to my taste in my pockets & my veins, I have an objection to out of them.[51]

There is a balance here between uncompromising philosophy—speaking truth to power—and accepting social limits, such as urging prudent concessions to avoid revolution. The errors of the *Zeitgeist* must be resisted, so that, in the language of the *Defence*, we can imagine that which we know. Shelley recommends courageous acts of will and hope, to hope until Hope creates from its own wreck the thing it contemplates. The kind of political life he says he avoided is apparently a total commitment to the reform movement as made by Cobbett or Carlile, and perhaps entertained in 1817 by the Hermit of Marlow. If virtue has withdrawn from one public realm, then Shelley proposes to create it in another, outside the ordinary political sphere. This sounds like the politics of the antipolitical developed by the anarchist Herbert Read.[52] As the elements of genuine society and free association expand, as the circle of truth increases its circumference, so the area dominated by power diminishes.

Despite the harsh view of politics expressed in the letter quoted above, Shelley does not repudiate the careful mediation of the Ideal embodied in *Hellas*. The truth must always be told, but the truth is always mediated—through particular cultures, particular historical moments, and particular words. Had he lived, Shelley would have continued to develop his ethical idealism in prose and poetry. As his technical proficiency improved dramatically over the years— from *Laon and Cythna* to *The Triumph of Life* is an astounding progress, especially given the by no means mediocre quality of the former—so did his thought gain in maturity, complexity, breadth, and subtlety. If there is a diminution of intellectual power in Shelley's last phase, I do not see it.

While Shelley himself continued to develop in ever more interesting ways, the actual situation for the political poet and leisure-class intellectual was contradictory and ambiguous—and would remain so throughout the nineteenth and twentieth centuries. Although a "radical" Shelley did indeed become a part of English working-class culture, another Shelley—the "ineffectual angel" of the late Victorians—served the interests of cultural and political reaction.[53] A source for this particular contradiction is the nature of the poet-prophet, who tries to mediate between an interest-ridden material world and a sphere of pure ideals, access to which is usually possible to someone from the leisure class. Although the realm of ideals is also the product of cultural creativity, representing the collective efforts of a transhistorical community, its democratic possibilities are vitiated by the class privilege that has usually attended a "cultured" education. As long as there is social inequality, the rebel from the privileged strata is as tied to contradiction as the rebel from the poorer classes who has to use the language and cultural heritage of his oppressors. In short, if Shelley had been poor and had acquired the education to write as complexly as he did, he would not have escaped dilemmas and problems, but endured new ones. The poet-prophet is the role he assigns himself to accommodate his attempt to be a disinterested writer and political analyst. The poet-prophet is both an idealist, belonging more to an imaginary than a real world, and a practical writer, who articulates the mediations of the ideal as they exist in the historical world. Ethical idealism is the logical outcome of the poet-prophet's quest for a coherent perspective; his is the unique situation of the disinterested author.

But is not the stance of being "disinterested" simply an illusion, an ideological obfuscation? Yes and no. Yes, it obscures Shelley's agrarian and leisure-class biases, many of which I have identified in the book, but no, it asserts something else, namely, the democratic ideal. He was committed to and tried to practice something akin to Jürgen Habermas's undistorted communication or the ideal speech situation, a mode of discourse governed not by coercion or merely selfish interests, but by "reason" understood in its most emancipatory sense.[54] Living at the beginning of the modern democratic movement, Shelley saw that no democracy worthy of the name was possible without socioeconomic equality, that is, socialism. Writing before the existence of self-proclaimed "socialist" societies, he also anticipated and objected to a socialism without democracy. He can be faulted at certain points for not being sufficiently self-reflexive, but his example is nevertheless impressive, especially considering the disastrous mistakes made by many political poets and intellectuals in the past few centuries. Despite many disappointments, political repression, personal tragedies, and the problem of finding a responsive audience, Shelley continued to believe in democracy and the ideal of equality; within the limits of his contradictory situation, he spoke for the hopes of the radical culture.

Notes

INTRODUCTION

1. H. N. Brailsford, *Shelley, Godwin, and Their Circle* (London: Williams and Norgate, 1913), overstated the case for Godwin's influence, but this was corrected from the 1930s to the 1950s by the work of numerous scholars: Carl Grabo, *The Magic Plant* (Chapel Hill: Univ. of North Carolina Press, 1936), and other books; Newman Ivy White's two-volume biography (New York: Alfred A. Knopf, 1940), and numerous articles; Carlos Baker, *Shelley's Major Poetry: The Fabric of a Vision* (Princeton: Princeton Univ. Press, 1948); James Notoupolos, *The Platonism of Shelley* (Durham: Duke Univ. Press, 1949); C. E. Pulos's study of Shelley's skepticism, *The Deep Truth* (Lincoln: Univ. of Nebraska Press, 1954); and especially Kenneth Neill Cameron's numerous articles on Shelley's politics, their sources and literary transformations—which culminated with *The Young Shelley: Genesis of a Radical* (New York: Macmillan, 1950). While I place Godwin, and more importantly, a philosophical anarchism, at the center of Shelley's literary project, I do not deny the significant influences elucidated by the scholars just mentioned. Although he was politically influenced by the entire radical tradition of his day, I also see a coherent thread running through his career which can be usefully identified as a philosophical anarchism, an extensively revised Godwinian perspective. Shelley's political trajectory anticipates, insofar as such things can be inferred, a number of radical tendencies, including the socialism of Marx as well as that of his libertarian and more moderate opponents. Eleanor Marx, George Bernard Shaw, and the anarchists are all correct, it seems to me, in finding Shelley part of their respective traditions: such is the contradictory nature of philosophical anarchism. Cf. Paul Foot, *Red Shelley* (London: Sidgwick and Jackson, 1980), who does not use the category of philosophical anarchism but tries to situate Shelley in the socialist tradition.

2. For Godwin's anarchism, see John P. Clark, *The Philosophical Anarchism of William Godwin* (Princeton: Princeton Univ. Press, 1977). Although he never uses the phrase "philosophical anarchism," Donald Reiman's account of Shelley's ethics in Chapter One of *Shelley's "The Triumph of Life": A Critical Study* (Urbana: Univ. of Illinois Press, 1965) describes an ethical idealism synonymous with philosophical anarchism. As I have finished my

own study I have become aware of P.M.S. Dawson's work, which parallels my own in some ways. See his article, " 'King Over Himself': Shelley's Philosophical Anarchism," *Keats-Shelley Memorial Bulletin*, 30 (1980), 16-35, and his book, *The Unacknowledged Legislator: Shelley and Politics* (Oxford: Clarendon Press, 1980). Although I agree with Dawson that Shelley was politically moderate (*usually*, but not always), with radical goals, I believe Dawson slights many instances of unmoderate radicalism; he treats the philosophical anarchism as though it justified only a moral revolution to precede institutional change, whereas I show that Shelley was more flexible, revising Godwin's ideas profoundly away from a rejection of politics. Our differences are most apparent when dealing with the texts of 1817, which he sees as cautionary statements urging moderation for the reform movement (pp. 69-75), while I demonstrate their radicalism to be more militant (Chapter Four). Whereas I emphasize Shelley's radical intentions undermined by political repression and other factors, Dawson does not believe Shelley tried hard to publish his most politically uncompromising texts (pp. 197-98).

3. "Shelley as Agrarian Reactionary," *Keats-Shelley Memorial Bulletin*, 30 (1980), 5-15.

4. For an interesting discussion of an "aristocratic" socialism, see the second chapter of Richard Gombin, *The Radical Tradition, A Study in Modern Revolutionary Thought*, trans. Rupert Swyer (New York: St. Martin's Press, 1979).

5. For a discussion of the crucial role of scarcity in radical theory, see Murray Bookchin, *Post-Scarcity Anarchism* (Berkeley: Ramparts Press, 1971), pp. 9-54, and Michael Harrington, *Socialism* (New York: Bantam, 1973), pp. 11-40.

6. Raymond Williams, *Keywords, A Vocabulary of Culture and Society* (New York: Oxford Univ. Press, 1976), pp. 87-91. E. P. Thompson, "The Poverty of Theory or An Orrery of Errors," in *The Poverty of Theory and Other Essays* (New York and London: Monthly Review Press, 1978).

ONE: VISIONARY RADICALISM AND RADICAL CULTURE

1. Charles Rosen, "Isn't It Romantic?" *New York Review of Books*, 20 (June 14, 1973), 12-18, in reviewing several new books of romantic scholarship, criticizes the tendency to depoliticize the romantic poets. Similarly, William Walling, "Hegel,—hélas!" *Partisan Review*, 42 (1975), 149-53, protests the dominant subjectivism in romantic studies. Carl Woodring has identified an important contradiction between the poetry and politics of the romantic poets. The philosophical basis of liberalism was empiricist, whereas the innovations in poetry were justified by appeals to organicism. *Politics in English Romantic Poetry* (Cambridge: Harvard Univ. Press, 1970), pp. 31-33. Marilyn Butler has offered a new way of viewing this problem by identifying as politically conservative the poetry of Wordsworth and Coleridge which esteems the retreat from urban society and the cultivation of a solitary

subjectivity. The politically progressive Keats, Peacock, and Shelley valued "nature," but not as antisocial retreat; rather, for them it was the foundation of a neoclassical paganism, which was an alternative to Christianity. Moreover, the liberal writers, committed to a public discourse and not a private language of the isolated self, were innovative in order to clarify their social vision and fulfill their responsibility as social critics. *Peacock Displayed, A Satirist in His Context* (London: Routledge and Kegan Paul, 1979), pp. 4; 104; 109; 303-306.

2. For the parliamentary reform movement before 1800, see E. P. Thompson, *The Making of the English Working Class* (New York: Vintage, 1963); Carl Cone, *The English Jacobins, Reformers in Late Eighteenth Century England* (New York: Charles Scribner's Sons, 1968); Albert Goodwin, *The Friends of Liberty, The English Democratic Movement in the Age of the French Revolution* (Cambridge: Harvard Univ. Press, 1979).

3. Goodwin, *The Friends of Liberty*, p. 164.

4. The pamphlet is from 1794, "Revolutions without Bloodshed, or Reformation preferable to Revolt," rpt. in G.D.H. Cole and A. W. Filson, *British Working Class Movements, Select Documents 1789-1875* (London: Macmillan, 1951), pp. 48-52.

5. Samuel Taylor Coleridge, *Conciones ad Populum*, in Lewis Patton and Peter Mann, eds., *The Collected Works of Samuel Taylor Coleridge*, I (London and Princeton: Routledge and Kegan Paul, and Princeton Univ. Press, 1971), 39.

6. William Godwin, *Considerations on Lord Grenville's and Mr. Pitt's Bills* . . . , in Jack W. Marken and Burton R. Pollin, eds., *Uncollected Writings by William Godwin* (Gainesville, Fla.: Scholars' Facsimiles and Reprints, 1968), p. 208.

7. John P. Clark, "On Anarchism in an Unreal World: Kramnick's View of Godwin and the Anarchists," *American Political Science Review*, 69 (1975), 163. Clark responds to Isaac Kramnick's provocative, if also largely inaccurate, article, "On Anarchism and the Real World: William Godwin and Radical England," *American Political Science Review*, 66 (1972), 114-28. Although Clark's refutation of Kramnick is convincing, the latter makes the interesting point that Godwin's evolutionary politics prefigures Marxian historicism in its assumption of gradual stages (122).

8. See Thompson, *The Making of the English Working Class*, pp. 70-73, (hereafter, cited as *Making*) for the "manipulated mob" and the "revolutionary crowd."

9. Samuel Taylor Coleridge, *The Statesman's Manual*, in Patton and Mann, VI, 38.

10. Sidney Pollard, *The Genesis of Modern Management* (Cambridge: Harvard Univ. Press, 1965), p. 180.

11. Richard Altick, *The English Common Reader* (Chicago: The Univ. of

Chicago Press, 1957), pp. 69-72; Altick's entire chapter, "The Time of Crisis, 1791-1800," is instructive.

12. On the eighteenth-century novel, the following were especially useful: J.M.S. Tompkins, *The Popular Novel in England 1770-1800* (1961; rpt. Westport: Greenwood Press, 1976); Leslie Fiedler, *Love and Death in the American Novel*, rev. ed. (New York: Dell, 1966), pp. 23-104; Ian Watt, *The Rise of the Novel* (1957; rpt. Berkeley and Los Angeles: Univ. of California Press, 1967), pp. 6-59.

13. Tompkins, p. 107.

14. For the "Jacobin" novelists, see Gary Kelly, *The English Jacobin Novel* (New York and London: Oxford Univ. Press, 1976); M. Ray Adams, *Studies in the Literary Backgrounds of English Radicalism* (Lancaster: Franklin and Marshall College Studies, 1947); Tompkins, pp. 296-328. The ideological ambiguities of "feeling" and "reason" as they are represented in the English novel are brilliantly analyzed in the first four chapters of Marilyn Butler's *Jane Austen and the War of Ideas* (Oxford: Clarendon Press, 1975).

15. Kenneth Neill Cameron, *The Young Shelley* (1950); Gerald McNiece, *Shelley and the Revolutionary Idea* (Cambridge: Harvard Univ. Press, 1969). Dawson, in *The Unacknowledged Legislator*, restores Godwin to a place of centrality.

16. Thanks to Mary Shelley's journal, we have a good idea of what Shelley read. Frederick L. Jones, ed., *Mary Shelley's Journal* (Norman: Univ. of Oklahoma Press, 1947).

17. See Nathaniel Brown, *Sexuality and Feminism in Shelley* (Cambridge: Harvard Univ. Press, 1979).

18. Wollstonecraft attacks economic injustice in nearly all her works. In *A Vindication of the Rights of Men* (1791; rpt. Gainesville, Fla.: Scholars' Facsimiles and Reprints, 1960), she finds most objectionable Burke's "contempt for the poor" (p. 142); she also protests against enclosures, wondering "why might not the industrious peasant be allowed to steal a farm from the heath?" (p. 148). In *A Vindication of the Rights of Woman* (1792; rpt. New York: W. W. Norton, 1975), she calls hereditary property the source of evil (in Chapter IX). In *Letters Written During a Short Residence in Sweden, Norway, and Denmark* (1796; rpt. Lincoln: Univ. of Nebraska Press, 1976), she frequently condemns the ill effects of commerce (pp. 119-20; 186-87; 190). And, of course, in the novel *Maria, or the Wrongs of Woman* (1798; rpt. New York: W. W. Norton, 1975), the economic distress of Jemima is prominent.

19. Paine revises his strict adherence to laissez-faire in *Agrarian Justice* (1796), in Philip Foner, ed., *The Complete Writings of Thomas Paine*, I (New York: Citadel Press, 1945), 605-23. Wordsworth's unpublished "Letter to the Bishop of Landaff" also advocates welfare measures within a capitalist economy. W.J.B. Owen and Jane W. Smyser, eds., *The Prose Works of William Wordsworth*, I (Oxford: Clarendon Press, 1974), 32-49.

20. For Fawcett and his influence, see M. Ray Adams, *Studies*, pp. 191-226.

21. Pollard, *Genesis*, p. 207. Karl Polanyi, *The Great Transformation* (1944; rpt. Boston: Beacon Press, 1957), suggests that the Speenhamland system of wage supplements delayed the formation of a labor market until the 1834 Poor Law Reform; thus, the period under consideration, 1789-1822, would be transitional, with remnants of paternalism coexisting with an emergent market economy.

22. Raymond Williams, *Culture and Society* (New York: Harper and Row, 1958), has a brilliant exposition on the question of culture.

23. In a slightly different form, this section appeared as "Godwin's Philosophy: A Revaluation," *Journal of the History of Ideas*, 39 (1978), 615-26.

24. For discussions of "subjectivity" that parallel my own ideas, see Michael Kosok's "Dialectics of Nature," and Paul Piccone's "Phenomenological Marxism," in Bart Grahl and Paul Piccone, eds., *Towards a New Marxism* (St. Louis: Telos Press, 1973), pp. 31-84; 133-58.

25. Godwin disowns "perfectibility" in *Thoughts Occasioned by the Perusal of Dr. Parr's Spital Sermon . . .* (London, 1801) in Marken and Pollin, *Uncollected Writings by William Godwin*, p. 336.

26. F.E.L. Priestley, "Introduction," in F.E.L. Priestley, ed., *Enquiry Concerning Political Justice*, III (Toronto: Univ. of Toronto Press, 1946), 11, 18-19, and 109. See Godwin's last ideas on necessity in *Thoughts on Man* (1832; rpt. New York: Augustus M. Kelley, 1969), pp. 226-42. Although I always quote from the third edition of *Political Justice*, it seems that Shelley preferred the first edition, at least in 1812. The next chapter deals more thoroughly with the Godwin-Shelley relationship.

27. Woodring, *Politics in English Romantic Poetry*, p. 37. E. P. Thompson repeats anti-Godwinian clichés in his otherwise excellent essay, "The Poverty of Theory," pp. 180-81.

28. Murry's analysis is cited by Burton R. Pollin, *Education and Enlightenment in the Works of William Godwin* (New York: Los Americas Publishing Co., 1962), p. 11.

29. Priestley, *Enquiry*, II, 231-32.

30. Godwin, *Thoughts on Man*, p. 244.

31. Ibid., p. 250.

32. Ibid., p. 257.

33. Priestley, *Enquiry*, I, 232-33.

34. The connection between Godwin's anarchism and radical Protestantism has been drawn by other critics, such as Woodcock and Pollin; the latter also cites Milton's *Areopagitica*, but in a different context. George Woodcock, *William Godwin* (London: Porcupine Press, 1946).

35. Priestley, *Enquiry*, I, 35.

36. Ibid., p. 151.

37. Ibid., p. 46.

38. Ibid., p. 414.

39. Ibid., pp. 343-44.

40. David McCracken, "Godwin's Literary Theory: The Alliance between Fiction and Political Philosophy," *Philological Quarterly*, 49 (1970), 128-32.

41. Mitzi Meyers, "Godwin's Changing Conception of *Caleb Williams*," *Studies in English Literature*, 12 (1972), 591-628.

42. William Godwin, *The Enquirer* (1798; rpt. New York: Augustus M. Kelley, 1965), pp. 129-46.

43. Ibid., pp. 135; 137.

44. See Roger Sharrock, "Godwin on Milton's Satan," *Notes and Queries*, 3rd ser., 9 (1962), 463-65.

45. Godwin, *The Enquirer*, p. 135.

46. Marken and Pollin, *Uncollected Writings*, p. 300.

47. One must not confuse the Byzantine legal procedures that were subject to numerous attacks, not just Godwin's, and the preconditions for rational discourse that Godwin absolutely affirmed. He wanted to liberate the jury system to permit full participation by jurists who would, of course, follow the rules of "reason" and open inquiry.

48. Priestley, *Enquiry*, II, 334.

49. Ibid., p. 463.

50. Ibid., I, 230.

51. Ibid., II, 347-48.

52. In the Priestley edition, this is part of a footnote where Godwin quotes Beccaria (II, 353, translated by K. Codell Carter, in his abridged edition of *Political Justice* [Oxford: Oxford Univ. Press, 1971], p. 256).

53. Elie Halévy quoting from Bentham's *Panopticon*, in *The Growth of Philosophic Radicalism* (Boston: Beacon Press, 1955), p. 83.

54. John Dings of S.U.N.Y. at Buffalo is responsible for suggesting in a graduate seminar the significance of Bentham and especially the importance of the *Panopticon* as a reverberating metaphor in the utilitarian worldview. Cf. Michel Foucault's development of the panoptical metaphor in *Surveiller et Punir* (Paris, 1975).

55. Godwin, *The Enquirer*, p. 370.

56. Pollin, *Education and Enlightenment* (1962).

57. Pollin, p. 60.

58. See James Preu, "Swift's Influence on Godwin's Doctrine of Anarchism," *Journal of the History of Ideas*, 15 (1954), 371-83; and William Godwin, *Of Population* (1820; rpt. New York: Augustus M. Kelley, 1964). See also Frederick Rosen, "The Principle of Population as Political Theory," *Journal of the History of Ideas*, 21 (1970), 33-48.

59. Godwin, *Of Population*, p. 615.

60. Priestley, *Enquiry*, I, 111-19.

61. Ibid., pp. 281-282.

62. Ibid., pp. 283-284.

63. Ibid., p. 271.

64. Ibid., pp. 252-253.

65. Ibid., p. 269.

66. Ibid., p. 167. Cf. Roger Poole's *Toward Deep Subjectivity* (London: Penguin Press, 1972).

67. Priestley, *Enquiry*, I, 68.

68. Ibid., II, Book VIII.

69. Ibid., I, 21.

70. The parallel with Kant is too obvious not to mention. A bias in favor of village life coupled with the ethical imperative has made Kant something of a favorite among certain anarchists. In addition to Proudhon, who was an outstanding Kantian, there are Paul Goodman and Robert Paul Wolff who derived much from Kant. Lukács' pre-Marxist phase was heavily influenced by Kant. For an apt Shelley-Kant comparison, see Reiman, *Shelley's "The Triumph of Life,"* p. 4.

71. Priestley, *Enquiry*, I, 335.

72. Ibid., p. 336.

73. See Clark, *Philosophical Anarchism* (1977).

74. Godwin, *Thoughts on Man*, pp. 7; 226-42; 436-55.

75. Judith Shklar, *After Utopia* (Princeton: Princeton Univ. Press, 1957), pp. 31-35.

76. C. Kegan Paul, *William Godwin: His Friends and Contemporaries*, I (London: Henry S. King, 1876), p. 11. See Jean de Palacio, "Godwin et la tentation de l'autobiographie (William Godwin et J.-J. Rousseau)," *Etudes Anglaises*, 27 (1974), 143-57.

77. Cf. Rudolf Storch, "Metaphors of Private Guilt and Social Rebellion in Godwin's *Caleb Williams*," *Journal of English Literary History*, 34 (1967), 188-207 (this journal is cited hereafter as *ELH*); Eric Rothstein, *Systems of Order and Inquiry in Later Eighteenth-Century Fiction* (Berkeley and Los Angeles: Univ. of California Press, 1975), pp. 208-42.

78. See the description of working-class life in André Parreaux, *Daily Life in England in the Reign of George III*, trans. Carola Congreve (London: George Allen and Unwin, 1969).

79. For Luddism, see Thompson, *Making*, pp. 269-313. See also Malcolm I. Thomis, *The Luddites* (New York: Schocken Books, 1972).

80. For laissez-faire liberalism, see Barry Gordon, *Political Economy in Parliament 1819-1823* (New York: Barnes and Noble, 1976), and Halévy, *The Growth of Philosophic Radicalism* (1955).

81. For the Ruffigny episode, see Ivanke Kovačević, *Fact into Fiction, English Literature and the Industrial Scene 1750-1850* (Leicester: Leicester Univ. Press, 1975), pp. 177-87.

82. Wollstonecraft, *Maria*, p. 152.

83. Max Horkheimer and Theodor Adorno, *The Dialectic of Enlight-*

enment, trans. John Cumming (1944; rpt. New York: Seabury Press, 1972), p. 119.

84. See Jacqueline Miller, who makes this point in "The Imperfect Tale: Articulation, Rhetoric, and Self in *Caleb Williams*," *Criticism*, 20 (1978), 366-82. A similar article by Jerrold E. Hogle suggests that Caleb unsuccessfully tries to discover a stable "character" not founded on pre-existing "texts." "The Texture of the Self in Godwin's *Things as They Are*," *Boundary 2*, 7 (1979), 261-81.

85. Lionel Trilling, *Sincerity and Authenticity* (Cambridge: Harvard Univ. Press, 1972), pp. 126-27.

86. Keith Hollingsworth, *The Newgate Novel 1830-1847* (Detroit: Wayne State Univ. Press, 1963), pp. 41-43.

87. For the role of language as constituting reality, see Earl R. Wasserman, *The Subtler Language* (Baltimore: The Johns Hopkins Univ. Press, 1959).

88. See Karl Kroeber, "Experience as History: Shelley's Venice, Turner's Carthage," *ELH*, 41 (1974), 321-39.

89. For the extreme experience in literature, see Trilling, *Sincerity and Authenticity*; Masao Miyoshi, *The Divided Self, A Perspective on the Literature of the Victorians* (New York and London: New York Univ. Press and Univ. of London Press, 1969); Georges Bataille, *Literature and Evil*, trans. Alastair Hamilton (1957; rpt. London: Calder and Boyars, 1973); Irving Massey, *The Uncreating Word, Romanticism and the Object* (Bloomington: Indiana Univ. Press, 1970), esp. Ch. 4, and *The Gaping Pig, Literature and Metamorphosis* (Berkeley and Los Angeles: Univ. of California Press, 1976); Susan Sontag, "The Pornographic Imagination," in *Styles of Radical Will* (New York: Dell, 1970).

90. Trilling, *Sincerity and Authenticity*, p. 39.

91. William Godwin, *Mandeville, A Tale of the Seventeenth Century*, III (Edinburgh: Archibald Constable, 1817), 113.

92. Ibid., II, 218.

93. Priestley, *Enquiry*, I, 129.

94. For the divided self in *Caleb Williams*, see Miyoshi, *The Divided Self*, pp. 23-29; Robert Kiely, *The Romantic Novel in England* (Cambridge: Harvard Univ. Press, 1972), pp. 81-97; Donald Roemer, "The Achievement of Godwin's *Caleb Williams*: The Proto-Byronic Squire Falkland," *Criticism*, 18 (1976), 43-56.

95. See Miller, "Imperfect Tale"; Gerald Barker, "Justice to *Caleb Williams*," *Studies in the Novel*, 6 (1974), 377-88.

96. *Thoughts Occasioned by the Perusal of Dr. Parr's Spital Sermon* . . . , in Marken and Pollin, *Uncollected Writings*, pp. 281-374.

TWO: THE MAKING OF A PHILOSOPHICAL ANARCHIST

1. Carl Grabo, *The Magic Plant* (1936), identifies Shelley's political vision as anarchist. F. A. Lea, *Shelley and the Romantic Revolution* (1945; rpt.

New York: Haskell House, 1971), also recognizes his anarchism. With the recent work of Art Young (*Shelley and Nonviolence* [The Hague and Paris: Mouton, 1975]), P.M.S. Dawson, and Roland Duerksen (whose "Shelley's Prometheus: Destroyer and Preserver," *Studies in English Literature*, 18 [1978], 625-36, does justice to the anarchist theme), perhaps Shelley's anarchism is finally being as recognized as it was when Brailsford wrote.

2. For the anarchist tradition, see George Woodcock, *Anarchism, A History of Libertarian Ideas and Movements* (Cleveland and New York: The World Publ. Co., 1962).

3. See Kingsley Widmer, *The Literary Rebel* (Carbondale and Edwardsville: Southern Illinois Univ. Press, 1965); Herbert Read, *To Hell With Culture* (New York: Schocken Books, 1963).

4. See Norman Cohn, *The Pursuit of the Millennium* (New York: Oxford Univ. Press, 1970); A. L. Morton, *The Everlasting Gospel, A Study in the Sources of William Blake* (London: Lawrence and Wishart, 1958).

5. Bookchin, *Post-Scarcity Anarchism*, p. 19.

6. Some critics have pointed to Shelley's anticipation of some Marxian ideas. Eleanor Marx and Edward Aveling, *Shelley's Socialism* (1888; rpt. Manchester: Leslie Praeger, 1947) records this comment by Karl Marx: "The real difference between Byron and Shelley is this; those who understand them and love them rejoice that Byron died at thirty-six, because if he had lived he would have become a reactionary *bourgeois*; they grieve that Shelley died at twenty-nine, because he was essentially a revolutionist and he would always have been one of the advanced guard of socialism." Another socialist, George Bernard Shaw, helped counter the sentimental depoliticization of Shelley: "Shaming of the Devil about Shelley," in *Pen Portraits and Reviews* (1892; rpt. London: Constable, 1931), pp. 236-46. For a Marxist-Leninist reading of Shelley, see Manfred Wojcik, "In Defense of Shelley," *Zeitschrift für Anglistik und Amerikanistik*, 11 (1963), 143-88, which is interesting, despite the propaganda for East Germany. See also Kenneth N. Cameron, "Shelley and Marx," *Wordsworth Circle*, 10 (1979), 234-39. Foot's *Red Shelley* portrays the poet as a socialist forerunner, but not a real socialist. Nevertheless, Foot concludes that "Shelley was a revolutionary, through and through" (p. 226).

7. The critic most sensitive to the actuality-potentiality dialectic in Shelley's work is Daniel Hughes, for whom the issue is ontological rather than political or social. See "Potentiality in *Prometheus Unbound*," *Studies in Romanticism*, 2 (1963), 107-26.

8. John V. Murphy, *The Dark Angel, Gothic Elements in Shelley's Works* (Lewisburg: Bucknell Univ. Press, 1975) discusses the novel and includes an excellent bibliography. Jerrold E. Hogle, "Shelley's Fiction: The 'Stream of Fate,' " *Keats-Shelley Journal*, 30 (1981), 78-99, also elucidates the "divided self" apparent in Shelley's novel.

9. The review of *Zastrozzi* appears in Newman I. White, *The Unextinguished Hearth* (Durham: Duke Univ. Press, 1938), pp. 33-35.

10. Roger Ingpen and Walter E. Peck, eds., *The Complete Works of Percy Bysshe Shelley*, V (1926-1930; rpt. New York: Gordian Press, 1965), 47.

11. Frederick L. Jones, ed., *The Letters of Percy Bysshe Shelley*, I (Oxford: Clarendon Press, 1964), 228.

12. See Daniel J. Hughes, "Coherence and Collapse in Shelley, With Special Reference to *Epipsychidion*," *ELH*, 28 (1961), 260-83.

13. Jones, *Letters*, I, 368-69.

14. Ingpen and Peck, *Complete Works*, V, 201-209.

15. Jones, *Letters*, I, 25. Cf. Gary Kelly, who emphasizes "unity of design" in *The English Jacobin Novel* (1976).

16. Jones, *Letters*, I, 27.

17. Cf. Kenneth N. Cameron's discussion of the homoerotic dimension in the Hogg-Shelley relationship in *The Young Shelley*, pp. 125-26. Lending support to my view that Godwin fulfilled certain Oedipal functions for Shelley is the unpublished verse letter to Graham of June 7, 1811, which names "Godwin" as the one human being most likely to offend his father. Neville Rogers, "An Unpublished Letter," *Keats-Shelley Memorial Bulletin*, 24 (1973), 22-23. For Oedipal configurations in Shelley's poetry, see Leon Waldoff, "The Father-Son Conflict in *Prometheus Unbound*," *The Psychoanalytic Review*, 62 (1975), 79-96.

18. Jones, *Letters*, I, 54-55.

19. Kenneth N. Cameron, ed., *Shelley and His Circle, 1773-1822*, II (Cambridge: Harvard Univ. Press, 1961), 760-61.

20. Cameron, *Shelley and His Circle*, II, 754-56; 775-78.

21. Cameron, II, 780-82.

22. The Abbé Barruel, *Memoirs, Illustrating the History of Jacobinism*, 4 vols. (Hartford, Conn.: Cornelius Davis, 1799).

23. Cf. James Rieger, *The Mutiny Within* (New York: George Braziller, 1967), pp. 63-68.

24. Jones, *Letters*, I, 116-17.

25. Ibid., p. 120.

26. Ibid., pp. 125; 127.

27. Ibid., pp. 150-51.

28. Ibid., p. 150.

29. Ibid., p. 314.

30. Ibid., p. 314.

31. Ibid., p. 152.

32. Ibid., p. 214.

33. Ibid., p. 218.

34. Ibid., p. 175.

35. Ibid., pp. 200-201.

36. Ibid., p. 320.

37. Ibid., p. 350.

38. Ibid., p. 269.

39. Ibid., p. 270.

40. Ibid., p. 235.

41. Ibid., p. 243.

42. Ibid., p. 263.

43. Ibid., p. 265.

44. Ibid., p. 239.

45. According to the *OED* (1933 edition) philanthropy signifies "Love of mankind; practical benevolence towards men in general," and only later in the nineteenth century does it come to be associated with charity. The *Anti-Jacobin* in 1797 called Tom Paine a "philanthropist," and William Godwin uses the phrase "universal philanthropy" to denote the highest ethical idealism in the 1801 *Thoughts Occasioned by the Perusal of Dr. Parr's Spital Sermon*, in Marken and Pollin, p. 333.

46. Ingpen and Peck, *Complete Works*, V, 265.

47. Jones, *Letters*, I, 197.

48. Ibid., p. 213.

49. P.M.S. Dawson, "Shelley and the Irish Catholics in 1812," *Keats-Shelley Memorial Bulletin*, 29 (1979), 27.

50. Jones, *Letters*, I, 223.

51. Frank O. Darvall, *Popular Disturbances and Public Disorder in Regency England* (1934; rpt. London: Oxford Univ. Press, 1969), p. 260.

52. Thompson, *Making*, p. 605.

53. Darvall, *Popular Disturbances*, p. 20.

54. A. Stanley Walker, "Peterloo, Shelley, and Reform," *PMLA*, 40 (1925), 130.

55. The execution statistics are derived from Hollingsworth, *The Newgate Novel*, p. 231. Hunt's *Examiner* regularly protested the large number of executions for property crimes.

56. Thompson, *Making*, p. 191. For the remarkable career of Richard Carlile, see: William Wickwar, *The Struggle for the Freedom of the Press, 1819-1832* (London: George Allen and Unwin, 1928); Thompson, *Making*, Ch. XVI; Guy Aldred, *Richard Carlile*, 3rd ed. (Glasgow: Strickland Press, 1941); George Holyoake, *The Life and Character of Richard Carlile* (London: Austin and Co., 1848); G.D.H. Cole, *Richard Carlile* (London: Fabian Society and Victor Gallancz, 1943).

57. Although the Hunts earned 511 pounds at the height of the *Examiner*'s popularity in 1811, the imprisonment and fine ruined them financially. Hunt had to borrow money from Shelley to go to Italy. George Dumas, *The Political History of Leigh Hunt's Examiner* (St. Louis: Washington Univ. Studies #19, 1949), p. 5. Leigh's brother, John, however, went to jail several other times in the 1820s.

58. Jones, *Letters*, I, 54.

59. Ibid., pp. 266-68.

60. A recent discussion of Shelley and repression: E. B. Murray, "The Trial of Mr. Perry, Lord Eldon, and Shelley's *Address to the Irish*," *Studies in Romanticism*, 17 (1978), 35-49.

61. See the quotation Louise Boas cites from Cobbett's *Political Register*, " 'Erasmus Perkins' and Shelley," *Modern Language Notes*, 80 (1955), 411-12; a correspondent complains that working-class radicals are imprisoned for writing material as blasphemous as *The Necessity of Atheism*, whose author is left alone. Shelley was aware of and troubled by the double standard (see his open letter to the *Examiner* protesting the imprisonment of Richard Carlile).

62. Cameron, *Young Shelley*, p. 147.

63. Richard Holmes, *Shelley, the Pursuit* (New York: E. P. Dutton, 1975), pp. 136-47.

64. Holmes, *Shelley, The Pursuit*, p. 145.

65. Newman I. White, *Shelley*, I (New York: Knopf, 1940), 247-48.

66. Donald Reiman, *Percy Bysshe Shelley* (New York: Twayne, 1969), p. 24.

67. Holmes, *Shelley, The Pursuit*, p. 161.

68. Holmes, *Shelley, The Pursuit*, pp. 177-98. Holmes's version runs counter to that of Cameron, *Young Shelley*, p. 234.

69. Jones, *Letters*, I, 294-95.

70. Dawson, p. 21.

71. Ingpen and Peck, *Complete Works*, V, 246-47.

72. Jones, *Letters*, I, 277.

73. Ingpen and Peck, *Complete Works*, V, 220.

74. Dawson, p. 26.

75. Ingpen and Peck, *Complete Works*, V, 206.

76. Ibid., p. 218.

77. Ibid., p. 219

78. Ibid., pp. 221-22.

79. Ibid., p. 221.

80. Ibid., p. 232.

81. Ibid., p. 234.

82. Ibid., p. 229.

83. Ibid., pp. 256-57.

84. Ibid., p. 256.

85. Priestley, *Enquiry*, I, 5.

86. See Peter Kropotkin, *The Great French Revolution, 1789-1793*, trans. N. F. Dryhurst (1909; rpt. New York: Schocken Books, 1971).

87. Ingpen and Peck, *Complete Works*, V, 253.

88. Ibid., p. 263.

89. Ibid., p. 254.

90. Ibid., p. 254.

91. Priestley, *Enquiry*, I, 164.

92. Ibid., p. 165.

93. Ibid., p. 161.

94. Ibid., p. 167.

95. Ingpen and Peck, *Complete Works*, V, 271-75.

96. Ibid., p. 284.

97. Ibid., p. 285.

98. Ibid., p. 291.

99. William Godwin, *Essays, Never Before Published* (London: Henry S. King, 1873). Godwin's own title was: "The Genius of Christianity Unveiled: in a Series of Essays."

100. See Edward Royle, ed., *The Infidel Tradition from Paine to Bradlaugh* (London: Macmillan, 1976), and *Victorian Infidels, The Origins of the British Secularist Movement 1791-1866* (Manchester: Univ. of Manchester Press, 1974).

101. "Shelley and *The Theological Inquirer*," an unpublished article.

102. For the text of *Queen Mab* I am using: Donald H. Reiman and Sharon B. Powers, eds., *Shelley's Poetry and Prose* (New York: W. W. Norton, 1977). Unless otherwise indicated, all quotations from Shelley's poetry are from this edition.

103. Thomas Hutchinson, ed., *Shelley, Poetical Works* (London: Oxford Univ. Press, 1970), pp. 808-809.

104. Hutchinson, *Poetical Works*, p. 805.

105. Ibid., p. 804.

106. Ibid., p. 831.

107. Ibid., p. 832.

THREE: ROMANTICISM AND RELIGION

1. See Cameron, *Shelley and His Circle*, IV, 911-1062. Pantheism is apparent in poems like "A Sabbath Walk," "Written on a beautiful day in Spring," and others.

2. Ingpen and Peck, *Complete Works*, VI, 25.

3. Cf. Earl R. Wasserman, *Shelley, A Critical Reading* (Baltimore: The Johns Hopkins Univ. Press, 1971), pp. 12-15.

4. Ingpen and Peck, *Complete Works* VI, 43.

5. Ibid., p. 29.

6. Ibid., pp. 38-39.

7. Ibid., pp. 48-49.

8. Ibid., p. 39.

9. Ibid., p. 41.

10. Ibid., pp. 53-54.

11. Ibid., pp. 54-56.

12. Ibid., p. 50.

13. Ibid., p. 155.

14. Ibid., p. 156.

15. Ibid., p. 160.

16. Ibid., p. 162.

17. Ibid., pp. 163-64.

18. White, *Shelley*, I, pp. 696-97. See also White's *Unextinguished Hearth*, pp. 45-46. Louise Boas, " 'Erasmus Perkins,' " 408-13.

19. Parks C. Hunter, Jr., "Shelley's *Alastor*, 683," *Explicator*, 29 (January 1971), Item 40, suggests a connection between Godwin's *St. Leon* and *Alastor* because in both instances a violation of natural boundaries results in human isolation.

20. The Wordsworth and Coleridge echoes have been discussed by numerous critics, including: Paul Mueschke and Earl Leslie Griggs, "Wordsworth as the Prototype of the Poet in Shelley's *Alastor*," *PMLA*, 49 (1934), 229-45; Joseph Raben, "Coleridge as the Prototype of the Poet in Shelley's *Alastor*," *Review of English Studies*, n.s., 17 (1966), 278-92. I am not claiming that Coleridge, Wordsworth, or Shelley were unequivocal pantheists for all or part of their careers, but a pantheistic theme is evident in numerous poems. Even in 1816 Shelley could emphasize imagination's relative autonomy from nature in "Mont Blanc," but my original point remains: with pantheism, however qualified, and a notion of inspiration, Shelley's poetry advanced beyond the rationalist limitations of *Queen Mab*. His least equivocal view of nature's divinity comes with *Prometheus Unbound*, while his greatest doubts concerning nature are in *The Triumph of Life*.

21. Jones, *Journal*, p. 15.

22. Cf. Charles Robinson, *Shelley and Byron, The Snake and the Eagle Wreathed in Fight* (Baltimore: The Johns Hopkins Univ. Press, 1976), pp. 14-40.

23. See the balanced view on this particular issue in Frank Jordan, Jr., ed., *The English Romantic Poets, A Review of Research and Criticism*, 3rd ed. (New York: Modern Language Association, 1972), pp. 354-55.

24. A. H. Koszul, *Shelley's Prose in the Bodleian Manuscripts* (London: Henry Froude, 1910).

25. James A. Notopoulos, *The Platonism of Shelley* (1949; rpt. New York: Octogon Books, 1969), pp. 326-33.

26. David Lee Clark, *Shelley's Prose* (Albuquerque: The Univ. of New Mexico Press, 1954), pp. 196-214.

27. Kenneth Neill Cameron, *The Golden Years* (Cambridge: Harvard Univ. Press, 1974), pp. 163-69.

28. Lady Shelley, ed., *Shelley Memorials* (Boston: Ticknor and Fields, 1859), pp. 273-308.

29. Notopoulos, *Platonism*, p. 326. See also his "The Dating of Shelley's Prose," *PMLA*, 58 (1943), 484-89. Koszul, *Shelley's Prose*, pp. 9-11. Rei-

man, *Percy Bysshe Shelley*, p. 60, offers the summer of 1817. See also his comments on the *Essay* in Donald Reiman, ed., *Shelley and His Circle*, V, 192, n. 5. Cameron, *The Golden Years*, p. 163. Clark, *Shelley's Prose*, p. 196. See also his argument for this dating, "Shelley's *Biblical Extracts*," *Modern Language Notes*, 66 (1951), 435-41. Dawson, *The Unacknowledged Legislator*, offers September-December, 1817 (p. 283).

30. Jones, *Letters*, I, 566-67.

31. See Thompson, *Making*, pp. 631-69.

32. Koszul, *Shelley's Prose*, p. 56.

33. Diogenes Laertius, *Lives of the Eminent Philosophers*, II, trans. R. D. Hicks (London and New York: William Heinemann and G. P. Putnam's Sons, 1925), 23-85.

34. Jones, *Letters*, I, 527.

35. Reiman, *Shelley and His Circle*, V, 86-87.

36. Ibid., pp. 195-96.

37. See Clark, "Shelley's *Biblical Extracts*," 435-41.

38. I use the pagination employed by Koszul, who reproduces Bodleian MS. Shelley adds. e. 4, which I have examined, finding no significant errors in Koszul's transcription.

39. For a discussion of Holbach's influence on Shelley, see Cameron, *The Young Shelley*, pp. 303-306.

40. See the comments on the Bible Society in the *Cambridge History of the Bible*, cited by R. J. White in his notes to Coleridge's *Second Lay Sermon*, in *The Collected Works of Samuel Taylor Coleridge*, VI, 166; 201.

41. Hutchinson, *Poetical Works*, p. 820, n. 1. The principal work of Elihu Palmer, the well-known American freethinker, was *Principles of Nature; or A Development of the Moral Causes of Happiness and Misery Amongst the Human Species* (London: J. W. Trust, 1819).

42. Ingpen and Peck, *Complete Works* VI, 38-39.

43. Foner, *Complete Writings of Thomas Paine*, I, 467-70.

44. R.H.M. Elwes, introd., *The Chief Works of Benedict de Spinoza*, trans. R.H.M. Elwes (New York: Dover Publications, 1951), pp. 4-278.

45. Ingpen and Peck, *Complete Works*, VII, 147. Claude Brew suggests that the "miracles" fragment and "On the Christian Religion" are two halves of the same text, written probably in 1812-1813, thus supporting my view that "miracles were analyzed by Shelley early in his career. "A New Shelley Text: Essay on Miracles and Christian Doctrine," *Keats-Shelley Memorial Bulletin*, 28 (1977), 10-28.

46. Ibid., pp. 227-28. Clark, *Shelley's Prose*, pp. 197-98.

47. Ingpen and Peck, *Complete Works*, VI, 228.

48. Koszul, *Shelley's Prose*, p. 34, n. 1.

49. Ibid., pp. 33-34.

50. Ibid., pp. 37-38.

51. E. P. Thompson's work makes this quite clear. See also Francis Hearn, *Domination, Legitimation, and Resistance, The Incorporation of the Nineteenth-Century English Working Class* (Westport: Greenwood Press, 1978).

52. Koszul, *Shelley's Prose*, pp. 38-39.

53. Ibid., p. 39.

54. Ibid., pp. 36-37.

55. Priestley, *Enquiry*, I, 349.

56. Koszul, *Shelley's Prose*, p. 40.

57. Ibid., p. 15.

58. Ibid., p. 16.

59. Ibid., p. 16.

60. Ibid., p. 17.

61. Ibid., pp. 24-25.

62. Ibid., p. 26.

63. Ibid., p. 32.

64. Ibid., p. 33.

65. Ingpen and Peck, *Complete Works*, VI, 38.

66. Koszul, *Shelley's Prose*, pp. 23-24.

67. Ibid., p. 22.

68. Elaine Pagels, "The Threat of the Gnostics," *The New York Review of Books*, 26 (Nov. 8, 1979), 37-45.

69. Cf. Cohn, *The Pursuit of the Millennium* (1970).

70. Koszul, *Shelley's Prose*, p. 24.

71. Ibid., p. 25.

72. Cf. Rieger, *The Mutiny Within* (1967).

73. Franco Venturi, *Utopia and Reform in the Enlightenment* (Cambridge: Cambridge Univ. Press, 1971), pp. 95-98.

74. Koszul, *Shelley's Prose*, p. 40.

75. Ibid., p. 41.

76. Ibid., p. 46.

77. Ibid., pp. 50-51.

FOUR: THE HERMIT OF MARLOW

1. A. Aspinall, ed., *The Letters of King George IV*, II (Cambridge: Cambridge Univ. Press, 1938), pp. 158-59.

2. *The Annual Register, or a View of the History, Politics, and Literature, 1816*, p. 111 (hereafter cited as *Annual Register*).

3. Ibid., p. iv.

4. Ibid., p. 93.

5. Ibid., p. iv.

6. Thompson, *Making*, p. 639, n. 2.

7. *Annual Register, 1817*, p. 6.

8. Ibid., pp. 8-9.

9. *Ibid.*, p. 10.

10. *Ibid.*, pp. 17-18.

11. William Cobbett, "To the Journeymen and Labourers of England, Wales, Scotland and Ireland," *The Political Register* (Nov. 2, 1816), 546-76.

12. W. H. Chaloner, ed., *The Autobiography of Samuel Bamford*, II, (New York: Augustus M. Kelley, 1967), 7.

13. Cobbett, "To the Journeymen," 560.

14. Ibid., p. 561.

15. Ibid., pp. 567-68.

16. Ibid., pp. 555-56.

17. Ibid., p. 557.

18. Ibid., p. 553.

19. Ibid., pp. 550ff.

20. *Annual Register, 1817*, p. 10.

21. Thompson, *Making*, p. 668.

22. Chaloner, *Autobiography*, II, 35-39.

23. Thompson, *Making*, p. 670.

24. Ingpen and Peck, *Complete Works*, VI, 63.

25. Ibid., p. 64.

26. Ibid., p. 65.

27. Jones, *Letters*, I, 533.

28. See Reiman, *Shelley and His Circle*, V, 156.

29. Jones, *Letters*, I, 533.

30. Most of the information concerning the people on the list I discovered in the *Dictionary of National Biography* (1908-1909 edition).

31. *The Examiner* (Jan. 19, 1817), 41.

32. Michael Roberts, *The Whig Party 1807-1812* (1939; rpt. London: Frank Cass and Co., 1965), pp. 272-74.

33. *Annual Register, 1817*, p. 30.

34. Peter Linebough, "The Tyburn Riot Against the Surgeons," in Hay et al., *Albion's Fatal Tree*, (New York: Pantheon Books, 1975), pp. 65-117.

35. *Examiner* (Dec. 15, 1816), 792.

36. Ibid., pp. 792-93.

37. Ibid., p. 793. It is ironic that Hazlitt, opponent of the "self-love" school in his 1805 work, *Essay on the Principles of Human Action*, should in this review be the exponent of "self-love" concepts that Shelley opposes. For a very different discussion of Shelley and Hazlitt, see Dawson, *The Unacknowledged Legislator*, pp. 230-34.

38. Ingpen and Peck, *Complete Works*, I, 239. I quote from the Ingpen and Peck edition of *Laon and Cythna*.

39. Ibid., p. 240.

40. Ibid., p. 245.

41. Ibid., p. 244.

42. Ibid., p. 242. Reiman, *Percy Bysshe Shelley*, p. 52, suggests the Spenserians are an attempt to exploit the popularity of *Childe Harold*. Alex Comfort, *Darwin and the Naked Lady* (London: Routledge and Kegan Paul, 1961), p. 82, discusses the Alexandrian novel parallel.

43. Ingpen and Peck, *Complete Works*, I, 247.

44. Ibid., p. 247.

45. Ibid., p. 240.

46. Ibid., p. 241.

47. See Reiman, *Percy Bysshe Shelley*, p. 51.

48. Frederick L. Jones, "Canto I of *The Revolt of Islam*," *Keats-Shelley Journal*, 9 (1960), 27-33.

49. See *Examiner* (June 1, 1817), 337-38.

50. *Examiner* (Dec. 8, 1816), 778.

51. McNiece, *Shelley and the Revolutionary Idea*, pp. 119ff.

52. *Annual Register, 1817*, p. 14.

53. Karl Marx, *The Eighteenth Brumaire of Louis Bonaparte* (New York: International Publishers, 1963), p. 15.

54. Reiman, *Shelley and His Circle*, V, 197.

55. *Annual Register, 1817*, pp. 26-27.

56. *Examiner* (Dec. 8, 1816), 778.

57. *Annual Register, 1817*, p. 7.

58. Chaloner, *Autobiography*, II, 43.

59. See *Examiner* (April 20, 1817), 248; 250.

60. Reiman, *Shelley and His Circle*, V, 196.

61. Ibid., p. 291.

62. *Annual Register, 1817*, p. 17. For Owen's attack on Christianity, see Reiman, *Shelley and His Circle*, V, 272-75.

63. *Annual Register, 1817*, p. 9.

64. See James Mill, *Commerce Defended* (1808; rpt. New York: Augustus M. Kelley, 1965).

65. Cobbett, "To the Journeymen," 562.

66. Ingpen and Peck, *Complete Works*, I, 242.

67. Chaloner, *Autobiography*, II, 165.

68. *Annual Register, 1817*, p. 6.

69. See *Black Dwarf* (April 23, 1817), 207.

70. *Black Dwarf* (Dec. 31, 1817), 813.

71. Chaloner, *Autobiography*, II, 110-11.

72. See Brian Wilkie, *Romantic Poets and Epic Tradition* (Madison and Milwaukee: The Univ. of Wisconsin Press, 1965), pp. 112-44.

73. Reiman, *Shelley and His Circle*, V, 163-64.

74. White, *The Unextinguished Hearth*, pp. 133-42.

75. Ibid., pp. 126-32.

76. *Examiner* (Nov. 9, 1817), 705-706; *Black Dwarf* (Nov. 12, 1817), 688-90.

77. Foner, *Complete Writings of Thomas Paine*, I, 260.

78. Ingpen and Peck, *Complete Works*, VI, 80.

79. Ibid., p. 74.

80. Ibid., pp. 77-79.

81. Ibid., p. 78.

82. Ibid., p. 79.

83. Ibid., p. 75.

84. Ibid., p. 82.

85. What I see as ambivalence, Foot perceives as a contradiction between Shelley's mild reformism and his revolutionary enthusiasm, with the latter ultimately predominating. *Red Shelley*, pp. 160-226. However, I believe that the poet's reformism was never unconnected with his utopian hope, and his preference for revolution was always qualified by a broad historical awareness. Foot's "contradiction," then, is an ahistorical category he imposes on the more dialectical and historically conscious Shelley.

FIVE: *PROMETHEUS UNBOUND* IN CONTEXT

1. Jones, *Letters*, II, 117.

2. I am quoting from the Hutchinson edition of the poem.

3. Hutchinson, *Poetical Works*, p. 167.

4. Reiman, *Percy Bysshe Shelley*, p. 63. See also Raymond D. Havens, "Rosalind and Helen," *Journal of English and Germanic Philology*, 30 (1931), 218-22, and Bennett Weaver, "Pre-Promethean Thought in Three Longer Poems of Shelley," *Philological Quarterly*, 29 (1950), 357-62.

5. For pastoral, see Raymond Williams, *The Country and the City* (New York: Oxford Univ. Press, 1973).

6. Cf. Daniel Cottom, "Violence and Law in the Waverley Novels," *Studies in Romanticism*, 20 (1981), 77-78, where he suggests that "exquisite suffering" beyond what is considered ordinary is a specifically aristocratic prerogative.

7. See Donald Reiman, "Structure, Symbol, and Theme in 'Lines written among the Euganean Hills,' " rpt. in Reiman and Powers, *Shelley's Poetry and Prose*, pp. 579-96.

8. Reiman, *Percy Bysshe Shelley*, p. 58.

9. Reiman, "Structure, Symbol, and Theme," in Reiman and Powers, *Shelley's Poetry and Prose*, p. 583.

10. Marie Louise Berneri, *Journey Through Utopia* (1950; rpt. New York: Schocken Books, 1971).

11. Frank and Fritzie Manuel, "Sketch for a Natural History of Paradise," *Daedalus*, 101 (1972), 106.

12. Ibid., p. 120.

13. Ibid., pp. 120-21.

14. Cohn, *The Pursuit of the Millennium*, pp. 127-47.

15. Ibid., p. 269.

16. Ibid., pp. 150-51.

17. Ibid., p. 173.

18. Ibid., p. 150.

19. Ibid., p. 151.

20. Ibid., p. 172.

21. A. Bartlett Giamatti, *The Earthly Paradise and the Renaissance Epic* (Princeton: Princeton Univ. Press, 1966), pp. 356-60.

22. Ibid., p. 359.

23. See Duerksen, "Shelley's Prometheus: Destroyer and Preserver," *Studies in English Literature* (1978).

24. See Wasserman, *Shelley, A Critical Reading*, pp. 258-60.

25. Jones, *Letters*, II, 47. In my discussion of freedom's preconditions, I am of course bringing to it the weight of a century's controversy, initiated principally by Marx, which is still continuing, but had barely begun in Shelley's day. Shelley expanded his ideas on preconditions beyond what he wrote in *Prometheus Unbound* in *A Philosophical View of Reform* and *A Defence of Poetry*, which articulated a surprisingly dialectical sense of historical change. Nevertheless, the typical emphasis in his later poetry is tenaciously ethical.

26. Roland Duerksen, "Shelley's 'Deep Truth' Reconsidered," *English Language Notes*, 13 (1975), 25-27.

27. See Hughes, "Potentiality in *Prometheus Unbound*," *Studies in Romanticism* (1963).

28. Kenneth N. Cameron, "The Political Symbolism of *Prometheus Unbound*," *P.M.L.A.*, 58 (1943), 728-53.

29. See Dawson, " 'King Over Himself': Shelley's Philosophical Anarchism," *Keats-Shelley Memorial Bulletin* (1980).

30. Hughes points this out in "Potentiality in *Prometheus Unbound*," *Studies in Romanticism* (1963).

31. Frederick Pottle, "The Role of Asia in the Dramatic Action of Shelley's *Prometheus Unbound*," in George Ridenour, ed., *Shelley, A Collection of Critical Essays* (Englewood Cliffs: Prentice-Hall, 1965), pp. 133-43.

32. G. M. Matthews, "A Volcano's Voice in Shelley," in Ridenour, *Shelley*, pp. 111-31. For the erotic dimension of the volcanic metaphor, see Northrop Frye, *A Study of Romanticism* (New York: Random House, 1968), pp. 123-24.

33. Lawrence Zillman, ed., *Shelley's Prometheus Unbound: The Text and Drafts* (New Haven: Yale Univ. Press, 1968), p. 134.

34. Lawrence Zillman, *Shelley's Prometheus Unbound, A Variorum Edition* (Seattle: Univ. of Washington Press, 1959), p. 490.

35. Hutchinson, *Poetical Works*, p. 825. Cf. Georges Poulet, "Timelessness and Romanticism," *Journal of the History of Ideas*, 15 (1954), 16-17.

36. See Irene Chayes, "Plato's *Statesman* Myth in Shelley and Blake,"

Comparative Literature, 13 (1961), 358-69.

37. Typical is Edward Bostetter, *The Romantic Ventriloquists* (1963; rpt. Seattle: Univ. of Washington Press, 1975), p. 193.

38. Wasserman, *Shelley,* pp. 255-305.

39. V. A. De Luca, "The Style of Millennial Announcement in *Prometheus Unbound,*" *Keats-Shelley Journal,* 28 (1979), 78-101.

40. Cf. Shelley's language describing Maddalo's pride in the Preface to *Julian and Maddalo,* in Reiman and Powers, *Shelley's Poetry and Prose,* p. 113. Charles E. Robinson has done more than anyone else to illustrate Byron's importance for Shelley in *Shelley and Byron* (1976). The Scrope Davies "find" confirms this view since one of the sonnets of 1816 is adamantly opposed to Byron's ironic fatalism. See Dewey Faulkner, "Shelley, Scrope Davies, and Shelley's Lost 1816 Notebook," *Yale Review,* 16 (1979), 44-54.

41. Jones, *Letters,* II, 58.

42. De Luca, "Style," 90-91.

43. Reiman and Powers, *Shelley's Poetry and Prose,* p. 112, n. 1.

44. Holmes, *Shelley, The Pursuit,* p. 447.

45. Wasserman, *Shelley, A Critical Reading,* p. 62.

46. Reiman and Powers, pp. 112-13.

47. Wasserman, p. 65.

48. Jones, *Letters* II, 47.

49. Wasserman, pp. 80-81. See also Bernard A. Hirsch, *"Julian and Maddalo* as Dramatic Dialogue," *Studies in Romanticism,* 17 (1978), 24.

50. Reiman and Powers, p. 237.

51. Ibid., p. 239.

52. Ibid., p. 240.

53. Ibid., p. 240.

54. Ibid., p. 239.

55. Ibid., p. 240.

56. Wasserman, pp. 84-128, emphasizes patriarchy.

57. Reiman and Powers, p. 238.

58. Robert Walmsley, *Peterloo: The Case Reopened* (New York: Augustus M. Kelley, 1969).

59. *Examiner* (Sept. 12, 1819), 578.

60. Thompson, *Making,* pp. 682-83.

61. Malcolm I. Thomis and Peter Holt, *Threats of Revolution in Britain, 1789-1848* (Hampden, Conn.: Archon Books, 1977).

62. Jones, *Letters,* I, 297.

63. For a different approach to the connections between the popular iconography and *The Mask of Anarchy,* see Richard Hendrix, "The Necessity of Response: How Shelley's Radical Poetry Works, *Keats-Shelley Journal,* 28 (1978), 45-69.

64. Stuart Curran, *Shelley's Annus Mirabilis* (San Marino: Huntington Library, 1975), p. 238, n. 3.

65. These pictures are reprinted in Edgell Rickword, ed., *Radical Squibs and Loyal Ripostes* (New York: Barnes and Noble, 1971), pp. 35-54; 83-98; 135-66.

66. Thompson, *Making*, p. 677.

67. Rickword, *Radical Squibs*, p. 24.

68. Ibid., p. 51.

69. Ibid., pp. 314-15.

70. Ibid., p. 38.

71. According to the *OED* (1933 edition), the first coin with Britannia inscribed on it was the 1672 copper halfpenny.

72. Rickword, *Radical Squibs*, p. 95.

73. Ibid., p. 96.

74. Ibid., p. 46.

75. *Examiner* (Sept. 19, 1819), 597.

76. Rickword, p. 166.

77. Ibid., p. 138. For the sexual dimensions of political powerlessness, see Michael Bell, "Social Control / Social Order / Social Art," *Sub-stance*, 22 (1979), 49-65.

78. Rickword, p. 13.

79. Ibid., p. 13.

80. Ibid., p. 43.

81. Ibid., p. 94.

82. John Franzosa, Wayne State University, has done psychoanalytically oriented work on the question of political "independence," and after talking with him I began to think along these lines.

83. Hearn, *Domination, Legitimation, and Resistance* (1978).

84. Cameron, *The Golden Years*, p. 625, n. 8.

85. Hutchinson, *Poetical Works*, p. 576.

86. Thompson, *Making*, p. 696. Richard Carlile's immediate reaction to Peterloo was not militant. He recommended abstention from excised consumer goods and bringing the soldiers to justice. *The Republican* (Aug. 27, 1819).

87. Thompson, *Making*, p. 697.

88. Ibid., p. 693.

89. Reiman, *Shelley and His Circle*, VI, 896.

90. Jones, *Letters*, II, 149.

91. Ibid., p. 164.

92. Reiman, *Shelley and His Circle*, V, 1107.

93. Frederick L. Jones, ed., *The Letters of Mary Wollstonecraft Shelley*, I (Norman: Univ. of Oklahoma Press, 1944), 96.

94. Jones, *Letters*, II, 201; 191.

95. Reiman, *Shelley and His Circle*, VI, 951-55.

96. John Bowring, ed., *The Works of Jeremy Bentham*, III (Edinburgh: William Tait, 1843), 443-597.

97. Ibid., p. 446.

98. See Halévy, *The Growth of Philosophic Radicalism*, for the Benthamite influence.

99. The *Examiner* closely followed Owen, whose speeches it also reprinted. See, for example, issues of: March 29, 1818; April 5, 1818; April 25, 1819; July 4, 1819.

100. For quotations from *A Philosophical View of Reform* I use the Ingpen and Peck text, but I check the accuracy of their transcription with the text reproduced by Reiman, *Shelley and His Circle*, VI, 961-1066.

101. Ingpen and Peck, *Complete Works*, VII, 43.

102. Ibid., p. 5.

103. See Peter Kropotkin, "The State: Its Historic Role," in Martin A. Miller, ed., *Selected Writings on Anarchism and Revolution, P. A. Kropotkin* (Cambridge, Mass.: The M.I.T. Press, 1970), pp. 210-65. Rudolf Rocker, *Nationalism and Culture*, trans. Ray E. Chase (1947; rpt. St. Paul: Michael E. Coughlin, 1978).

104. Ingpen and Peck, *Complete Works*, VII, 6.

105. Ibid., p. 7.

106. Ibid., p. 7.

107. Ibid., pp. 7-8.

108. Ibid., p. 9.

109. Ibid., pp. 17-18; 50.

110. Ibid., p. 11.

111. Ibid., p. 11.

112. Ibid., pp. 44-45.

113. Ibid., pp. 40-41.

114. Ibid., p. 25.

115. Ibid., pp. 25-27.

116. Ibid., p. 27. Cf. a letter written to the *Examiner* by H. Hodson, a. weaver, who complained that 16 hours labor brings in only 10 shillings, when such labor used to bring in 20 shillings (Sept. 20, 1818), 603-605.

117. Ingpen and Peck, *Complete Works*, VII, 27.

118. Ibid., pp. 28-29. Reiman's text reveals a few interesting cross-outs: "speculators in the funds"; "master manufa"—i.e., manufacturers; "bank directors"; "insurance office keepers." *Shelley and His Circle*, VI, 1016.

119. Ingpen and Peck, *Complete Works*, VII, 37-39.

120. Ibid., p. 34.

121. Ingpen and Peck, *Complete Works*, VI, 291.

122. Ingpen and Peck, *Complete Works*, VII, 53.

123. Ibid., p. 54.

124. Ibid., p. 48.

125. Ibid., p. 48.

126. Ibid., p. 49.

127. Ibid., p. 48.

128. Ibid., p. 51.

129. Ibid., p. 45.

130. Ibid., p. 43.

131. Ibid., p. 19.

132. Ibid., p. 20.

133. See the discussion of Lowther and Brougham in the *Examiner* (July 15, 1818), 417-18.

134. Jones, *Letters*, II, 26.

135. Ibid., p. 135.

136. Cameron, *Golden Years*, pp. 626-27, n. 1. See also Jack Benoit Gohn, "Did Shelley Know Wordsworth's *Peter Bell*?", *Keats-Shelley Journal*, 28 (1979), 20-24.

137. Thompson, *Making*, pp. 26-76.

138. Ibid., p. 667.

139. Reiman and Powers, *Shelley's Poetry and Prose*, p. 344, n. 5.

140. Thompson, *Making*, pp. 746-48.

141. *Political Register* (Sept. 19, 1818), 121-22.

142. For an account of Carlile, see Chapter Two, n. 56.

143. Jones, *Letters*, II, 136.

144. Ibid., p. 137.

145. Ibid., p. 143.

146. Ibid., p. 144.

147. Holmes, *Shelley, The Pursuit*, p. 593.

148. Cf. Hutchinson, *Poetical Works*, pp. 571-72, with George Edward Woodberry, *The Shelley Notebook in the Harvard College Library* (Cambridge: John Barnard Associates, 1929), pp. 149-50. For Medwin's text, see *Athenaeum* (Dec. 8, 1832), 794.

149. Hutchinson, p. 573. Cf. Woodberry, p. 16. For Medwin's text, see *Athenaeum* (Aug. 25, 1832), 554.

150. Hutchinson, p. 573.

151. H. Buxton Forman, *Note Books of Percy Bysshe Shelley*, II (Boston: The Bibliophile Society, 1911), 175-79.

152. Hutchinson, p. 574.

153. Forman, II, 182.

154. William McTaggart, *England in 1819: Church, State and Poverty* (London: Keats-Shelley Memorial Association, 1970).

155. Quotations from "England" are from the Harvard Notebook.

156. Quotations from "People of England" are from Forman, II, 175-79.

157. Quotations are from the McTaggart edition.

158. Forman, II, 182.

159. *Examiner* issues from Feb. 15, April 12, and May 3, 1818.

160. A. L. Morton, *A People's History of England* (New York: International Publishers, 1938), p. 378.

161. *Examiner* (Sept. 20, 1818), 603-605.

162. *Examiner* (Sept. 13, 1818), 582-83.

163. *Examiner* (Aug. 29, 1819), 558.

164. Gordon, *Political Economy in Parliament*, p. 80.

165. Zillman, *Shelley's Prometheus Unbound, a Variorum Edition*, p. 10.

166. Richard Caldwell, " 'The Sensitive Plant' as an Original Fantasy," *Studies in Romanticism*, 15 (1976), 221-52.

167. Wasserman, *Shelley*, pp. 154-79.

168. If Elsie Mayer is correct, then the poem was written in the summer of 1819, during his grief over William's death. "Notes on the Composition of 'A Vision of the Sea,' " *Keats-Shelley Journal*, 28 (1979), 17-20.

169. Reiman and Powers, *Shelley's Poetry and Prose*, p. 226, n. 5.

170. *Examiner* (Mar. 26, 1820), 193; 197-98.

171. Robert Malcolmson, *Popular Recreations in English Society 1700-1850* (Cambridge: Cambridge Univ. Press, 1973), pp. 5-6.

172. Ibid., p. 117.

173. Francis Hearn, "Towards a Critical Theory of Play," *Telos*, 30 (Winter, 1976-77), 145.

174. See, for example, *Examiner* (May 10, 1818), and his Christmas essays.

175. See Northrop Frye, *A Study of Romanticism*, pp. 123-24.

SIX: DEFENDING THE IMAGINATION

1. Marken and Pollin, *Uncollected Writings*, p. 432.

2. Marken and Pollin, pp. 57-58.

3. Janet M. Todd, ed., *A Wollstonecraft Anthology* (Bloomington: Indiana Univ. Press, 1977), p. 177.

4. William Godwin, *Life of Chaucer*, I (1803; rpt. New York: AMS Press, 1974), 393.

5. Paul, *William Godwin*, II, 10-11.

6. Thomas Love Peacock, *Memoirs of Shelley and Other Essays and Reviews*, ed. Howard Mills (New York: New York Univ. Press, 1970), p. 118. When I capitalize Poetry or Poet, I do so to indicate Shelley's unique sense of both; when I do not capitalize either, I am using the terms in their ordinary meanings.

7. Ibid., p. 122.

8. Reiman and Powers, *Shelley's Poetry and Prose*, p. 481.

9. Ibid., p. 480.

10. Ibid., pp. 474-75.

11. Ibid., p. 475.

12. Ibid., p. 477.

13. Ingpen and Peck, *Complete Works*, VII, 62.
14. Reiman and Powers, *Shelley's Poetry and Prose*, p. 481.
15. Ibid., p. 482.
16. Ingpen and Peck, VI, 213.
17. Reiman and Powers, *Shelley's Poetry and Prose*, pp. 486-87.
18. Ibid., p. 487.
19. Ibid., p. 487.
20. Ibid., pp. 487-88.
21. Ingpen and Peck, *Complete Works*, VI, 270.
22. Ibid., p. 291.
23. Reiman and Powers, *Shelley's Poetry and Prose*, p. 488.
24. Ibid., p. 489.
25. Ibid., p. 490.
26. Ibid., p. 491.
27. Ibid., p. 492.
28. Ibid., pp. 491-93.
29. Ibid., p. 497.
30. Ibid., p. 496.
31. Ibid., p. 497.
32. Ibid., p. 499.
33. Ibid., p. 498.
34. Ibid., p. 496.
35. Ingpen and Peck, *Complete Works*, VII, 10.
36. Reiman and Powers, *Shelley's Poetry and Prose*, pp. 500-501.
37. Ibid., p. 501.
38. Ibid., p. 502.
39. Ibid., p. 503.
40. Ibid., p. 505.
41. Eleanor Wilner, *Gathering the Winds: Visionary Imagination and Radical Transformation of Self and Society* (Baltimore: The Johns Hopkins Univ. Press, 1974), p. 41. In this paragraph I employ the masculine pronouns because Wilner does not discuss female shamans or romantic bards.
42. Ingpen and Peck, *Complete Works*, VII, 75-76.
43. See Reiman and Powers, *Shelley's Poetry and Prose*, p. 313, n. 1, suggesting the conflict between the mechanical and the imaginative. See also James M. Hall, "The Spider and the Silkworm: Shelley's 'Letter to Maria Gisborne,' " *Keats-Shelley Memorial Bulletin*, 20 (1969), 1-10.
44. Cf. David Davie, "Shelley's Urbanity," in M. H. Abrams, ed., *English Romantic Poets, Modern Essays in Criticism* (New York: Oxford Univ. Press, 1960), pp. 307-25.
45. Brown, *Sexuality and Feminism in Shelley* (1979) discusses Shelleyan androgyny.
46. Although most likely the "Bruce" receiving a copy of the pamphlet is William Bruce, the Irish Presbyterian, it could be James George Bruce.

47. *Examiner* (June 4, 1820), 360.

48. *Examiner* (May 7, 1820), 291.

49. *Examiner* (April 9, 1820), 232-33 (and later issues as well).

50. *Examiner* (July 9, 1820), 442.

51. *Examiner* (Aug. 30, 1818), 548-50. Cited by Cameron, *Golden Years*, p. 357. See also Roland Bartel, "Shelley and Burke's Swinish Multitude," *Keats-Shelley Journal*, 18 (1969), 4-9.

52. C. E. Pulos, "Shelley and Malthus," *PMLA*, 67 (1952), 113-24. Cameron, *Golden Years*, p. 357.

53. Pulos, 120-24.

54. Quotations from the play are from Hutchinson, *Poetical Works*.

55. Cameron, *Golden Years*, p. 529.

56. *Examiner* (Feb. 22, 1818), 119.

57. Jones, *Letters*, II, 434.

58. Reiman and Powers, *Shelley's Poetry and Prose*, p. 373.

59. Ibid., n. 1.

60. Hughes, "Coherence and Collapse in Shelley, With Particular Reference to *Epipsychidion*," *ELH*, 28 (1961), 260-83.

61. Ibid., p. 274.

62. Reiman and Powers, p. 373.

63. Hughes, 278.

64. Wasserman, *Shelley*, pp. 462; 472.

65. Milton Wilson, *Shelley's Later Poetry* (New York: Columbia Univ. Press, 1959), pp. 235; 252.

66. Ross Woodman, *The Apocalyptic Vision in the Poetry of Shelley* (Toronto: Univ. of Toronto Press, 1964), pp. 3; 158-79.

67. Cameron, *Golden Years*, pp. 422-31; also, Reiman, *Shelley and His Circle*, V, 399-418.

68. Wasserman, *The Subtler Language*, p. 321.

69. See Irving Massey, on Shelleyan memory, in "Shelley's 'Music, When Soft Voices Die': Text and Meaning," *Journal of English and Germanic Philology*, 59 (1960), 430-38.

70. Curran, *Shelley's Annus Mirabilis*, p. 165. Cf. Daniel Hughes' statement on the poet's self-destruction: Prometheus "is *sacrificed* like the Bard of the West Wind in order that the great age of millennium and apocalypse can come to consciousness." "Prometheus Made Capable Poet in Act One of *Prometheus Unbound*," *Studies in Romanticism*, 17 (1978), 4.

71. Carlos Baker, *Shelley's Major Poetry*, pp. 245-46.

SEVEN: AN ETHICAL IDEALISM

1. Jones, *Letters*, II, 436.

2. Ibid., p. 156.

3. Reiman, *Shelley and His Circle*, VI, 641-47.

4. Jones, *Letters*, II, 339.

5. Ibid., p. 398.

6. Ibid., pp. 406-407. Cf. Timothy Webb, *The Violet in the Crucible* (Oxford: Clarendon Press, 1976), pp. 154-62.

7. Jones, *Letters*, II, 156.

8. Cameron, *Golden Years*, pp. 375-81; Woodring, *Politics in English Romantic Poetry*, pp. 313-19.

9. Margery Weiner, *The Sovereign Remedy, Europe After Waterloo* (London: Constable, 1971), p. 163.

10. Jones, *Letters*, II, 234.

11. Ibid., pp. 266-67.

12. Ibid., pp. 290-91.

13. Weiner, *Sovereign Remedy*, p. 161.

14. Bolton King, *A History of Italian Unity*, I (1899; rpt. New York: Russell and Russell, 1924), 24-27.

15. Weiner, p. 62.

16. *Examiner* (Nov. 4, 1821), 689-92; cited by Cameron, *Golden Years*, p. 376.

17. Jones, *Letters*, II, 406.

18. Ibid., pp. 298; 302.

19. Ibid., pp. 304-305.

20. Ibid., p. 382, n. 8.

21. Ibid., p. 382.

22. White, *The Unextinguished Hearth*, pp. 269-271.

23. Hutchinson, *Poetical Works*, p. 478.

24. Ibid., pp. 478-79.

25. Reiman and Powers, *Shelley's Poetry and Prose*, p. 410.

26. Wasserman, *Shelley*, pp. 374-413.

27. Judith Chernaik, *The Lyrics of Shelley* (Cleveland: The Press of Case Western Reserve Univ., 1972), pp. 210-19.

28. See Jones, *Letters*, II, 353.

29. Reiman and Powers, p. 437, n. 1.

30. Jones, *Letters*, II, 219-20. The Hutchinson text of the play is in a corrupt state, with a nonexistent fifth scene, and needs the correction provided by the articles of R. B. Woodings: " 'A Devil of a Nut to Crack': Shelley's *Charles the First*," *Studia Neophilogica*, 40 (1968), 216-37; "Shelley's 'Widow Bird,' " *Review of English Studies*, 19 (1968), 411-14; "Shelley's Sources for *Charles the First*," *Modern Language Review*, 64 (1969), 267-75.

31. See, e.g., Walter F. Wright, "Shelley's Failure in *Charles the First*," *ELH*, 8 (1941), 41-46; N. I. White, "Shelley's *Charles the First*," *Journal of English and Germanic Philology*, 21 (1922), 431-41.

32. See Jones, *Letters*, II, 436.

33. See ibid., pp. 388; 394.

34. See, for example, David Hume, *The History of England*, IV (New York: Worthington Co., 1889), 443.

35. Reiman and Powers, *Shelley's Poetry and Prose*, p. 410.

36. Bulstrode Whitelocke, *Memorials of the English Affairs* (London: Nathaniel Ponder, 1682), p. 18.

37. Ibid., p. 37.

38. Stephen Orgel, *The Illusion of Power, Political Theater in the English Renaissance* (Berkeley and Los Angeles: Univ. of California Press, 1975), pp. 79-83.

39. Reiman and Powers, *Shelley's Poetry and Prose*, p. 491.

40. Forman, *Note Books*, III, 104.

41. Ibid., p. 105.

42. For scene iv, see Woodings, " 'A Devil of a Nut to Crack': *Shelley's Charles the First*," 230-33.

43. I am in basic agreement with Donald Reiman's interpretation of the poem in *Shelley's "The Triumph of Life": A Critical Study*, pp. 19-86, and disagree with the line of criticism presented by Ann Shealy, *Journey Through the Unapparent* (Hicksville: Exposition Press, 1974).

44. Reiman and Powers, *Shelley's Poetry and Prose*, p. 491.

45. Ibid., p. 458, n. 5.

46. Reiman, *Shelley's "The Triumph of Life*," pp. 34-35.

47. Reiman and Powers, p. 459, n. 7.

48. Reiman, *Shelley's "The Triumph of Life*," p. 40.

49. Edward Duffy, *Rousseau in England, The Context for Shelley's Critique of the Enlightenment* (Berkeley and Los Angeles: Univ. of California Press, 1979).

50. If Shelley had been more familiar with Kant's work, especially his ethics, he would have been more favorable to him.

51. Jones, *Letters*, II, 442.

52. Herbert Read, *The Politics of the Unpolitical* (London, 1943), rpt. in *To Hell With Culture* (1963).

53. See Sylva Norman, *Flight of the Skylark* (Norman: Univ. of Oklahoma Press, 1954), for the history of Shelley's reputation in nineteenth-century England. For his reception by the English working class, see Y. V. Kovalev, "The Literature of Chartism," *Victorian Studies*, 7 (1958), 117-38; W. C. Bebbington, "Social Protest in Some Minor Poets of the Nineteenth Century," *Ariel*, 6 (1975), 36-56; M. Saddiq Kallim, *The Social Orpheus, Shelley and the Owenites* (Lahore, Pakistan: Government College, 1973); White, *Shelley*, II, 389-411; Foot, *Red Shelley*, pp. 227-73.

54. For an introduction to Habermas, see T. A. McCarthy, "A Theory of Communicative Competence," in Paul Connerton, ed., *Critical Sociology, Selected Readings* (New York: Penguin, 1976), pp. 470-97.

Index

Index

Williams, Raymond (*cont.*)
  322n, 336n
Wilner, Eleanor, 255-56, 343n
Wilson, Milton, 272, 344n
Winstanley, Gerrard, 153
Winters, J., 119
Wojcik, Manfred, 326n
Wolff, Robert Paul, 324n
Wollstonecraft, Mary, 5, 8-10, 13-14,
  25-26, 31, 125, 248, 321n
Woodcock, George, 322n, 326n
Woodings, R. B., 345n, 346n
Woodman, Ross, 272, 344n
Woodring, Carl, 319n, 322n, 345n
Wooler, Jonathan, 115, 124, 129, 132,

133, 207; *see also Black Dwarf*
Wordsworth, William, 7, 9, 78-79, 84-
  88, 101-102, 106, 121-23, 126, 143,
  218-24, 230, 236, 259, 269, 273,
  284-85, 319-20n, 320n
Wright, John (of Liverpool), 130
Wright, Walter E., 345n
Wyvill, Rev. Christopher, 4

Yeats, William B., 255, 314
Young, Art, 326n
Young, Arthur, 111

Zillman, Lawrence, 342n

LIBRARY OF CONGRESS CATALOGING IN PUBLICATION DATA

Scrivener, Michael Henry, 1948-
Radical Shelley.
Bibliography: p.
Includes index.
1. Shelley, Percy Bysshe, 1792-1822—Philosophy. 2. Shelley, Percy Bysshe, 1792-
1822—Political and social views. 3. Anarchism and anarchists
in literature. 4. Utopias in literature. I. Title.
PR5442.P5S35 1982   821'.7   82-3770
ISBN 0-691-06525-X   AACR2